Foundations of Analysis
in Operations Research

OPERATIONS RESEARCH
AND INDUSTRIAL ENGINEERING

Consulting Editor: J. William Schmidt

Virginia Polytechnic Institute and State University
Blacksburg, Virginia

Applied Statistical Methods, *I. W. Burr*

Mathematical Foundations of Management Science and Systems Analysis, *J. William Schmidt*

Urban Systems Models, *Walter Helly*

Introduction to Discrete Linear Controls: Theory and Application, *Albert B. Bishop*

Integer Programming: Theory, Applications, and Computations, *Hamdy A. Taha*

Transform Techniques for Probability Modeling, *Walter C. Giffin*

Analysis of Queueing Systems, *J. A. White, J. W. Schmidt, and G. K. Bennett*

Models for Public Systems Analysis, *Edward J. Beltrami*

Computer Methods in Operations Research, *Arne Thesen*

Cost-Benefit Analysis: A Handbook, *Peter G. Sassone and William A. Schaffer*

Modeling of Complex Systems, *V. Vemuri*

Applied Linear Programming: For the Socioeconomic and Environmental Sciences, *Michael R. Greenberg*

Foundations of Analysis in Operations Research, *J. William Schmidt and Robert P. Davis*

Foundations of Decision Support Systems, *Robert H. Bonczek, Clyde W. Holsapple, and Andrew B. Whinston*

Foundations of Analysis in Operations Research

J. William Schmidt

Robert P. Davis

Department of Industrial Engineering and Operations Research
Virginia Polytechnic Institute and State University
Blacksburg, Virginia

 1981

ACADEMIC PRESS
A Subsidiary of Harcourt Brace Jovanovich, Publishers

New York   London   Toronto   Sydney   San Francisco

To my wife, Shirley
R. P. D.

To five wonderful children:
Suzanne, Billy, Patty, Kurt, and Cathy
J. W. S.

ACADEMIC PRESS, INC.
111 Fifth Avenue, New York, New York 10003

United Kingdom Edition published by
ACADEMIC PRESS, INC. (LONDON) LTD.
24/28 Oval Road, London NW1 7DX

Library of Congress Cataloging in Publication Data

Schmidt, Joseph William.
Foundations of analysis in operations research.

(Operations research and industrial engineering)
Includes index.
1. Operations research––Mathematics. I. Davis,
Robert Pratt, Date, joint author. II. Title.
T57.6.S318   001.4'24   80–987
ISBN 0–12–626850–9

PRINTED IN THE UNITED STATES OF AMERICA

81 82 83 84   9 8 7 6 5 4 3 2 1

Contents

Preface

Until the end of the eighteenth century, nearly all products were manufactured by individual artisans and craftsmen. With the advent of new manufacturing technology in the late eighteenth and early nineteenth centuries came the Industrial Revolution. Early advances occurred in England and spread quickly throughout Europe. While technological breakthroughs led to more efficient production processes, the cost of associated manufacturing equipment was beyond the capital resources of individual craftsmen. To take advantage of the mass production available through the application of new technology, and the concomitant penetration of massive markets for the goods produced, enterprises possessing sufficient capital organized men and machines into what has become known as the factory system.

The factory system was the result of the application of scientific techniques to manufacturing and persists as a fundamental characteristic of modern industry. However, by today's standards the organizations that characterized the Industrial Revolution would be considered to be rather primitive. Today larger companies employ thousands of workers, deal in billions of dollars, manufacture hundreds of products, and service a multitude of markets. The service industries, including banks, hospitals, insurance companies, consulting firms, and governments, are faced with operational complexities similar to those noted for the manufacturing industry.

The complexity of today's business operations, aggressive competition, and government controls have made the job of the manager increasingly difficult. It is no longer possible for one individual to be aware of the details of every characteristic of the firm or to make all decisions regarding its operation. Even within a manager's relatively small span of control the factors affecting his decisions are often so numerous and their effects so pervasive that "seat of the pants" decisions are no longer acceptable. As a result, effective decision making often requires the availability of information analyzed and summarized in a timely fashion.

Much of the analysis of operational systems is through system models that are synthetic representations of physical systems. A system model relates those variables which affect the performance of the system to a measure (or measures) of systems performance in a logical manner. By experimenting with the model, the effects of various management decisions can be explored.

The analytical results obtained from a model must always be tempered with experienced judgment, since there usually exist factors that cannot be accounted for in the model. However, an analysis of the system through the use of a reasonable model usually provides valuable input to managerial decisions. While a system model may take many forms, it usually includes the logical relationships between the variables affecting system performance and some measure (or measures) of system performance. These relationships are frequently expressed in a mathematical form. By altering values of the variables in these relationships, the manager or analyst can determine the effect of a variety of conditions on the operational effectiveness of the system described by the model.

The analysis of operations through mathematical models is usually included in the activities of operations research, management science, systems analysis, and industrial engineering. While the Industrial Revolution resulted from the application of science to the development of hardware for more efficient and effective production, mathematical modeling and model analysis have brought the techniques of science to bear upon decision processes. Although the initial applications of these techniques can be traced to the early part of this century, their widespread use is usually dated to the efforts of the military in the United States and England during World War II. With the cessation of hostilities and with the advent of the digital computer for commercial use in the 1950s, the use of mathematical modeling spread to the private sector and has grown rapidly since.

Over the past three decades research in quantitative methods for decision analysis has taken two paths. First, investigators have pursued methods for describing the behavior of systems through mathematical models. These investigations have led to the emergence of queueing (or waiting line) theory, reliability theory, quality control, production control, inventory theory, and engineering economy, to name but a few. At the same time a great deal of research has been devoted to the analysis of mathematical models to determine optimal conditions for system operation, the sensitivity of system performance to changing conditions, variation in system performance under a given set of operational conditions, and transformation techniques to simplify the development and analysis of system models. These efforts have led to developments such as linear programming, dynamic programming, and search procedures; and to the application of Laplace and Fourier transforms, probability theory, stochastic processes, and experimental statistics to the analysis of decision problems.

Purpose and Scope of the Text

This text is designed to provide the reader with a foundation in those mathematical concepts that form the basis for the development and analysis of mathematical models. It is assumed that the reader has an operational knowledge of integral and differential calculus. The major objective of this work is to provide the student of operations research or a related discipline with a discussion of these mathematical foundations in a context that is intended to support the transition from undergraduate calculus to the applications-oriented techniques of operations research. To accomplish this objective, we have chosen to present the material contained in this volume both in greater depth and in a less mathematically rigorous manner than is found in existing textbooks.

The emphasis throughout this presentation is on developing a conceptual understanding of, and an interpretive capability with, the mathematics of operations research, and not on presenting proofs for their own sake. This is not to say that proofs are unnecessary, but rather that the student should first be prepared to interpret the concepts underlying the mathematical tools at his disposal, and in so doing be then prepared to grasp both the rationale and significance of the methodologies to which he or she is exposed. Our hope is that the student, armed with such a perspective, will achieve a greater understanding of more rigorously defined topics in operations research and will be prepared to accomplish this aim in an expeditious fashion.

Practitioners in research, analysis, and design have long held fast (in spirit at least) to the tenet that the system under study, and its operational characteristics, should dictate the modeling approach, and not that the modeling familiarity of the analyst should dictate his description of the system. This is an easy thing to state but quite another to accomplish, regardless of how true it may be. It is our belief that a conceptually oriented, interpretive perspective is of definite utility to the analyst in the quest for a model that, as accurately as possible, describes the system under study. Although not very pedagogical, we believe in the need for, and importance of, gaining a "feel" for the system and its operation—to interpret its operational characteristics and environment. We ask the reader to consider the following.

(1)   First, you must *see*, but that is not enough; you must then take time to *observe*.

(2)   Next, you must *think*, but that is not enough; you must then take time to *reason*.

(3)   Then, you must *realize* what needs to be done, but that is not enough; you must then take time to *understand* "why" and the consequences.

(4)   Now, you must *plan* well your actions, but that is not enough; you must then take time to *implement*, and perhaps *adapt,* your plans.

(5)   Once accomplished, you must *tell* what you have done, but that is not enough; you must then take time to *interpret* what you have accomplished, its meaning and consequences, so that others may also *see*.

Organization of the Text

Four areas of mathematics having important applications in operations research are presented in this text: linear algebra, classical optimization, discrete calculus, and transform methods. The first chapter is devoted to a review of the fundamentals of calculus. This chapter will probably serve as a review for students in engineering, operations research, and quantitatively oriented management programs. However, an understanding of the topics in Chapter 1 is necessary for study of the primary topics of the text contained in Chapters 2–6.

Chapter 2 contains a fundamental treatment of linear algebra. The topics treated here include basic matrix operations, the determinant and inverse of a matrix, vectors, vector spaces, transformations, the solution of simultaneous linear equations, quadratic forms, definiteness, and convex spaces. This material has direct application to the solution of problems in operations research, serving as a foundation for the techniques of classical optimization treated in Chapters 3 and 4, and those of linear programming and Markov chains in Chapter 7.

Chapters 3 and 4 focus on the concepts and applications of classical optimization theory. Chapter 3 contains a treatment of the basic concepts of system optimization and the techniques that may be applied to unconstrained optimization problems. Chapter 4 then extends the analysis to constrained optimization. Since the optimization techniques presented require an understanding of matrix operations and quadratic forms, the reader should have a thorough understanding of the material in Chapter 2 up to and including quadratic forms before pursuing the material contained in Chapters 3 and 4.

In Chapter 5 the reader is introduced to the fundamentals of discrete calculus. Here the techniques of analysis for functions of a discrete variable are treated, including differencing, summation of series, optimization, and numerical methods.

Operational methods that are useful in systems analysis are presented in Chapter 6. The major emphasis of this chapter is on transform methods and their applications. The basis of all of the transforms presented is the Fourier transform. In addition, the continuous transforms treated include the Laplace transform, the moment-generating and characteristic functions, and the Mellin transform. The discrete transforms discussed include the geometric and Z transforms and the moment-generating and characteristic functions. The primary application of each of these transforms is in probability modeling. In addition, the use of the Laplace transform in solving differential equations is discussed as is the application of the geometric transform to the solution of difference equations.

A final discussion is included in Chapter 7, one which directly relates the material presented herein to specific operations research methodologies.

Throughout the text, examples are given to illustrate both applications of the concepts that are presented and inherent characteristics of mathematical models and solution methodologies. Further, additional practice problems and references are provided at the end of each chapter to permit the student to reinforce and extend his understanding.

Uses of the Text

A primary motivation in the development of this work was to provide a text to be used by undergraduate students of industrial engineering, operations research, and management science in an intermediate course, building upon their mathematical background in direct preparation for a first course in operations research methodology. In effect, this book is intended to be used to reinforce the student's transition from mathematics for its own sake to the applications-oriented mathematics of operations research. Further, the book is intended to promote a questioning attitude and an interpretive posture to be assumed by the student as studies in opeations research are continued.

We also perceive a need for such a text by (1) students who pursue graduate study in operations research with no formal undergraduate background in the subject, and (2) practitioners in industry who come to the realization that such methodologies can enhance their ability to design, analyze, and control systems. In both of these cases, the text is designed to be suitable for independent study.

Chapter 1 | Mathematical Foundations

INTRODUCTION

Those who manage or control systems of men and equipment face the continuing problem of improving system performance. The problem may be one of reducing the cost of operation while maintaining an acceptable level of service, increasing profit of current operations, providing a higher level of service without increasing cost, maintaining a profitable operation while meeting imposed government regulations, or "improving" one aspect of product quality without reducing quality in another. When faced with situations such as these, the manager, engineer, or analyst will probably have to change the mode of operation of the system in some way. The problem is then, What elements of system operation should be changed and how should they be changed to achieve the goal sought?

To identify methods for improvement of system operation one might simply experiment with the system. If the objective is to improve product quality, the production manager might try a variety of materials, manufacturing processes, and/or product designs and see whether or not any of these variations achieves the goal of quality improvement to an acceptable degree. This approach may be acceptable given sufficient time and resources for experimentation. On the other hand, the production manager may already know what must be done to improve quality. In this case his problem is not what needs to be done but rather implementation of the solution of which he is already aware. However, if he does not have a solution at hand and does not have the time and/or resources for experimentation with the physical system, his next alternative would be a synthetic representation, or model, of the physical system which could be used to describe the effect of a variety of proposed solutions.

1

A *model* may be thought of as an entity which captures the *essence* of reality without the *presence* of reality. A photograph is a model of the reality portrayed in the picture. Blood pressure may be used as a model of the health of an individual. A pilot sales campaign may be used to model the response of individuals to a new product. Finally, a mathematical equation may be used to model the energy contained in a given material. In each case the model captures some aspect of the reality it attempts to represent.

Since a model only captures certain aspects of reality, it may be inappropriate for use in a particular application because it captures the wrong elements of reality. Temperature is a model of climatic conditions but may be inappropriate if one is interested in barometric pressure. A photograph of a person is a model of that individual but provides little information regarding his or her academic achievement. An equation which predicts annual sales of a particular product is a model of that product but is of little value if we are interested in the cost of production per unit. Thus the usefulness of a model is dependent upon the aspect of reality it represents.

A model may prove to be inadequate even when it attempts to capture the appropriate element (or elements) of reality if it does so in a distorted or biased manner. An equation predicting monthly sales volume may be exactly what the sales manager is looking for but could lead to serious losses if it consistently yields estimates of sales which are high. A thermometer which reads too high (or low) would be of little use in medical diagnosis. Hence a useful model is one which captures the proper elements of reality with acceptable accuracy.

In this text the focus of attention will be on operations appropriate for the analysis of mathematical models. A mathematical model is an equation, inequality, or system of equations or inequalities which represents certain aspects of the physical system modeled. Models of this type are used extensively in the physical sciences, engineering, business, and economics. This is not intended to imply that mathematical models are the only models used in these areas, nor that they are necessarily used more often than other types of models. However, mathematical models do have important application throughout both the public and private sectors of the economy.

As already mentioned, a model offers the analyst a tool which he can manipulate in his analysis of the system under study, without disturbing the system itself. For example, suppose that a mathematical model has been developed to predict annual sales as a function of unit selling price. If the production cost per unit is known, total annual profit for any given selling price can easily be calculated. To determine the selling price which will yield the maximum total profit, various values for selling price can be introduced into the model one at a time, the sales resulting noted, and the total profit per year computed for each value of selling price examined. By trial and error the analyst could determine the selling price which will maximize total annual profit.

In the example just cited the analyst is interested in operating on the model to determine the optimal product selling price. This operation is referred to as *optimization* and is frequently an important part of the analysis of systems. In Chapters 3, 4, and 5 methods for optimizing mathematical models which are more efficient than trial-and-error procedures will be discussed in detail. However, before discussing optimization, a knowledge of matrices, determinants, and quadratic forms is required, and these topics are treated in Chapter 2. Frequently the model formulated to describe the system involves a system of simultaneous linear equations which must be solved for the values of the variables included. This problem is treated in Chapter 2. Many models in use today are linear in form and are optimized through a technique known as *linear programming* (see Chapter 7). Fundamental to linear programming is a knowledge of vector spaces, and this topic is also presented in Chapter 2. In some situations the mathematical model of the system studied is a function of discrete rather than continuous variables. The analytical tools which apply to such models are introduced in Chapter 5. A mathematical model is occasionally easier to analyze if it is reexpressed through a transformation. Transforms and their applications will be discussed in Chapter 6.

The primary purpose of this text is to introduce the reader to analytical techniques which can be applied to mathematical models in order to efficiently solve the system problems with which he is faced. However, the techniques presented in the chapters which follow are of value only if they are applied to a model which is a valid representation of those elements of the physical system of interest. In the next section of this chapter a brief discussion of model development is presented. This is followed by a review of the fundamentals of differential and integral calculus. The review of calculus is intended for the reader who has had at least a full year of calculus but needs to refresh his background. However, this review should not be considered to be equivalent to the material covered in an introductory sequence of courses in the calculus.

MATHEMATICAL MODELS

Ideally, if the mathematical model is a valid representation of the performance of the system, by the application of appropriate analytical techniques the solution obtained from the model should also be the solution to the system problem. Thus the effectiveness of the results of the application of any operational technique is largely a function of the degree to which the model represents the system studied.

To define those conditions which will lead to the solution of a systems problem, the analyst must first identify a criterion by which the performance of the system may be measured. This criterion is often referred to as the *measure of system performance* or the *measure of effectiveness*. In business applications the measure of effectiveness is often either cost or profit, while this measure is more often defined in terms of a benefit-to-cost ratio in governmental applications.

The mathematical model which describes the behavior of the measure of effectiveness is called the *objective function*. If the objective function is to describe the behavior of the measure of effectiveness, it must capture the relationship between that measure and those variables which cause it to vary. System variables can be categorized as decision variables and uncontrollable variables. A *decision variable* is a variable which can be directly controlled by the analyst or his superiors while an *uncontrollable variable* is a variable which cannot be directly controlled. In practice it is virtually impossible to capture the precise relationship between all system variables and the measure of effectiveness through a mathematical equation. Instead, the analyst must strive to identify those variables which most significantly affect the measure of effectiveness, and then attempt to logically define the mathematical relationship between these variables and the measure of effectiveness. This mathematical relationship is the objective function which is used to evaluate the performance of the system under study.

Formulation of a meaningful objective function is usually a tedious and frustrating task. Attempts at development of the objective function may meet with failure. This result may occur because the analyst chooses the wrong set of variables for inclusion in the model or, if this set is adequate, because he fails to identify the proper relationship between these variables and the measure of effectiveness. Returning to the drawing board, the analyst attempts to discover additional variables which may improve his model while discarding those which seem to have little or no bearing. However, whether or not these factors do in fact improve the model can only be determined after formulation and testing of new models that include the additional variables. The entire process of variable selection and rejection and model formulation may require multiple reiteration before a satisfactory objective function is developed. The analyst hopes to achieve some improvement in the model at each iteration, although such consistent good fortune is not usually the case. More often ultimate success is preceded by a string of frustrating failures and small successes.

At each stage of the development process the analyst must judge the adequacy, or validity, of the model. Two criteria are frequently employed in this determination. The first involves experimentation with the model: subjecting the model to a variety of conditions and recording the associated values of the measure of effectiveness given by the model in each case. If the measure of effectiveness varies in a counterintuitive manner with a succession of input conditions, then there may be reason to believe that the objective function is invalid. For example, suppose that a model is developed which is intended to estimate the market value of single-family homes. The model is to express market value in dollars as a function of square feet of living area, number of bedrooms, number of bathrooms, and lot size. After developing the model the analyst applies the model to the valuation of several homes, having different values for the characteristics mentioned above, and finds that market value tends to decrease as the square feet of living area increases. Since this result is at variance with reality, the analyst would question the validity of the model. On the other hand, suppose that the model is such that home value is an increasing function of each of the four characteristics cited, as we should generally expect. Although this result is encouraging, it does not necessarily imply that the model is a valid representation of reality, since the rate of increase with each variable may be inappropriately high or low.

The second stage of model validation calls for a comparison of model results with those achieved in reality. To accomplish this, the analyst subjects the model to conditions which have been experienced in the physical system. If the model is a valid representation of the behavior of the physical system, then the results produced by the model and the physical system should be similar when the experimental conditions are the same. To illustrate let us return to the property valuation model discussed above. Suppose that the model developed was given by

$$f(x_1, x_2, x_3, x_4) = 15x_1 + 750x_2 + 1000x_3 + 1200x_4 \qquad (1.1)$$

where $f(x_1, x_2, x_3, x_4)$ is the estimated market value of the home and x_1 is square feet of living area, x_2 the number of bedrooms, x_3 the number of bathrooms, and x_4 the lot size in acres. To validate the model, suppose the analyst randomly selects ten homes in the area under study which have sold in the past month. He records the values of x_1, x_2, x_3, x_4 and the sale price for each. The next step is to obtain an estimate of market value for each property from the model. As an illustration suppose that the ten homes selected and the validation results are as given in Table 1.1. A casual examination of the difference between the estimate of market value and actual sale price for each property would indicate that the model is inadequate. The average absolute error is $11,750.40, and the error in estimation reaches a value of $24,313.00 for property number 9.

Table 1.1

Validation for the Objective Function in Eq. (1.1)

Home number	x_1	x_2	x_3	x_4	Actual sale price ($)	Estimated sale price from $f(x_1, x_2, x_3, x_4)$ ($)
1	1070	2	1	0.15	29,700.00	18,730.00
2	1742	3	2	0.30	37,200.00	30,740.00
3	1228	2	1	0.57	19,000.00	21,604.00
4	3826	4	3	2.02	83,400.00	65,814.00
5	2237	2	2	4.29	64,000.00	42,203.00
6	1897	3	1	1.37	43,900.00	33,349.00
7	2642	3	2	0.64	64,500.00	44, 648.00
8	873	2	1	0.26	24,400.00	15,907.00
9	3111	3	3	0.81	77,200.00	52,887.00
10	1638	3	2	0.31	41,500.00	29,192.00

In the case cited above the model may have been invalid because sufficient characteristics of homes were not included, because the relationship between the characterisitcs included and sale price were improperly formulated, or both. Unfortunately the validation attempt may provide little information regarding the reason for the inadequacy of the model tested. However, it is sometimes helpful to examine those conditions for which the model estimates and the results derived from the physical system depart most significantly. Indentification of those conditions under which the model seems to be most inadequate may provide a clue to the reason for the departure of the model from reality. Consider another example in which model development is described in more detail.

Example 1.1 The quality of production lots at a manufacturing plant is believed to be a function of the production rate, the lot size, and the time between successive maintenance periods. While the direct cost of production decreases as each of these variables increases the proportion of defective units can be expected to increase. However, the nature of the relationship between proportion defective and production rate, lot size, and time between successive maintenance periods is unknown. To estimate the cost of defective units included in production lots and therefore the total cost of production, a mathematical model is to be developed which will estimate the proportion of defective units produced. The model should estimate proportion defective within ± 0.01. The data in Table 1.2 has been collected for 40 production lots.

The approach adopted for development of the mathematical model is called *least squares analysis* or *regression analysis*. In applying this technique the analyst hypothesizes a functional relationship for the model that includes undetermined coefficients. The technique then defines the values of

Table 1.2

Observed Values of Proportion Defective for 40 Combinations of Values of
Production rate, Time between Maintenance Periods, and Lot Size

Lot number i	Production rate (units/day) x_1	Time between maintenance periods (days) x_2	Lot size (units) x_3	Proportion defective p
1	5100	5	4000	0.089
2	8700	7	7000	0.146
3	2900	10	6000	0.113
4	5500	5	7000	0.098
5	3500	7	1000	0.070
6	9900	4	6000	0.132
7	5700	9	1000	0.108
8	6000	5	6000	0.098
9	1900	10	7000	0.109
10	7200	5	2000	0.090
11	4000	10	8000	0.140
12	6300	4	3000	0.081
13	4600	10	3000	0.116
14	1100	1	6000	0.042
15	5800	3	1000	0.073
16	6500	7	3000	0.100
17	2800	5	3000	0.061
18	2500	5	4000	0.053
19	5700	3	5000	0.092
20	1900	11	5000	0.100
21	3700	9	6000	0.113
22	7400	8	6000	0.131
23	9500	8	6000	0.162
24	4900	10	5000	0.119
25	4600	1	5000	0.077
26	5900	9	5000	0.120
27	1400	9	7000	0.095
28	6900	10	5000	0.139
29	2500	3	7000	0.070
30	9600	7	4000	0.136
31	7000	2	6000	0.103
32	3600	11	2000	0.102
33	7900	6	3000	0.117
34	3700	8	5000	0.089
35	7300	8	6000	0.140
36	6800	7	5000	0.113
37	4200	11	2000	0.118
38	7700	8	7000	0.139
39	1100	7	8000	0.081
40	3000	7	3000	0.065

these coefficients so that the sum of the squares of the differences between the estimated values and the observed values of the measure of effectiveness is minimized. In this case, let p_i be the observed value of proportion defective for the ith lot, $\hat{p}_i$ the estimated value of proportion defective for the ith lot, and n the sample size (number of lots for which observations are available). Application of least squares analysis yields values of the undetermined coefficients such that $\sum_{i=1}^{n}(\hat{p}_i - p_i)^2$ is minimized.

Since simplicity, for practical reasons, is a desirable characteristic of any mathematical model, let us first attempt to estimate the value of proportion defective as a function of one of the independent variables x_1, x_2, or x_3, where x_1 is the production rate, x_2 the time between maintenance periods, and x_3 the lot size. That is, we will first develop models of the form

$$\hat{p} = b_1 x_1 \tag{1.2}$$

$$\hat{p} = b_2 x_2 \tag{1.3}$$

$$\hat{p} = b_3 x_3 \tag{1.4}$$

and assess the acceptability or validity of each. Based upon least squares analysis we obtain

$$\hat{p} = 0.00001788 x_1 \tag{1.5}$$

$$\hat{p} = 0.01367515 x_2 \tag{1.6}$$

$$\hat{p} = 0.00001921 x_3 \tag{1.7}$$

To determine the validity of each model the estimated value of proportion defective $\hat{p}_i$ is compared with the observed value p_i. A summary of this analysis is given in Table 1.3, where absolute error is given by $e = |\hat{p} - p|$.

As the results in Table 1.3 indicate, the model in Eq. (1.5) fails to estimate proportion defective within ± 0.01 in 65.0% of the cases examined; the model in Eq. (1.6), 87.5% of the time; that in Eq. (1.7), 80.0% of the time. Since a linear function of one variable is not acceptable, we will try linear functions of two variables. The relationships analyzed are of the form

$$\hat{p} = b_1 x_1 + b_2 x_2 \tag{1.8}$$

$$\hat{p} = b_1 x_1 + b_3 x_3 \tag{1.9}$$

$$\hat{p} = b_2 x_2 + b_3 x_3 \tag{1.10}$$

and as a result of least squares analysis are given explicitly by

$$\hat{p} = 0.00000987 x_1 + 0.00745536 x_2 \tag{1.11}$$

$$\hat{p} = 0.00001097 x_1 + 0.00000918 x_3 \tag{1.12}$$

$$\hat{p} = 0.00841685 x_2 + 0.00000881 x_3 \tag{1.13}$$

The validation analysis for Eq. (1.11), (1.12), and(1.13) is summarized in Table 1.4. In this case the estimating equations failed to achieve the

Table 1.3

Validation Analysis for Eq. (1.5), (1.6), and (1.7)

Absolute error interval	$\hat{p} = 0.00001788x_1$ Frequency	$\hat{p} = 0.01367515x_2$ Frequency	$p = 0.00001921x_3$ Frequency
$0.000 \leqslant e \leqslant 0.002$	3	0	0
$0.002 < e \leqslant 0.004$	1	3	4
$0.004 < e \leqslant 0.006$	1	1	2
$0.006 < e \leqslant 0.008$	3	1	2
$0.008 < e \leqslant 0.010$	6	0	0
$0.010 < e \leqslant 0.012$	2	1	1
$0.012 < e \leqslant 0.014$	0	0	3
$0.014 < e \leqslant 0.016$	2	3	1
$0.016 < e \leqslant 0.018$	1	2	3
$0.018 < e \leqslant 0.020$	0	0	1
$0.020 < e \leqslant 0.022$	0	5	0
$0.022 < e \leqslant 0.024$	3	1	4
$0.024 < e \leqslant 0.026$	2	1	2
$0.026 < e \leqslant 0.028$	0	2	0
$0.028 < e \leqslant 0.030$	0	6	0
$0.030 < e$	16	14	17
Total	40	40	40

Table 1.4

Validation Analysis for Eq. (1.11), (1.12), and (1.13)

Absolute error interval	$\hat{p} = 0.0000098x_1$ $+ 0.00745536x_2$ Frequency	$\hat{p} = 0.00001097x_1$ $+ 0.00000918x_3$ Frequency	$\hat{p} = 0.00841685x_2$ $+ 0.00000881x_3$ Frequency
$0.000 \leqslant e \leqslant 0.002$	4	2	1
$0.002 < e \leqslant 0.004$	5	4	2
$0.004 < e \leqslant 0.006$	4	5	2
$0.006 < e \leqslant 0.008$	4	2	2
$0.008 < e \leqslant 0.010$	6	2	4
$0.010 < e \leqslant 0.012$	2	1	3
$0.012 < e \leqslant 0.014$	1	1	0
$0.014 < e \leqslant 0.016$	4	2	3
$0.016 < e \leqslant 0.018$	4	3	1
$0.018 < e \leqslant 0.020$	2	2	2
$0.020 < e \leqslant 0.022$	0	1	2
$0.022 < e \leqslant 0.024$	2	4	3
$0.024 < e \leqslant 0.026$	1	2	4
$0.026 < e \leqslant 0.028$	1	1	0
$0.028 < e \leqslant 0.030$	0	2	0
$0.030 < e$	0	6	11
Total	40	40	40

Table 1.5

Validation Analysis for Eq. (1.15)

Absolute error interval	$\hat{p} = 0.00000829x_1 + 0.00575154x_2 + 0.00000452x_3$
	Frequency
$0.000 \leqslant e \leqslant 0.002$	10
$0.002 < e \leqslant 0.004$	8
$0.004 < e \leqslant 0.006$	8
$0.006 < e \leqslant 0.008$	7
$0.008 < e \leqslant 0.010$	0
$0.010 < e \leqslant 0.012$	4
$0.012 < e \leqslant 0.014$	2
$0.014 < e \leqslant 0.016$	1
Total	40

desired accuracy 42.5%, 62.5%, and 72.5% of the time, respectively, and hence all three equations must be judged inadequate.

Deriving a linear relationship of the form

$$\hat{p} = b_1x_1 + b_2x_2 + b_3x_3 \tag{1.14}$$

yields

$$\hat{p} = 0.00000829x_1 + 0.00575154x_2 + 0.00000452x_3 \tag{1.15}$$

and leads to the validation analysis in Table 1.5. In this case the model fails to achieve the required accuracy for 17.5% of the lots observed and yields results within ± 0.016 in all cases.

To further improve the model for estimation of proportion defective we will plot the error in estimation in Eq. (1.15) versus x_1, x_2, and x_3 in an attempt to identify consistent influence of one of these variables on proportion defective. In particular, we will attempt to identify a shift in the sign of the error as each of these variables is increased. The graph of the error in estimation e, where

$$e = \hat{p} - p \tag{1.16}$$

is shown in Fig. 1.1. The reader will note that there is no apparent functional variation in e with x_1 or x_3. However, e tends to assume negative values for small and large values of x_2 while taking on positive values in between. Variation of this type may indicate that the expression in Eq. (1.15) should include a different or additional term in x_2. We will first attempt to replace x_2 in Eq. (1.15) by x_2^2. That is,

$$\hat{p} = b_1x_1 + b_2x_2^2 + b_3x_3 \tag{1.17}$$

Application of the method of least squares yields

$$\hat{p} = 0.00000964x_1 + 0.00050669x_2^2 + 0.00000538x_3 \tag{1.18}$$

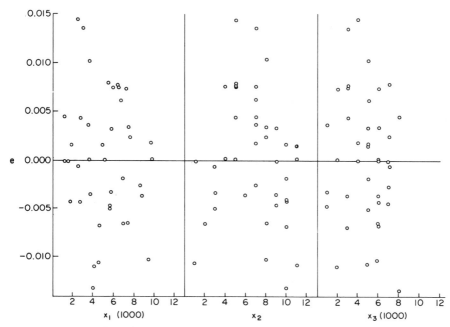

Fig. 1.1 Plot of error e versus x_1, x_2, and x_3 for the model in Eq. (1.15).

The valdiation analysis for this model is given in Table 1.6. Since the error in estimation was within ± 0.01 in each case, this model would be accepted as an adequate estimator of proportion defective for this application. ∎

The approach to model development illustrated in Example 1.1, least squares analysis or regression analysis, is by no means the only approach or even that most frequently used to define the relationship between the measure of system performance and the variables that affect that measure. In a similar vein the criterion for a satisfactory model and the associated

Table 1.6

Validation Analysis for Eq. (1.18)

Absolute error interval	$\hat{p} = 0.00000964x_1 + 0.00050669x_2^2 + 0.00000538x_3$
	Frequency
$0.000 \leqslant e \leqslant 0.002$	3
$0.002 < e \leqslant 0.004$	11
$0.004 < e \leqslant 0.006$	20
$0.006 < e \leqslant 0.008$	6
Total	40

validation analysis in Example 1.1 must be treated as unique to the problem discussed in that example. However, several general observations with respect to validation of mathematical models are noteworthy.

Before the validity of a model can be assessed, the criterion or criteria for model validity must be defined. In Example 1.1 the criterion for validity was the proportion of model-generated values which deviated from corresponding observed values by more than ± 0.01. One may question the objective merit of this criterion. That is, why is the model valid if it estimates proportion defective within ± 0.01? Why not ± 0.05 or ± 0.02? The answers to these questions depend upon the ultimate use of the model and the effect of errors in estimation on the overall performance of the manufacturing system. In any case, the ultimate criterion for model validity will include a certain amount of subjective judgment. Hence, the model finally accepted as a valid representation of reality is in fact only an approximate representation based upon subjective judgment.

In Example 1.1 a single criterion was chosen for validation purposes. In practice several criteria for model validity are usually specified, and it is unusual when the model finally accepted satisfies all of the criteria. In some cases the criteria chosen may be unrealistically restrictive. In other cases the analyst or team chosen to address the problem may not possess the capability necessary for formulation of the model required. In the final analysis one attempts to develop a model which satisfies the criteria for validity as nearly as possible. In the course of this endeavor, a series of models will probably be developed and rejected. The final result of the analysis will either be rejection of all models developed and termination of the project or acceptance of one of the models as "good enough" for the purposes intended. In this context "good enough" does not mean that the model necessarily satisfies all criteria for validity, but rather that it is at least better than anything else which is available and is better than nothing at all.

The preceding discussion of model validation implies that there is real-world data available which may be used to assess the performance of the model. However, if the data itself is unreliable it provides no basis for validation. A similar result occurs if no relevant data is available on the system modeled. Finally a comparison of model results with those obtained from the system may not be possible because the system modeled does not exist at the present time but is rather a proposal for future development. In any of these cases validation of the model will usually rest on judgments which are purely intuitive. In such situations the analyst must ask himself and other knowledgeable individuals whether the results of the model seem reasonable given the conditions of application of the model. Even when data is available for validation purposes one can anticipate that it will be insufficient either in quantity or variety to provide a basis for complete validation. Thus, in the final analysis the analyst must expect to exercise a good deal of subjective judgment based upon intuition before arriving at a satisfactory model.

FUNDAMENTALS OF DIFFERENTIAL AND INTEGRAL CALCULUS

As we have already pointed out, a mathematical model consists of an equation or set of equations which approximate the behavior of the system modeled. These equations relate one or more measures of system performance to those variables which influence the measure of performance. These variables may be either discrete or continuous. In this section we will discuss some of the characteristics of functions of continuous variables which are particularly important in mathematical modeling and in the subsequent analysis of mathematical models.

Functions of a Single Variable

Consider a variable x defined on the open interval (a, b). An interval (a, b) is said to be *open* if it does not include its end points, a and b in this case. On the other hand, a *closed interval* $[a, b]$ includes its end points, a and b. If x assumes an infinite number of values on some *finite* nonzero open interval, then x is said to be a continuous variable. For example, suppose that x is temperature measured in degrees centigrade. If we choose an open interval $(0, 10)$, then x can assume an infinite number of values on that interval. Now suppose that x is the number of cars on a parking lot. On any finite open interval x can assume only the integer values included on the interval. For example, on the open interval $(0, 8)$ x can assume the values $1, 2, 3, 4, 5, 6$ and 7 only and therefore is a discrete variable.

In Chapters 3 and 4 we shall be concerned with optimization of mathematical functions of continuous variables. In the case of functions of one or more continuous variables we shall employ the derivative. However, the derivative exists only if the function is continuous at the point at which the derivative is evaluated. In turn, continuity is dependent upon the existence of the limit of the function. Hence a discussion of limits, continuity, and the derivative is in order before pursuing the fundamentals of optimization theory.

Limits

Formally defined, the limit of a function $f(x)$ as x approaches the value a, expressed as $\lim_{x \to a} f(x)$, where a is called the *limit point*, is L if for every $\epsilon > 0$ there exists a $\delta > 0$ such that $|f(x) - L| < \epsilon$ whenever $|x - a|$

$< \delta$. This statement means that $f(x)$ approaches L as x approaches a if, as the difference between x and a decreases, the difference between $f(x)$ and L decreases.

Example 1.2   Show that

$$\lim_{x \to 2} f(x) = 4, \quad \text{where} \quad f(x) = x^2$$

and x can approach 2 through values less than 2 and values greater than 2.

Let us first examine $f(x)$ as x approaches 2 through values of x less than 2, where the limit is expressed by $\lim_{x \to 2-} f(x)$. In attempting to define $\lim_{x \to 2-} f(x)$ we are interested in the behavior of $f(x)$ for x near but less than 2. For $x < 2$, $|x - 2| = (2 - x)$. We will choose x on the interval $(1, 2)$ and examine $f(x)$ as x approaches 2 on this open interval. If $1 < x < 2$,

$$|x^2 - 4| = |(x - 2)(x + 2)|$$

On the interval $(1, 2)$, $(x + 2) \leqslant 4$. Therefore,

$$|x^2 - 4| \leqslant 4(2 - x)$$

For $(2 - x) < \delta$,

$$|x^2 - 4| < 4\delta$$

Letting $\epsilon = 4\delta$, whenever $(2 - x) < \delta$, $|x^2 - 4| < \epsilon$. Now considering the behavior of $f(x)$ as x approaches 2 through values of x greater than 2, we choose x on the interval $(2, 3)$, where

$$|x^2 - 4| = |(x - 2)(x + 2)| \leqslant 5(x - 2)$$

When $(x - 2) < \delta$,

$$f(x) < 5\delta$$

Letting $\epsilon = 5\delta$, $|x^2 - 4| < \epsilon$ whenever $(x - 2) < \delta$ and $\lim_{x \to 2+} f(x) = 4$. Since x^2 approaches 4 as x approaches 2 (through values of x greater than and less than 2), $\lim_{x \to 2} f(x) = 4$.   ∎

As implied in Example 1.2, the limit of a function exists at a point $x = a$ if and only if the left- and right-hand limits, $\lim_{x \to a-} f(x)$ and $\lim_{x \to a+} f(x)$ respectively, are finite and equal. That is, $\lim_{x \to a} f(x) = L$ if and only if

$$\lim_{x \to a-} f(x) = \lim_{x \to a+} f(x) = L \tag{1.19}$$

where L is a finite number. The limit of $f(x)$ does not exist if

(1)   the left- or right-hand limits tend to $\pm \infty$,
(2)   the left- or right-hand limits are undefined, and
(3)   the left- and right-hand limits exist but are unequal.

To illustrate these three cases consider the functions defined by

(a) $f(x) = \begin{cases} \dfrac{1}{a-x}, & x \leqslant a \\ x, & x > a \end{cases}$

(b) $g(x) = \sin(x), \quad -\infty < x < \infty$

(c) $h(x) = \begin{cases} 2x, & x \leqslant a \\ 5x, & x > a \end{cases}$

In the case of $f(x)$, $\lim_{x \to a-} f(x) = \infty$ and $\lim_{x \to a+} f(x) = a$. Since $\lim_{x \to a-} f(x)$ is undefined because it is infinite, the limit does not exist. Now consider $\lim_{x \to \infty} g(x)$. Here we consider only the left-hand limit since the limit from the right has no meaning. Since $\sin(x)$ is a bounded function, $g(x)$ does not approach infinity as $x \to \infty$. However, the behavior of $g(x)$ cannot be defined as $x \to \infty$. Hence $\lim_{x \to \infty} g(x)$ is undefined and therefore does not exist. In the case of $h(x)$,

$$\lim_{x \to a-} h(x) = 2a \quad \text{and} \quad \lim_{x \to a+} h(x) = 5a$$

For $a \neq 0$, $\lim_{x \to a-} h(x) \neq \lim_{x \to a+} h(x)$ and $\lim_{x \to a} h(x)$ does not exist.

The reader should note that $\lim_{x \to a} f(x)$ refers to the behavior of $f(x)$ close to a but not at a itself. For example, suppose

$$f(x) = \begin{cases} x^2, & x < 2 \\ 10, & x = 2 \\ x^2, & x > 2 \end{cases}$$

As shown in Example 1.2, $\lim_{x \to 2} f(x) = 4$ but $f(2) = 10$. Hence the limiting value of a function at a point a may be different from the value of the function at that point.

The following relationships are useful in evaluating the limit of the sum, difference, product, or ratio of functions. If $\lim_{x \to a} f(x) = L_1$ and $\lim_{x \to a} g(x) = L_2$, then

$$\lim_{x \to a} [f(x) \pm g(x)] = L_1 \pm L_2 \tag{1.20}$$

$$\lim_{x \to a} [f(x)g(x)] = L_1 L_2 \tag{1.21}$$

$$\lim_{x \to a} [f(x)/g(x)] = L_1/L_2 \quad \text{if} \quad L_2 \neq 0 \tag{1.22}$$

Frequently we are interested in the behavior of a function as x increases or decreases without limit, that is, as $x \to \infty$ or $x \to -\infty$. In such cases we cannot evaluate the limit from above and below since the limit point is infinite. Thus $\lim_{x \to \infty} f(x)$ is equivalent to $\lim_{x \to \infty-} f(x)$ and $\lim_{x \to -\infty} f(x)$ is equivalent to $\lim_{x \to -\infty+} f(x)$. Finally, if $f(x)$ increases or decreases indefinitely as $x \to a$, the limit does not exist but is expressed as $\lim_{x \to a} f(x) = \pm \infty$.

Continuity

If the limit of a function at a given point a and its value there are equal, then the function is said to be *continuous* at that point. That is, $f(x)$ is continuous at $x = a$ if and only if

$$\lim_{x \to a} f(x) = f(a) \tag{1.23}$$

As the definition and the word itself imply, continuity conveys the notion of unbroken flow. Continuity of mathematical functions may be thought of in that sense. If one were to graph a continuous function over a closed interval, the function could be traced without ever lifting the pencil from the paper. On the other hand, discontinuity carries with it the notion of a break in flow, and this is the case where a function is discontinuous at one or more points, as illustrated in Fig. 1.2 through 1.5.

Derivative

The derivative of a function at a point a is often thought of as the rate of change in the function at that point, or the slope of a straight line tangent to the function at that point. Suppose that we examine a function $f(x)$ at the points x_0 and $x_0 + \Delta x$. The slope b of the line joining $f(x_0)$ and $f(x_0 + \Delta x)$ is given by

$$b = \frac{f(x_0 + \Delta x) - f(x_0)}{\Delta x} \tag{1.24}$$

If we take the limit of Eq. (1.24) as $\Delta x \to 0$, we obtain the derivative of $f(x)$ at x_0 denoted by

$$f'(x_0), \quad (d/dx)f(x_0), \quad \text{or} \quad (d/dx)f(x)|_{x = x_0}$$

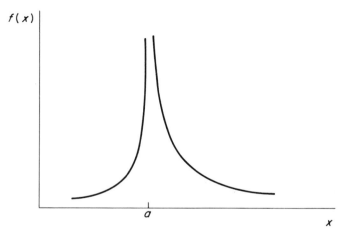

Fig. 1.2   Discontinuity at $x = a$ where $\lim_{x \to a} f(x)$ does not exist.

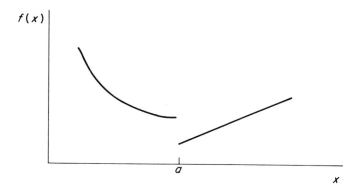

Fig. 1.3 Discontinuity at $x = a$ where $\lim_{x \to a} f(x)$ does not exist.

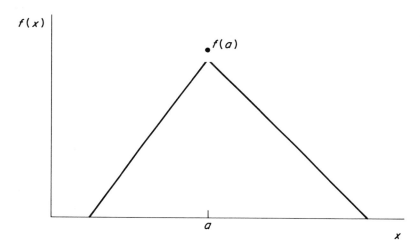

Fig. 1.4 Discontinuity at $x = a$ where $\lim_{x \to a} f(x)$ exists but $\lim_{x \to a} f(x) \neq f(a)$.

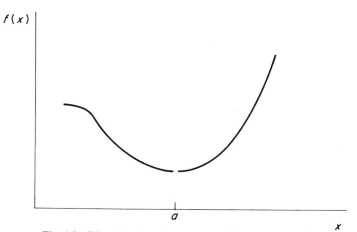

Fig. 1.5 Discontinuity at $x = a$ where $f(x)$ is undefined.

and is defined as

$$f'(x_0) = \lim_{\Delta x \to 0} \frac{f(x_0 + \Delta x) - f(x_0)}{\Delta x} \qquad (1.25)$$

For the derivative to exist at x_0, $f(x)$ must be continuous there. However, continuity is not a sufficient condition for existence of the derivative. That is, the limit in Eq. (1.25) may not exist even though $f(x)$ is continuous at x_0. Hence continuity is said to be a necessary but not a sufficient condition for existence of the derivative.

Example 1.3   Find the derivative of $f(x)$ at x_0, where

$$f(x) = x^2$$

As a result of our discussion of limits and continuity we may show that $f(x)$ is continuous for all finite values of x_0. Now

$$f'(x_0) = \lim_{\Delta x \to 0} \frac{(x_0 + \Delta x)^2 - x_0^2}{\Delta x}$$

if the limit exists. Evaluating this limit yields

$$\lim_{\Delta x \to 0} \frac{(x_0 + \Delta x)^2 - x_0^2}{\Delta x} = \lim_{\Delta x \to 0} \frac{\left[x_0^2 + 2x_0\Delta x + (\Delta x)^2\right] - x_0^2}{\Delta x}$$

$$= \lim_{\Delta x \to 0} \left[2x_0 + \Delta x\right] = 2x_0 \quad \blacksquare$$

Example 1.4   Show that the derivative of $f(x)$ does not exist at x_0 even though $f(x)$ is continuous at x_0, where

$$f(x) = \begin{cases} 5x, & x < x_0 \\ 5x^2/x_0, & x \geqslant x_0 \end{cases}$$

For the left- and right-hand limits of $f(x)$ at x_0 we have

$$\lim_{x \to x_0-} f(x) = 5x_0 \qquad \text{and} \qquad \lim_{x \to x_0+} f(x) = 5x_0$$

Since

$$\lim_{x \to x_0-} f(x) = \lim_{x \to x_0+} f(x)$$

the limit of $f(x)$ exists at $x = x_0$, and since $f(x_0) = \lim_{x \to x_0} f(x)$, $f(x)$ is continuous at x_0. Now let us attempt to define $f'(x_0)$. If $f'(x_0)$ exists, then

$$\lim_{\Delta x \to 0-} \frac{f(x_0 + \Delta x) - f(x_0)}{\Delta x} = \lim_{\Delta x \to 0+} \frac{f(x_0 + \Delta x) - f(x_0)}{\Delta x}$$

Now

$$\lim_{\Delta x \to 0-} \frac{f(x_0 + \Delta x) - f(x_0)}{\Delta x} = \lim_{\Delta x \to 0-} \frac{5(x_0 + x) - 5x_0}{\Delta x}$$

$$= \lim_{\Delta x \to 0-} [5] = 5$$

For the right-hand limit we have

$$\lim_{\Delta x \to 0+} \frac{f(x_0 + \Delta x) - f(x_0)}{\Delta x} = \lim_{\Delta x \to 0+} \frac{5\dfrac{(x_0 + \Delta x)^2}{x_0} - 5x_0}{\Delta x}$$

$$= \lim_{\Delta x \to 0+} \frac{\dfrac{5\left[x_0^2 + 2x_0\Delta x + (\Delta x)^2\right]}{x_0} - 5x_0}{\Delta x}$$

$$= \lim_{\Delta x \to 0+} \left[10x_0 + \frac{5\Delta x}{x_0}\right] = 10x_0$$

Since the left- and right-hand limits are unequal, the limit defined for the derivative does not exist and the derivative itself does not exist. ∎

Let $f(x)$ and $g(x)$ be functions for which $f'(x)$ and $g'(x)$ exist on the open interval (a, b). The following properties can be stated:

(1) $$\frac{d}{dx}\left[f(x) \pm g(x)\right] = f'(x) \pm g'(x) \tag{1.26}$$

(2) $$\frac{d}{dx}\left[f(x)g(x)\right] = f(x)g'(x) + g(x)f'(x) \tag{1.27}$$

(3) $$\frac{d}{dx}\left[\frac{f(x)}{g(x)}\right] = \frac{g(x)f'(x) - f(x)g'(x)}{\left[g(x)\right]^2}, \qquad g(x) \neq 0 \tag{1.28}$$

In our discussion of limits we mentioned that the limit of the ratio is equal to the ratio of the limits. Consider the case where $\lim_{x \to a} f(x) = \lim_{x \to a} g(x) = 0$ or $\lim_{x \to x} f(x) = \lim_{x \to a} g(x) = \infty$. The expression $\lim_{x \to a}\left[f(x)/g(x)\right]$ is called an *indeterminate form* since the ratio of the limits is $0/0$ or ∞/∞. If $\lim_{x \to a}\left[f(x)/g(x)\right]$ exists, the derivative can be used to resolve an indeterminate form. Specifically, if $f(x)$ and $g(x)$ are differentiable on the interval (b, c) and

(1) $g'(x) \neq 0$ for x on (b, c)

(2) $\lim_{x \to a} f(x) = \lim_{x \to a} g(x) = 0$ or $\lim_{x \to a} f(x) = \lim_{x \to a} g(x) = \infty$

(3) $\lim_{x \to a}\left[f'(x)/g'(x)\right] = L$ $\tag{1.29}$

then

$$\lim_{x \to a} \left[f(x)/g(x) \right] = L$$

This result is known as L'Hôpital's rule.

Example 1.5   Define

$$\lim_{x \to \infty} \frac{x^2}{e^x}$$

Since

$$\lim_{x \to \infty} x^2 = \lim_{x \to \infty} e^x = \infty$$

the limit of the ratio is indeterminate. Applying Eq. (1.29), where $f(x) = x^2$ and $g(x) = e^x$, we have

$$\lim_{x \to \infty} \left[\frac{f'(x)}{g'(x)} \right] = \lim_{x \to \infty} \left[\frac{2x}{e^x} \right] \tag{1.30}$$

Since

$$\lim_{x \to \infty} 2x = \lim_{x \to \infty} e^x = \infty$$

the expression in Eq. (1.30) is still indeterminate. Reapplying L'Hôpital's rule yields

$$\lim_{x \to \infty} \left[f''(x)/g''(x) \right] = \lim_{x \to \infty} \left[\frac{2}{e^x} \right] = 0$$

since $\lim_{x \to \infty} (2) = 2$ and $\lim_{x \to \infty} (e^x) = \infty$. ■

Example 1.6   The efficiency of an operator is a function of the time he spends on the job. If t is the number of years of experience of an operator, then $f(t)$, his expected efficiency at time t, is given by

$$f(t) = b \left[1 - e^{-\lambda t} \right]$$

where λ and b are constants which vary from operator to operator. What is the maximum of operator efficiency and how long will it take an operator to achieve 98% of maximum efficiency?

$f(t)$ is an increasing function of t; maximum efficiency is attained as $t \to \infty$. Now

$$\lim_{t \to \infty} f(t) = \lim_{t \to \infty} b \left[1 - e^{\lambda t} \right] = \lim_{t \to \infty} (b) - (b) \lim_{t \to \infty} e^{-\lambda t} = b$$

The operator achieves 98% of maximum efficiency at time t when

$$f(t)/b = 0.98 \qquad \text{or} \qquad f(t) = 0.98b$$

Hence the required value of t is given by

$$1 - e^{-\lambda t} = 0.98 \qquad \text{and} \qquad t = 3.91/\lambda \quad ■$$

Example 1.7 A long-distance operator handles telephone calls on a first come, first served basis. The probability that a call arrives in a small increment of time Δt is $\lambda \Delta t$, where λ is the arrival rate. The probability that the operator connects a call in time Δt is $\mu \Delta t$, where μ is the service rate. If a call is placed when the operator is busy, the calling party hangs up and calls at a later time. Let $P_0(t)$ be the probability the operator is idle at time t, and let $P_1(t)$ be the probability the operator is servicing a call at time t. Find the rate of change of $P_0(t)$ and the steady-state values of $P_0(t)$ and $P_1(t)$. The steady state of a function $f(t)$ is given by $\lim_{t \to \infty} f(t)$ if the limit exists.

The rate of change of a function is given by its derivative. To find the derivatives of $P_0(t)$ and $P_1(t)$ we must first find $P_0(t + \Delta t)$ and $P_1(t + \Delta t)$. We first note that

$$P_0(t) + P_1(t) = 1$$

since the operator must either be idle or busy at any time t. $P_0(t + \Delta t)$ can be expressed by

$$P_0(t + \Delta t) = P_0(t) \quad [\text{probability of 0 calls in } \Delta t]$$

$$+ P_0(t) \quad [\text{probability of 1 call and 1 service in } \Delta t]$$

$$+ P_0(t) \quad [\text{probability of 2 calls and 2 services in } \Delta t]$$

$$\vdots$$

$$+ P_0(t) \quad [\text{probability of } n \text{ calls and } n \text{ services in } \Delta t]$$

$$\vdots$$

$$+ P_1(t) \quad [\text{probability of 0 calls and 1 service in } \Delta t]$$

$$+ P_1(t) \quad [\text{probability of 1 call and 2 services in } \Delta t]$$

$$\vdots$$

$$+ P_1(t) \quad [\text{probability of } n \text{ calls and } n + 1 \text{ services in } \Delta t]$$

$$\vdots$$

Now

Probability of n calls in $\Delta t = (\lambda \Delta t)^n, \ n > 0,$
Probability of n services in Δt given n or more handled during Δt
$\quad = (\mu \Delta t)^n, \ n > 0,$
Probability of 0 calls in $\Delta t = 1 - \lambda \Delta t,$

Probability of 0 services in

$$\Delta t = \begin{cases} 1 \text{ if system empty during } \Delta t \\ 1 - \mu\Delta t \text{ if system not empty during } \Delta t \end{cases}$$

and

$$P_0(t + \Delta t) = P_0(t)(1 - \lambda\Delta t) + \sum_{n=1}^{\infty} P_0(t)(\lambda\Delta t)^n(\mu\Delta t)^n$$

$$+ P_1(t)\mu\Delta t(1 - \lambda\Delta t) + \sum_{n=1}^{\infty} P_1(t)(\lambda\Delta t)^n(\mu\Delta t)^{n+1}$$

Therefore

$$\frac{P_0(t + \Delta t) - P_0(t)}{\Delta t} = -\lambda P_0(t) + \sum_{n=1}^{\infty} P_0(t)(\lambda\mu)^n(\Delta t)^{2n-1}$$

$$+ \mu P_1(t) - \lambda\mu\Delta t P_1(t) + \sum_{n=1}^{\infty} P_1(t)(\lambda\mu)^{2n+1}(\Delta t)^{2n}$$

and $(d/dt)P_0(t)$ is given by

$$\frac{d}{dt} P_0(t) = \lim_{\Delta t \to 0} \left[-\lambda P_0(t) + \sum_{n=1}^{\infty} P_0(t)(\lambda\mu)^n(\Delta t)^{2n-1} + \mu P_1(t) \right.$$

$$\left. - \lambda\mu\Delta t P_1(t) + \sum_{n=1}^{\infty} P_1(t)(\lambda\mu)^{2n+1}(\Delta t)^{2n} \right]$$

$$= -\lambda P_0(t) + \mu P_1(t)$$

$$= -\lambda P_0(t) + \mu[1 - P_0(t)]$$

$$= \mu - (\lambda + \mu)P_0(t)$$

In the steady state $\lim_{t \to \infty} (d/dt)P_0(t) = 0$. Let

$$\lim_{t \to \infty} P_0(t) = P_0$$

Then

$$\lim_{t \to \infty} [\mu - (\lambda + \mu)P_0(t)] = 0 \quad \text{and} \quad P_0 = \frac{\mu}{\lambda + \mu}$$

Since $P_0(t) + P_1(t) = 1$,

$$P_1 = \frac{\lambda}{\lambda + \mu} \quad \blacksquare$$

Higher-Order Derivatives

As we shall see in our treatment of classical optimization theory, the analyst is sometimes interested in derivatives of order higher than the first, where $f'(x)$ is called the *first derivative* of $f(x)$. The *second derivative* of $f(x)$ is simply the first derivative of the first derivative of $f(x)$ and is denoted $f''(x)$. In general, the *nth derivative* of $f(x)$, denoted $f^n(x)$, is given by $(d/dx)f^{n-1}(x)$.

Knowledge of the first m derivatives of a function leads to a convenient method for approximating the function. We shall find such approximations particularly useful in classical optimization theory. Let $f(x)$ be a continuous function on the closed interval $[a, b]$. If the first m derivatives, $f^i(x)$, $i = 1, 2, \ldots, m$, exist and are continuous on (a, b), then for x and x_0 on (a, b) there exists a point x_1 on the open interval (x_0, x) if $x_0 < x$ and on (x, x_0) if $x < x_0$ such that

$$f(x) = f(x_0) + \sum_{i=1}^{n-1} \frac{(x - x_0)^i}{i!} f^i(x_0) + \frac{(x - x_0)^n}{n!} f^n(x_1) \quad (1.31)$$

where $n \leq m$. This result is called *Taylor's mean-value theorem*. The expression $[(x - x_0)^n/n!]f^n(x_1)$ is called the *remainder term* and expresses the error when $f(x)$ is approximated by

$$f(x) \cong f(x_0) + \sum_{i=1}^{n-1} \frac{(x - x_0)^i}{i!} f^i(x_0) \quad (1.32)$$

Equation (1.32) is a polynomial approximation for $f(x)$ at a point x near x_0. As the degree of the polynomial increases the accuracy of the approximation also increases as shown in the following example.

Example 1.8 Approximate $f(x)$ using first-, second-, and third-degree Taylor polynomials on the interval $(1, 2)$, where

$$f(x) = xe^x$$

For each approximation estimate the maximum error.
In each case we let $x_0 = 1.5$. At $x_0 = 1.5$ we have

$$f(x_0) = 6.722534$$
$$f'(x_0) = e^x + xe^x|_{x=x_0} = 11.204223$$
$$f''(x_0) = 2e^x + xe^x|_{x=x_0} = 15.685912$$
$$f'''(x_0) = 3e^x + xe^x|_{x=x_0} = 20.167601$$

Let $f_1(x)$, $f_2(x)$, and $f_3(x)$ be the first-, second-, and third-degree Taylor polynomial approximations to $f(x)$. Then

$$f_1(x) = f(x_0) + \frac{x - x_0}{1} f'(x_0)$$

$$= 6.722534 + (x - 1.5)(11.204223) = -10.083801 + 11.204223x$$

$$f_2(x) = f(x_0) + \frac{x - x_0}{1} f'(x_0) + \frac{(x - x_0)^2}{2} f''(x_0)$$

$$= 6.722534 + (x - 1.5)(11.204223) + (0.5)(x - 1.5)^2(15.685912)$$

$$= 7.562851 - 12.324645x + 7.842956x^2$$

$$f_3(x) = f(x_0) + \frac{x - x_0}{1} f'(x_0) + \frac{(x - x_0)^2}{2} f''(x_0) + \frac{(x - x_0)^3}{6} f'''(x_0)$$

$$= 6.7225344 + (x - 1.5)(11.204223) + (0.5)(x - 1.5)^2(15.685912)$$

$$+ (0.1667)(x - 1.5)^3(20.167601)$$

$$= -3.783706 + 10.368438x - 7.285775x^2 + 3.361939x^3$$

The remainder term for these approximations will be denoted by $R_1(x_1)$, $R_2(x_1)$, and $R_3(x_1)$, respectively, where x_1 lies between x and x_0 and is given by

$$R_1(x_1) = \frac{(x - x_0)^2}{2!} f''(x_1)$$

$$= (x - 1.5)^2(e^{x_1} + 0.5x_1e^{x_1})$$

$$R_2(x_1) = \frac{(x - x_0)^3}{3!} f'''(x_1)$$

$$= (x - 1.5)^3(0.5e^{x_1} + 0.1667x_1e^{x_1})$$

$$R_3(x_1) = \frac{(x - x_0)^4}{4!} f^4(x_1)$$

$$= (x - 1.5)^4(0.1667e^{x_1} + 0.0417x_1e^{x_1})$$

Let us now examine the magnitude of $R_i(x_1)$, $i = 1, 2, 3$, that is, $|R_i(x_1)|$. For x on the interval $(1.0, 1.5)$ the maximum value of $|R_i(x_1)|$ occurs when $x_1 = 0.0$ and is given by $x_1 = 2.0$ when x lies on $(1.5, 2.0)$. Hence for x on $(1.0, 1.5)$,

$$|R_1(x_1)| \leqslant 7.842956(1.5 - x)^2$$

$$|R_2(x_1)| \leqslant 3.361491(1.5 - x)^3$$

$$|R_3(x_1)| \leqslant 1.027427(1.5 - x)^4$$

and for x on $(1.5, 2.0)$,

$$|R_1(x_1)| \leqslant 14.778112(x - 1.5)^2$$

$$|R_2(x_1)| \leqslant 6.158039(x - 1.5)^3$$

$$|R_3(x_1)| \leqslant 1.847264(x - 1.5)^4$$

Now let us examine the actual and approximate values of $f(x)$ for each approximation and the actual and maximum estimated absolute errors. These results are summarized in Table 1.7. As this example illustrates, the error in the approximation decreases for all $x \neq x_0$ as the degree of the approximating polynomial increases. In addition, for each polynomial approximation, the error resulting decreases as x approaches x_0. ∎

Table 1.7

Summary of the Results of Example 1.8

x	$f(x)$	$f_1(x)$	$f_2(x)$	$f_3(x)$	max $|R_1(x_1)|$	$\begin{array}{c}|f(x) - \\ f_1(x)|\end{array}$	max $|R_2(x_1)|$	$\begin{array}{c}|f(x) - \\ f_2(x)|\end{array}$	max $|R_3(x_1)|$	$\begin{array}{c}|f(x) - \\ f_3(x)|\end{array}$
1.1	3.3045	2.2408	3.4957	3.2805	1.2549	1.0637	0.2151	0.1911	0.0263	0.0240
1.2	3.9841	3.3612	4.0671	3.9763	0.7059	0.6229	0.0908	0.0830	0.0083	0.0078
1.3	4.7700	4.4817	4.7954	4.7684	0.3137	0.2895	0.0269	0.0253	0.0016	0.0016
1.4	5.6772	5.6021	5.6805	5.6771	0.0784	0.0752	0.0034	0.0033	0.0001	0.0001
1.5	6.7225	6.7225	6.7225	6.7225	0.0000	0.0000	0.0000	0.0000	0.0000	0.0000
1.6	7.9249	7.8430	7.9214	7.9247	0.1478	0.0819	0.0062	0.0035	0.0002	0.0001
1.7	9.3057	8.9634	9.2771	9.3040	0.5911	0.3423	0.0493	0.0286	0.0030	0.0018
1.8	10.8894	10.0838	10.7897	10.8804	1.3300	0.8056	0.1663	0.0997	0.0150	0.0090
1.9	12.7032	11.2042	12.4591	12.6742	2.3645	1.4990	0.3941	0.2441	0.0473	0.0290

Integration

Consider the problem of finding the area under a function $f(x)$ for x on the closed interval $[a, b]$, such as that shown in Fig. 1.6. We might estimate the area by first approximating the function by a series of rectangles each of width Δ_n, where n is the number of rectangles used in the approxima-

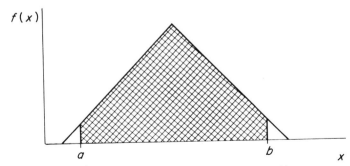

Fig. 1.6   Area under $f(x)$ on the interval $[a, b]$.

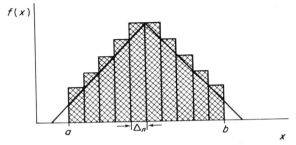

Fig. 1.7   Outer area approximation to the area under $f(x)$ on the interval $[a, b]$.

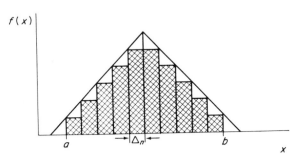

Fig. 1.8   Inner area approximation to the area under $f(x)$ on the interval $[a, b]$.

tion. The sum of the areas of the approximating rectangles is then an estimate of the area under the function. The approximating rectangle may be constructed either as shown in Fig. 1.7 or Fig. 1.8. The approximation in Fig. 1.7 is called the *outer area* and that in Fig. 1.8 the *inner area*. Let $\overline{A}_n$ and $\underline{A}_n$ be the outer and inner area approximations where each approximation includes n rectangles. Then $\underline{A}_n \leqslant \overline{A}_n$. However, as n increases $\underline{A}_n$ and $\overline{A}_n$ will become better approximations to the true area under $f(x)$ for x on the interval $[a, b]$. If

$$\lim_{n \to \infty} \underline{A}_n = \lim_{n \to \infty} \overline{A}_n \qquad (1.33)$$

then the area under the function $f(x)$ exists and is called the integral of $f(x)$ defined by

$$\int_a^b f(x)\,dx = \lim_{n \to \infty} \underline{A}_n = \lim_{n \to \infty} \overline{A}_n \qquad (1.34)$$

If a function $f(x)$ is continuous at all but a finite number of points on the interval $[a, b]$, then the integral of $f(x)$ exists on that interval. For example, suppose that $f(x)$ is continuous throughout $[a, b]$ except at c' and c'', where $a < c' < c'' < b$. Then

$$\int_a^b f(x)\,dx = \int_a^{c'} f(x)\,dx + \int_{c'}^{c''} f(x)\,dx + \int_{c''}^b f(x)\,dx \qquad (1.35)$$

Thus a function may not even be defined at a finite set of points on $[a, b]$, and yet its integral will still exist if it is continuous elsewhere.

If the *limits of integration* a and b are constant, the resulting integral is referred to as a *definite integral*. Suppose that x is an arbitrary point on the interval $[a, b]$ and that $F'(x) = f(x)$. Then $F(x)$ is called the *antiderivative* of $f(x)$ or the *indefinite integral* of $f(x)$. The antiderivative of $f(x)$ can be used to evaluate the definite integral of $f(x)$. That is,

$$\int_a^b f(x)\,dx = F(b) - F(a) \qquad (1.36)$$

The relationship in Eq. (1.36) is called the *fundamental theorem* of *integral calculus* and allows us to evaluate the definite integral of $f(x)$ between any limits a and b for which $F(x)$ is defined.

While Eq. (1.34) can be used to define the indefinite or definite integral, the process can be rather tedious. More often than not the analyst will resort to a table of indefinite and definite integrals, although these tables possess a limited number of forms. In those cases where the antiderivative cannot be detremined directly, the method of *integration by parts* may be useful. Suppose we wish to determine $\int_a^b f(x)\,dx$ where $f(x)$ can be expressed as $h(x)g'(x)$. Then

$$\int_a^b f(x)\,dx = \int_a^b h(x)g'(x)\,dx = g(x)h(x)\Big|_a^b - \int_a^b g(x)h'(x)\,dx \qquad (1.37)$$

Obviously we attempt to define $g'(x)$ and $h(x)$ so that $\int_a^b g(x)h'(x)\,dx$ is more easily resolved than $\int_a^b h(x)g'(x)\,dx$. To illustrate the method of integration by parts, consider the following example.

Example 1.9 The probability density function of the gamma random variable is

$$f(x) = \begin{cases} 0, & -\infty < x < 0 \\ \dfrac{\lambda^\alpha}{\Gamma(\alpha)} \, x^{\alpha-1} e^{-\lambda x}, & 0 \leqslant x < \infty \end{cases}$$

where $\lambda > 0$, $\alpha > 0$. The cumulative distribution function of a random variable is defined by

$$F(x) = \int_{-\infty}^{x} f(y)\,dy$$

if x is a continuous random variable. Find the cumulative distribution function of the gamma random variable if α is integer valued. Note that for the integer α,

$$\Gamma(\alpha) = (\alpha - 1)! = (\alpha - 1)(\alpha - 2)(\alpha - 3) \cdots 3 \cdot 2 \cdot 1$$

For the gamma random variable $F(x)$ is defined by

$$F(x) = \int_{-\infty}^{x} f(y)\,dy$$

$$= \int_{-\infty}^{0} 0\,dy + \int_{0}^{x} \frac{\lambda^\alpha}{\Gamma(\alpha)} \, y^{\alpha-1} e^{\lambda y}\,dy$$

$$= \int_{0}^{x} \frac{\lambda^\alpha}{\Gamma(\alpha)} \, y^{\alpha-1} e^{-\lambda y}\,dy$$

We will attempt to obtain an expression for $F(x)$ by successive application of integration by parts. Letting

$$h(y) = \frac{(\lambda y)^{\alpha-1}}{(\alpha-1)!}, \qquad g'(y) = \lambda e^{-\lambda y}$$

we have

$$h'(y) = \lambda \frac{(\lambda y)^{\alpha-2}}{(\alpha-2)!}, \qquad g(y) = -e^{-\lambda y}$$

and

$$F(x) = -\left. \frac{(\lambda y)^{\alpha-1}}{(\alpha-2)!} \, e^{-\lambda y} \right|_{0}^{x} - \int_{0}^{x} - \lambda \frac{(\lambda y)^{\alpha-2}}{(\alpha-2)!} \, e^{-\lambda y}\,dy$$

$$= -\frac{(\lambda x)^{\alpha-1}}{(\alpha-1)!} \, e^{\lambda x} + \int_{0}^{x} \lambda \frac{(\lambda y)^{\alpha-2}}{(\alpha-2)!} \, e^{-\lambda y}\,dy$$

Again applying integration by parts, let

$$h(y) = \frac{(\lambda y)^{\alpha - 2}}{(\alpha - 2)!}, \qquad g'(y) = \lambda e^{-\lambda y}$$

Then

$$h'(y) = \lambda \frac{(\lambda y)^{\alpha - 3}}{(\alpha - 3)!}, \qquad g(y) = -e^{-\lambda y}$$

and

$$F(x) = -\frac{(\lambda x)^{\alpha - 1}}{(\alpha - 1)!} e^{-\lambda x} + \left[-\frac{(\lambda y)^{\alpha - 2}}{(\alpha - 2)!} e^{-\lambda y} \Big|_0^x - \int_0^x - \lambda \frac{(\lambda y)^{\alpha - 3}}{(\alpha - 3)!} e^{-\lambda y} \, dy \right]$$

$$= -\frac{(\lambda x)^{\alpha - 1}}{(\alpha - 1)!} e^{-\lambda x} - \frac{(\lambda x)^{\alpha - 2}}{(\alpha - 2)!} e^{-\lambda x} + \int_0^x \lambda \frac{(\lambda y)^{\alpha - 3}}{(\alpha - 3)!} e^{-\lambda y} \, dy$$

$$= -\sum_{i=1}^{2} \frac{(\lambda x)^{\alpha - i}}{(\alpha - i)!} e^{-\lambda x} + \int_0^x \lambda \frac{(\lambda y)^{\alpha - 3}}{(\alpha - 3)!} e^{-\lambda y} \, dy$$

Applying the method of integration by parts again, we have

$$h(y) = \frac{(\lambda y)^{\alpha - 3}}{(\alpha - 3)!}, \qquad g'(y) = \lambda e^{-\lambda y}$$

and

$$h'(y) = \lambda \frac{(\lambda y)^{\alpha - 4}}{(\alpha - 4)!}, \quad g(y) = -e^{-\lambda y}$$

Finally

$$F(x) = -\sum_{i=1}^{2} \frac{(\lambda x)^{\alpha - i}}{(\alpha - i)!} e^{\lambda x} + \left[-\frac{(\lambda y)^{\alpha - 3}}{(\alpha - 3)!} e^{-\lambda x} \Big|_0^x - \int_0^x - \lambda \frac{(\lambda y)^{\alpha - 4}}{(\alpha - 4)!} e^{-\lambda y} \, dy \right]$$

$$= -\sum_{i=1}^{3} \frac{(\lambda x)^{\alpha - i}}{(\alpha - 1)!} e^{-\lambda x} + \int_0^x \lambda \frac{(\lambda y)^{\alpha - 4}}{(\alpha - 4)!} e^{-\lambda y} \, dy$$

The first three applications would lead us to guess that after j applications $F(x)$ would be given by

$$F(x) = \sum_{i=1}^{j} \frac{(\lambda x)^{\alpha - i}}{(\alpha - i)!} e^{\lambda x} + \int_0^x \lambda \frac{(\lambda y)^{\alpha - j - 1}}{(\alpha - j - 1)!} e^{-\lambda y} \, dy$$

If this form is in fact correct, then integration of this form by parts should lead to the expression

$$F(x) = -\sum_{i=1}^{j+1} \frac{(\lambda x)^{\alpha - i}}{(\alpha - i)!} e^{-\lambda x} + \int_0^x \frac{(\lambda y)^{\alpha - j - 2}}{(\alpha - j - 2)!} e^{-\lambda y} dy \qquad (1.38)$$

Let

$$h(y) = \frac{(\lambda y)^{\alpha - j - 1}}{(\alpha - j - 1)!}, \qquad g'(y) = \lambda e^{-\lambda y}$$

which yields

$$h'(y) = \lambda \frac{(\lambda y)^{\alpha - j - 2}}{(\alpha - j - 2)!}, \qquad g(y) = -e^{-\lambda y}$$

and

$$F(x) = -\sum_{i=1}^{j} \frac{(\lambda x)^{\alpha - i}}{(\alpha - i)!} e^{-\lambda x}$$

$$+ \left[-\frac{(\lambda y)^{\alpha - j - 1}}{(\alpha - j - 1)!} e^{-\lambda y} \Big|_0^x - \int_0^x - \lambda \frac{(\lambda y)^{\alpha - j - 2}}{(\alpha - j - 2)!} e^{-\lambda y} dy \right]$$

$$= \sum_{i=1}^{j+1} \frac{(\lambda x)^{\alpha - i}}{(\alpha - i)!} e^{-\lambda x} + \int_0^x \lambda \frac{(\lambda y)^{\alpha - j - 2}}{(\alpha - j - 2)!} e^{-\lambda y} dy$$

Thus the expression in Eq. (1.38) holds for all $j \leq \alpha - 2$. Letting $j = \alpha - 2$, we have

$$F(x) = -\sum_{i=1}^{\alpha - 1} \frac{(\lambda x)^{\alpha - i}}{(\alpha - i)!} e^{-\lambda x} + \int_0^x \lambda e^{-\lambda y} dy$$

$$= -\sum_{i=1}^{\alpha - 1} \frac{(\lambda x)^{\alpha - i}}{(\alpha - i)!} e^{-\lambda x} - e^{-\lambda y} \Big|_0^x$$

$$= 1 - \sum_{i=1}^{\alpha} \frac{(\lambda x)^{\alpha - i}}{(\alpha - i)!} e^{-\lambda x} \quad \blacksquare \qquad (1.39)$$

The method used to develop the expression in Eq. (1.39) is called *proof by induction*. The general approach taken in a proof by induction starts with the iterative application of a technique (integration by parts in Example 1.9) which gives the first, second, third, etc., terms in a sequence. That is, the technique is applied to the first term to generate the second, to the second term to generate the third, etc. An attempt is made to generate a sufficient number of terms to recognize a pattern to the sequence. Once the pattern is identified the mathematical expression for the jth term in the sequence is defined. The technique used to obtain the initial terms in the sequence is then applied to the jth term to generate the $(j + 1)$st term. If the $(j + 1)$st term is equal to the jth term when j is increased by one, the proof is complete. If not, the general term specified is in error. The latter case usually arises when the initial sequence of terms generated is insufficient in number to specify a unique general term.

Example 1.10 Show that

$$\int_0^\infty \lambda \frac{(\lambda x)^{\alpha - 1}}{(\alpha - 1)!} e^{-\lambda x} dx = 1$$

where λ is positive valued and α is a postive integer.

From example 1.9

$$F(x) = 1 - \sum_{i=1}^{\alpha} \frac{(\lambda x)^{\alpha - i}}{(\alpha - i)!} e^{-\lambda x}$$

From Eq. (1.36) we have

$$\int_a^b \lambda \frac{(\lambda x)^{\alpha - 1}}{(\alpha - 1)!} e^{-\lambda x} dx = F(b) - F(a)$$

Now

$$F(0) = 1 - e^{\lambda x} \sum_{i=1}^{\alpha - 1} \frac{(\lambda x)^{\alpha - i}}{(\alpha - i)!} e^{-\lambda x} \Bigg|_{x=0} = 0$$

For $b = \infty$ we cannot give specific definition to $F(b)$ since $F(x)$ is not continuous at $x = \infty$. In cases such as this we define $F(\infty)$ as

$$F(\infty) = \lim_{x \to \infty} F(e)$$

Thus

$$F(\infty) = \lim_{x \to \infty} \left[1 - \sum_{i=1}^{\alpha} \frac{(\lambda x)^{\alpha - i}}{(\alpha - i)!} e^{-\lambda x} \right]$$

$$= 1 - \sum_{i=1}^{\alpha} \lim_{x \to \infty} \left[\frac{(\lambda x)^{\alpha - i}}{(\alpha - i)!} e^{-\lambda x} \right]$$

$$= 1 - \sum_{i=1}^{\alpha} \frac{\lambda^{\alpha - i}}{(\alpha - i)!} \lim_{x \to \infty} \left[\frac{x^{\alpha - i}}{e^{\lambda x}} \right]$$

The limit of $x^{\alpha - i}/e^{\lambda x}$ as $x \to \infty$ is indeterminate. To resolve this indeterminate form we will apply L'Hôpital's rule, which yields

$$\lim_{x \to \infty} \left[\frac{x^n}{e^{\lambda x}} \right] = \lim_{x \to \infty} \left[\frac{nx^{n-1}}{\lambda e^{\lambda x}} \right]$$

for positive integer n. Differentiating x^n and $e^{\lambda x}$ n times with respect to x leads to

$$\lim_{x \to \infty} \left[\frac{x^n}{e^{\lambda x}} \right] = \lim_{x \to \infty} \left[\frac{n!}{\lambda^n e^{\lambda x}} \right] = \frac{n!}{\lambda^n \lim_{x \to \infty} e^{\lambda x}} = 0$$

Therefore

$$\lim_{x} \left[\frac{x^\alpha}{e^{\lambda x}} \right] = 0$$

for all postive, finite, integer valued α. Hence

$$F(\infty) = 1$$

and

$$\int_0^\infty \lambda \frac{(\lambda x)^{\alpha - 1}}{(\alpha - 1)!} e^{-x} \, dx = 1 - 0 = 1 \quad \blacksquare$$

Functions of Several Variables

The concepts for functions of a single variable discussed in the preceding section may be extended of functions of several variables. A function $f(x)$ of a single variable was defined on an open or closed interval of values for x. However, if we consider $f(x_1, x_2)$, the function is defined for combinations of x_1 and x_2 on a plane rather than a line, or the points for which $f(x_1, x_2)$ is defined lie in 2-dimensional space. Let us define S_n as the n-dimensional space on which the values of $x_1, x_2, \ldots, x_n$ are defined. A *boundary point* for S_n is the n-dimensional analog of an end point for an interval which is a 1-dimensional space. Let us construct an n-dimensional sphere with center at $(x_1, x_2, \ldots, x_n)$ and radius $\epsilon > 0$ called a neighborhood. If $(x_1, x_2, \ldots, x_n)$ is a boundary point for S_n, then some points in the n-dimensional sphere will lie inside S_n and some will lie outside, no matter how small we make ϵ, provided $\epsilon > 0$. A *closed space* is a space which includes *all* of its boundary points and will be denoted $[S_n]$. An *open space* is a space which includes *none* of its boundary points and will be denoted (S_n). A space which includes some but not all of its boundary points is partially open and partially closed and will be expressed simply as S_n. To illustrate, consider the space S_2, where x_1 may assume any value such that $a \leqslant x_1 < b$ and x_2 may assume any value such that $c < x_2 \leqslant d$. S_2 is shown graphically in Fig. 1.9. The boundary points for the closed portion of the space are the points on the solid lines, and the boundary points for the open portion of the space are the points on the dashed lines.

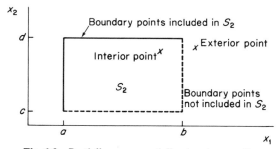

Fig. 1.9 Partially open, partially closed space S_2.

An *interior point* for the space S_n is a point which lies within S_n and which is not a boundary point for S_n. An *exterior point* for S_n is a point which does not lie within S_n and which is not a boundary point for S_n. To determine whether an arbitrarily selected point is an interior, exterior, or boundary point for S_n, we examine an ϵ *neighborhood* of points about the point in question. For example, consider the point $(x_1, x_2, \ldots, x_n)$. We construct an n-dimensional sphere of radius $\epsilon > 0$ about $(x_1, x_2, \ldots, x_n)$. If we can select a positive value of ϵ such that all points in the sphere are contained in S_n, then $(x_1, x_2, \ldots, x_n)$ is an interior point for S_n. On the other hand, if we can find some $\epsilon > 0$ such that every point in the sphere does not belong to S_n, then $(x_1, x_2, \ldots, x_n)$ is an exterior point for S_n. Finally, if every sphere contains some points which belong to S_n and some which do not, no matter how small $\epsilon > 0$, then $(x_1, x_2, \ldots, x_n)$ is a *boundary point* for S_n.

Limits

As it pertains to functions of a single variable, the limiting value of a function expresses the behavior of the function as the variable approaches the limit point. The concept of a limit is the same for functions of several variables. Let **x** be a point with coordinates $(x_1, x_2, \ldots, x_n)$ and **a** a point with coordinates $(a_1, a_2, \ldots, a_n)$. For functions of a single variable $\lim_{x \to a} f(x)$ exists if

$$\lim_{x \to a-} f(x) = \lim_{a \to a+} f(x) \tag{1.40}$$

An alternative statement would be that $\lim_{x \to a} f(x) = L$ if $f(x)$ approaches L for all possible paths of approach of x to a. In this case there are only two possible paths of approach of x to a: through values of x less than a and through values of x greater than a. However, for functions of several variables **x** may approach the limit point **a** through many paths. For example, in Fig. 1.10 four possible paths of approach to **a** are shown, and there are infinitely many more.

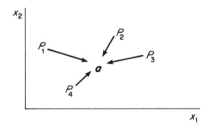

Fig. 1.10   Four paths of approach to **a**.

Let

$$\lim_{\substack{\mathbf{x}\to\mathbf{a}\\P}} f(\mathbf{x})$$

be the limit of $f(\mathbf{x})$ as $\mathbf{x}$ approaches **a** over path P. Then

$$\lim_{\mathbf{x}\to\mathbf{a}} f(\mathbf{x}) = L \qquad (1.41)$$

if and only if

$$\lim_{\substack{\mathbf{x}\to\mathbf{a}\\P}} f(\mathbf{x}) = L \qquad (1.42)$$

for all possible paths of approach P.

Continuity

   The concept of continuity of a function of several variables is defined in a manner analogous to that for a function of a single variable. That is, $f(\mathbf{x})$ is continuous at the point **a** if and only if

$$\lim_{\mathbf{x}\to\mathbf{a}} (\mathbf{x}) = f(\mathbf{a}) \qquad (1.43)$$

Derivative

   As in the case of functions of a single variable, the derivative of a function of several variables expresses the rate of change in the function. However, in the case of functions of several variables we must specify the direction in which we wish to take the derivative. The *partial derivative* identifies the rate of change in the function along one of the coordinate axes. The partial derivative of $f(\mathbf{x})$ along the coordinate axis x_i will be denoted by $(\partial/\partial x_i)f(\mathbf{x})$ or $f_i(\mathbf{x})$ and is defined as

$$f_i(\mathbf{x})$$

$$= \lim_{\Delta x_i \to 0} \left[\frac{f(x_1, x_2, \ldots, x_{i-1}, x_i + \Delta x_i, x_{i+1}, \ldots, x_n) - f(x_1, x_2, \ldots, x_n)}{\Delta x_i} \right]$$

$$(1.44)$$

if the limit exists. Operationally, $f_i(\mathbf{x})$ is calculated by taking the first derivative of $f(\mathbf{x})$ with respect to x_i, where $x_1, x_2, \ldots, x_{i-1}, x_{i+1}, \ldots, x_n$ are treated as constants. As in the case of functions of a single variable, the second partial derivative is simply the first partial derivative of the first partial derivative. The notation $f_{ij}(\mathbf{x})$ or $(\partial^2/\partial x_i \, \partial x_j)f(\mathbf{x})$ defines the second partial derivative of $f(\mathbf{x})$ with respect to x_i and x_j and can be defined as

$$f_{ij}(\mathbf{x}) = \frac{\partial}{\partial x_j} f_i(\mathbf{x}) = \frac{\partial}{\partial x_i} f_j(\mathbf{x}) \tag{1.45}$$

Thus the value of $f_{ij}(\mathbf{x})$ is the same whether we take the first partial derivative of $f_i(\mathbf{x})$ with respect to x_j or the first partial derivative of $f_j(\mathbf{x})$ with respect to x_i.

Example 1.11   Given the function

$$f(\mathbf{x}) = (x_1 - 1)^2 + (x_2 + 1)^2 + 2x_1^2 x_2^2$$

determine $f_1(\mathbf{x})$, $f_2(\mathbf{x})$, $f_{12}(\mathbf{x})$, and $f_{21}(\mathbf{x})$ at $\mathbf{x} = (-2, 2)$.

To find $f_1(\mathbf{x})$ we treat x_2 as a constant and take the simple derivative of $f(\mathbf{x})$ with respect to x_1:

$$f_1(\mathbf{x}) = 2(x_1 - 1) + 4x_1 x_2^2$$

In a similar manner,

$$f_2(\mathbf{x}) = 2(x_2 + 1) + 4x_1^2 x_2$$

and at $\mathbf{x} = (-2, 2)$,

$$f_1(\mathbf{x})|_{(-2, 2)} = 2(-2 - 1) + 4(-2)(2)^2 = -38$$

$$f_2(\mathbf{x})|_{(-2, 2)} = 2(2 + 1) + 4(-2)^2(2) = 38$$

For $f_{12}(\mathbf{x})$ and $f_{21}(\mathbf{x})$ we have

$$f_{12}(\mathbf{x}) = \frac{\partial}{\partial x_2} f_1(\mathbf{x}) = 8x_1 x_2$$

and

$$f_{21}(\mathbf{x}) = \frac{\partial}{\partial x_1} f_2(\mathbf{x}) = 8x_1 x_2$$

Thus

$$f_{12}(\mathbf{x})|_{(-2, 2)} = f_{21}(\mathbf{x})|_{(-2, 2)} = -32 \quad \blacksquare$$

In some instances the analyst is interested not in the rate of change of $f(\mathbf{x})$ along one of the coordinate axes but rather in the rate of change of $f(\mathbf{x})$ in some other direction in the space of definition of $\mathbf{x}$. For example, we might be interested in the rate of change in a function of the two variables x_1, x_2 along a direction at a $45°$ angle with the coordinate axes as

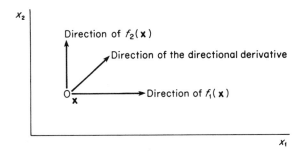

Fig. 1.11 Directions for $f_1(x)$, $f_2(x)$ and the directional derivative taken in a direction at a 45° angle with the coordinate axes.

shown in Fig. 1.11. The rate of change in such a direction is given by the directional derivative. Before defining the directional derivative we must define the direction in which the derivative is to be taken. A direction is defined as a vector $(b_1, b_2, \ldots, b_n)$ of unit length. An extensive discussion of vectors is given in Chapter 2. For our present purpose a *vector* may simply be thought of as a point in n-dimensional space, where the elements denote projections along each of the n coordinate axes. *The length of a vector* $(x_1, x_2, \ldots, x_n)$ is the distance of the point from the origin $(0, 0, \ldots, 0)$ and is measured by $\sqrt{x_1^2 + x_2^2 + \cdots + x_n^2}$. Thus, if $(b_1, b_2, \ldots, b_n)$ is a vector of unit length,

$$\sqrt{b_1^2 + b_2^2 + \cdots b_n^2} = 1 \qquad (1.46)$$

The rate of change of $f(x)$ in the direction $(b_1, b_2, \ldots, b_n)$ is called the *directional derivative* and is defined by

$$\nabla_{\mathbf{b}} f(\mathbf{x}) = \lim_{\lambda \to 0} \frac{f(x_1 + \lambda b_1, x_2 + \lambda b_2, \ldots, x_n + \lambda b_n) - f(x_1, x_2, \ldots, x_n)}{\lambda}$$
$$(1.47)$$

where

$$\mathbf{b} = (b_1, b_2, \ldots, b_n) \qquad (1.48)$$

The reader will note that if $b_i = 1$ and $b_j = 0$ for all $j \neq i$,

$$\nabla_{\mathbf{b}} f(\mathbf{x}) = f_i(\mathbf{x}) \qquad (1.49)$$

For convenience the directional derivative is usually computed by

$$\nabla_{\mathbf{b}} f(\mathbf{x}) = \sum_{i=1}^{n} b_i f_i(\mathbf{x}) \qquad (1.50)$$

Example 1.12 Find the directional derivative of the function in Example 1.11 in the direction $(1/\sqrt{2}, -1/\sqrt{2})$ at the point $(-2, 2)$.

From Example 1.11,

$$f_1(\mathbf{x}) = 2(x_1 - 1) + 4x_1x_2^2$$
$$f_2(\mathbf{x}) = 2(x_2 + 1) + 4x_1^2x_2$$

and

$$\nabla_\mathbf{b} f(\mathbf{x}) = \sqrt{0.5}\left[2(x_1 - 1) + 4x_1x_2^2\right] - \sqrt{0.5}\left[2(x_1 + 1) + 4x_1^2x_2\right]$$
$$= \sqrt{2}\,(x_1 - x_2 - 2) + 2\sqrt{2}\,x_1x_2(x_2 - x_1)$$

where

$$\mathbf{b} = \left(1/\sqrt{2}\,, -1/\sqrt{2}\,\right) \qquad \text{at} \quad x = (-2, 2)$$

and

$$\nabla_\mathbf{b} f(\mathbf{x}) = \sqrt{2}\,(-6) + 2\sqrt{2}\,(-2)(2)(4) = -38\sqrt{2} \quad \blacksquare$$

Example 1.13 The tensile strength of a particular alloy is a function of the proportions of materials A and B. If x_1 and x_2 are the proportions of A and B, respectively, then tensile strength is given by $f(\mathbf{x})$, where

$$f(\mathbf{x}) = x_1e^{x_1} + 2x_2e^{x_2/2} + x_1/(20x_2)$$

The manufacturer wishes to increase the tensile strength of the alloy by a slight amount and can do so in one of three ways:

(1) increase x_1 only,
(2) increase x_2 only; or
(3) increase x_1 and x_2 in equal amounts.

Which alternative will yield the greatest rate of increase in tensile strength if the current values of x_1 and x_2 are 0.06 and 0.10, respectively?

The rate of increase in $f(\mathbf{x})$ at $(0.06, 0.10)$ is given by the directional derivative. The directional derivative for $f(\mathbf{x})$ is given by

$$\nabla_\mathbf{b} f(\mathbf{x}) = b_1\left(e^{x_1} + x_1e^{x_1} + \frac{1}{20x_2}\right) + b_2\left(2e^{x_2/2} + x_2e^{x_2/2}\frac{x_1}{20x_2^2}\right)$$

for any direction $\mathbf{b} = (b_1, b_2)$. At $\mathbf{x} = (0.06, 0.10)$, $\nabla_\mathbf{b} f(\mathbf{x})$ is given by

$$\nabla_\mathbf{b} f(\mathbf{x}) = b_1(1.0618 + 0.0637 + 0.5000) + b_2(2.1025 + 0.2103 - 0.3000)$$
$$= 1.6255b_1 + 2.0128b_2$$

The three permissible alternatives call for increases in x_1 and x_2 in the directions $(1, 0)$, $(0, 1)$, or $(1/\sqrt{2}\,, 1/\sqrt{2}\,)$. For $\mathbf{b} = (1, 0)$,

$$\nabla_\mathbf{b} f(\mathbf{x}) = 1.6255$$

For $\mathbf{b} = (0, 1)$,

$$\nabla_{\mathbf{b}} f(\mathbf{x}) = 2.0128$$

and for $\mathbf{b} = (1/\sqrt{2}, 1/\sqrt{2})$,

$$\nabla_{\mathbf{b}} f(\mathbf{x}) = 2.5727$$

Since the rate of increase in tensile strength is greatest for small and equal incremental increases in both x_1 and x_2, the third alternative is the most desirable. ■

Knowledge of the first m partial derivatives of a function of several variables leads us to an extension of Taylor's mean-value theorem for functions of several variables. If $f(\mathbf{x})$ is continuous on the closed space $[S_n]$, where $\mathbf{x} = (x_1, x_2, \ldots, x_m)$, and if the first n partial derivatives of $f(\mathbf{x})$ with respect to x_k, $k = 1, 2, \ldots, m$, exist and are continuous on (S_n), then for $\mathbf{x}$ and $\mathbf{x}_0 = (x_{01}, x_{02}, \ldots, x_{0m})$ on (S_n) there exists a point $\mathbf{x}_1 = (x_{11}, x_{12}, \ldots, x_{1m})$ on the line segment joining $\mathbf{x}$ and $\mathbf{x}_0$ such that

$$f(\mathbf{x}) = f(\mathbf{x}_0) + \sum_{i=1}^{n-1} \frac{1}{i!} D^i f(\mathbf{x}) \bigg|_{\mathbf{x}_0} + R_n(\mathbf{x}) \bigg|_{\mathbf{x}_1} \tag{1.51}$$

where D^i is a differential operator defined by

$$D^i = \left[\sum_{k=1}^{m} (x_k - x_{0k}) \frac{\partial}{\partial x_k} \right]^i \tag{1.52}$$

and

$$R_n(\mathbf{x}) \bigg|_{\mathbf{x}_1} = \frac{1}{n!} D^n f(\mathbf{x}) \bigg|_{\mathbf{x}_1} \tag{1.53}$$

For example, if $n = 2$,

$$f(\mathbf{x}) = f(\mathbf{x}_0) + \sum_{k=1}^{m} (x_k - x_{0k}) \frac{\partial}{\partial x_k} f(\mathbf{x}) \bigg|_{\mathbf{x}_0} + R_2(\mathbf{x}) \bigg|_{\mathbf{x}_1} \tag{1.54}$$

and

$$R_2(\mathbf{x}) \bigg|_{\mathbf{x}_1} = \frac{1}{2} \sum_{k=1}^{m} \sum_{j=1}^{m} (x_k - x_{0k})(x_j - x_{0j}) \frac{\partial^2}{\partial x_k \partial x_j} f(\mathbf{x}) \bigg|_{\mathbf{x}_1} \tag{1.55}$$

For $n = 3$ we have

$$f(\mathbf{x}) = f(\mathbf{x}_0) + \sum_{k=1}^{m} (x_k - x_{0k}) \frac{\partial}{\partial x_k} f(\mathbf{x}) \bigg|_{\mathbf{x}_0} + \frac{1}{2} \sum_{k=1}^{m} \sum_{j=1}^{m} (x_k - x_{0k})(x_j - x_{0j})$$

$$\frac{\partial^2}{\partial x_k \partial x_j} f(\mathbf{x})|_{\mathbf{x}_0} + R_3(\mathbf{x})|_{\mathbf{x}_1} \tag{1.56}$$

and

$$R_3(\mathbf{x})\bigg|_{\mathbf{x}_1} = \frac{1}{6!} \sum_{k=1}^{m} \sum_{j=1}^{m} \sum_{l=1}^{m} (x_k - x_{0k})(x_j - x_{0j})(x_l - x_{0l}) \frac{\partial^3}{\partial x_k \partial x_j \partial x_l} f(\mathbf{x})\bigg|_{\mathbf{x}_1}$$

$$(1.57)$$

As in the case of functions of a single variable, as $\mathbf{x}$ approaches $\mathbf{x}_0$ the error in the approximation decreases for all n. Further, as n increases the error in the approximation will decrease for all $\mathbf{x} \neq \mathbf{x}_0$.

Integration

The integral of a function of several variables or the *multiple integral* is a simple extension of the integral of a function of a single variable. Geometrically the double integral of a function of two variables represents the volume under the surface described by the function. To illustrate, consider the function shown in Fig. 1.12. The volume under the function is given by $\int_a^b \int_c^d f(x_1, x_2)\, dx_2\, dx_1$.

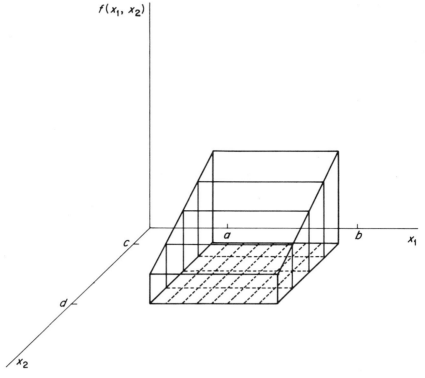

Fig. 1.12 Volume included under the function $f(x_1, x_2)$ for $a \leqslant x_1 \leqslant b$ and $c \leqslant x_2 \leqslant d$.

In general the rules for multiple integration follow those for integarion of functions of a single variable. For example, let

$$I = \int_a^b \int_{c(x_1)}^{d(x_1)} f(x_1, x_2)\, dx_2\, dx_1 \tag{1.58}$$

Consider the inside integral first. From the fundamental theorem of integral calculus,

$$\int_{c(x_1)}^{d(x_1)} f(x_1, x_2)\, dx_2 = F[d(x_1)] - F[c(x_1)] \tag{1.59}$$

and

$$I = \int_a^b \{ F[d(x_1)] - F[c(x_1)] \}\, dx_1 \tag{1.60}$$

Hence a multiple integration may be carried out through successive applications of integration of a function of a single variable.

SUMMARY

In this chapter we have attempted to introduce the student to models, model development, and validation, and to review the fundamentals of the calculus. While this text is not directly concerned with model development, it does focus on analysis of mathematical models. The basic concepts of calculus presented here are vital to the development of many of the analytical techniques discussed in Chapters 3, 4 and 6 and have direct analogies in discrete variable calculus, which is presented in Chapter 5. While this treatment of calculus is primarily intended for the purpose of review, we have attempted to present the material in detail sufficient to the needs of the reader who is not familiar with some of the topics treated. However, the reader with no prior knowledge of calculus will probably require a more detailed treatment of basic calculus before pursuing the topics in the chapters which follow.

PROBLEMS

1. Show that

$$\lim_{x \to a} k = k$$

2. For each of the following functions determine the required limit if it exists.

$$\lim_{x \to 2} \frac{x^2 - 2}{x^2 - 3}, \qquad \lim_{x \to 1} x^2(x - 4), \qquad \lim_{x \to 4} (x^2 + x + 1)$$

3. Show that

$$f(x) = x^3 - 2x^2 + x$$

is continuous at $x = 4$.

4. Show that

$$f(x) = \begin{cases} e^{-x}, & x \leqslant 1 \\ x, & x > 1 \end{cases}$$

is not continuous at $x = 1$.

5. Show that

$$f(x) = \begin{cases} x, & x \leqslant 5 \\ 10 - x, & x > 5 \end{cases}$$

is continuous at $x = 1$.

6. Let

$$f(x) = \frac{25}{(x-5)^2}$$

Show that $f(x)$ is discontinuous at $x = 5$.

7. Show that

$$f(x) = \begin{cases} x + 1, & x \leqslant 1 \\ (x + 1)^2, & x > 1 \end{cases}$$

is discontinuous at $x = 1$.

8. Show that

$$f(x) = \frac{1}{x-1}$$

is continuous at every point on the open interval $(1, b)$, but is not continuous on the closed interval $[1, b]$, where b is a finite constant.

9. Show that

$$f(x) = \begin{cases} x \sin(1/x), & x \neq 0 \\ 0, & x = 0 \end{cases}$$

is continuous at $x = 0$.

10. If

$$f(x) = \begin{cases} x, & x \leqslant 5 \\ 10 - x, & x > 5 \end{cases}$$

show that the derivative of $f(x)$ does not exist at $x = 5$.

11. Evaluate each of the following limits using L'Hôpital's rule:

$$\lim_{x \to 0} \frac{x^3}{x^2 + x}, \qquad \lim_{x \to \infty} \frac{e^{-x}}{x}, \qquad \lim_{x \to \infty} \frac{x}{e^x}$$

12. Determine the first, second, and third derivatives of the following functions:

$$f(x) = x^4 - 3x^3 + x, \qquad f(x) = x^2 - 4, \qquad f(x) = xe^{-x}$$

13. Find all of the first, second, and third partial derivatives of

$$f(\mathbf{x}) = 3x_1^2 + x_2^3 - 3x_1 x_2^2 + x_1 x_2^4 + x_1 e^{-x_2}$$

14. Find the points at which the first derivative vanishes for the following function:

$$f(x) = ax^3 + bx^2 + cx + d$$

15. For the function given in Problem 14 find the points at which the second derivative vanishes.

16. The cost $C(s)$ of producing a certain product is given by

$$C(s) = C_1 \int_0^s \lambda(s - x)e^{-\lambda x}\,dx + C_2 \int_s^\infty \lambda(x - s)e^{-\lambda x}\,dx$$

where C_1 is the cost per unit of overproduction and C_2 is the unit cost of producing too little. λ is the average demand rate and s is the number of units manufactured. Derive an expression for the rate of change of production cost with respect to s.

17. For the function in Problem 16 show that the second derivative of $C(s)$ with respect to s is always positive.

18. For the function defined in Problem 13 find the directional derivative in the directions $(1/\sqrt{2}\,,\ 1/\sqrt{2}\,),\ (-1/\sqrt{2},\ 1/\sqrt{2}\,),\ (1/\sqrt{2}\,,\ -1/\sqrt{2}\,),\ (-1/\sqrt{2}\,,\ -1/\sqrt{2}\,).$

19. Let

$$f(\mathbf{x}) = x_1^2 + 2x_1 x_2 + x_2^2$$

Find the directional derivative of $f(\mathbf{x})$ at $\mathbf{x} = (2, 2)$ in the direction $(\sqrt{\alpha},\ \sqrt{1 - \alpha}\,)$ and plot the directional derivative for $0 \leqslant \alpha \leqslant 1$.

20. Let

$$F(x) = \int_{a(x)}^{b(x)} f(x, y)\,dy$$

The derivative of $F(x)$ with respect to x can be expressed as

$$\frac{d}{dx}F(x) = \int_{a(x)}^{b(x)} \frac{d}{dx}f(x, y)\,dy + \left[\frac{d}{dx}b(x)\right]f[x, b(x)] - \left[\frac{d}{dx}a(x)\right]f[x, a(x)]$$

If

$$F(x) = a\int_0^x (x - y)g(y)\,dy + b\int_x^\infty (y - x)g(y)\,dy$$

show that

$$\frac{d}{dx}F(x) = 0 \qquad \text{when} \qquad \int_0^x g(y)\,dy = \frac{b}{a + b}$$

if

$$\int_0^x g(y)\,dy = 1 - \int_x^\infty g(y)\,dy$$

21. Approximate the function

$$f(x) = e^{-x^2}$$

using a second-degree Taylor polynomial on the interval $(2, 3)$. Estimate the maximum error in the approximation at $x = 2.1, 2.2, \ldots, 2.9$ and compare the maximum estimated error with the actual error in the approximation.

22. Solve Problem 21 using a third-degree Taylor polynomial.

23. The expected number of rejectable units in manufacturing lots of size L is given by

$$R(\delta) = L\left[\int_{-\infty}^{\mu - \delta} f(x \mid u)\,dx + \int_{\mu + \delta}^\infty f(x \mid u)\,dx\right]$$

where

$$f(x \mid u) = \frac{1}{\sigma\sqrt{2\pi}}\,e^{-(x - u)^2/(2\sigma^2)}$$

Develop a second-degree Taylor polynomial approximation for $R(\delta)$ if

$$L = 10,000, \qquad \mu = 3, \qquad \sigma = 1$$

Hint: Use the relationship in Problem 20.

24. Show that

$$\int_0^\infty \lambda e^{-\lambda x}\, dx = 1$$

for all $\lambda > 0$.

25. Evaluate the following integrals:

$$\int_{-\infty}^\infty \frac{x}{\sqrt{2\pi}}\, e^{-x^2/2}\, dx, \qquad \int_a^b \frac{x}{b-a}\, dx, \qquad \int_0^\infty \lambda x^2 e^{-\lambda x}\, dx$$

26. Integrate the following:

$$\int_0^\infty \int_0^\infty \lambda \mu e^{-\lambda x_1 - \mu x_2}\, dx_1\, dx_2$$

$$\int_0^T \int_0^{x_1} \frac{1}{x_1 T}\, dx_2\, dx_1 \qquad \text{where } T \text{ is a positive constant}$$

$$\int_0^\infty \int_0^{x_2} 4x_1^2(x_2 - x_1)e^{-(x_1 + x_2)}\, dx_1\, dx_2$$

27. Given the function

$$f(\mathbf{x}) = 4x_1(x_2 - x_1)e^{-(x_1 + x_2)}$$

show that

$$f(\mathbf{x}) \neq \int_0^{x_2} f(\mathbf{x})\, dx_1 \int_{x_1}^\infty f(\mathbf{x})\, dx_2$$

28. The probability density function of the random variables x_1 and x_2 is given by

$$f(x_1, x_2) = \lambda \mu^2 x_2 e^{-\lambda x_1 - \mu x_2}, \qquad 0 < x_1 < \infty, \quad 0 < x_2 < \infty$$

The marginal probability density functions of x_1 and x_2 are given by

$$g(x_1) = \int_0^\infty f(x_1, x_2)\, dx_2$$

$$h(x_2) = \int_0^\infty f(x_1, x_2)\, dx_1$$

If $f(x_1, x_2) = g(x_1)h(x_2)$, then x_1 and x_2 are said to be *independent random variables*. Are x_1 and x_2 independently distributed in this case?

29. The joint probability density function of x_1 and x_2 is given by

$$f(x_1, x_2) = 1/(x_1 T), \qquad 0 < x_2 < x_1 < T$$

Using the definition of independence in Problem 28, are x_1 and x_2 independently distributed random variables?

Suggested Further Reading

Baumol, W. (1961). "Economic Theory and Operations Analysis." Prentice-Hall, Englewood Cliffs, New Jersey.

Buck, R. C. (1956). "Advanced Calculus." McGraw-Hill, New York.

Fulks, W. (1961). "Advanced Calculus." Wiley (Interscience), New York.

Giffin, W. C. (1971). "Introduction to Operations Engineering." Irwin, Homewood, Illinois.

Gue, R. L., and Thomas, M. E. (1968). "Mathematical Methods in Operations Research." Macmillan, New York.

Schmidt, J. W. (1974). "Mathematical Foundations for Management Science and Systems Analysis." Academic Press, New York.

Taha, H. A. (1971). "Operations Research: An Introduction." Macmillan, New York.

Wagner, H. M. (1969). "Principles of Operations Research." Prentice-Hall, Englewood Cliffs, New Jersey.

Chapter 2 | Linear Algebra

INTRODUCTION

Linear algebra is as fundamental to the formulation and analysis of mathematical models as calculus. In Chapters 3 and 4 we shall use the determinants of matrices and the analysis of quadratic forms to identify points which maximize or minimize functions of several continuous variables.

In addition to their use in conjunction with other analytical techniques, the concepts of linear algebra are useful in the formulation and solution of many mathematical models frequently treated in operations research. Linear programming, discussed in Chapter 7, is founded on the principles of linear vector spaces. Basic matrix operations are important in the formulation and analysis of Markov processes. Matrix solutions for a set of simultaneous linear equations are basic to the development of empirical mathematical models through the method of least squares.

This chapter is composed of three sections. The first deals with the definition of a matrix, its properties, and basic matrix operations including calculation of the determinant and the inverse of a matrix. The second treats vectors, vector spaces, and convex spaces: vectors, vector spaces and convex spaces are defined; the conditions for independence and orthogonality of vectors are presented, as is their application to identification of a basis for a vector space; this section is concluded with a discussion of the properties and applications of convex spaces. The final section of this chapter is devoted to quadratic forms and their analysis and includes a discussion of eigenvalues and eigenvectors and the use of eigenvalues in the analysis of quadratic forms.

The topics in the first section may already be familiar to the reader. In this case the first section will serve as a review. However, this section should also provide adequate preparation for study of the remainder of the text for the student without a background in matrix algebra.

FUNDAMENTALS OF MATRIX ALGEBRA

Definitions

A *matrix* is defined as any 2-dimensional array of numbers or functions. If A is a matrix with *elements* a_{ij}, then A is given by

$$A = \begin{bmatrix} a_{11} & a_{12} & \cdots & a_{1n} \\ a_{21} & a_{22} & \cdots & a_{2n} \\ \vdots & \vdots & & \vdots \\ a_{m1} & a_{m2} & \cdots & a_{mn} \end{bmatrix} \tag{2.1}$$

The *order* of a matrix is defined by the number of rows and columns in the matrix. The order of the matrix in Eq. (2.1) is then $m \times n$. If the matrix contains either a single column or a single row then the matrix is called a *vector*. For example, the vector **x** defined by

$$\mathbf{x} = \begin{bmatrix} x_1 \\ x_2 \\ \vdots \\ x_m \end{bmatrix} \tag{2.2}$$

is called a *column vector* since it is a vector comprised of one column. On the other hand, the vector **y** defined by

$$\mathbf{y} = \begin{bmatrix} y_1 & y_2 & \cdots & y_n \end{bmatrix} \tag{2.3}$$

is called a *row vector* since it is comprised of one row. A matrix which contains one row and one column is called a *scalar*; thus it is simply a number and is usually denoted by a lower-case letter.

A matrix with an equal number of rows and columns is called a *square*

Fundamentals of Matrix Algebra 47

matrix. If a square matrix has n rows and columns, then its order is said to be n. Let the square matrix A be defined by

$$A = \begin{bmatrix} a_{11} & a_{12} & \cdots & a_{1n} \\ a_{21} & a_{22} & \cdots & a_{2n} \\ \vdots & \vdots & & \vdots \\ a_{n1} & a_{n2} & \cdots & a_{nn} \end{bmatrix} \qquad (2.4)$$

The elements a_{ij} for which $i = j$ are referred to as the *diagonal elements.*

There are several square matrices which are of particular importance in matrix theory and its applications. If a square matrix is such that corresponding off diagonal elements are equal, then the matrix is said to be *symmetric.* That is, if A is a symmetric matrix, then $a_{ij} = a_{ji}$ for all i and j. The *identity matrix*, denoted I, is a symmetric matrix such that $a_{ij} = 0$ for all $i \neq j$ and $a_{ii} = 1$ for all i. That is,

$$I = \begin{bmatrix} 1 & 0 & 0 & \cdots & 0 \\ 0 & 1 & 0 & \cdots & 0 \\ 0 & 0 & 1 & \cdots & 0 \\ \vdots & \vdots & \vdots & & \vdots \\ 0 & 0 & 0 & \cdots & 1 \end{bmatrix} \qquad (2.5)$$

If A is a symmetric matrix such that $a_{ij} = 0$, $i \neq j$, and $a_{ii} = k$ for all i, then A is said to be a *scalar matrix.* If A is a square matrix such that $a_{ij} = 0$ for all $i > j$, then A is said to be an *upper triangular matrix* and is called a *lower triangular matrix* if $a_{ij} = 0$ for all $i < j$. A matrix which is both upper triangular and lower triangular, that is $a_{ij} = 0$ for $i \neq j$, is referred to as a *diagonal matrix.*

Basic Matrix Operations

Two matrices A and B are conformable for addition and subtraction if and only if A and B are of the same order. If A and B are $m \times n$ matrices, where

$$A = \begin{bmatrix} a_{11} & a_{12} & \cdots & a_{1n} \\ a_{21} & a_{22} & \cdots & a_{2n} \\ \vdots & \vdots & & \vdots \\ a_{m1} & a_{m2} & \cdots & a_{mn} \end{bmatrix} \qquad (2.6)$$

48   2 **Linear Algebra**

and

$$
B = \begin{bmatrix}
b_{11} & b_{12} & \cdots & b_{1n} \\
b_{21} & b_{22} & \cdots & b_{2n} \\
\vdots & \vdots & & \vdots \\
b_{m1} & b_{m2} & \cdots & b_{mn}
\end{bmatrix}
\tag{2.7}
$$

then

$$
A \pm B = \begin{bmatrix}
a_{11} \pm b_{11} & a_{12} \pm b_{12} & \cdots & a_{1n} \pm b_{1n} \\
a_{21} \pm b_{21} & a_{22} \pm b_{22} & \cdots & a_{2n} \pm b_{2n} \\
\vdots & \vdots & & \vdots \\
a_{m1} \pm b_{m1} & a_{m2} \pm b_{m2} & \cdots & a_{mn} \pm b_{mn}
\end{bmatrix}
\tag{2.8}
$$

Hence to add or subtract two matrices of the same order we simply add or subtract corresponding elements.

Example 2.1 Given the following matrices, find $A + B$ and $A - B$:

$$
A = \begin{bmatrix} 3 & 1 & 2 \\ 4 & 1 & 8 \\ 1 & 1 & 4 \\ 3 & 1 & 7 \end{bmatrix}, \qquad
B = \begin{bmatrix} 0 & 1 & 5 \\ 1 & 8 & 2 \\ 0 & 7 & 0 \\ 4 & 6 & 5 \end{bmatrix}
$$

Since A and B are of the same order, they are conformable for addition and subtraction. For $A + B$ we have

$$
A + B = \begin{bmatrix}
3+0 & 1+1 & 2+5 \\
4+1 & 1+8 & 8+2 \\
1+0 & 1+7 & 4+0 \\
3+4 & 1+6 & 7+5
\end{bmatrix}
$$

$$
= \begin{bmatrix} 3 & 2 & 7 \\ 5 & 9 & 10 \\ 1 & 8 & 4 \\ 7 & 7 & 12 \end{bmatrix}
$$

$A - B$ is given by

$$
A - B = \begin{bmatrix}
3-0 & 1-1 & 2-5 \\
4-1 & 1-8 & 8-2 \\
1-0 & 1-7 & 4-0 \\
3-4 & 1-6 & 7-5
\end{bmatrix}
$$

$$
= \begin{bmatrix} 3 & 0 & -3 \\ 3 & -7 & 6 \\ 1 & -6 & 4 \\ -1 & -5 & 2 \end{bmatrix} \quad \blacksquare
$$

If A and B are conformable for addition and subtraction and $A - B$ is a *zero* or *null matrix*, then $A = B$, where a null matrix is a matrix with all elements equal to zero. Hence two matrices A and B with elements a_{ij} and b_{ij} are equal if the following conditions hold:

(1) A and B are of the same order;
(2) $a_{ij} = b_{ij}$ for all i and j.

To multiply two matrices the order of multiplication must be recognized. If A is conformable to B for multiplication, then the product matrix AB is defined. If BA is defined, then B is said to be conformable to A for multiplication. A is conformable to B for multiplication if the number of columns in A is equal to the number of rows in B. Hence the product matrix AB is defined if and only if A is of order (m, n) and B is of order (n, p). However, if $m \neq p$, the product matrix BA is not defined or B is not conformable to A for multiplication. If A is an (m, n) matrix with elements a_{ij} and B is an (n, p) matrix with elements b_{jk}, then the product matrix AB is of order (m, p) and the element in the ith row and kth column of AB is given by $\sum_{j=1}^{n} a_{ij} b_{jk}$, $i = 1, 2, \ldots, m$, $j = 1, 2, \ldots, p$. That is,

$$
AB = \begin{bmatrix} a_{11} & a_{12} & \cdots & a_{1n} \\ a_{21} & a_{22} & \cdots & a_{2n} \\ \vdots & \vdots & & \vdots \\ a_{m1} & a_{m2} & \cdots & a_{mn} \end{bmatrix} \begin{bmatrix} b_{11} & b_{12} & \cdots & b_{1p} \\ b_{21} & b_{22} & \cdots & b_{2p} \\ \vdots & \vdots & & \vdots \\ b_{n1} & b_{n2} & \cdots & b_{np} \end{bmatrix}
$$

$$
= \begin{bmatrix} \sum_{j=1}^{n} a_{1j} b_{j1} & \sum_{j=1}^{n} a_{1j} b_{j2} & \cdots & \sum_{j=1}^{n} a_{1j} b_{jp} \\ \sum_{j=1}^{n} a_{2j} b_{j1} & \sum_{j=1}^{n} a_{2j} b_{j2} & \cdots & \sum_{j=1}^{n} a_{2j} b_{jp} \\ \vdots & \vdots & & \vdots \\ \sum_{j=1}^{n} a_{mj} b_{j1} & \sum_{j=1}^{n} a_{mj} b_{j2} & \cdots & \sum_{j=1}^{n} a_{mj} b_{jp} \end{bmatrix} \quad (2.9)
$$

It should be noted that even when AB *and* BA are defined they are not *necessarily* equal.

Example 2.2 Let

$$
A = \begin{bmatrix} 3 & 4 \\ 2 & 1 \\ 0 & 2 \end{bmatrix}, \qquad B = \begin{bmatrix} 3 & 3 & 1 \\ 1 & 4 & 2 \\ 6 & 7 & 8 \end{bmatrix}, \qquad C = \begin{bmatrix} 1 & 6 & 2 \\ 0 & 1 & 0 \\ 1 & 0 & 1 \end{bmatrix}
$$

Determine whether the product matrices AB, BA, AC, CA, BC, and CB are defined, and determine the product matrices which are defined.

As A is a $(3, 2)$ matrix, B a $(3, 3)$ matrix, and C a $(3, 3)$ matrix, AB and AC are not defined. The remaining four product matrices are defined and are given by

$$BA = \begin{bmatrix} (3)(3) + (3)(2) + (1)(0) & (3)(4) + (3)(1) + (1)(2) \\ (1)(3) + (4)(2) + (2)(0) & (1)(4) + (4)(1) + (2)(2) \\ (6)(3) + (7)(2) + (8)(0) & (6)(4) + (7)(1) + (8)(2) \end{bmatrix}$$

$$= \begin{bmatrix} 15 & 17 \\ 11 & 12 \\ 32 & 47 \end{bmatrix}$$

$$CA = \begin{bmatrix} (1)(3) + (6)(2) + (2)(0) & (1)(4) + (6)(1) + (2)(2) \\ (0)(3) + (1)(2) + (0)(0) & (0)(4) + (1)(1) + (0)(2) \\ (1)(3) + (0)(2) + (1)(0) & (1)(4) + (0)(1) + (1)(2) \end{bmatrix}$$

$$= \begin{bmatrix} 15 & 14 \\ 2 & 1 \\ 3 & 6 \end{bmatrix}$$

$$BC = \begin{bmatrix} (3)(1) + (3)(0) + (1)(1) & (3)(6) + (3)(1) + (1)(0) & (3)(2) + (3)(0) + (1)(1) \\ (1)(1) + (4)(0) + (2)(1) & (1)(6) + (4)(1) + (2)(0) & (1)(2) + (4)(0) + (2)(1) \\ (6)(1) + (7)(0) + (8)(1) & (6)(6) + (7)(1) + (8)(0) & (6)(2) + (7)(0) + (8)(1) \end{bmatrix}$$

$$= \begin{bmatrix} 4 & 21 & 7 \\ 3 & 10 & 4 \\ 14 & 43 & 20 \end{bmatrix}$$

$$CB = \begin{bmatrix} (1)(3) + (6)(1) + (2)(6) & (1)(3) + (6)(4) + (2)(7) & (1)(1) + (6)(2) + (2)(8) \\ (0)(3) + (1)(1) + (0)(6) & (0)(3) + (1)(4) + (0)(7) & (0)(1) + (1)(2) + (0)(8) \\ (1)(3) + (0)(1) + (1)(6) & (1)(3) + (0)(4) + (1)(7) & (1)(1) + (0)(2) + (1)(8) \end{bmatrix}$$

$$= \begin{bmatrix} 21 & 41 & 29 \\ 1 & 4 & 2 \\ 9 & 10 & 9 \end{bmatrix}$$

It should be noted that even though BC and CB are defined, $BC \neq CB$. ∎

A matrix B may be multiplied by a scalar c and this is referred to as *scalar multiplication*. Scalar multiplication is defined by

$$cB = \begin{bmatrix} cb_{11} & cb_{12} & \cdots & cb_{1n} \\ cb_{21} & cb_{22} & \cdots & cb_{2n} \\ \vdots & \vdots & & \vdots \\ cb_{m1} & cb_{m2} & \cdots & cb_{mn} \end{bmatrix} \qquad (2.10)$$

Hence scalar multiplication is accomplished by simply multiplying each element in the matrix by the scalar.

The *transpose* of a matrix is obtained by interchanging its rows and columns. If the matrix A is defined by

$$A = \begin{bmatrix} a_{11} & a_{12} & \cdots & a_{1n} \\ a_{21} & a_{22} & \cdots & a_{2n} \\ \vdots & \vdots & & \vdots \\ a_{m1} & a_{m2} & \cdots & a_{mn} \end{bmatrix} \tag{2.11}$$

then its transpose, denoted A^T, is given by

$$A^T = \begin{bmatrix} a_{11} & a_{21} & \cdots & a_{m1} \\ a_{12} & a_{22} & \cdots & a_{m2} \\ \vdots & \vdots & & \vdots \\ a_{1n} & a_{2n} & \cdots & a_{mn} \end{bmatrix} \tag{2.12}$$

Thus if A is of order (m,n), then A^T is of order (n,m). If A and B are conformable for addition then

$$(A \pm B)^T = A^T \pm B^T \tag{2.13}$$

If A is conformable to B for multiplication, then

$$(AB)^T = B^T A^T \tag{2.14}$$

If A is a symmetric matrix, and therefore square,

$$A^T = A \tag{2.15}$$

Example 2.3   A company makes four products, numbered 1 to 4. These products require man-hours of processing time in each of three departments, designated A, B, and C. Item 1 takes 2 hours in A, 4 hours in B, and 3 hours in C. Item 2 takes 1 hour in A, 1 hour in B, and 2 hours in C. Item 3 takes 3 hours in A, 2 hours in B, and 1 hour in C. Item 4 takes 4 hours in A, 2 hours in B, and 3 hours in C. The man-hour cost of processing in department A is $6 per hour, in B is $8 per hour, and in C is $10 per hour. Use matrix methods to find:

(a)   the processing cost of each item;
(b)   the departmental man-hour requirements if daily demand is for 150 units of item 1, 200 of item 2, 300 of item 3, and 100 of item 4;
(c)   the total daily processing cost.

Let P be the processing time matrix, $\mathbf{d}$ the demand vector, and $\mathbf{c}$ the hourly cost vector. Then

$$
P = \begin{array}{c} \\ 1 \\ 2 \\ 3 \\ 4 \end{array} \overset{\displaystyle A \; B \; C}{\left[\begin{array}{ccc} 2 & 4 & 3 \\ 1 & 1 & 2 \\ 3 & 2 & 1 \\ 4 & 2 & 3 \end{array}\right]}, \qquad \mathbf{d}^{\mathrm{T}} = \overset{\text{products}}{\left[\begin{array}{cccc} 150 & 200 & 300 & 100 \end{array}\right]}
$$

$$
\overset{\text{departmehts}}{\mathbf{c}^{\mathrm{T}} = \left[\begin{array}{ccc} 6 & 8 & 10 \end{array}\right]}
$$

For part (a),

$$
Pc = \begin{array}{c} \left[\begin{array}{c} \$74 \\ \$34 \\ \$44 \\ \$70 \end{array}\right] \end{array} \begin{array}{c} 1 \\ 2 \\ 3 \\ 4 \end{array}
$$

For part (b),

departmental requirements vector $\quad \mathbf{r}^{\mathrm{T}} = \mathbf{d}^{\mathrm{T}}P = \overset{\displaystyle A \qquad B \qquad C}{\left[\begin{array}{ccc} 1800 & 1600 & 1450 \end{array}\right]}$

and for part (c),

$$
\text{total daily cost} = \mathbf{r}^{\mathrm{T}}\mathbf{c} = \$38,100. \quad \blacksquare
$$

The Determinant and Inverse of a Matrix

Suppose that a company manufactures two solvents A and B. Each unit of A requires a_{11} units of raw material R_1 and a_{21} units of raw material R_2, while each unit of B produced requires a_{12} units of R_1 and a_{22} units of R_2. If the total number of units of R_1 available is b_1 and the number of units of R_2 available is b_2, determine the number of units x_1 of A and x_2 of B which can be produced.

The total number of units of R_1 consumed in the production of x_1 units of A and x_2 units of B is $a_{11}x_1 + a_{12}x_2$, and the number of units of R_2 consumed is $a_{21}x_1 + a_{22}x_2$. Therefore,

$$
a_{11}x_1 + a_{12}x_2 = b_1 \tag{2.16}
$$

$$
a_{21}x_1 + a_{22}x_2 = b_2 \tag{2.17}
$$

Solving for x_1 in terms of x_2 yields

$$
x_1 = (b_1 - a_{12}x_2)/a_{11} \tag{2.18}
$$

Substituting the expression for x_1 in (2.18) into Eq. (2.17) and solving for x_2, we have

$$
x_2 = \frac{b_2 - a_{21}x_1}{a_{22}} = \frac{-a_{12}b_1 + a_{11}b_2}{a_{11}a_{22} - a_{12}a_{21}} \tag{2.19}
$$

and

$$x_1 = \frac{a_{22}b_1 - a_{21}b_2}{a_{11}a_{22} - a_{12}a_{21}} \tag{2.20}$$

Equations (2.19) and (2.20) can be expressed in matrix form as

$$\begin{bmatrix} x_1 \\ x_2 \end{bmatrix} = \frac{1}{a_{11}a_{22} - a_{12}a_{21}} \begin{bmatrix} a_{22}b_1 - a_{21}b_2 \\ -a_{12}b_1 + a_{11}b_2 \end{bmatrix}$$

$$= \frac{1}{a_{11}a_{22} - a_{12}a_{21}} \begin{bmatrix} a_{22} & -a_{21} \\ -a_{12} & a_{11} \end{bmatrix} \begin{bmatrix} b_1 \\ b_2 \end{bmatrix}$$

The expression $a_{11}a_{22} - a_{12}a_{21}$ is called the *determinant* of the matrix A, denoted $|A|$ or $\det(A)$, where

$$A = \begin{bmatrix} a_{11} & a_{12} \\ a_{21} & a_{22} \end{bmatrix} \tag{2.21}$$

The matrix

$$\begin{bmatrix} \dfrac{a_{22}}{|A|} & -\dfrac{a_{21}}{|A|} \\ -\dfrac{a_{12}}{|A|} & \dfrac{a_{11}}{|A|} \end{bmatrix}$$

is called the *inverse* of A and is denoted A^{-1}. The inverse possesses the property that

$$AA^{-1} = A^{-1}A = I \tag{2.22}$$

Although the inverse and therefore the determinant are important in solving systems of simultaneous linear equations, they also have important applications in other areas, as we shall see later in this and in succeeding chapters.

The determinant of a matrix exists only if the matrix is square. If the value of the determinant is zero, then the associated matrix is said to be *singular*. The determinant of a (2, 2) matrix is given by

$$|A| = a_{11}a_{22} - a_{12}a_{21} \tag{2.23}$$

and by

$$|A| = a_{11}a_{22}a_{33} + a_{12}a_{23}a_{31} + a_{13}a_{32}a_{21}$$
$$- a_{13}a_{22}a_{31} - a_{23}a_{32}a_{11} - a_{33}a_{21}a_{12} \tag{2.24}$$

for (3, 3) matrices. For matrices of higher order the expression for the determinant is more complicated. This complexity can be reduced by application of the cofactor method. However, before introducing the co-factor method, it will be necessary to introduce the concepts of the minor and cofactor of an element.

Let M_{ij} be the matrix remaining after deletion of the ith row and jth column. If A is an (n,n) matrix, then M_{ij} is of order $(n-1, n-1)$ for all i and j. The determinant of M_{ij}, $|M_{ij}|$, is called the *minor* of element a_{ij}.

Example 2.4 Find the minors for each element a_{ij} in the matrix A, where

$$A = \begin{bmatrix} 1 & 4 & 6 \\ 2 & 1 & 1 \\ 3 & 2 & 1 \end{bmatrix}$$

The matrices M_{ij} are defined as follows:

$$M_{11} = \begin{bmatrix} 1 & 1 \\ 2 & 1 \end{bmatrix}, \quad M_{12} = \begin{bmatrix} 2 & 1 \\ 3 & 1 \end{bmatrix}, \quad M_{13} = \begin{bmatrix} 2 & 1 \\ 3 & 2 \end{bmatrix}$$

$$M_{21} = \begin{bmatrix} 4 & 6 \\ 2 & 1 \end{bmatrix}, \quad M_{22} = \begin{bmatrix} 1 & 6 \\ 3 & 1 \end{bmatrix}, \quad M_{23} = \begin{bmatrix} 1 & 4 \\ 3 & 2 \end{bmatrix}$$

$$M_{31} = \begin{bmatrix} 4 & 6 \\ 1 & 1 \end{bmatrix}, \quad M_{32} = \begin{bmatrix} 1 & 6 \\ 2 & 1 \end{bmatrix}, \quad M_{33} = \begin{bmatrix} 1 & 4 \\ 2 & 1 \end{bmatrix}$$

Applying Eq. (2.23) to each of the matrices M_{ij}, we have the minors $|M_{ij}|$ given by

$$|M_{11}| = -1, \quad |M_{12}| = -1, \quad |M_{13}| = 1$$
$$|M_{21}| = -8, \quad |M_{22}| = -17, \quad |M_{23}| = -10$$
$$|M_{31}| = -2, \quad |M_{32}| = -11, \quad |M_{33}| = -7 \quad \blacksquare$$

The *cofactor* of an element a_{ij}, sometimes called the *signed minor*, is given by

$$A_{ij} = (-1)^{i+j}|M_{ij}| \tag{2.25}$$

Example 2.5 Find the cofactor of each element in the matrix A in Example 2.4.

To compute the cofactor of the element a_{ij} of the matrix in Example 2.4 we simply multiply the minor of a_{ij}, $|M_{ij}|$, by $(-1)^{i+j}$. Hence

$$A_{11} = (-1)^{1+1}(-1) \qquad A_{12} = (-1)^{1+2}(-1) \qquad A_{13} = (-1)^{1+3}(1)$$
$$= -1, \qquad\qquad = 1, \qquad\qquad = 1$$

$$A_{21} = (-1)^{2+1}(-8) \qquad A_{22} = (-1)^{2+2}(-17) \qquad A_{23} = (-1)^{2+3}(-10)$$
$$= 8, \qquad\qquad = -17, \qquad\qquad = 10$$

$$A_{31} = (-1)^{3+1}(-2) \qquad A_{32} = (-1)^{3+2}(-11) \qquad A_{33} = (-1)^{3+3}(-7)$$
$$= -2, \qquad\qquad = 11, \qquad\qquad = -7 \quad \blacksquare$$

The *cofactor method* allows the analyst to compute the determinant using the elements in any *one* row *or* column and their associated cofactors. If A is an (n, n) matrix with elements a_{ij} and associated cofactors A_{ij}, then

$$|A| = \sum_{i=1}^{n} a_{ij} A_{ij} \qquad (2.26)$$

for any choice of j or

$$|A| = \sum_{j=1}^{n} a_{ij} A_{ij} \qquad (2.27)$$

for any choice of i. Equations (2.26) and (2.27) define the cofactor method. Since $A_{ij} = (-1)^{i+j} |M_{ij}|$ and since M_{ij} is of order $(n-1, n-1)$ if A is (n, n), the cofactor method allows the analyst to compute the determinant of an (n, n) matrix by computing the determinants of n $(n-1, n-1)$ matrices. Thus through repeated application of the cofactor method we can reduce the computation of the determinant of an (n, n) matrix to computation of the determinants of a series of $(3, 3)$ matrices which may be evaluated using Eq. (2.24). To reduce the effort further one would usually apply the cofactor method to the row or column containing the maximum number of elements for which $a_{ij} = 0$.

Example 2.6   Evaluate the determinant of the matrix A, where

$$A = \begin{bmatrix} 1 & 4 & 2 & 0 \\ 0 & 1 & 0 & 2 \\ 7 & 1 & 0 & 4 \\ 8 & 2 & 0 & 1 \end{bmatrix}$$

using first a row expansion and second a column expansion through the cofactor method.

Since $a_{2j} = 0, j = 1, 3$, the cofactor method is applied to the second row.

$$|A| = \sum_{i=1}^{4} a_{2j} A_{2j} = a_{22} A_{22} + a_{24} A_{24}$$

since $a_{21} = a_{23} = 0$. Now

$$M_{22} = \begin{bmatrix} 1 & 2 & 0 \\ 7 & 0 & 4 \\ 8 & 0 & 1 \end{bmatrix}, \qquad M_{24} = \begin{bmatrix} 1 & 4 & 2 \\ 7 & 1 & 0 \\ 8 & 2 & 0 \end{bmatrix}$$

Applying Eq. (2.24), we have

$$|M_{22}| = 64 - 14 = 50, \qquad |M_{24}| = 28 - 16 = 12$$

and

$$A_{22} = (-1)^{2+2}(50) = 50, \qquad A_{24} = (-1)^{2+4}(12) = 12$$

$|A|$ is then given by

$$|A| = (1)(50) + (2)(12) = 74$$

Since the third column contains three zero elements, the cofactor method is most conveniently applied to this column. Hence,

$$|A| = \sum_{i=1}^{4} a_{i3}A_{i3} = a_{13}A_{13}$$

Now

$$M_{13} = \begin{bmatrix} 0 & 1 & 2 \\ 7 & 1 & 4 \\ 8 & 2 & 1 \end{bmatrix}$$

and

$$|M_{13}| = 32 + 28 - 16 - 7 = 37$$

Hence

$$A_{13} = (-1)^{1+3}(37) = 37$$

and

$$|A| = (2)(37) = 74 \quad \blacksquare$$

The following properties of determinants are useful in many applications of matrix methods:

(1)   Interchanging any two rows (columns) of a square matrix reverses the sign of the determinant.

(2)   If any two rows (columns) of a square matrix are equal, the determinant of the matrix is zero.

(3)   If any row or column of a square matrix is zero, the determinant of the matrix is zero.

(4)   If A is a square matrix,

$$|A^{\mathrm{T}}| = |A| \tag{2.28}$$

(5)   If a square matrix is such that one row (column) is a common multiple of another row (column), then the determinant of the matrix is zero.

(6)   If two (n, n) square matrices A and B are identical except that one row (column) of B is k times the corresponding row (column) of A, then

$$|B| = k|A| \tag{2.29}$$

(7)   If A and B are square matrices of order (n, n), then

$$|AB| = |A||B| \tag{2.30}$$

(8)   If A is an (n, n) scalar matrix with diagonal elements equal to

k, then

$$|A| = k^n \tag{2.31}$$

(9) $|I| = 1$ (2.32)

(10) If A is an (n, n) matrix and k is a scalar, then

$$|kA| = k^n|A| \tag{2.33}$$

(11) If a common multiple of row (column) i of A is added to row (column) k of A, the determinant of A is unchanged.

The determinant is used to define the rank of a matrix. The matrix A is said to be of *rank* k, denoted $r(A) = k$, if there exists at least one nonsingular square submatrix in A of order k and if all square submatrices of order $k + i$, $i \geqslant 1$ (if any), are singular. If A is a nonsingular square matrix of order k, then the rank of A is also of order k since it contains no square submatrices of order greater than k. On the other hand, if A is of order (m, n) where $m > n$, then the rank of A cannot be greater than n since there are no square submatrices in A which have order greater than n.

Example 2.7 Determine the rank of the matrix A, where

$$A = \begin{bmatrix} 2 & 3 & 0 & 0 \\ 2 & 3 & 1 & 0 \\ 0 & 0 & 1 & 0 \end{bmatrix}$$

A contains four square submatrices of order 3 given by

$$A_1 = \begin{bmatrix} 2 & 3 & 0 \\ 2 & 3 & 1 \\ 0 & 0 & 1 \end{bmatrix}, \qquad A_2 = \begin{bmatrix} 2 & 3 & 0 \\ 2 & 3 & 0 \\ 0 & 0 & 0 \end{bmatrix}$$

$$A_3 = \begin{bmatrix} 2 & 0 & 0 \\ 2 & 1 & 0 \\ 0 & 1 & 0 \end{bmatrix}, \qquad A_4 = \begin{bmatrix} 3 & 0 & 0 \\ 3 & 1 & 0 \\ 0 & 1 & 0 \end{bmatrix}$$

As the determinant of each of these submatrices is zero, the rank of A must be less than 3. Now examining square submatrices of order 2, we find that the submatrix obtained by deleting the second and fourth columns and the third row of A is given by

$$B = \begin{bmatrix} 2 & 0 \\ 2 & 1 \end{bmatrix}$$

and is nonsingular. Hence A has rank 2. ∎

The inverse of a square matrix exists if and only if the matrix is *nonsingular*, where the matrix is nonsingular if $|A| \neq 0$. If A is a nonsingular square matrix, then the inverse of A, denoted A^{-1}, is defined so that $A^{-1}A = I$ or $AA^{-1} = I$. To determine the inverse of A we use the *adjoint matrix* adj(A). The adjoint of a matrix is the transpose of the matrix of cofactors. Hence to compute adj(A) we calculate the cofactor A_{ij} of each element a_{ij}, replace a_{ij} by A_{ij}, and take the transpose of the matrix of cofactors. Thus if

$$A = \begin{bmatrix} a_{11} & a_{12} & \cdots & a_{1n} \\ a_{21} & a_{22} & \cdots & a_{2n} \\ \vdots & \vdots & & \vdots \\ a_{n1} & a_{n2} & \cdots & a_{nn} \end{bmatrix} \tag{2.34}$$

then

$$\text{adj}(A) = \begin{bmatrix} A_{11} & A_{21} & \cdots & A_{n1} \\ A_{12} & A_{22} & \cdots & A_{n2} \\ \vdots & \vdots & & \vdots \\ A_{1n} & A_{2n} & \cdots & A_{nn} \end{bmatrix} \tag{2.35}$$

The *inverse* of A is then defined by

$$A^{-1} = \text{adj}(A)/|A| \tag{2.36}$$

Example 2.8   Find the inverse of the matrix given in Example 2.6 if the inverse exists.

From Example 2.6 we have $|A| = 74$. Since $|A| \neq 0$, the inverse of A exists. The minors of the elements of A are given by

$$|M_{11}| = \begin{vmatrix} 1 & 0 & 2 \\ 1 & 0 & 4 \\ 2 & 0 & 1 \end{vmatrix} = 0, \quad |M_{12}| = \begin{vmatrix} 0 & 0 & 2 \\ 7 & 0 & 4 \\ 8 & 0 & 1 \end{vmatrix} = 0, \quad |M_{13}| = \begin{vmatrix} 0 & 1 & 2 \\ 7 & 1 & 4 \\ 8 & 2 & 1 \end{vmatrix} = 37, \quad |M_{14}| = \begin{vmatrix} 0 & 1 & 0 \\ 7 & 1 & 0 \\ 8 & 2 & 0 \end{vmatrix} = 0$$

$$|M_{21}| = \begin{vmatrix} 4 & 2 & 0 \\ 1 & 0 & 4 \\ 2 & 0 & 1 \end{vmatrix} = 14, \quad |M_{22}| = \begin{vmatrix} 1 & 2 & 0 \\ 7 & 0 & 4 \\ 8 & 0 & 1 \end{vmatrix} = 50, \quad |M_{23}| = \begin{vmatrix} 1 & 4 & 0 \\ 7 & 1 & 4 \\ 8 & 2 & 1 \end{vmatrix} = 93, \quad |M_{24}| = \begin{vmatrix} 1 & 4 & 2 \\ 7 & 1 & 0 \\ 8 & 2 & 0 \end{vmatrix} = 12$$

$$|M_{31}| = \begin{vmatrix} 4 & 2 & 0 \\ 1 & 0 & 2 \\ 2 & 0 & 1 \end{vmatrix} = 6, \quad |M_{32}| = \begin{vmatrix} 1 & 2 & 0 \\ 0 & 0 & 2 \\ 8 & 0 & 1 \end{vmatrix} = 32, \quad |M_{33}| = \begin{vmatrix} 1 & 4 & 0 \\ 0 & 1 & 2 \\ 8 & 2 & 1 \end{vmatrix} = 61, \quad |M_{34}| = \begin{vmatrix} 1 & 4 & 2 \\ 0 & 1 & 0 \\ 8 & 2 & 0 \end{vmatrix} = -1$$

$$|M_{41}| = \begin{vmatrix} 4 & 2 & 0 \\ 1 & 0 & 2 \\ 1 & 0 & 4 \end{vmatrix} = -4, \quad |M_{42}| = \begin{vmatrix} 1 & 2 & 0 \\ 0 & 0 & 2 \\ 7 & 0 & 4 \end{vmatrix} = 28, \quad |M_{43}| = \begin{vmatrix} 1 & 4 & 0 \\ 0 & 1 & 2 \\ 7 & 1 & 4 \end{vmatrix} = 58, \quad |M_{44}| = \begin{vmatrix} 1 & 4 & 2 \\ 0 & 1 & 0 \\ 7 & 1 & 0 \end{vmatrix} = -1$$

Multiplying $|M_{ij}|$ by $(-1)^{i+j}$, we obtain the matrix of cofactors given by

$$\begin{bmatrix} 0 & 0 & 37 & 0 \\ -14 & 50 & -93 & 12 \\ 6 & -32 & 61 & 16 \\ 4 & 28 & -58 & -14 \end{bmatrix}$$

and the adjoint matrix is

$$\text{adj}(A) = \begin{bmatrix} 0 & -14 & 6 & 4 \\ 0 & 50 & -32 & 28 \\ 37 & -93 & 61 & -58 \\ 0 & 12 & 16 & -14 \end{bmatrix}$$

The inverse of matrix A is then

$$A^{-1} = \text{adj}(A)/|A|$$

$$= \begin{bmatrix} 0 & -14/74 & 6/74 & 4/74 \\ 0 & 50/74 & -32/74 & 28/74 \\ 37/74 & -93/74 & 61/74 & -58/74 \\ 0 & 12/74 & 16/74 & -14/74 \end{bmatrix}$$

To check our calculation of the inverse we will calculate the product matrix $A^{-1}A$. If $A^{-1}A = I$, then A^{-1} given above is the inverse of A:

$$A^{-1}A = \begin{bmatrix} 0 & -14/74 & 6/74 & 4/74 \\ 0 & 50/74 & -32/74 & 28/74 \\ 37/74 & -93/74 & 61/74 & -58/74 \\ 0 & 12/74 & 16/74 & -14/74 \end{bmatrix} \begin{bmatrix} 1 & 4 & 2 & 0 \\ 0 & 1 & 0 & 2 \\ 7 & 1 & 0 & 4 \\ 8 & 2 & 0 & 1 \end{bmatrix}$$

$$= \begin{bmatrix} 1 & 0 & 0 & 0 \\ 0 & 1 & 0 & 0 \\ 0 & 0 & 1 & 0 \\ 0 & 0 & 0 & 1 \end{bmatrix} \blacksquare$$

The following properties hold if the inverse of the matrices A and B exist:

(1) If A is a symmetric matrix, A^{-1} is also symmetric.
(2) $(A^{-1})^{-1} = A$ (2.37)
(3) $(A^{\mathrm{T}})^{-1} = (A^{-1})^{\mathrm{T}}$ (2.38)
(4) If A is conformable to B for multiplication and A and B are square matrices, then

$$(AB)^{-1} = B^{-1}A^{-1}$$ (2.39)

(5) The inverse of a matrix is unique. That is, if

$$A^{-1}A = I \quad \text{and} \quad C^{-1}A = I$$

then

$$C = A$$

(6) If A is a scalar matrix, then A^{-1} is a scalar matrix.

VECTORS AND VECTOR SPACES

Vectors

As already mentioned, a matrix having either a single row or a single column is called a vector. Unless otherwise stated, all reference to vectors will be to column vectors. The *dimension* of a vector is defined by the number of elements in the vector. Hence an *n-dimensional vector* is a column vector having n rows. An n-dimensional vector represents a point in a space having n coordinate axes. Hence the vectors $\mathbf{x}_1$ and $\mathbf{x}_2$ defined by

$$\mathbf{x}_1 = \begin{bmatrix} 3 \\ 2 \end{bmatrix}, \qquad \mathbf{x}_2 = \begin{bmatrix} 4 \\ 1 \\ 3 \end{bmatrix}$$

are points in 2- and 3-dimensional space, respectively. Graphical representations of $\mathbf{x}_1$ and $\mathbf{x}_2$ are shown in Figs. 2.1 and 2.2. The elements of a vector represent the projection of that vector on the corresponding coordinate axis, as shown by the dashed lines in Figs. 2.1 and 2.2. If all the elements of the vector are zero, the vector is denoted Ø, called the *zero* or *null vector* and may be taken as the *origin* of the coordinate system.

In the discussion of the directional derivative, the concept of a direction or direction vector was introduced. A *direction* or *direction vector* is simply a vector of unit length. Thus if $\mathbf{x}$ is an n-dimensional direction,

$$\sqrt{x_1^2 + x_2^2 + \cdots + x_n^2} = 1 \tag{2.40}$$

As the name direction or direction vector would imply, this vector tells us

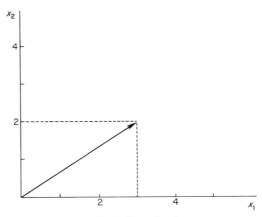

Fig. 2.1   The 2-dimensional vector $\mathbf{x}_1$.

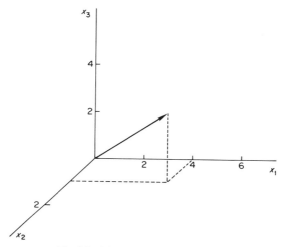

Fig. 2.2 The 3-dimensional vector x_2.

something about the direction we would have to move in were we to proceed in a straight line from the origin to the point represented by the vector. The elements of the direction vector indicate the size of the step necessary along each coordinate axis necessary to move one unit in the direction defined by the direction vector.

The *distance* between two vectors x_1 and x_2 is denoted $|x_1 - x_2|$ or $|x_2 - x_1|$ and is defined by

$$|x_1 - x_2| = \sqrt{(x_{11} - x_{21})^2 + (x_{12} - x_{22})^2 + \cdots + (i_{1n} - x_{2n})}$$

$$= \sqrt{(x_1 - x_2)^T(x_1 - x_2)} \tag{2.41}$$

where x_1 and x_2 are n-dimensional vectors with elements x_{1i} and x_{2i}, $i = 1, 2, \ldots n$, respectively. The distance between two vectors or points in space is the length of a straight-line segment connecting the two vectors. If, in Eq. (2.41), x_2 is a vector with elements $x_{2i} = 0$ for all i, then x_2 represents the origin. The distance of a vector from the origin is called the *length of the vector* and is denoted $|x_1|$.

It should be recalled that a vector is a special matrix, and thus the operations of addition, subtraction, and multiplication of vectors are governed by the rules of matrix addition, subtraction, and multiplication. These rules suggest that the distance between two vectors has meaning only if the vectors are of the same dimension.

If a set of vectors, $x_1, x_2, \ldots, x_m$ have the same dimension, then they may be added or subtracted. If $\alpha_1, \alpha_2, \ldots, \alpha_m$ are arbitrary scalars, then a *linear combination* of $\mathbf{x}_1, \mathbf{x}_2, \ldots, \mathbf{x}_m$ is defined by

$$\mathbf{y} = \alpha_1\mathbf{x}_1 + \alpha_2\mathbf{x}_2 + \cdots + \alpha_m\mathbf{x}_m \qquad (2.42)$$

where $\mathbf{y}$ is a vector having the same dimension as each of the vectors in the linear combination.

Two vectors $\mathbf{x}_1$, $\mathbf{x}_2$ having the same dimension are *orthogonal* or perpendicular if the angle between them is $90°$. Based upon this definition of orthogonality it may be shown that two vectors are orthogonal if

$$\mathbf{x}_1^T\mathbf{x}_2 = \mathbf{x}_2^T\mathbf{x}_1 = 0 \qquad (2.43)$$

A set of vectors $\mathbf{x}_1, \mathbf{x}_2, \ldots, \mathbf{x}_m$ having the same dimension is said to be *mutually orthogonal* if

$$\mathbf{x}_i^T\mathbf{x}_j = 0 \qquad (2.44)$$

for all $i \neq j$. That is, if every combination of two distinct vectors from the set are orthogonal, then the set is mutually orthogonal.

Example 2.9 Find the length of the following two vectors, determine the distance between them, and determine whether they are orthogonal:

$$\mathbf{x}_1 = \begin{bmatrix} 1 \\ 0 \\ 0 \end{bmatrix}, \qquad \mathbf{x}_2 = \begin{bmatrix} 0 \\ 4 \\ 3 \end{bmatrix}$$

The lengths of $\mathbf{x}_1$ and $\mathbf{x}_2$ are given by

$$|\mathbf{x}_1| = \sqrt{(1)^2 + (0)^2 + (0)^2} = 1$$

$$|\mathbf{x}_2| = \sqrt{(0)^2 + (4)^2 + (3)^2} = 5$$

Since $\mathbf{x}_1$ and $\mathbf{x}_2$ are both 3-dimensional vectors, the distance between them is defined and is given by

$$|\mathbf{x}_1 - \mathbf{x}_2| = \sqrt{(1 - 0)^2 + (0 - 4)^2 + (0 - 3)^2} = \sqrt{26}$$

To determine whether $\mathbf{x}_1$ and $\mathbf{x}_2$ are orthogonal we compute $\mathbf{x}_1^T\mathbf{x}_2$ or $\mathbf{x}_2^T\mathbf{x}_1$.

$$\mathbf{x}_1^T\mathbf{x}_2 = \begin{bmatrix} 1 & 0 & 0 \end{bmatrix} \begin{bmatrix} 0 \\ 4 \\ 3 \end{bmatrix} = 0$$

and $\mathbf{x}_1$ and $\mathbf{x}_2$ are orthogonal to one another. ∎

A set of n-dimensional vectors $\mathbf{x}_1, \mathbf{x}_2, \ldots, \mathbf{x}_m$ is *linearly independent* if and only if

$$\sum_{i=1}^{m} k_i\mathbf{x}_i = \emptyset \qquad (2.45)$$

implies that $k_i = 0$, $i = 1, 2, \ldots, m$, where the k_i are scalars. If the condition for independence is satisfied for a given set of vectors, then no vector within the set can be expressed as a linear combination of the remaining vectors. In this sense each vector in the set is not dependent upon the others. A set of vectors that are not linearly independnet is said to be *linearly dependent*. A set of vectors that are mutually orthogonal is also linearly independent. However, linear independence does not imply orthogonality.

Example 2.10 Show that the vectors x_1, x_2, and x_3 are linearly independent but are not mutually orthogonal, where

$$x_1 = \begin{bmatrix} 1 \\ 0 \\ 3 \end{bmatrix}, \qquad x_2 = \begin{bmatrix} 0 \\ 2 \\ 0 \end{bmatrix}, \qquad x_3 = \begin{bmatrix} 2 \\ 0 \\ 1 \end{bmatrix}$$

To satisfy the condition for linear independence the relationship

$$k_1 x_1 + k_2 x_2 + k_3 x_3 = \varnothing$$

must lead to the conclusion that $k_1 = k_2 = k_3 = 0$. From the definition of x_1, x_2 and x_3,

$$k_1 x_1 + k_2 x_2 + k_3 x_3 = \begin{bmatrix} k_1 \\ 0 \\ 3k_1 \end{bmatrix} + \begin{bmatrix} 0 \\ 2k_2 \\ 0 \end{bmatrix} + \begin{bmatrix} 2k_3 \\ 0 \\ k_3 \end{bmatrix} = \begin{bmatrix} 0 \\ 0 \\ 0 \end{bmatrix}$$

and we must solve for the values of k_1, k_2, and k_3 which satisfy the system of simultaneous linear equations given by

$$k_1 + \qquad 2k_3 = 0$$
$$2k_2 \qquad = 0$$
$$3k_1 + \qquad k_3 = 0$$

From the second equation, $k_2 = 0$. From the first and third equations, $k_1 = -2k_3$ and $k_1 = -k_3/3$. The only values of k_1 and k_3 which satisfy both relationships are $k_1 = 0$ and $k_3 = 0$. Hence the only solution for the system of simultaneous linear equations is $k_1 = k_2 = k_3 = 0$, and the vectors x_1, x_2, and x_3 are linearly independent.

To determine whether x_1, x_2, and x_3 are mutually orthogonal as a set we compute $x_1^T x_2$, $x_1^T x_3$, and $x_2^T x_3$, yielding

$$x_1^T x_2 = \begin{bmatrix} 1 & 0 & 3 \end{bmatrix} \begin{bmatrix} 0 \\ 2 \\ 0 \end{bmatrix} = 0$$

$$x_1^T x_3 = \begin{bmatrix} 1 & 0 & 3 \end{bmatrix} \begin{bmatrix} 2 \\ 0 \\ 1 \end{bmatrix} = 5$$

$$x_2^T x_3 = \begin{bmatrix} 0 & 2 & 0 \end{bmatrix} \begin{bmatrix} 2 \\ 0 \\ 1 \end{bmatrix} = 0$$

Hence $\mathbf{x}_1$ and $\mathbf{x}_2$ are orthogonal, as are $\mathbf{x}_2$ and $\mathbf{x}_3$. However, since $\mathbf{x}_1$ and $\mathbf{x}_3$ are not orthogonal, the set of vectors $\mathbf{x}_1$, $\mathbf{x}_2$, and $\mathbf{x}_3$ is not mutually orthogonal. ∎

Example 2.11 Show that if the vectors $\mathbf{x}_1$, $\mathbf{x}_2$, . . . , $\mathbf{x}_n$ are mutually orthogonal, they are also linearly independent.

First choose k_1, k_2, . . . , k_n such that

$$\sum_{i=1}^{n} k_i \mathbf{x}_i = \varnothing$$

Now choose *any* vector $\mathbf{x}_j$ from the set $\mathbf{x}_1$, $\mathbf{x}_2$, . . . , $\mathbf{x}_n$ and form the product

$$\mathbf{x}_j^{\mathrm{T}}\left(\sum_{i=1}^{n} k_i \mathbf{x}_i\right) = \mathbf{x}_j^{\mathrm{T}}\phi$$

Since ϕ is the zero vector, $\mathbf{x}_j \phi = 0$. Now, since $\mathbf{x}_1$, $\mathbf{x}_2$, . . . , $\mathbf{x}_n$ are mutually orthogonal,

$$\mathbf{x}_j^{\mathrm{T}}\mathbf{x}_i = 0 \qquad \text{for} \quad i \neq j$$

and

$$\mathbf{x}_j^{\mathrm{T}}\mathbf{x}_j \neq 0$$

Hence

$$\mathbf{x}_j^{\mathrm{T}}\left(\sum_{i=1}^{n} k_i \mathbf{x}_i\right) = \sum_{i=1}^{n} k_i \mathbf{x}_j^{\mathrm{T}}\mathbf{x}_i = k_j \mathbf{x}_j^{\mathrm{T}}\mathbf{x}_j = 0$$

Since $\mathbf{x}_j^{\mathrm{T}}\mathbf{x}_j$ is a nonzero scalar, $k_j \mathbf{x}_j^{\mathrm{T}}\mathbf{x}_j = 0$ if and only if

$$k_j = 0$$

Since $\mathbf{x}_j$ is any vector from the set $\mathbf{x}_1$, $\mathbf{x}_2$, . . . , $\mathbf{x}_n$, $k_j = 0, j = 1, 2, . . . , n$, and $\mathbf{x}_1$, $\mathbf{x}_2$, . . . , $\mathbf{x}_n$ are linearly independent. ∎

Consider the set of vectors $\mathbf{x}_1$, $\mathbf{x}_2$, . . . , $\mathbf{x}_r$, $\mathbf{x}_{r+1}$, . . . , $\mathbf{x}_n$, where $\mathbf{x}_1$, $\mathbf{x}_2$, . . . , $\mathbf{x}_r$ are linearly independent, while each $\mathbf{x}_j$ in the set $\mathbf{x}_{r+1}$, . . . , $\mathbf{x}_n$ can be expressed by a linear combination of $\mathbf{x}_1, \mathbf{x}_2, . . . , \mathbf{x}_r$. Specificially, let

$$\mathbf{x}_j = \sum_{i=1}^{r} k_{ji} \mathbf{x}_i, \qquad j = r + 1, r + 2, . . . , n$$

Now let X be the matrix with columns $\mathbf{x}_1$, $\mathbf{x}_2$, . . . , $\mathbf{x}_r$, . . . , $\mathbf{x}_n$. Then

$$X = \begin{bmatrix} \mathbf{x}_1 & \mathbf{x}_2 & \cdots & \mathbf{x}_r & \mathbf{x}_{r+1} & \cdots & \mathbf{x}_n \end{bmatrix}$$

$$= \begin{bmatrix} \mathbf{x}_1 & \mathbf{x}_2 & \cdots & \mathbf{x}_r & \sum_{i=1}^{r} k_{r+1, i} \mathbf{x}_i & \cdots & \sum_{i=1}^{r} k_{ni} \mathbf{x}_i \end{bmatrix}$$

Now let us examine the determinant of X. The reader will recall from the properties of the determinant that the addition of a common mutliple of column i of X to column k of X does not change the determinant of X. Now to the $(r + 1)$st column of X add successively $-k_{r+1,1}\mathbf{x}_1$, $-k_{r+1,2}\mathbf{x}_2, \ldots, -k_{r+1,r}\mathbf{x}_r$. This reduces the $(r + 1)$st column of X to a zero vector. In a similar manner we can reduce each of the columns of X from $r + 1$ to n to a zero vector without changing $|X|$. Let X_T be the new matrix with columns $r + 1$ through n composed of zero vectors. Since $|X| = |X_T|$ and since X_T has at least one column with zero elements, $|X_T| = 0$ and $|X| = 0$. Hence if X is a matrix composed of columns which form a linearly dependent set of vectors, then $|X| = 0$. However, if X is composed of columns which form a linearly independent set of vectors, then $|X| \neq 0$ since no column of X can be reduced to zero by successively adding common multiples of other columns to it.

In the case just cited we assumed that the vectors $\mathbf{x}_1, \mathbf{x}_2, \ldots, \mathbf{x}_r$ were linearly independent, while $\mathbf{x}_{r+1}, \ldots, \mathbf{x}_n$ were assumed to be linearly dependent upon $\mathbf{x}_1, \mathbf{x}_2, \ldots, \mathbf{x}_r$. Defining the matrix X as before, it can be shown that if r of the columns of X are linearly independent, then X has rank r. Thus we may determine the number of linearly independent vectors in a given set by determining the rank of the matrix composed of columns formed by the vectors in the set.

Vector Spaces

A *space* may be thought of as a collection of vectors each having the same dimension. Of particular interest are vector spaces and convex spaces. Convex spaces will be discussed in the next section, and we shall show that a vector space is also convex. However, a convex space is not necessarily a vector space.

Let χ_n be a set of n-dimensional vectors $\mathbf{x}_i$, and let k be a scalar. Let $\mathbf{x}_1$ and $\mathbf{x}_2$ be any two vectors, distinct or not, in χ_n. Now define the vectors $\mathbf{y}_1$ and $\mathbf{y}_2$ by

$$\mathbf{y}_1 = k\mathbf{x}_1 \tag{2.46}$$

$$\mathbf{y}_2 = \mathbf{x}_1 + \mathbf{x}_2 \tag{2.47}$$

If $\mathbf{y}_1$ and $\mathbf{y}_2$ also belong to χ_n for all choices of real k and $\mathbf{x}_1$ and $\mathbf{x}_2$, then χ_n is called a *vector space*. Conversely, if for any real k the vector $k\mathbf{x}_1$ does not belong to χ_n or for any $\mathbf{x}_1$ and $\mathbf{x}_2$ contained in χ_n the vector $\mathbf{x}_1 + \mathbf{x}_2$ does not belong to χ_n, then χ_n is not a vector space.

Associated with every vector space is its dimension. The *dimension of a vector space* is given by the dimension of the vectors included in the vector space.

Example 2.12   The space χ_3 includes the four 3-dimensional vectors defined by

$$\cdot \mathbf{x}_1 = \begin{bmatrix} 2 \\ 2 \\ 2 \end{bmatrix}, \qquad \mathbf{x}_2 = \begin{bmatrix} 4 \\ 3 \\ 6 \end{bmatrix}, \qquad \mathbf{x}_3 = \begin{bmatrix} 2 \\ 1 \\ 7 \end{bmatrix}, \qquad \mathbf{x}_4 = \begin{bmatrix} 0 \\ 0 \\ 1 \end{bmatrix}$$

Is χ_3 a vector space?

Let $k = 2$. Then

$$y_1 = k\mathbf{x}_1 = \begin{bmatrix} 4 \\ 4 \\ 4 \end{bmatrix}$$

Since the vector $\mathbf{y}_1$ is not contained in the original set, χ_3 is not a vector space. Alternatively, the vector $\mathbf{y}_2 = \mathbf{x}_1 + \mathbf{x}_2$ does not belong to the original set, and this too demonstrates that χ_3 is not a vector space. ∎

Example 2.13   Let χ_2 be the set of all 2-dimensional vectors such that any vector $\mathbf{x}$ in χ_2 can be expressed by

$$\mathbf{x} = \begin{bmatrix} 2n \\ n \end{bmatrix}$$

where n must be an integer. Is χ_2 a vector space?

Consider any two vectors in χ_2 defined by

$$\mathbf{x}_1 = \begin{bmatrix} 2n \\ n \end{bmatrix}, \qquad \mathbf{x}_2 = \begin{bmatrix} 2m \\ m \end{bmatrix}$$

where m and n are integers. Then

$$\mathbf{y}_2 = \mathbf{x}_1 + \mathbf{x}_2 = \begin{bmatrix} 2(n + m) \\ n + m \end{bmatrix}$$

Now for all vectors in χ_2 the first element must be an even integer while the second element must be an integer, odd or even. The first element of $\mathbf{y}_2$, $2(m + n)$, is an even integer since m and n are integers. The second element of $\mathbf{y}_2$, $n + m$, is an integer. Hence we cannot reject χ_2 as a vector space at this point. Now choose $k = 1/2$ and let n be an odd integer. Then

$$\mathbf{y}_1 = k\mathbf{x}_1 = \tfrac{1}{2}\begin{bmatrix} 2n \\ n \end{bmatrix} = \begin{bmatrix} n \\ n/2 \end{bmatrix}$$

Since the first element of $\mathbf{y}_1$ is not an even integer and $n/2$ is not an integer, $\mathbf{y}_1$ does not belong to χ_2 and χ_2 is not a vector space. ∎

Example 2.14   Let χ_3 be a space composed of all 3-dimensional vectors $\mathbf{x}$ of the form

$$\mathbf{x} = \begin{bmatrix} b \\ b \\ b \end{bmatrix}$$

where b is any real number. Is χ_3 a vector space?

Let x_1 and x_2 be defined by

$$\mathbf{x}_1 = \begin{bmatrix} b \\ b \\ b \end{bmatrix}, \qquad \mathbf{x}_2 = \begin{bmatrix} c \\ c \\ c \end{bmatrix}$$

where b and c are any real numbers. Then $\mathbf{x}_1$ and $\mathbf{x}_2$ belong to χ_3. Now

$$\mathbf{y}_2 = \mathbf{x}_1 + \mathbf{x}_2 = \begin{bmatrix} b + c \\ b + c \\ b + c \end{bmatrix}$$

also belongs to χ_3 since its elements are real and equal. Let k be any real number. Then

$$\mathbf{y}_1 = k\mathbf{x}_1 = \begin{bmatrix} kb \\ kb \\ kb \end{bmatrix}$$

belongs to χ_3 since it is a 3-dimensional vector with elements which are real and equal. Since χ_3 satisfies the conditions for a vector space, χ_3 is a vector space. ∎

The definition of a vector space leads immediately to several properties of vector spaces. Every vector space must contain the zero vector. Since k can assume any real value on $(-\infty, \infty)$, we may choose $k = 0$. If $\mathbf{x}_1$ is any vector which belongs to the vector space χ_n, then

$$\mathbf{y}_1 = k\mathbf{x}_1 = \phi \tag{2.48}$$

Hence if χ_n is a vector space, it must contain ϕ. In addition, the zero vector is a vector space itself since $k\phi = \phi$ and $\phi + \phi = \phi$. A vector space either contains one and only one vector, the zero vector, or it contains infinitely many vectors. We have just shown that ϕ is a vector space, and thus a vector space may contain one and only one vector. Now let $\mathbf{x}_1 \neq \phi$ be an n-dimensional vector belonging to χ_n. If χ_n is a vector space, then $k\mathbf{x}_1$ must also belong to χ_n for every choice of k. But since $\mathbf{x}_1 \neq \phi$ and since k may assume all values on the interval $(-\infty, \infty)$, there are an infinite number of vectors $k\mathbf{x}_1$ which must belong to χ_n if χ_n is a vector space. Thus if χ_n contains one nonzero vector, it must contain infinitely many vectors.

A vector space may not be composed of vectors of the form

$$\mathbf{x} = \begin{bmatrix} x_1 \\ x_2 \\ \vdots \\ x_n \end{bmatrix}$$

where any element x_i is constrained so that $x_i \leqslant b$, $x_i < b$, $x_i \geqslant b$, $x_i > b$, where b is a finite real number. Suppose that χ_n is composed of n-

dimensional vectors such that $x_i \geqslant b$. Now choose a vector $\mathbf{x}_1$ from χ_n such that $x_i = b$. Then $k\mathbf{x}_1$ does not belong to χ_n if $k > 1$, and χ_n cannot be a vector space. Finally if $\mathbf{x}_1, \mathbf{x}_2, \ldots, \mathbf{x}_m$ are n-dimensional vectors belonging to the vector space χ_n and $k_1, k_2, \ldots, k_n$ are scalars, then $\sum_{i=1}^m k_i \mathbf{x}_i$ also belongs to χ_n.

In our discussion of linear transformations we will require an understanding of the notion of a subspace. Let χ_n and ψ_n be n-dimensional vector spaces such that χ_n is comprised of vectors $\mathbf{x}$ and ψ_n of vectors $\mathbf{y}$. If every $\mathbf{y}$ which belongs to ψ_n also belongs to χ_n, then ψ_n is a *subspace* of χ_n. It should be noted that every $\mathbf{x}$ belonging to χ_n may not belong to ψ_n.

In the analysis of practical problems involving the concepts of vector spaces, the analyst is usually concerned with Euclidean space. An *n-dimensional Euclidean space*, denoted E_n, is the collection of all n-dimensional vectors of the form

$$\mathbf{x} = \begin{bmatrix} x_1 \\ x_2 \\ \vdots \\ x_n \end{bmatrix}$$

where the elements of $\mathbf{x}$ may assume any real value on the interval $(-\infty, \infty)$. Based upon the definition, E_n is obviously a vector space.

The *span* of E_n is defined as a set of n-dimensional vectors $\mathbf{x}_1$, $\mathbf{x}_2, \ldots, \mathbf{x}_m$ belonging to E_n such that any vector in E_n can be expressed as a linear combination of that set. That is, suppose that $\mathbf{y}_1$ is any vector in E_n and $\mathbf{x}_1, \mathbf{x}_2, \ldots, \mathbf{x}_m$ are n-dimensional vectors which also belong to E_n and span E_n. Then

$$\mathbf{y}_1 = \sum_{i=1}^m k_i \mathbf{x}_i \tag{2.49}$$

for appropriate choice of the scalars $k_1, k_2, \ldots, k_m$. Thus from a spanning set of vectors for E_n the analyst may generate any other vector belonging to E_n. A spanning set for n-dimensional Euclidean space must be composed of no fewer than n vectors although more than n vectors may also span E_n.

Let us choose a set of m vectors belonging to E_n and form all possible linear combinations, where $m < n$. That is,

$$\mathbf{y} = \sum_{i=1}^m k_i \mathbf{x}_i$$

The set of vectors $\mathbf{y}$ thus generated will form a vector space which is a subspace of E_n. For example, let

$$\mathbf{x}_1 = \begin{bmatrix} 1 \\ 0 \\ 0 \end{bmatrix}, \qquad \mathbf{x}_2 = \begin{bmatrix} 0 \\ 1 \\ 0 \end{bmatrix}$$

Then y is given by

$$y = \begin{bmatrix} k_1 \\ k_2 \\ 0 \end{bmatrix}$$

The vectors y are 3-dimensional and belong to E_3. However, each vector in this set lies in the $x_1 x_2$ plane and thus in a subspace of E_3.

Example 2.15   Let

$$x_1 = \begin{bmatrix} 1 \\ 0 \\ 1 \end{bmatrix}, \qquad x_2 = \begin{bmatrix} 0 \\ 0 \\ 4 \end{bmatrix}, \qquad x_3 = \begin{bmatrix} 2 \\ 0 \\ 0 \end{bmatrix}$$

Do the vectors x_1, x_2, and x_3 span 3-dimensional Euclidean space?

If x_1, x_2, and x_3 span E_3, then any vector in E_3, say y_1, may be expressed by

$$y_1 = \sum_{i=1}^{3} k_i x_i$$

for an appropriate choice of k_i, $i = 1, 2, 3$. Now

$$y_1 = \begin{bmatrix} k_1 + 2k_3 \\ 0 \\ k_1 + 4k_2 \end{bmatrix}$$

Hence the element y_{12} of y_1 is always zero for this linear combination. However, E_3 contains all 3-dimensional vectors including those for which the second element is nonzero. Hence every vector in E_3 cannot be generated by x_1, x_2, and x_3, and these vectors do not span E_3. ■

Example 2.16   Do the vectors

$$x_1 = \begin{bmatrix} 2 \\ 0 \end{bmatrix}, \qquad x_2 = \begin{bmatrix} 4 \\ 1 \end{bmatrix}, \qquad x_3 = \begin{bmatrix} 2 \\ 2 \end{bmatrix}$$

span E_2?

A linear combination of x_1, x_2, and x_3 yields the vector

$$y_1 = \begin{bmatrix} 2k_1 + 4k_2 + 2k_3 \\ k_2 + 2k_3 \end{bmatrix}$$

Now let y_1 be any vector in E_2 defined by

$$y_1 = \begin{bmatrix} b \\ c \end{bmatrix}$$

where b and c are real numbers on the interval $(-\infty, \infty)$. To determine whether or not x_1, x_2, and x_3 form a spanning set we must determine whether or not values of k_1, k_2, and k_3 can be defined such that

$$\begin{bmatrix} b \\ c \end{bmatrix} = \begin{bmatrix} 2k_1 + 4k_2 + 2k_3 \\ k_2 + 2k_3 \end{bmatrix}$$

From the second row of the vectors to the left and right of the equality $k_2 = c - 2k_3$, and from the first row $k_1 = (b - 4k_2 - 2k_3)/2$. Thus $k_2 = c - 2k_3$, $k_1 = (b - 4c + 6k_3)/2$ yields the required solution for any value of k_3, b, and c, and x_1, x_2, and x_3 span E_2. It should be noted that x_1 and x_2 also span E_2. ∎

In n-dimensional Euclidean space no more than n vectors may be linearly independent, although one may choose an infinite number of combinations of n linearly independent vectors. In addition, if the vectors x_1, x_2, . . . , x_n are linearly independent, then any subset of these vectors is also linearly independent. The notions of linear independence and a spanning set of vectors lead to the definition of the basis for a vector space.

A basis for n-dimensional Euclidean space is a set of vectors which are linearly independent and which span the space. Since no more than n such vectors may be linearly independent and no fewer than n may span E_n, every basis for n-dimensional Euclidean space is composed of exactly n vectors. However, there exists an infinite number of sets of vectors which satisfy the criteria for a basis. Identification of the basis for E_n is often important in the solution of problems for which the space of possible solutions is a subspace of E_n. Since every vector in E_n may be expressed as a linear combination of the basis vectors, the solution to many problems can be determined merely by manipulation of the basis vectors. This property is particularly important in linear programming.

A rather obvious choice of vectors as a basis for E_n is the set of n unit vectors. The vector x_i is a *unit vector* if one of its elements is unity and its remaining elements are zero. Let x_i be the unit vector with $x_i = 1$ and $x_j = 0$ for $j \neq i$. Then

$$x_1 = \begin{bmatrix} 1 \\ 0 \\ \vdots \\ 0 \\ \vdots \\ 0 \end{bmatrix}, \quad x_2 = \begin{bmatrix} 0 \\ 1 \\ \vdots \\ 0 \\ \vdots \\ 0 \end{bmatrix}, \ldots, \quad x_i = \begin{bmatrix} 0 \\ 0 \\ \vdots \\ 1 \\ \vdots \\ 0 \end{bmatrix}, \ldots \quad x_n = \begin{bmatrix} 0 \\ 0 \\ \vdots \\ 0 \\ \vdots \\ 1 \end{bmatrix}$$

$$(2.50)$$

Since $x_i^T x_j = 0$ for $i \neq j$, we have a mutually orthogonal set of vectors and thus a set of independent vectors. Since

$$\mathbf{y}_1 = \sum_{i=1}^{n} k_i \mathbf{x}_i = \begin{bmatrix} k_1 \\ k_2 \\ \vdots \\ k_i \\ \vdots \\ k_n \end{bmatrix} \tag{2.51}$$

this set of vectors also spans E_n and hence forms a basis for E_n.

Example 2.17 Determine whether or not the following set of vectors is a basis for E_3:

$$\mathbf{x}_1 = \begin{bmatrix} 3 \\ 1 \\ 2 \end{bmatrix}, \qquad \mathbf{x}_2 = \begin{bmatrix} 2 \\ 1 \\ 1 \end{bmatrix}, \qquad \mathbf{x}_3 = \begin{bmatrix} 1 \\ 1 \\ 1 \end{bmatrix}$$

If $\mathbf{x}_1$, $\mathbf{x}_2$, and $\mathbf{x}_3$ form a basis for E_3, then they must be linearly independent and span E_3. First testing for linear independence we have

$$k_1 \mathbf{x}_1 + k_2 \mathbf{x}_2 + k_3 \mathbf{x}_3 = \begin{bmatrix} 3k_1 + 2k_2 + k_3 \\ k_1 + k_2 + k_3 \\ 2k_1 + k_2 + k_3 \end{bmatrix} = \emptyset$$

Since $k_1 = k_2 = k_3 = 0$ is the only solution for this system of equations, $\mathbf{x}_1$, $\mathbf{x}_2$, and $\mathbf{x}_3$ are linearly independent. If $\mathbf{x}_1$, $\mathbf{x}_2$, and $\mathbf{x}_3$ span E_3, then any vector in E_3 can be generated by an appropriate linear combination of $\mathbf{x}_1$, $\mathbf{x}_2$, and $\mathbf{x}_3$. Let

$$\mathbf{y} = \begin{bmatrix} a \\ b \\ c \end{bmatrix}$$

where the elements of $\mathbf{y}$ are any real numbers. If $\mathbf{x}_1$, $\mathbf{x}_2$, and $\mathbf{x}_3$ span E_3, then we should be able to form a linear combination of these three vectors which will yield the vector $\mathbf{y}$. For

$$\begin{bmatrix} a \\ b \\ c \end{bmatrix} = \begin{bmatrix} 3k_1 + 2k_2 + k_3 \\ k_1 + k_2 + k_3 \\ 2k_1 + k_2 + k_3 \end{bmatrix}$$

we have the solution

$$k_1 = -b + c, \qquad k_2 = a + b - 2c, \qquad k_3 = -a + b + c$$

and $\mathbf{x}_1$, $\mathbf{x}_2$, and $\mathbf{x}_3$ span E_3 and hence are a basis for E_3. ∎

Linear Transformations

A transformation is a mapping of points in one space into another. For example, suppose we define the vector $\mathbf{y}$ in E_2 in terms of the vector $\mathbf{x}$, also in E_2, by the transformation

$$\mathbf{y} = \begin{bmatrix} 2x_1 + 3x_2 \\ x_1 + 4x_2 \end{bmatrix}$$

or

$$y_1 = 2x_1 + 3x_2$$
$$y_2 = x_1 + 4x_2$$

Now let us consider the mapping of the points $\mathbf{x}_1$, $\mathbf{x}_2$, $\mathbf{x}_3$, and $\mathbf{x}_4$ defined by

$$\mathbf{x}_1 = \begin{bmatrix} 2 \\ 2 \end{bmatrix}, \qquad \mathbf{x}_2 = \begin{bmatrix} 5 \\ 2 \end{bmatrix}, \qquad \mathbf{x}_3 = \begin{bmatrix} 1 \\ 4 \end{bmatrix}, \qquad \mathbf{x}_4 = \begin{bmatrix} 1 \\ 6 \end{bmatrix}$$

in the $y_1 y_2$ plane. For the transformation defined, the points $\mathbf{x}_1$, $\mathbf{x}_2$, $\mathbf{x}_3$, and $\mathbf{x}_4$ are mapped into the points $\mathbf{y}_1$, $\mathbf{y}_2$, $\mathbf{y}_3$, and $\mathbf{y}_4$ defined by

$$\mathbf{y}_1 = \begin{bmatrix} 10 \\ 10 \end{bmatrix}, \qquad \mathbf{y}_2 = \begin{bmatrix} 16 \\ 13 \end{bmatrix}, \qquad \mathbf{y}_3 = \begin{bmatrix} 14 \\ 17 \end{bmatrix}, \qquad \mathbf{y}_4 = \begin{bmatrix} 20 \\ 25 \end{bmatrix}$$

The points $\mathbf{x}_i$, $i = 1, 2, 3, 4$, and $\mathbf{y}_i$, $i = 1, 2, 3, 4$, are shown graphically in Fig. 2.3a and 2.3b respectively. For this transformation the points in the $x_1 x_2$ (E_2) plane were simply transformed into new points in the $y_1 y_2$ (E_2) plane. This transformation could have been written as

$$\mathbf{y} = A\mathbf{x}$$

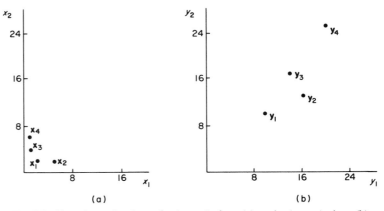

Fig. 2.3 Transformation from the (x_1, x_2)-plane (a) to the (y_1, y_2)-plane (b).

where

$$A = \begin{bmatrix} 2 & 3 \\ 1 & 4 \end{bmatrix}$$

In this case the transformation is from E_2 to E_2.

Let us denote $T(\mathbf{x})$ as a transformation which defines a vector $\mathbf{y}$ for each and every vector $\mathbf{x}$, where $\mathbf{x}$ is a vector in E_n and $\mathbf{y}$ a vector in E_m and where m and n may or may not be equal. A *linear transformation* $T(\mathbf{x})$ defines a correspondence which maps each vector $\mathbf{x}$ in E_n into a vector $\mathbf{y}$ in E_m such that for all $\mathbf{x}_1$ and $\mathbf{x}_2$ in E_n and all scalars k_1 and k_2,

$$T(k_1\mathbf{x}_1 + k_2\mathbf{x}_2) = k_1 T(\mathbf{x}_1) + k_2 T(\mathbf{x}_2) \tag{2.52}$$

If the transformation $T(\mathbf{x})$ is a *matrix transformation* defined by

$$T(\mathbf{x}) = A\mathbf{x} \tag{2.53}$$

where A is called the *matrix of the transformation*, $\mathbf{x}$ is a vector in E_n, and A is of order (m, n), then the transformation is indeed linear since

$$T(k_1\mathbf{x}_1 + k_2\mathbf{x}_2) = A[k_1\mathbf{x}_1 + k_2\mathbf{x}_2] = k_1 A\mathbf{x}_1 + k_2 A\mathbf{x}_2 = k_1 T(\mathbf{x}_1) + k_2 T(\mathbf{x}_2) \tag{2.54}$$

Hence every matrix transformation is a linear transformation.

A linear transformation $\mathbf{y} = A\mathbf{x}$ is said to be *one-to-one* if and only if for each vector $\mathbf{x}$ there is only one vector $\mathbf{y}$ and for each vector $\mathbf{y}$ there is only one vector $\mathbf{x}$. If the matrix of the transformation A is nonsingular, then

$$\mathbf{x} = A^{-1}\mathbf{y} \tag{2.55}$$

and the transformation is one-to-one. It should be noted that if $\mathbf{x}$ belongs to E_n and $\mathbf{y}$ to E_m, then a linear transformation from E_m to E_n cannot be one-to-one if $n \neq m$, since the matrix of the transformation A has no inverse in this case.

Example 2.18 Show that the linear transformation $\mathbf{y} = A\mathbf{x}$ is not one-to-one, where $\mathbf{x}$ belongs to E_3, $\mathbf{y}$ to E_2, and

$$A = \begin{bmatrix} 2 & 1 & 2 \\ 3 & 0 & 1 \end{bmatrix}$$

For this transformation every vector $\mathbf{x}$ will yield a vector $\mathbf{y}$. However, since A^{-1} does not exist, the transformation is not one-to-one. For example, for

$$\mathbf{x}_1 = \begin{bmatrix} 1 \\ 1 \\ 1 \end{bmatrix} \quad \text{and} \quad \mathbf{x}_2 = \begin{bmatrix} 5 \\ 17 \\ -11 \end{bmatrix}$$

we have

$$\mathbf{y} = \begin{bmatrix} 5 \\ 4 \end{bmatrix}$$

Since two distinct vectors **x** lead to the same vector **y**, the transformation is not one-to-one. ∎

Suppose that the vectors **y** are generated by the transformation $\mathbf{y} = A\mathbf{x}$, where **x** is any vector belonging to E_n and A is of order $(m \times n)$. The dimension of the vectors **y** will be m and the collection of vectors **y** generated by the transformation will be a vector subspace χ_m of E_m which may be E_m itself. To demonstrate this property consider the following example.

Example 2.19   Let **x** be any 3-dimensional vector such that

$$\mathbf{x} = \begin{bmatrix} x_1 \\ x_2 \\ x_3 \end{bmatrix}$$

Show that the collection of vectors **y** generated by $\mathbf{y} = A\mathbf{x}$ for all vectors **x** is a vector space, where

$$A = \begin{bmatrix} 1 & 0 & 1 \\ 1 & 1 & -1 \end{bmatrix}$$

The vector **y** is defined by

$$\mathbf{y} = \begin{bmatrix} x_1 & + x_3 \\ x_1 + x_2 - x_3 \end{bmatrix}$$

The dimension of the vector **y** is obviously 2. To show that the collection of vectors **y** generated by the collection of **x** is the vector space E_2, let $\mathbf{x}_1$ and $\mathbf{x}_2$ be any vectors of the form defined by **x**. Then

$$\mathbf{x}_1 = \begin{bmatrix} x_1' \\ x_2' \\ x_3' \end{bmatrix}, \qquad \mathbf{x}_2 = \begin{bmatrix} x_1'' \\ x_2'' \\ x_3'' \end{bmatrix}$$

and the resulting transformed vectors $\mathbf{y}_1$ and $\mathbf{y}_2$, are given by

$$\mathbf{y}_1 = \begin{bmatrix} x_1' & + x_3' \\ x_1' + x_2' - x_3' \end{bmatrix}, \qquad \mathbf{y}_2 = \begin{bmatrix} x_1'' & + x_3'' \\ x_1'' + x_2'' - x_3'' \end{bmatrix}$$

Now since

$$k_1\mathbf{y}_1 = \begin{bmatrix} k_1(x_1' & + x_3') \\ k_1(x_1' + x_2' - x_3') \end{bmatrix}$$

and

$$\mathbf{y}_1 + \mathbf{y}_2 = \begin{bmatrix} (x_1' + x_1'') & + (x_3' + x_3'') \\ (x_1' + x_1'') & + (x_2' + x_2'') & - (x_3' + x_3'') \end{bmatrix}$$

belong to the set of vectors defined by **y**, this set is a vector space and is E_2. ∎

Example 2.20   Let **x** be any 4-dimensional vector belonging to E_4, and let A be the transformation matrix defined by

$$A = \begin{bmatrix} 2 & 4 & 2 & 4 \\ 1 & 2 & 0 & 0 \\ 0 & 0 & 2 & 4 \end{bmatrix}$$

Define the vector space generated by the transformation $\mathbf{y} = A\mathbf{x}$.

From the transformation matrix A we have

$$\mathbf{y} = \begin{bmatrix} 2x_1 + 4x_2 + 2x_3 + 4x_4 \\ x_1 + 2x_2 \\ 2x_3 + 4x_4 \end{bmatrix}$$

or

$$\mathbf{y} = (x_1 + 2x_2)\begin{bmatrix} 2 \\ 1 \\ 0 \end{bmatrix} + (x_3 + 2x_4)\begin{bmatrix} 2 \\ 0 \\ 2 \end{bmatrix}$$

Since the scalars $(x_1 + 2x_2)$ and $(x_3 + 2x_4)$ may assume any real values, the collection of vectors **y** is defined by all possible linear combinations of the vectors $[2 \quad 1 \quad 0]^T$ and $[2 \quad 0 \quad 2]^T$, and those two vectors span the space of vectors defined by **y**.

As we have already indicated, the space spanned by a set of vectors is a vector space and the set of vectors defined by **y** forms a vector space. In this case the vector space defined by the collection of vectors **y** is a plane in E_3, as shown in Fig. 2.4. ■

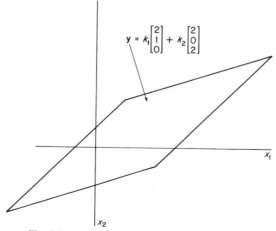

Fig. 2.4   Vector space for **y** in Example 2.20.

The transformation matrix provides important information regarding the dimension of the collection of vectors **y** resulting from the transformation and the dimension of the subspace to which those vectors belong. In Example 2.20 the collection of vectors resulting from the transformation were 3-dimensional but were restricted to a 2-dimensional plane within E_3. If the transformation matrix A is of order $(m \times n)$ and rank r, then the vectors **y** resulting from the transformation will be of dimension m but will be restricted to an r-dimensional subspace of E_m. This point can be illustrated by examination of the matrix of the transformation in Example 2.20, where A is of order (3×4) and rank 2, indicating that the vectors **y** will be 3-dimensional but restricted to a 2-dimensional subspace of E_3. On the other hand, in Example 2.18 A is of order (2×3) and rank 2, and hence the vectors resulting from the transformation are 2-dimensional and comprise E_2.

SIMULTANEOUS LINEAR EQUATIONS

Consider the following system of linear equations where the a_{ij} and b_i are constants and the x_j are unknown:

$$
\begin{aligned}
a_{11}x_1 + a_{12}x_2 + \cdots + a_{1n}x_n &= b_1 \\
a_{21}x_1 + a_{22}x_2 + \cdots + a_{2n}x_n &= b_2 \\
&\vdots \\
a_{n1}x_1 + a_{n2}x_2 + \cdots + a_{nn}x_n &= b_n
\end{aligned}
\tag{2.56}
$$

We may solve this set of equations for the values of $x_1, x_2, \ldots, x_n$ using methods similar to those illustrated in the preceding section. However, the computational effort can be reduced through matrix methods. Define the matrix A and the vectors **b** and **x** as follows:

$$
A = \begin{bmatrix} a_{11} & a_{12} & \cdots & a_{1n} \\ a_{21} & a_{22} & \cdots & a_{2n} \\ \vdots & \vdots & & \vdots \\ a_{n1} & a_{n2} & \cdots & a_{nn} \end{bmatrix}, \quad \mathbf{b} = \begin{bmatrix} b_1 \\ b_2 \\ \vdots \\ b_n \end{bmatrix}, \quad \mathbf{x} = \begin{bmatrix} x_1 \\ x_2 \\ \vdots \\ x_n \end{bmatrix}
$$

The set of simultaneous equations in (2.56) may be expressed as

$$
A\mathbf{x} = \mathbf{b} \tag{2.57}
$$

If A is a nonsingular matrix, we may solve for the vector **x** as follows:

$$
A^{-1}A\mathbf{x} = A^{-1}\mathbf{b} \tag{2.58}
$$

or

$$
I\mathbf{x} = A^{-1}\mathbf{b}
$$

since $A^{-1}A = I$, the identity matrix. Multiplying the identity matrix by any matrix B to which I is conformable for multiplication yields the original matrix B. Hence $I\mathbf{x} = \mathbf{x}$ and the solution vector $\mathbf{x}^*$ is

$$\mathbf{x}^* = A^{-1}\mathbf{b} \tag{2.59}$$

Example 2.21 Solve the following system of simultaneous linear equations:

$$3x_1 + x_2 + x_3 = 100$$
$$x_1 + 3x_2 + x_3 = 200$$
$$x_1 + x_2 + 3x_3 = 300$$

For the matrix A and the vector $\mathbf{b}$ we have

$$A = \begin{bmatrix} 3 & 1 & 1 \\ 1 & 3 & 1 \\ 1 & 1 & 3 \end{bmatrix}, \qquad \mathbf{b} = \begin{bmatrix} 100 \\ 200 \\ 300 \end{bmatrix}$$

Now

$$|A| = 20$$

Since $|A| \neq 0$, the inverse of A exists. The adjoint of A is given by

$$\text{adj}(A) = \begin{bmatrix} 8 & -2 & -2 \\ -2 & 8 & -2 \\ -2 & -2 & 8 \end{bmatrix}$$

and

$$A^{-1} = \begin{bmatrix} 0.40 & -0.10 & -0.10 \\ -0.10 & 0.40 & -0.10 \\ -0.10 & -0.10 & 0.40 \end{bmatrix}$$

Hence

$$\mathbf{x}^* = \begin{bmatrix} 0.40 & -0.10 & -0.10 \\ -0.10 & 0.40 & -0.10 \\ -0.10 & -0.10 & 0.40 \end{bmatrix} \begin{bmatrix} 100 \\ 200 \\ 300 \end{bmatrix} = \begin{bmatrix} -10 \\ 40 \\ 90 \end{bmatrix} \quad \blacksquare$$

In Eq. (2.57), if the matrix A is singular, either no solution $\mathbf{x}^*$ exists or infinitely many solutions exist. The set of n equations defined in Eq. (2.57) yields n linear planes in n-dimensional space. If A is nonsingular, then the solution vector $\mathbf{x}^*$ is the point of simultaneous intersection of the n planes. If A is singular and no solution exists, then there is no point $\mathbf{x}$ at which all of the planes simultaneously intersect. Finally, if A is singular and infinitely many solutions exist, then there are infinitely many points $\mathbf{x}^*$ at which the n planes simultaneously intersect.

The concept of the rank of a matrix may be used to determine whether the solution to a system of n simultaneous linear equations in n unknowns is a unique point, does not exist, or consists of an infinite number of points. In the set of simultaneous equations $A\mathbf{x} = \mathbf{b}$, where A is $(n \times n)$ and $\mathbf{x}$ and $\mathbf{b}$ are n-dimensional vectors, if A is nonsingular, then the system of equations has a unique solution. In terms of the rank of A, if the rank of A is n, then a unique solution exists for the solution to $A\mathbf{x} = \mathbf{b}$. If the rank of A is less than n, then either no solution exists or an infinite number of solutions exist. To determine which case exists we augment the matrix A by the addition of an $(n + 1)$st column composed of the vector $\mathbf{b}$. We will denote the augmented matrix by $(A \,|\, \mathbf{b})$. Then

$$(A \,|\, \mathbf{b}) = \begin{bmatrix} a_{11} & a_{12} & \cdots & a_{1n} & b_1 \\ a_{21} & a_{22} & \cdots & a_{2n} & b_2 \\ \vdots & & & & \\ a_{n1} & a_{n2} & \cdots & a_{nn} & b_n \end{bmatrix} \tag{2.60}$$

If $r(A) = r(A \,|\, \mathbf{b}) = m < n$, then the system of simultaneous equations has an infinite number of solutions. If $r(A) < r(A \,|\, \mathbf{b})$, then the system of simultaneous equations has no solution. Finally, if $r(A) = r(A \,|\, \mathbf{b}) = n$, the system of simultaneous equations has a unique solution. It should be noted that since A is $(n \times n)$ and $(A \,|\, \mathbf{b})$ is $(n \times n + 1)$, $r(A \,|\, \mathbf{b})$ can never exceed n and $r(A \,|\, \mathbf{b}) \geqslant r(A)$. Thus $r(A) \leqslant r(A \,|\, \mathbf{b}) \leqslant n$.

In the examples which follow we shall illustrate the use of the rank of A and $(A \,|\, \mathbf{b})$ in determining the existence of a solution for a set of simultaneous linear equations and the uniqueness of the solution, if it exists. However, an interpretation of the results discussed here is in order. First let us consider the case where $r(A) = n$. If $r(A) = n$, then A is nonsingular and the system of equations $A\mathbf{x} = \mathbf{b}$ may be solved by

$$\mathbf{x}^* = A^{-1}\mathbf{b}$$

Since the inverse of A is unique, $\mathbf{x}^*$ is unique and only one solution to the system of equations exists.

Now let us consider the case where $r(A) < r(A \,|\, \mathbf{b})$. Since $r(A \,|\, \mathbf{b})$ must be less than or equal to n, $r(A) < r(A \,|\, \mathbf{b})$ implies $r(A) < n$ and A^{-1} does not exist. If $r(A) < r(A \,|\, \mathbf{b})$, then the largest *nonvanishing* determinant in $(A \,|\, \mathbf{b})$, that which determines the rank of $(A \,|\, \mathbf{b})$, must contain elements from the column vector $\mathbf{b}$. Conversely, if at least one of the largest nonvanishing determinants in $(A \,|\, \mathbf{b})$ contains elements from A only, then $r(A) = r(A \,|\, \mathbf{b})$, but this cannot be since we have assumed $r(A) < r(A \,|\, \mathbf{b})$. Now assume $r(A) = m$ and $r(A \,|\, \mathbf{b}) = k$, where $m < k$. Since the rank of $(A \,|\, \mathbf{b})$ specifies the number of linearly independent columns in $(A \,|\, \mathbf{b})$, there are k columns in $(A \,|\, \mathbf{b})$ which are linearly independent, and one of these columns is $\mathbf{b}$. Let the columns of A be the vectors $\mathbf{a}_1, \mathbf{a}_2, ..., \mathbf{a}_n$ and the elements of $\mathbf{x}$ be $x_1, x_2, \ldots, x_n$. Then $A\mathbf{x} = \mathbf{b}$ implies

$$\sum_{i=1}^{n} x_i \mathbf{a}_i = \mathbf{b} \qquad (2.61)$$

Let $\mathbf{a}_1, \mathbf{a}_2, \ldots, \mathbf{a}_{k-1}, \mathbf{b}$ be a set of k linearly independent vectors in $(A \mid \mathbf{b})$. Then $\mathbf{a}_k, \mathbf{a}_{k+1}, \ldots, \mathbf{a}_n$ can be expressed as a linear combination of $\mathbf{a}_1, \mathbf{a}_2, \ldots, \mathbf{a}_{k-1}, \mathbf{b}$. Let

$$\mathbf{a}_j = \sum_{t=1}^{k-1} p_{jt} \mathbf{a}_t + p_{jk} \mathbf{b}, \qquad j = k, k+1, \ldots, n \qquad (2.62)$$

Then

$$\sum_{i=1}^{n} x_i \mathbf{a}_i = \sum_{i=1}^{k-1} x_i \mathbf{a}_i + \sum_{i=k}^{n} x_i \left[\sum_{t=1}^{k-1} p_{it} \mathbf{a}_t + p_{ik} \mathbf{b} \right]$$

$$= \sum_{i=1}^{k-1} x_i \mathbf{a}_i + \sum_{t=1}^{k-1} \mathbf{a}_t \sum_{i=k}^{n} x_i p_{it} + \sum_{i=k}^{n} p_{ik} x_i \mathbf{b} \qquad (2.63)$$

But $\sum_{i=k}^{n} x_i p_{it}$ is simply a scalar, which we shall denote y_t. Hence

$$\sum_{i=1}^{n} x_i \mathbf{a}_i = \sum_{i=1}^{k-1} x_i \mathbf{a}_i + \sum_{t=1}^{k-1} y_t \mathbf{a}_t + y_k \mathbf{b} = \mathbf{b} \qquad (2.64)$$

Thus $A\mathbf{x} = \mathbf{b}$ is equivalent to

$$\sum_{i=1}^{k-1} (x_i + y_i) \mathbf{a}_i = (1 - y_k) \mathbf{b} \qquad (2.65)$$

or dividing both sides by the scalar $(1 - y_k)$,

$$\sum_{i=1}^{k-1} \frac{(x_i + y_i)}{(1 - y_k)} \mathbf{a}_i = \mathbf{b} \qquad (2.66)$$

But since $\mathbf{a}_1, \mathbf{a}_2, \ldots, \mathbf{a}_{k-1}, \mathbf{b}$ are linearly independent, $\mathbf{b}$ cannot be expressed as a linear combination of $\mathbf{a}_1, \mathbf{a}_2, \ldots, \mathbf{a}_{k-1}$, and there is no solution for Eq. (2.66) and hence no solution for $A\mathbf{x} = \mathbf{b}$. Such a set of equations is said to be *inconsistent*.

Finally consider the case where $r(A) = r(A \mid \mathbf{b}) = k$. Since $r(A) = k$, there are k linearly independent column vectors $\mathbf{a}_1, \mathbf{a}_2, \ldots, \mathbf{a}_k$ in A. Since $r(A \mid \mathbf{b}) = k$ and A is a submatrix of $(A \mid \mathbf{b})$, $\mathbf{b}$ can be expressed as a linear combination of $\mathbf{a}_1, \mathbf{a}_2, \ldots, \mathbf{a}_k$. Thus there is a solution for

$$\sum_{i=1}^{k} x_i \mathbf{a}_i = \mathbf{b} \qquad (2.67)$$

where $x_j = 0$ for $j = k+1, k+2, \ldots, n$. Now let us express the linearly dependent vectors $\mathbf{a}_k, \mathbf{a}_{k+1}, \ldots, \mathbf{a}_n$ as

$$\mathbf{a}_j = \sum_{t=1}^{k} p_{jt}\mathbf{a}_t, \qquad j = k, k+1, \ldots, n \tag{2.68}$$

Then $A\mathbf{x}$ can be expressed as

$$\begin{aligned} A\mathbf{x} &= \sum_{i=1}^{k} x_i\mathbf{a}_i + \sum_{i=k+1}^{n} x_i \sum_{t=1}^{k} p_{it}\mathbf{a}_t \\ &= \sum_{i=1}^{k} x_i\mathbf{a}_i + \sum_{t=1}^{k} \mathbf{a}_t \sum_{i=k+1}^{n} x_i p_{it} \end{aligned} \tag{2.69}$$

Let the scalar $\sum_{i=k+1}^{n} x_i p_{it}$ be denoted y_t. Then

$$A\mathbf{x} = \sum_{i=1}^{k} (x_i + y_i)\mathbf{a}_i = \mathbf{b} \tag{2.70}$$

Letting $x_i + y_i = z_i$ in Eq. (2.70), we have

$$A\mathbf{x} = \sum_{i=1}^{k} z_i\mathbf{a}_i = \mathbf{b} \tag{2.71}$$

We have already shown that one solution for $A\mathbf{x} = \mathbf{b}$ exists by Eq. (2.67) which is equivalent to that given in Eq. (2.70) if $y_i = 0$, $i = 1, 2, \ldots, k$. Hence a solution for Eq. (2.71) also exists. But $z_i = (x_i + y_i)$ for $i = 1, 2, \ldots, k$, and any combination of x_i and y_i yielding an appropriate value for z_i is a solution for Eq. (2.71). Since there are an infinite number of combinations of x_i and y_i yielding a given value of z_i, Eq. (2.71) has an infinite number of solutions and hence so does $A\mathbf{x} = \mathbf{b}$.

When $r(A) = r(A \mid \mathbf{b}) = k$ and $k < n$, then $n - k$ of the equations are linear combinations of the remaining k equations. These $n - k$ equations are said to be *redundant* in that the restrictions which they place upon the solution $\mathbf{x}^*$ are already implied by the k nonredundant equations.

Example 2.22   Plot the surfaces defined by the system of equations in Example 2.21 and define the point of simultaneous intersection $\mathbf{x}^*$.

The planes representing the equations in Example 2.21 are shown in Fig. 2.5 along with the point of their simultaneous intersection, $\mathbf{x}^*$. ■

Example 2.23   Show that there are an infinite number of solutions for the system of linear equations defined by

$$x_1 + x_3 = 8$$
$$-(6/10)x_1 + x_3 = -48/10$$
$$(1/8)x_1 + x_3 = 1$$

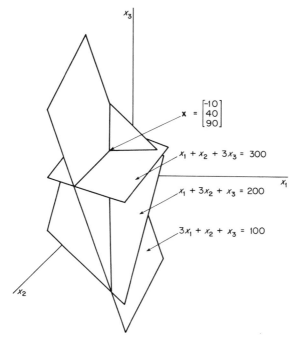

Fig. 2.5 Intersection of the planes in Example 2.22.

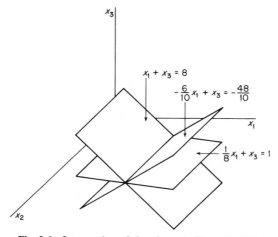

Fig. 2.6 Intersection of the planes in Example 2.23.

The coefficient of x_2 is zero in all three equations and the matrix A is

$$A = \begin{bmatrix} 1 & 0 & 1 \\ -6/10 & 0 & 1 \\ 1/8 & 0 & 1 \end{bmatrix}$$

and $|A| = 0$. Now $r(A) = 2$. Defining $(A \,|\, \mathbf{b})$ as

$$(A \,|\, \mathbf{b}) = \begin{bmatrix} 1 & 0 & 1 & 8 \\ -6/10 & 0 & 1 & -48/10 \\ 1/8 & 0 & 1 & 1 \end{bmatrix}$$

we note that $r(A \,|\, \mathbf{b}) = 2$. Since $r(A) = r(A \,|\, \mathbf{b}) < 3$, the system of equations should have an infinite number of solutions. The planes represented by this system of equations are shown in Fig. 2.6 and show that $x_1^* = 8$, $x_3^* = 0$, and any value of x_2 yields a solution to this system of equations. Hence the system of equations has an infinite number of solutions. ∎

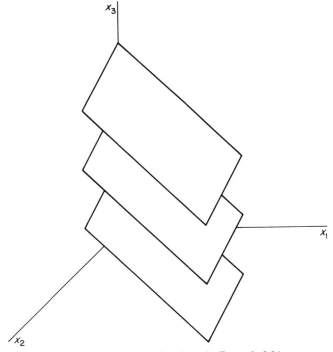

Fig. 2.7 Graph of the planes in Example 2.24.

Example 2.24 Show that there is no solution for the following system of linear equations:

$$x_1 + x_2 + x_3 = 20$$
$$x_1 + x_2 + x_3 = 25$$
$$x_1 + x_2 + x_3 = 15$$

The matrix A is defined by

$$A = \begin{bmatrix} 1 & 1 & 1 \\ 1 & 1 & 1 \\ 1 & 1 & 1 \end{bmatrix}$$

Since the two rows of A are equal, $|A| = 0$. Forming the augmented matrix $(A \mid \mathbf{b})$, we have

$$(A \mid \mathbf{b}) = \begin{bmatrix} 1 & 1 & 1 & 20 \\ 1 & 1 & 1 & 25 \\ 1 & 1 & 1 & 15 \end{bmatrix}$$

Now $r(A) = 1$ and $r(A \mid \mathbf{b}) = 2$. Since $r(A) < r(A \mid \mathbf{b})$, the system of equations has no solution. As shown in Fig. 2.7, the planes represented by this system of linear equations are parallel and thus do not intersect. Since the planes do not intersect at a common point, there is no solution to the system of equations. ∎

THE GAUSS ELIMINATION METHOD

Gaussian elimination is an iterative procedure which may be used for finding the determinant and inverse of a matrix as well as for solving a system of simultaneous linear equations. This procedure is computationally efficient and is often used to solve such problems on a digital computer. The Gauss elimination method is based upon the repeated application of row operations to a matrix A, where a *row operation* consists of adding a scalar multiple of one row of A to another row of A. The reader will recall from property (11) of determinants that such an operation does not change the determinant of A. Hence if a sequence of row operations on A leads to the matrix A', then $|A'| = |A|$. The purpose of the successive application of row operations is to obtain a matrix A' which is in upper triangular form (see Fig. 2.8). Recall that an upper triangular matrix is a square matrix A, where $a_{ij} = 0$, $i > j$. The matrix A' is termed an *equivalent matrix* in that the determinant of A' is equal to the determinant of A.

Once the elimination process is complete (that is, we have A'), the value of the determinant can be obtained from the product of the principal

$$
\begin{bmatrix}
a_{11} & a_{12} & \cdots & a_{1n} \\
a_{21} & a_{22} & \cdots & a_{2n} \\
\vdots & \vdots & & \vdots \\
a_{n1} & a_{n2} & \cdots & a_{nn}
\end{bmatrix}
\xrightarrow[\text{operations}]{\text{elementary row}}
\begin{bmatrix}
a'_{11} & a'_{12} & \cdots & a'_{1n} \\
0 & a'_{22} & \cdots & a'_{2n} \\
\vdots & \vdots & & \vdots \\
0 & 0 & & a'_{nn}
\end{bmatrix}
$$

Fig. 2.8   The Gauss elimination method.

diagonal elements of A'. In effect,

$$\det(A) = (-1)^k \det(A') = (-1)^k (a'_{11})(a'_{22}) \cdots (a'_{nn}). \qquad (2.72)$$

Here k denotes the number of row interchanges which have been made in accomplishing the elimination process. The following two examples illustrate the application of the Gauss elimination method for finding the value of the determinant of a square matrix.

Example 2.25   Find the value of the determinant of the following matrix:

$$
A = \begin{bmatrix}
1 & 1 & 1 \\
-1 & 1 & -2 \\
0 & 2 & -1
\end{bmatrix}
$$

To start we add the first row to the second, giving

$$
\begin{bmatrix}
1 & 1 & 1 \\
0 & 2 & -1 \\
0 & 2 & -1
\end{bmatrix}
$$

Add -1 times the second row to the third row:

$$
A' = \begin{bmatrix}
1 & 1 & 1 \\
0 & 2 & -1 \\
0 & 0 & 0
\end{bmatrix}
$$

The value of $\det(A)$ is then equal to zero since one of the principal diagonal elements of A' is equal to zero:

$$|A| = (1)(2)(0) = 0 \quad \blacksquare$$

Example 2.26   Find the value of the determinant of the following matrix:

$$
A = \begin{bmatrix}
1 & 3 & 2 \\
-2 & 1 & 3 \\
3 & -5 & -1
\end{bmatrix}
$$

Adding 2 times the first row to the second leads to

$$\begin{bmatrix} 1 & 3 & 2 \\ 0 & 7 & 7 \\ 3 & -5 & -1 \end{bmatrix}$$

Add -3 times the first row to the third row:

$$\begin{bmatrix} 1 & 3 & 2 \\ 0 & 7 & 7 \\ 0 & -14 & -7 \end{bmatrix}$$

Add 2 times the second row to the third row:

$$A' = \begin{bmatrix} 1 & 3 & 2 \\ 0 & 7 & 7 \\ 0 & 0 & 7 \end{bmatrix}$$

$$|A| = (1)(7)(7) = 49 \quad \blacksquare$$

Simultaneous Linear Equations

The procedure of Gauss elimination can also be applied to the solution of simultaneous linear equations. Before describing how this is accomplished, consider the following structural characteristics of systems of linear equations.

A system of linear equations, defined algebraically by

$$\sum_{j=1}^{n} a_{ij} x_j = b_i, \qquad i = 1, \ldots, m \qquad (2.73)$$

and for which at least one solution, $\mathbf{x}^*$, exists can be classified according to the number of variables (n) and equations (m) represented by the system. When the number of equations is less than the number of variables ($m < n$), the system is said to be *underdetermined*. When the number of equations is equal to the number of variables ($m = n$), the system is said to be *exactly determined*. When the number of equations is greater than the number of variables ($m > n$), the system is said to be *overdetermined*.

The dimensionality of the space represented by the system is equal to the number of unique variables present in the system (n). Each equation represents a condition which must be satisfied by a point ($\mathbf{x}^*$) in the space defined, and as such reduces the number of degrees of freedom (i.e., dimensionality of the region in which the point may lie) available to a point by one. When the number of degrees of freedom is reduced to zero ($m = n$), a unique point is defined (a point being a geometrical entity of zero dimension). However, this is only true if each condition (equation) is unique, or nonredundant, and does not violate one of the other conditions; that is, it is not inconsistent. A system of n equations that are linearly independent in n variables has one unique solution point. As we have mentioned, the system of n equations in n unique variables, written in matrix notation

$$A\mathbf{x} = \mathbf{b} \qquad (2.74)$$

has one unique solution if $\det(A) \neq 0$. The solution to the exactly determined system of equations (2.74) can be obtained in a manner similar to that employed in finding the determinant of a square matrix.

To accomplish this, the matrix A is first augmented with the vector of right-hand-side values $\mathbf{b}$ as $(A \,|\, \mathbf{b})$. Now, as before, elementary row operations are employed to convert the partition A into its equivalent upper triangular form A'. Note that these row operations also involve the augmented elements from the vector $\mathbf{b}$, which is converted to its equivalent form $\mathbf{b}'$ by these operations. The consequence of the elimination process is to produce an *equivalent* system of linear equations,

$$A'\mathbf{x} = \mathbf{b}' \qquad (2.75)$$

(See Fig. 2.9). This system is equivalent to the original system in that the same solution, $\mathbf{x}^*$, satisfies both systems of equations. However, this solution is directly obtainable from the latter system by back substitution. Note that the value of x_n^* is directly obtainable from the nth equation of the latter system. Further, the value of x_{n-1}^* can be obtained from the $(n-1)$st equation, once the value of x_n^* is known, and so on. The following example will illustrate the solution of a system of simultaneous linear equations using Gauss elimination.

$$(A/\mathbf{b}) \xrightarrow[\text{operations}]{\text{elementary row}} (A/\mathbf{b}')$$

Fig. 2.9 Gauss elimination on $(A \,|\, \mathbf{b})$.

Example 2.27 Find the solution to the following system of linear equations:

$$x_1 + 3x_2 + 2x_3 = 6$$
$$-2x_1 + x_2 + 3x_3 = 4$$
$$3x_1 - 5x_2 - x_3 = 1$$

The augmented matrix is

$$(A \,|\, \mathbf{b}) = \begin{bmatrix} 1 & 3 & 2 & 6 \\ -2 & 1 & 3 & 4 \\ 3 & -5 & -1 & 1 \end{bmatrix}$$

Note that the A matrix is the same as in the preceding example; consequently the row operations are the same as those employed in finding A' in that example. The sequence of augmented matrices obtained through these operations is summarized below:

$$\begin{bmatrix} 1 & 3 & 2 & 6 \\ 0 & 7 & 7 & 16 \\ 0 & -14 & -7 & -17 \end{bmatrix}$$

after operations 1 and 2;

$$(A' \mid \mathbf{b}') = \begin{bmatrix} 1 & 3 & 2 & 6 \\ 0 & 7 & 7 & 16 \\ 0 & 0 & 7 & 15 \end{bmatrix}$$

after operation 3.

The resulting equivalent system of equations is then

$$x_1 + 3x_2 + 2x_3 = 6$$
$$7x_2 + 7x_3 = 16$$
$$7x_3 = 15$$

The value of x_3 is obtained directly from the third equation:

$$x_3^* = 15/7.$$

The value of x_2 is obtained from the second equation:

$$7x_2^* = 16 - 7x_3^*$$
$$= 16 - 7(15/7)$$
$$x_2^* = 1/7$$

The value of x_1 is obtained from the first equation:

$$x_1^* = 6 - 2x_3^* - 3x_2^*$$
$$= 6 - 2(15/7) - 3(1/7)$$
$$= 9/7$$

The vector $\mathbf{x}^*$ which identifies the solution to this system of simultaneous linear equations is

$$\mathbf{x}^* = \begin{bmatrix} 9/7 \\ 1/7 \\ 15/7 \end{bmatrix} \quad \blacksquare$$

The Inverse of a Square Matrix

Having described how the Gauss elimination method can be employed to solve a system of simultaneous linear equations, we are now prepared to show how this same basic procedure can be used to obtain the inverse of a matrix. As already indicated, if a matrix A is nonsingular, then the matrix has associated with it a unique inverse matrix A^{-1} having the following property:

$$AA^{-1} = A^{-1}A = I \qquad (2.76)$$

where I is an identity matrix.

As indicated by Eq. (2.76), the inverse matrix is a uniform transformation matrix that converts the set of row (or column) vectors of A into the mutually orthogonal set that collectively comprises an identity matrix. Considering the above relationship in a slightly different way, let us decompose the matrix A^{-1} and the matrix I into their respective column vectors as follows:

$$(A)(\mathbf{b}_1 \cdots \mathbf{b}_n) = (\mathbf{i}_1 \cdots \mathbf{i}_n). \qquad (2.77)$$

Observe that the elements of each column vector of the inverse $\mathbf{b}_k$ must be such that

$$A\mathbf{b}_k = \mathbf{i}_k, \qquad k = 1, \ldots, n \qquad (2.78)$$

in order to satisfy the matrix equation (2.77). In effect, we can obtain the values of the inverse matrix, one column at a time, by solving a set of simultaneous linear equations, one set of equations for each column of the inverse. Note that the matrix of detached coefficients A is the same for each system of equations to be solved.

To obtain the inverse of a square matrix, we first form the augmented matrix $(A \mid I)$ where, in this instance, the identity matrix represents collectively each of the right-hand-side values from the n systems of equations identified by (2.78). Gauss elimination is then performed on this augmented matrix to convert A into its equivalent upper triangular form A'. This being accomplished, we have $(A' \mid I')$. As before, we have now defined the following equivalent *systems* of simultaneous linear equations:

$$(A')(\mathbf{b}_1 \cdots \mathbf{b}_n) = (\mathbf{i}'_1 \ldots \mathbf{i}'_n) \qquad (2.79)$$

The solutions to each of these systems $\mathbf{b}_k^*$, $k = 1, \ldots, n$, are then the respective column vectors of the inverse matrix A^{-1}.

Example 2.28 Find the inverse of the following matrix:

$$A = \begin{bmatrix} 1 & 3 & 2 \\ -2 & 1 & 3 \\ 3 & -5 & -1 \end{bmatrix}$$

Augmenting A with the identity matrix gives

$$\begin{bmatrix} 1 & 3 & 2 & 1 & 0 & 0 \\ -2 & 1 & 3 & 0 & 1 & 0 \\ 3 & -5 & -1 & 0 & 0 & 1 \end{bmatrix}$$

Note that the A matrix is the same as in the two preceding examples. Consequently, the same elementary row operations are required to convert the portion A into A'. Applying these operations gives the following augmented matrix:

$$
\begin{array}{cc}
A' & I'
\end{array}
$$
$$
\left[\begin{array}{ccc|ccc}
1 & 3 & 2 & 1 & 0 & 0 \\
0 & 7 & 7 & 2 & 1 & 0 \\
0 & 0 & 7 & 1 & 2 & 1
\end{array}\right]
$$

The columns of the inverse are then obtained, one column at a time, by treating each column of I' as if it were the reduced right-hand-side vector from a system of simultaneous linear equations. That is, use the first column of I' to obtain the first column vector of A^{-1}, the second column of I' to obtain the second column vector of A^{-1}, etc. For example,

$$
\left[\begin{array}{ccc}
1 & 3 & 2 \\
0 & 7 & 7 \\
0 & 0 & 7
\end{array}\right]
\left[\begin{array}{c}
b_{11} \\
b_{21} \\
b_{31}
\end{array}\right]
=
\left[\begin{array}{c}
1 \\
2 \\
1
\end{array}\right]
$$

and the solution is

$$b_{31}^* = 1/7$$
$$7b_{21} = 2 - 7b_{31} = 2 - 7(1/7) = 1$$
$$b_{21}^* = 1/7$$
$$b_{11} = 1 - 2b_{31} - 3b_{21} = 1 - 2(1/7) - 3(1/7) = 2/7$$
$$b_{11}^* = 2/7$$

In similar fashion, the remaining column vectors of A^{-1} are obtained to yield the following inverse:

$$
A^{-1} =
\left[\begin{array}{ccc}
2/7 & -1/7 & 1/7 \\
1/7 & -1/7 & -1/7 \\
1/7 & 2/7 & 1/7
\end{array}\right]
\quad \blacksquare
$$

The inverse matrix has a number of important applications in operations research and systems analysis. Of these, one of the most important is its use in the solution of simultaneous linear equations. In this regard, if the system of equations

$$A\mathbf{x} = \mathbf{b}$$

is premultiplied by the inverse of A, that is, A^{-1}, then the result is to transfrom the right-hand-side vector into a vector of solution values $\mathbf{x}^*$ for the system of equations. This, of course, assumes that the system of equations is independent and exactly determined. Doing this yields

$$A^{-1}A\mathbf{x} = A^{-1}\mathbf{b} \tag{2.80}$$

$$I\mathbf{x} = \mathbf{x}^* \tag{2.81}$$

or

$$
\begin{aligned}
x_1 & & & = x_1^* \\
& x_2 & & = x_2^* \\
& & \ddots & \quad \vdots \\
& & x_n & = x_n^*
\end{aligned}
$$

Recalling the system of equations given in Example 2.27 and noting that the inverse matrix obtained in the preceding example is the inverse of the A matrix in Example 2.28, the solution to this system of equations could have been obtained by the following:

$$A^{-1}\mathbf{b} = \mathbf{x}^*$$

or

$$
\begin{bmatrix} 2/7 & -1/7 & 1/7 \\ 1/7 & -1/7 & -1/7 \\ 1/7 & 2/7 & 1/7 \end{bmatrix}
\begin{bmatrix} 6 \\ 4 \\ 1 \end{bmatrix} =
\begin{bmatrix} 9/7 \\ 1/7 \\ 15/7 \end{bmatrix}
$$

At this point the reader may question the need for going to the trouble of finding the inverse just to be able to find the solution to a system of simultaneous linear equations, when the same approach could be applied to find this solution in a more straightforward manner. Although there are a number of examples that could be given to illustrate the utility of the inverse beyond that of its direct application to systems of linear equations, we prefer to delay these illustrations until they can be shown in the context of operations research methodologies (that is, until Chapter 7). For the present, we will illustrate the utility of the inverse in determining what effect a variation in the right-hand-side vector $\Delta\mathbf{b}$ will have on the solution values $\mathbf{x}^*$ for a system of simultaneous linear equations. Given that we have a system of simultaneous linear equations whose right-hand-side vector $\mathbf{b}$ may vary by some arbitrary amount $\Delta\mathbf{b}$, let us show how any such variation can be accounted for in terms of the individual component variations of the solution vector $\mathbf{x}^*$. Consider the matrix equation

$$A\mathbf{x} = \mathbf{b} + \Delta\mathbf{b} \tag{2.82}$$

and observe that premultiplying both sides of the equation by A^{-1} gives

$$I\mathbf{x} = \mathbf{x}^* + A^{-1}\Delta\mathbf{b} \tag{2.83}$$

Then for any specific values of $\Delta\mathbf{b}_i$, $i = 1, \ldots, n$, we can obtain the corresponding new solution values directly by expanding the terms on the right-hand side of Eq. (2.83) and then substituting the values for Δb_i, $i = 1, \ldots, n$. To illustrate this, we return again to the system of equations employed in Example 2.27.

Example 2.29   What would be the effect of an arbitrary variation in the right-hand-side vector of the following system of equations?

$$\begin{bmatrix} 1 & 3 & 2 \\ -2 & 1 & 3 \\ 3 & -5 & -1 \end{bmatrix} \begin{bmatrix} x_1 \\ x_2 \\ x_3 \end{bmatrix} = \begin{bmatrix} 6 \\ 4 \\ 1 \end{bmatrix} + \begin{bmatrix} \Delta b_1 \\ \Delta b_2 \\ \Delta b_3 \end{bmatrix}$$

Premultiplying by A^{-1} gives

$$Ix = x^* + \begin{bmatrix} 2/7 & -1/7 & 1/7 \\ 1/7 & -1/7 & -1/7 \\ 1/7 & 2/7 & 1/7 \end{bmatrix} \begin{bmatrix} \Delta b_1 \\ \Delta b_2 \\ \Delta b_3 \end{bmatrix}$$

Expanding the right-hand-side components of the above equation gives the following solution for **x** in terms of the potential variations in the right-hand-side vector $\Delta \mathbf{b}$.

$$x_1 = 9/7 + 2/7\,\Delta b_1 - 1/7\,\Delta b_2 + 1/7\,\Delta b_3$$
$$x_2 = 1/7 + 1/7\,\Delta b_1 - 1/7\,\Delta b_2 - 1/7\,\Delta b_3$$
$$x_3 = 15/7 + 1/7\,\Delta b_1 + 2/7\,\Delta b_2 + 1/7\,\Delta b_3 \quad \blacksquare$$

Examining the effect of variations in the right-hand-side vector of a system of simultaneous linear equations, as illustrated above, is a primary aspect of *sensitivity analysis* in linear programming. This will be discussed in more detail in Chapter 7.

Example 2.30   Raoul LaFong, the well known building contractor, has an opportunity to purchase quantities of mosaic stones which are used in exterior building decoration. The quantities to be sold must be purchased in total. They are as follows:

> blue stones   3/4 tons
> green stones   1 ton
> white stones   2 tons

Raoul can use these stones in the following three mixtures for wall decorations:

> mixture 1   green/blue   ratio 3/2
> mixture 2   green/white   ratio 2/3
> mixture 3   blue/white   ratio 1/4

He would like to find quantities of each of these mixtures which can be made from the above supply of stones for which all the stones purchased will be fully utilized. What are these quantities?

If no stones are used in his own work he can sell the mixtures for the following prices:

mixture 1 $0.05/lb
mixture 2 $0.03/lb
mixture 3 $0.02/lb

If he can purchase this load of stones for $0.002/lb, how much profit can be made from the sale of all of each mixture? If he can purchase an additional quantity of green stones from another source for $0.005/lb, how many addiitonal pounds of green stones should he purchase?

First we will define quantities of each mixture which will consume all of the stones to be purchased:

$$
\begin{aligned}
(3/5)x_1 + (2/5)x_2 \qquad\qquad &= 2000 \text{ lb} \quad \text{(green stones)} \\
(2/5)x_1 \qquad\qquad + (1/5)x_3 &= 1500 \text{ lb} \quad \text{(blue stones)} \\
+ (3/5)x_2 + (4/5)x_3 &= 4000 \text{ lb} \quad \text{(white stones)}
\end{aligned}
$$

where x_1 is the number of pounds of mixture 1, x_2 the number of pounds of mixture 2, and x_3 the number of pounds of mixture 3. Solving for $\mathbf{x}^*$,

$$
A^{-1} = \begin{bmatrix} 3/5 & 8/5 & -2/5 \\ 8/5 & -12/5 & 3/5 \\ -6/5 & 9/5 & 4/5 \end{bmatrix}, \qquad \mathbf{x}^* = \begin{bmatrix} 2000 \\ 2000 \\ 3500 \end{bmatrix}
$$

Consequently, he can produce 2000 lb of mixture 1, 2000 lb of mixture 2, and 3500 lb of mixture 3.

Second, the cost of this load of stones is $15.00. The revenue from the sale of all mixtures is $0.05(2000) + $0.03(2000) + $0.02(3500) = $230. The potential profit to be made from the sale of these three mixtures is then $215.

The third question regarding the number of additional pounds of green stones to purchase is resolved as follows. First, we must determine the potential additional profit to be obtained from these additional stones, if any. Then we must determine how many additional pounds could be effectively used in the production of the three mixtures. To answer both of these questions, we must first find the effect on the solution values caused by a variation in the right-hand side of the first equation:

$$
\mathbf{x} = \begin{bmatrix} 2000 \\ 2000 \\ 3500 \end{bmatrix} + \begin{bmatrix} 3/5 & 8/5 & -2/5 \\ 8/5 & -12/5 & 3/5 \\ -6/5 & 9/5 & 4/5 \end{bmatrix} \begin{bmatrix} \Delta b_1 \\ 0 \\ 0 \end{bmatrix}
$$

$$
\mathbf{x} = \mathbf{x}^* + A^{-1}\Delta\mathbf{b}
$$

$$
\mathbf{x} = \begin{bmatrix} 2000 + 3/5\,\Delta b_1 \\ 2000 + 8/5\,\Delta b_1 \\ 3500 - 6/5\,\Delta b_1 \end{bmatrix} = \mathbf{x}^* + \Delta\mathbf{x}
$$

The potential profit from each additional pound of green stones is then the revenue generated,

$$0.05(3/5\,\Delta b_1) + 0.03(8/5\,\Delta b_1) + 0.02(-6/5\,\Delta b_1) = 0.054\,\Delta b_1$$

minus the cost per pound, $0.005\,\Delta b_1$, which is then

$$\text{change in profit} = \Delta P = (0.054 - 0.005)\,\Delta b_1 = \$0.049\,\Delta b_1$$

From this we know that these additional green stones have a potential value which is greater than their cost. We must now determine the limitations which exist in procuring them. Note that as Δb_1 increases, both x_1 and x_2 will increase. However, as Δb_1 increases, x_3 will decrease. Since a value of x_3 which is negative would not make sense (i.e., we could not have less than zero mixture 3), our purchase of green stone will be limited by the restriction that

$$x_3 = 3500 - 6/5\,\Delta b_1 \geqslant 0.$$

We should observe that any increase in Δb_1 which would cause x_3 to have a negative value, according to the original system of equations, would have the following interpretation. We would use all of the white stones in mixture 2 and all of the blue stones in mixture 1, and would then have none of these colored stones left to mix with the excess of green stones that were purchased. The limit on the purchase of green stones is then defined by

$$6/5\,\Delta b_1 \leqslant 3500$$

$$\Delta b_1 \leqslant 2916\tfrac{2}{3} \text{ lb}$$

The number of additional pounds of green stones that the contractor should purchase, if he intends to sell the resulting mixtures, is then $2916\tfrac{2}{3}$ lb. From this additional purchase he could realize an additional profit of

$$\Delta P = \$0.049(2916\tfrac{2}{3}) = \$142.92. \quad \blacksquare$$

CONVEX SPACES

In many problems in systems analysis the solution to the problem is constrained to a set of points within a vector space but not including the entire space itself. This is a recurring problem in mathematical programming. In many cases the space of feasible solutions for the problem, where a solution is simply a vector in the feasible space, is convex. In this section we shall discuss the properties of convex spaces and their applications to one area of mathematical programming, linear programming.

Let $x_1, x_2, \ldots, x_m$ be a set of vectors belonging to the space χ_n (not necessarily a vector space) and let y be expressed as the linear combination given by

$$y = \sum_{i=1}^{m} \lambda_i x_i \qquad (2.84)$$

If we restrict λ_i, $i = 1, 2, \ldots, m$, to nonnegative values such that

$$\sum_{i=1}^{m} \lambda_i = 1 \qquad (2.85)$$

then y is said to be formed by a *convex combination* of $x_1, x_2, \ldots, x_m$. If we restrict our attention to two vectors, x_1 and x_2, then the convex combination is given by

$$y = \lambda x_1 + (1 - \lambda) x_2 \qquad (2.86)$$

where $0 \leqslant \lambda \leqslant 1$. If we vary λ from 0 to 1 we obtain a straight-line segment connecting x_1 and x_2. Thus the convex combination defined in Eq. (2.86) defines each vector on the line segment joining x_1 and x_2.

Let the space χ_2 in E_2 be defined by all vectors x such that

$$x_1 + x_2 \geqslant 8$$
$$2x_1 + x_2 \leqslant 16$$
$$-x_1 + x_2 \leqslant 8$$

The space χ_2 is shown in Fig. 2.10. If χ_2 is a convex space, then a convex combination of any two vectors within χ_2 will yield another vector within χ_2. If we examine χ_2 as shown in Fig. 2.10, it is obvious that a line segment

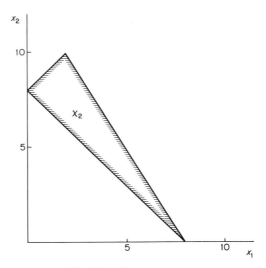

Fig. 2.10   Convex space χ_2.

between any two points in χ_2 will yield a continuum of points all of which are in χ_2 and χ_2 is a convex space. In general, then, χ_n is a *convex space* if a line segment between any two points in χ_n is contained entirely in χ_n. In terms of convex combinations of points or vectors, χ_n is a convex space if every convex combination of two points in χ_n yields another point in χ_n.

Example 2.31 Let χ_2 be composed of all vectors satisfying the inequalities given by

$$x_1 + x_2 \geqslant 4$$
$$x_1 + x_2 \leqslant 10$$
$$x_1 - x_2 \leqslant 5$$
$$x_1 \geqslant 0$$
$$x_2 \geqslant 0$$

Sketch the space defined by all convex combinations of the vectors x_1, x_2, and x_3, where

$$x_1 = \begin{bmatrix} 5 \\ 2 \end{bmatrix}, \quad x_2 = \begin{bmatrix} 3 \\ 5 \end{bmatrix}, \quad x_3 = \begin{bmatrix} 2 \\ 4 \end{bmatrix}$$

The space χ_2 is shown graphically in Fig. 2.11. Let C be the space defined by all convex combinations of x_1, x_2, and x_3. The space C is bounded by straight-line segments joining x_1 and x_2, x_1 and x_3, and x_2 and x_3 and is shown in Fig. 2.11. ∎

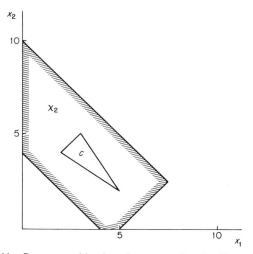

Fig. 2.11 Convex combination of x_1, x_2, and x_3 for Example 2.31.

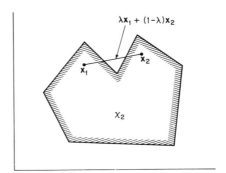

Fig. 2.12 Space χ_2, which is not convex.

If we select two points within χ_n, $\mathbf{x}_1$ and $\mathbf{x}_2$, and the point $\mathbf{y}_1 = \lambda\mathbf{x}_1 + (1 - \lambda)\mathbf{x}_2$, $0 \leqslant \lambda \leqslant 1$, does not lie within χ_n, then χ_n cannot be a convex space. An example of a space which is not convex is illustrated in Fig. 2.12.

Let $\mathbf{b}$ and $\mathbf{x}$ be n-dimensional vectors and k a scalar. Then the equation

$$\mathbf{b}^T\mathbf{x} = k \tag{2.87}$$

defines a *hyperplane* in n-dimensional Euclidean space. In 2 dimensions a hyperplane is a straight line, and is a plane in 3-dimensional space. A hyperplane divides E_n into two *half-spaces* defined by

$$\mathbf{b}^T\mathbf{x} \leqslant k \tag{2.88}$$

and

$$\mathbf{b}^T\mathbf{x} > k \tag{2.89}$$

respectively. In 2 dimensions the half-space in Eq. (2.88) includes all points on one side of the line defined by $\mathbf{b}^T\mathbf{x} = k$, and Eq. (2.89) defines the half-space including all points on the other side of that line. The space defined by $\mathbf{b}^T\mathbf{x} \leqslant k$ is *closed* since it includes its boundary points, while that defined by $\mathbf{b}^T\mathbf{x} > k$ is *open*.

If we select any two points in the same half-space and connect them by a straight line, then each point on the line segment will lie within the same half-space. Hence a half-space is always convex. This can be shown as follows. Let the half-space of interest be defined by Eq. (2.88). Then any two vectors $\mathbf{x}_1$ and $\mathbf{x}_2$ in this half-space must satisfy the inequalities

$$\mathbf{b}^T\mathbf{x}_1 \leqslant k \tag{2.90}$$

$$\mathbf{b}^T\mathbf{x}_2 \leqslant k \tag{2.91}$$

Now let us form a convex combination of $\mathbf{x}_1$ and $\mathbf{x}_2$ by

$$\mathbf{y} = \lambda\mathbf{x}_1 + (1 - \lambda)\mathbf{x}_2 \tag{2.92}$$

where $0 \leqslant \lambda \leqslant 1$. Multiplying both sides of Eq. (2.92) by $\mathbf{b}^T$, we have

$$\mathbf{b}^T\mathbf{y} = \mathbf{b}^T\big[\lambda\mathbf{x}_1 + (1 - \lambda)\mathbf{x}_2\big] = \lambda\mathbf{b}^T\mathbf{x}_1 + (1 - \lambda)\mathbf{b}^T\mathbf{x}_2 \qquad (2.93)$$

Since $\mathbf{b}^T\mathbf{x}_1 \leqslant k$ and $\mathbf{b}^T\mathbf{x}_2 \leqslant k$, we have

$$\mathbf{b}^T\mathbf{y} \leqslant \lambda k + (1 - \lambda)k \leqslant k$$

and $\mathbf{y}$ belongs to the same half-space as $\mathbf{x}_1$ and $\mathbf{x}_2$.

The *intersection of m half-spaces* defines the set of points or vectors common to all m half-spaces if the set is not empty. In Example 2.31 we dealt with the half-spaces defined by

$$x_1 + x_2 \geqslant 4$$
$$x_1 + x_2 \leqslant 10$$
$$x_1 - x_2 \leqslant 5$$
$$x_1 \geqslant 0$$
$$x_2 \geqslant 0$$

The intersection of these half-spaces is the set of all vectors $\mathbf{x}$ which satisfies each of these inequalities and is defined by χ_2 in Fig. 2.11. If there are no vectors or points which simultaneously lie in all half-spaces defining the intersection, then the intersection is *empty*. For example, consider the two half-spaces defined by

$$x_1 + x_2 \leqslant 10$$
$$x_1 + x_2 > 20$$

Since there are no points which simultaneously lie above the line $x_1 + x_2 = 20$ and below or on the line $x_1 + x_2 = 10$, the intersection of these two half-spaces is empty. If the intersection of m half-spaces is not empty, then it is convex.

An *extreme point of a convex space* is a point in the space which cannot be expressed as a convex combination of any two distinct points in the convex space. In Fig. 2.13 there are five extreme points, denoted w_i, $i = 1, 2, \ldots, 5$. An extreme point for a convex space χ_n is always a boundary point for χ_n, but the converse is not necessarily true. As shown in Fig. 2.13, a boundary point lies on one of the hyperplanes bounding the convex space and may be defined by a convex combination of extreme points. An extreme point for a convex space may be defined in terms of intersecting bounding hyperplanes. A *bounding hyperplane* for a convex space χ_n is a hyperplane which contains boundary points for χ_n. An extreme point for a convex space χ_n will always lie in χ_n at the *intersection of n bounding hyperplanes*. It can be shown that every point in the convex space χ_n can be expressed as a convex combination of at least some of the extreme points of χ_n.

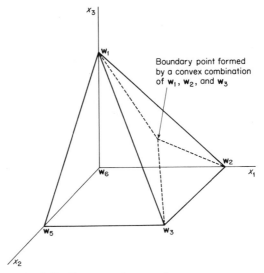

Fig. 2.13   Extreme points w_i, of a convex space.

Example 2.32   Given the convex space χ_3 defined by

$$x_1 + x_2 + x_3 \leqslant 20$$
$$x_1 + x_2 + x_3 \geqslant 10$$
$$x_1 \geqslant 0$$
$$x_2 \geqslant 0$$
$$x_3 \geqslant 0$$

determine the extreme points for χ_3.

Every extreme point for χ_n lies at the intersection of n bounding hyperplanes if the intersection exists. In this case the convex space is 3-dimensional. Hence an extreme point may lie at the intersection of any three hyperplanes. Since χ_3 is defined by five hyperplanes, there are $\binom{5}{3} = 10$ possible intersections of three hyperplanes, although some of these intersections may not exist. Let us denote by $H_1, H_2, \ldots, H_5$ the hyperplanes defined by

$$H_1:\quad x_1 + x_2 + x_3 = 20$$
$$H_2:\quad x_1 + x_2 + x_3 = 10$$
$$H_3:\quad x_1 = 0$$
$$H_4:\quad x_2 = 0$$
$$H_5:\quad x_3 = 0$$

The intersection of H_1, H_2, and H_3 is the set of values of x_1, x_2, and x_3

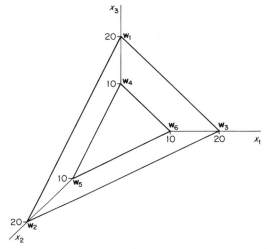

Fig. 2.14   Extreme points w_i, $i = 1, 2, \ldots, b$, for the convex space defined in Example 2.32.

which simultaneously satisfies the first three equations. In this case the intersection does not exist since the hyperplanes H_1 and H_2 do not intersect. The ten possible intersections are shown in Table 2.1. Where the intersection exists there is an extreme point at the intersection. As indicated in Table 2.1, there are six extreme points for χ_3. While the intersection of H_3, H_4, and H_5 exists, the point of intersection is not an extreme point, since it does not belong to the intersection of all five half-spaces and therefore does not belong to χ_3. The convex space χ_3 and its extreme points are shown in Fig. 2.14. ∎

Table 2.1

Intersecting Bounding Hyperplanes and Extreme Points for Example 2.32

Intersecting hyperplanes	Existence of intersection	Extreme point	Comments
H_1, H_2, H_3	Nonexistent		
H_1, H_2, H_4	Nonexistent		
H_1, H_2, H_5	Nonexistent		
H_1, H_3, H_4	Exists	$w_1 = (0, 0, 20)$	
H_1, H_3, H_5	Exists	$w_2 = (0, 20, 0)$	
H_1, H_4, H_5	Exists	$w_3 = (20, 0, 0)$	
H_2, H_3, H_4	Exists	$w_4 = (0, 0, 10)$	
H_2, H_3, H_5	Exists	$w_5 = (0, 10, 0)$	
H_2, H_4, H_5	Exists	$w_6 = (10, 0, 0)$	
H_3, H_4, H_5	Exists		Solution not in χ_3

A convex space formed by the intersection of half-spaces may be expressed in general as

$$\mathbf{b}_1^T\mathbf{x} \leqslant k_1$$
$$\mathbf{b}_2^T\mathbf{x} \leqslant k_2$$
$$\vdots$$
$$\mathbf{b}_m^T\mathbf{x} \leqslant k_m \tag{2.94}$$

where $\mathbf{b}_i$ and $\mathbf{x}$ are n-dimensional column vectors. Now let $\mathbf{b}_i^T$ be the ith row of the $m \times n$ matrix B and k_i the ith element in the column vector $\mathbf{k}$. Then the set of inequalities in Eq. (2.94) may be expressed by

$$B\mathbf{x} \leqslant \mathbf{k} \tag{2.95}$$

In Example 2.32, B would be defined as

$$B = \begin{bmatrix} 1 & 1 & 1 \\ -1 & -1 & -1 \\ -1 & 0 & 0 \\ 0 & -1 & 0 \\ 0 & 0 & -1 \end{bmatrix}$$

and $\mathbf{k}$ by

$$\mathbf{k} = \begin{bmatrix} 20 \\ -10 \\ 0 \\ 0 \\ 0 \end{bmatrix}$$

where both sides of the last four inequalities are multiplied by -1 to express the inequalities in the form $\mathbf{b}_i^T\mathbf{x} \leqslant k_i$.

Example 2.33 (Linear Programming) The vector $\mathbf{x}^*$ is to be determined such that

$$c_1x_1 + c_2x_2 + \cdots + c_2x_n$$

is minimized subject to the constraints

$$a_{11}x_1 + a_{12}x_2 + \cdots + a_{1n}x_n \leqslant k_1$$
$$a_{21}x_1 + a_{22}x_2 + \cdots + a_{2n}x_n \leqslant k_2$$
$$\vdots$$
$$a_{m1}x_1 + a_{m2}x_2 + \cdots + a_{mn}x_n \leqslant k_m$$
$$x_i \geqslant 0, \qquad i = 1, 2, \ldots, n$$

Show that $\mathbf{x}^*$ lies at an extreme point of the convex set (assumed to be nonempty) defined by the set of inequality constraints.

The minimization problem defined here is referred to as a *linear programming problem*. Letting

$$\mathbf{c} = \begin{bmatrix} c_1 \\ c_2 \\ \vdots \\ c_n \end{bmatrix}, \qquad A = \begin{bmatrix} a_{11}a_{12} & \cdots & a_{1n} \\ a_{21}a_{22} & \cdots & a_{2n} \\ \vdots & & \vdots \\ a_{m1}a_{m2} & \cdots & a_{mn} \end{bmatrix}, \qquad \mathbf{k} = \begin{bmatrix} k_1 \\ k_2 \\ \vdots \\ k_m \end{bmatrix}$$

the problem may be reexpressed as

$$\mathbf{c}^T\mathbf{x} = \min \tag{2.96}$$
$$\text{s.t.}$$
$$A\mathbf{x} \leqslant \mathbf{k} \tag{2.97}$$
$$\mathbf{x} \geqslant \emptyset \tag{2.98}$$

where the notation s.t. means "subject to the constraints," here given by $A\mathbf{x} \leqslant \mathbf{k}$ and $\mathbf{x} \geqslant \emptyset$. Let the extreme points of the convex space χ_n defined by $A\mathbf{x} \leqslant \mathbf{k}$, $\mathbf{x} \geqslant \emptyset$ be $\mathbf{w}_1, \mathbf{w}_2, \ldots, \mathbf{w}_r$. Let $\mathbf{w}_j$ be the extreme point such that

$$\mathbf{c}^T\mathbf{w}_j \leqslant \mathbf{c}^T\mathbf{w}_i, \qquad i = 1, 2, \ldots, r$$

Now choose any point $\mathbf{x}$ in χ_n such that $\mathbf{x}$ is not an extreme point. As already mentioned, any point in a convex space may be expressed as a convex combination of at least some of the extreme points of χ_n. Assume that $\mathbf{x}$ can be expressed as a convex combination of the extreme points $\mathbf{w}_1, \mathbf{w}_2, \ldots, \mathbf{w}_t$. Then

$$\mathbf{x} = \sum_{i=1}^{t} \lambda_i\mathbf{w}_i \qquad \text{and} \qquad \mathbf{c}^T\mathbf{x} = \sum_{i=1}^{t} \lambda_i\mathbf{c}^T\mathbf{w}_i$$

Now

$$\mathbf{c}^T\mathbf{w}_i \geqslant \mathbf{c}^T\mathbf{w}_j$$

by definition of $\mathbf{w}_j$. Thus

$$\sum_{i=1}^{t} \lambda_i\mathbf{c}^T\mathbf{w}_i \geqslant \sum_{i=1}^{t} \lambda_i\mathbf{c}^T\mathbf{w}_j \geqslant \mathbf{c}^T\mathbf{w}_j \sum_{i=1}^{t} \lambda_i \geqslant \mathbf{c}^T\mathbf{w}_j$$

and

$$\mathbf{c}^T\mathbf{x} \geqslant \mathbf{c}^T\mathbf{w}_j$$

Hence if the extreme point $\mathbf{w}_j$ yields the minimum solution for $\mathbf{c}^T\mathbf{x}$ *among all of the extreme points*, then $\mathbf{w}_j$ yields a solution for $\mathbf{c}^T\mathbf{x}$ which is less than or equal to any solution vector belonging to χ_n. The vector $\mathbf{w}_j$ is referred to as the *minimizing extreme point solution*. ∎

The result obtained in Example 2.33 is extremely important in solving linear programming problems such as that formulated in Eq. (2.96)–(2.98). The convex space χ_n defined by $A\mathbf{x} \leqslant k$, $\mathbf{x} \geqslant \varnothing$, contains a finite number of extreme points, but an infinite number of vectors $\mathbf{x}$ if χ_n is not empty. Since the vector $\mathbf{x}^*$ which minimizes $\mathbf{c}^T\mathbf{x}$ lies at an extreme point, our search for $\mathbf{x}^*$ is limited to examination of the extreme points of χ_n. Now there may be other points in χ_n which yield a value for $\mathbf{c}^T\mathbf{x}$ equal to the minimizing extreme point solution. However, no point in χ_n can yield a value for $\mathbf{c}^T\mathbf{x}$ which is less than that given by the minimizing extreme point.

Frequently an optimization problem formulated as a linear programming problem calls for maximization of $\mathbf{c}^T\mathbf{x}$ rather than minimization. In this case the problem is stated as

$$\mathbf{c}^T\mathbf{x} = \max \tag{2.99}$$
$$\text{s.t.}$$
$$A\mathbf{x} \leqslant \mathbf{k} \tag{2.100}$$
$$\mathbf{x} \geqslant \varnothing \tag{2.101}$$

As in the case of the minimization problem, a vector $\mathbf{x}^*$ which maximizes $\mathbf{c}^T\mathbf{x}$ can always be found at an extreme point of the convex space defined by $A\mathbf{x} \leqslant \mathbf{k}$, $\mathbf{x} \geqslant \varnothing$.

Example 2.34 A company manufactures three types of solvents: A, B, and C. For each unit of A, B, and C produced, a profit of \$5.00, \$7.00, and \$3.00 is realized. The same two raw materials, I and II, are used in the production of all three solvents, but in different quantities. The quantities of each raw material required to produce one unit of each solvent are shown in Table 2.2. The company has available 1000 units of raw material I and 2000 units of raw material II. Determine the number of units of A, B, and C, x_1, x_2, and x_3 respectively, which should be produced to maximize profit.

Table 2.2

Materials Requirements for Production of 1 Unit of Solvents A, B, and C in Example 2.34

Solvents	Units of materials required for production	
	I	II
A	10	2
B	2	20
C	5	10

The profit model to be maximized is

$$\text{profit} = 5x_1 + 7x_2 + 3x_3$$

The volume of raw materials consumed in the production of x_1 units of A, x_2 units of B, and x_3 units of C cannot exceed the supply on hand. Thus

$$10x_1 + 2x_2 + 5x_3 \leqslant 1000$$
$$2x_1 + 20x_2 + 10x_3 \leqslant 2000$$

Since production of a negative quantity of any solvent is impossible, we have the additional restrictions

$$x_1 \geqslant 0$$
$$x_2 \geqslant 0$$
$$x_3 \geqslant 0$$

and the linear programming problem is defined as

$$5x_1 + 7x_2 + 3x_3 = \max$$

s.t.

$$10x_1 + 2x_2 + 5x_3 \leqslant 1000$$
$$2x_1 + 20x_2 + 10x_3 \leqslant 2000$$
$$x_1 \geqslant 0$$
$$x_2 \geqslant 0$$
$$x_3 \geqslant 0$$

We know that a vector $\mathbf{x}^*$ which maximizes $\mathbf{c}^T\mathbf{x}$ lies at an extreme point of the convex space defined by the constraints. Hence we need only identify the extreme points of the convex space defined by the constraint set χ_3, evaluate $\mathbf{c}^T\mathbf{x}$ at each, and choose as our solution that extreme point which maximizes $\mathbf{c}^T\mathbf{x}$.

The bounding hyperplanes for the convex space will be denoted H_1, $H_2, \ldots, H_6$ and are defined by

$$
\begin{aligned}
H_1 &: \quad 10x_1 + 2x_2 + 5x_3 = 1000 \\
H_2 &: \quad 2x_1 + 20x_2 + 10x_3 = 2000 \\
H_3 &: \quad x_1 = 0 \\
H_4 &: \quad x_2 = 0 \\
H_5 &: \quad x_3 = 0
\end{aligned}
$$

Each extreme point of χ_3 must lie at the intersection of three bounding hyperplanes and belong to χ_3. The extreme points for χ_3 are given in Table 2.3. The reader will note that the intersections of H_1, H_3, and H_5 and H_2, H_4, and H_5 yield vectors which do not belong to χ_3 as defined by the constraint set. The intersection of H_1, H_3, and H_5 is at $\mathbf{x} = [0 \quad 500 \quad 0]^T$. Substituting these values of x_1, x_2, and x_3 into the second constraint yields

$$2x_1 + 20x_2 + 10x_3 = 10000 > 2000$$

which is in violation of the second constraint and is therefore outside χ_3. In a similar manner the intersection of H_2, H_4, and H_5 violates the first constraint and is therefore outside χ_3. Since an extreme point must belong to χ_3, neither of these points can be an extreme point for χ_3. As Table 2.3 indicates, the profit is maximized subject to the constraints on raw material availability when 81.63 units of A, 91.84 units of B, and 0.00 units of C are produced, yielding a profit of \$1051.03. ■

For a more detailed discussion of linear programming and its applications the reader should see Chapter 7.

Table 2.3

Extreme Points for χ_3 in Example 2.34

Intersecting hyperplanes	Existence of intersection	Intersection	Extreme point?	$c^T x$ (\$)
H_1, H_2, H_3	Exists	$x_1 = 0, x_2 = 0, x_3 = 200$	Yes	600.00
H_1, H_2, H_4	Exists	$x_1 = 0, x_2 = 0, x_3 = 200$	Yes	600.00
H_1, H_2, H_5	Exists	$x_1 = 81.63, x_2 = 91.84, x_3 = 0$	Yes	1051.03
H_1, H_3, H_4	Exists	$x_1 = 0, x_2 = 0, x_3 = 200$	Yes	600.00
H_1, H_3, H_5	Exists	$x_1 = 0, x_2 = 500, x_3 = 0$	No, outside χ_3	—
H_1, H_4, H_5	Exists	$x_1 = 100, x_2 = 0, x_3 = 0$	Yes	500.00
H_2, H_3, H_4	Exists	$x_1 = 0, x_2 = 0, x_3 = 200$	Yes	600.00
H_2, H_3, H_5	Exists	$x_1 = 0, x_2 = 100, x_3 = 0$	Yes	700.00
H_2, H_4, H_5	Exists	$x_1 = 1000, x_2 = 0, x_3 = 0$	No, outside χ_3	—
H_3, H_4, H_5	Exists	$x_1 = 0, x_2 = 0, x_3 = 0$	Yes	0.00

QUADRATIC FORMS

In the next two chapters we shall deal with the problem of finding the maximum or minimum of a continuous function of one or more variables. The objective of problems of this nature is to define the value of each variable so that the function achieves either its maximum or minimum at that combination of values. In our attempt to identify the minimum or maximum of continuous functions, we first shall evaluate the first partial derivative of the funciton with respect to each variable and set each partial derivative equal to zero. For continuous functions of n variables, setting each of the n first partial derivatives equal to zero leads to a system of n simultaneous equations in n unknowns. If one or more solutions to this set of equations exists, then the points or vectors associated with the set of solutions are called stationary points and represent points at which a maximum or minimum for the function may exist. Having identified a set of points which are candidates for a maximum or minimum for the function, one problem will be to determine which represents the maximum or minimum, if any.

In Chapter 3 we shall show that a continuous function of several variables can be represented as a quadratic form, the subject of this section, in an ϵ neighborhood of any point for which the function is defined for sufficiently small $\epsilon > 0$. By examining the quadratic form in the ϵ neighborhood of each stationary point, we shall obtain information which will assist us in identifying the maximum or minimum for the function.

Undoubtedly quadratic forms have their most important applications in the area of optimization. However, quadratic forms also have important applications in the statistical analysis of data, particularly in the analysis of variance and regression analysis.

A quadratic form q may be defined by

$$q = \mathbf{x}^T A \mathbf{x} \tag{2.102}$$

where

$$\mathbf{x} = \begin{bmatrix} x_1 \\ x_2 \\ \vdots \\ x_n \end{bmatrix}, \qquad A = \begin{bmatrix} a_{11} & a_{12} & \cdots & a_{1n} \\ a_{12} & a_{22} & \cdots & a_{2n} \\ \vdots & \vdots & & \vdots \\ a_{1n} & a_{2n} & \cdots & a_{nn} \end{bmatrix}$$

Here A is a symmetric matrix referred to as the *matrix of the quadratic form*. Expansion of Eq. (2.102) leads to a quadratic equation of the form

$$\begin{aligned} q &= \sum_{i=1}^{n} \sum_{j=1}^{n} a_{ij} x_i x_j \\ &= \sum_{i=1}^{n} a_{ii} x_i^2 + 2 \sum_{i=1}^{n-1} \sum_{j=i+1}^{n} a_{ij} x_i x_j \end{aligned} \tag{2.103}$$

Let A_i be the *submatrix* of matrix A defined by

$$A_i = \begin{bmatrix} a_{11} & a_{12} & \cdots & a_{1i} \\ a_{12} & a_{22} & \cdots & a_{2i} \\ \vdots & \vdots & & \vdots \\ a_{1i} & a_{2i} & \cdots & a_{ii} \end{bmatrix} \tag{2.104}$$

$|A_i|$ is called the *ith leading principal minor of A*. Any quadratic form q can be expressed as

$$q = \sum_{i=1}^{n} \frac{|A_i|}{|A_{i-1}|} z_i^2 \tag{2.105}$$

where $|A_0| = 1$ and z_i is a function of $x_1, x_2, \ldots, x_n$. That is, a quadratic form such as that given in Eq. (2.103) can be expressed as a sum of squares of the form in Eq. (2.105) by an appropriate transformation. This transformation is based upon successive completion of squares and is illustrated in the following example.

Example 2.35   Reduce the quadratic form

$$q = 2x_1^2 - x_1 x_2 + x_2^2$$

to a sum of squares.

Let

$$q = 2\left[x_1^2 - (1/2)x_1 x_2 \right] + x_2^2$$

Completing the square in the term in square brackets we have

$$q = 2\left[x_1^2 - (1/2)x_1 x_2 + (1/16)x_2^2 \right] - (1/8)x_2^2 + x_2^2$$

$$= 2\left[x_1 - (1/4)x_2 \right]^2 + (7/8)x_2^2$$

Let

$$z_1 = x_1 - (1/4)x_2, \qquad z_2 = x_2$$

Then

$$q = 2z_1^2 + (7/8)z_2^2 \quad \blacksquare$$

Example 2.36   Express the quadratic form in Example 2.35 as a sum of squares using the relationship in Eq. (2.105).

The matrix of the quadratic form in Example 2.35 is

$$A = \begin{bmatrix} 2 & -1/2 \\ -1/2 & 1 \end{bmatrix}$$

Now $A_1 = 2$ and $|A_1| = 2$. $|A_2|$ is given by

$$|A_2| = (2)(1) - (-1/2)(-1/2) = 2 - (1/4) = 7/4$$

Then

$$q = (|A_1|/|A_0|)z_1^2 + (|A_2|/|A_1|)z_2^2 = 2z_1^2 + (7/8)z_2^2 \quad \blacksquare$$

A quadratic form $\mathbf{x}^T A \mathbf{x}$ is said to be *positive definite* if and only if $\mathbf{x}^T A \mathbf{x} > 0$ for all $\mathbf{x} \neq \emptyset$. $\mathbf{x}^T A \mathbf{x}$ is *negative definite* if and only if $\mathbf{x}^T A \mathbf{x} < 0$ for all $\mathbf{x} \neq \emptyset$. $\mathbf{x}^T A \mathbf{x}$ is *positive semidefinite* if and only if $\mathbf{x}^T A \mathbf{x} \geqslant 0$ for all $\mathbf{x} \neq \emptyset$ and $\mathbf{x}^T A \mathbf{x} = 0$ for some $\mathbf{x} \neq \emptyset$ and *negative semidefinite* if and only if $\mathbf{x}^T A \mathbf{x} \leqslant 0$ for all $\mathbf{x} \neq \emptyset$ and $\mathbf{x}^T A \mathbf{x} = 0$ for some $\mathbf{x} \neq \emptyset$. Finally, $\mathbf{x}^T A \mathbf{x}$ is *indefinite* if $\mathbf{x}^T A \mathbf{x} < 0$ for some $\mathbf{x} \neq \emptyset$ and $\mathbf{x}^T A \mathbf{x} > 0$ for other $\mathbf{x} \neq \emptyset$.

Leading Principal Minor Test

The leading principal minors of the matrix of a quadratic from can be used to determine whether the quadratic form is positive definite, negative definite, or indefinite; although semidefiniteness cannot be determined in this manner. Recalling that q may be expressed as

$$q = \sum_{i=1}^{n} \frac{|A_i|}{|A_{i-1}|} z_i^2 = \sum_{i=1}^{n} \sum_{j=1}^{n} a_{ij} x_i x_j$$

if $|A_i| > 0$ for all i, then q must be positive for all vectors $\mathbf{z}$, where

$$\mathbf{z} = \begin{bmatrix} z_1 \\ z_2 \\ \vdots \\ z_n \end{bmatrix}$$

However, associated with every vector $\mathbf{z} \neq 0$ is a vector $\mathbf{x} \neq 0$, and associated with every vector $\mathbf{x} \neq 0$ is a vector $\mathbf{z} \neq 0$. Hence if $q > 0$ for all $\mathbf{z}$, then $q > 0$ for all $\mathbf{x}$ and q is positive definite.

If $|A_i|$ alternate in sign so that $|A_1| < 0$, $|A_2| > 0$, $|A_3| < 0, \dots$, then $q < 0$. Hence q is negative definite if and only if $|A_i| < 0$ for odd i and $|A_i| > 0$ for even i. If $|A_i| \neq 0$ for all i and $|A_i|/|A_{i-1}| < 0$ for some i and $|A_j|/|A_{j-1}| > 0$ for some j, then q is indefinite.

Example 2.37   Determine whether the following quadratic forms are positive definite, negative definite, or indefinite:

(a) $q = x_1^2 - 2x_1 x_2 - 4x_2^2 + 8x_1 x_3 + 3x_3^2$;
(b) $q = -2x_1^2 - 4x_2^2 - 2x_1 x_3 + 2x_2 x_3 - 2x_3^2$;
(c) $q = x_1^2 - 2x_1 x_2 + x_2^2 + 2x_1 x_3 + 3x_3^2$.

In part (a) the matrix of the quadratic form is defined by

$$A = \begin{bmatrix} 1 & -1 & 4 \\ -1 & -4 & 0 \\ 4 & 0 & 3 \end{bmatrix}$$

The leading principal minors of A are given by

$$|A_1| = 1, \qquad |A_2| = -5, \qquad |A_3| = 49$$

Since $|A_1|/|A_0| > 0$ and $|A_2|/|A_1| < 0$, q is indefinite. The matrix of the quadratic form in part (b) is

$$A = \begin{bmatrix} -2 & 0 & -1 \\ 0 & -4 & 1 \\ -1 & 1 & -2 \end{bmatrix}$$

and the leading principal minors of A are

$$|A_1| = -2, \qquad |A_2| = 8, \qquad |A_3| = -10$$

Since the leading principal minors alternate in sign starting with a negative, the quadratic form is negative definite. The matrix of the quadratic form in part (c) is

$$A = \begin{bmatrix} 1 & -1 & 1 \\ -1 & 1 & 0 \\ 1 & 0 & 3 \end{bmatrix}$$

The leading principal minors of A are given by

$$|A_1| = 1, \qquad |A_2| = 0, \qquad |A_3| = -1$$

Since $|A_2| = 0$, the leading principal minors do not tell us anything about the definiteness of q. ∎

Example 2.38   Show that if $|A_i| \geqslant 0$ for all i but $|A_i| = 0$ for at least one value of i, we cannot conclude that the quadratic form $\mathbf{x}^T A \mathbf{x}$ is positive semidefinite.

Let

$$q = -x_2^2 + 4x_1 x_3 + 6x_2 x_3 + 4x_3^2$$

The matrix of this quadratic form is given by

$$A = \begin{bmatrix} 0 & 0 & 2 \\ 0 & -1 & 3 \\ 2 & 3 & 4 \end{bmatrix}$$

where

$$|A_1| = 0, \qquad |A_2| = 0, \qquad |A_3| = 4$$

Thus $|A_i| \geqslant 0$ for all i. However, for

$$\mathbf{x} = \begin{bmatrix} 0 \\ 1 \\ 0 \end{bmatrix}$$

$q = -1$, while for

$$\mathbf{x} = \begin{bmatrix} 0 \\ 1 \\ 1 \end{bmatrix}$$

$q = 9$. Hence q is indefinite, and the fact that $|A_i| \geqslant 0$ does not lead us to the conclusion that q is positive semidefinite. ∎

As illustrated in the preceding examples, an analysis of the leading principal minors of the matrix of the quadratic form provides the analyst with a tool for determining whether the form is positive or negative definite.

In addition, if each leading principal minor is nonzero, this analysis may also be used to determine whether the matrix is indefinite or not. However, if $|A_i| = 0$ for some i, we may only conclude that the quadratic form is neither positive nor negative definite. In the latter case the quadratic form may be positive semidefinite, negative semidefinite, or indefinite. The significance of the definiteness of a quadratic form will become fully apparent in succeeding chapters dealing with optimization of functions of several continuous variables.

Example 2.39 The following equation has been developed as an approximation to the cost $C(\mathbf{x})$ of production per unit when x_1, x_2, x_3, and x_4 units of products A, B, C, and D, respectively, are manufactured. The estimating equation

$$C(\mathbf{x}) = 40x_1^2 - 20x_1x_2 + 60x_2^2 + 34x_3^2 - 28x_1x_3 - 22x_2x_3$$
$$+ 104x_4^2 - 38x_1x_4 - 20x_3x_4$$

seems to represent the cost of production per unit fairly well for values of x_1, x_2, x_3, and x_4 observed in the past. However, since cost cannot be negative for positive values of x_i, $i = 1, 2, 3, 4$, the equation must be tested to see whether this condition is satisfied. Determine whether the approximating equation will generate negative values of cost for any positive values of x_i, $i = 1, 2, 3, 4$.

The cost model $C(\mathbf{x})$ is a quadratic form. If the matrix of the quadratic form is positive definite, then $C(\mathbf{x}) > 0$ for both negative and positive values of x_i, $i = 1, 2, 3, 4$, and is therefore positive for all nonnegative values of x_i. The matrix of the quadratic form is given by

$$A = \begin{bmatrix} 40 & -10 & -14 & -19 \\ -10 & 60 & -11 & 0 \\ -14 & -11 & 34 & -10 \\ -19 & 0 & -10 & 104 \end{bmatrix}$$

and the leading principal minors of A are

$$|A_1| = 40, \qquad |A_2| = 2{,}300, \qquad |A_3| = 58{,}520, \qquad |A_4| = 4{,}802{,}321.$$

Since $|A_i| > 0$ for all i, $C(\mathbf{x})$ is positive definite and therefore assumes positive values for every nonzero choice of x_1, x_2, x_3, and x_4 and therefore for all nonnegative values. ∎

Eigenvalues

The tests for definiteness presented in the preceding section proved conclusive only when $|A_i| \neq 0$ for all i. Specifically, if $|A_i| = 0$, the test for definiteness leads to the conclusion that the quadratic form is either negative semidefinite, positive semidefinite, or indefinite, but does not reveal which of these is the case. This problem can be resolved by evaluating the eigenvalues of the matrix of the quadratic form. That is, the eigenvalue test will completely specify the definiteness of the quadratic form. While the eigenvalue test may be considered a more complete test for definiteness of a quadratic form than the leading principal minor test, it is more tedious from a computational point of view and is often employed only when the leading principal minor test is inconclusive.

Let A be a symmetric matrix of order n, $\mathbf{x}$ an n-dimensional vector, and λ a scalar such that

$$A\mathbf{x} = \lambda\mathbf{x} \tag{2.106}$$

for some $\mathbf{x} \neq \varnothing$. Each vector $\mathbf{x}$ satisfying Eq. (2.106) is called an *eigenvector* and the associated scalar λ an *eigenvalue*. Eigenvectors are often referred to as characteristic vectors, latent vectors, or invariant vectors, while eigenvalues are also called characteristic roots or latent roots. Equation (2.106) may be expressed as

$$(\lambda I - A)\mathbf{x} = \varnothing \tag{2.107}$$

where I is the identity matrix. The solution vector for Eq. (2.107) is nonzero if and only if

$$|\lambda I - A| = 0 \tag{2.108}$$

Evaluation of $|\lambda I - A|$ yields an nth-degree polynomial in λ called the *characteristic equation* of A. Solution of the characteristic equation for λ leads to the n eigenvalues for the matrix A.

Example 2.40   Find the eigenvalues for the matrix A given by

$$A = \begin{bmatrix} 4 & 0 & -1 \\ 0 & 2 & 0 \\ -1 & 0 & 4 \end{bmatrix}$$

The characteristic equation of A is

$$|\lambda I - A| = 0$$

where

$$|\lambda I - A| = \begin{vmatrix} \lambda - 4 & 0 & 1 \\ 0 & \lambda - 2 & 0 \\ 1 & 0 & \lambda - 4 \end{vmatrix}$$

$$= (\lambda - 4)^2(\lambda - 2) - (\lambda - 2) = (\lambda - 2)\left[(\lambda - 4)^2 - 1\right]$$

Letting λ_1, λ_2, and λ_3 be the solutions for the third-degree polynomial in λ $|\lambda I - A| = 0$, we have

$$\lambda_1 = 2, \qquad \lambda_2 = 3, \qquad \lambda_3 = 5 \quad \blacksquare$$

Associated with the n eigenvalues for the symmetric matrix A of order n is a set of n distinct eigenvectors. The set of eigenvalues for a symmetric matrix need not be distinct. If A is a symmetric matrix of order n with $k < n$ identical eigenvalues, then that eigenvalue is said to be of *multiplicity* k. If a particular eigenvalue has multiplicity k, then there are k distinct eigenvectors associated with that eigenvalue. Whether the set of eigenvalues is distinct or not, the associated eigenvectors form a mutually orthogonal set. This result may be shown without difficulty for distinct eigenvalues, although proof of the more general case is beyond the scope of this text. Let λ_1 and λ_2 be two distinct eigenvalues and $\mathbf{x}_1$ and $\mathbf{x}_2$ the associated eigenvectors for the symmetric matrix A. Then

$$A\mathbf{x}_1 = \lambda_1\mathbf{x}_1 \tag{2.109}$$

and

$$A\mathbf{x}_2 = \lambda_2\mathbf{x}_2 \tag{2.110}$$

Then

$$\mathbf{x}_2^T A\mathbf{x}_1 = \lambda_1\mathbf{x}_2^T\mathbf{x}_1 \tag{2.111}$$

and

$$\mathbf{x}_1^T A\mathbf{x}_2 = \lambda_2\mathbf{x}_1^T\mathbf{x}_2 \tag{2.112}$$

But

$$\mathbf{x}_1^T A\mathbf{x}_2 = \mathbf{x}_2^T A\mathbf{x}_1 \tag{2.113}$$

Hence

$$\lambda_1\mathbf{x}_2^T\mathbf{x}_1 = \lambda_2\mathbf{x}^T\mathbf{x}_2 \tag{2.114}$$

since $\lambda_1 \neq \lambda_2$ and $\mathbf{x}_2^T\mathbf{x}_1 = \mathbf{x}_1^T\mathbf{x}_2$, Eq. (2.114) is valid only if $\mathbf{x}_1^T\mathbf{x}_2 = 0$, which implies orthogonality of $\mathbf{x}_1$ and $\mathbf{x}_2$.

Example 2.41 Find the set of mutually orthogonal set of eigenvectors for the matrix in Example 2.40.
From example 2.40,

$$A = \begin{bmatrix} 4 & 0 & -1 \\ 0 & 2 & 0 \\ -1 & 0 & 4 \end{bmatrix}$$

For $\lambda_1 = 2$ we have

$$(\lambda_1 I - A)\mathbf{x}_1 = \begin{bmatrix} -2 & 0 & 1 \\ 0 & 0 & 0 \\ 1 & 0 & -2 \end{bmatrix} \begin{bmatrix} x_{11} \\ x_{12} \\ x_{13} \end{bmatrix} = \begin{bmatrix} 0 \\ 0 \\ 0 \end{bmatrix}$$

which leads to

$$\mathbf{x}_1 = \begin{bmatrix} 0 \\ b \\ 0 \end{bmatrix}$$

For $\lambda_2 = 3$,

$$(\lambda_2 I - A)\mathbf{x}_2 = \begin{bmatrix} -1 & 0 & 1 \\ 0 & 1 & 0 \\ 1 & 0 & -1 \end{bmatrix} \begin{bmatrix} x_{21} \\ x_{22} \\ x_{23} \end{bmatrix} = \begin{bmatrix} 0 \\ 0 \\ 0 \end{bmatrix}$$

and

$$\mathbf{x}_2 = \begin{bmatrix} a \\ 0 \\ a \end{bmatrix}$$

For $\lambda_3 = 5$,

$$(\lambda_3 I - A)\mathbf{x}_3 = \begin{bmatrix} 1 & 0 & 1 \\ 0 & 3 & 0 \\ 1 & 0 & 1 \end{bmatrix} \begin{bmatrix} x_{31} \\ x_{32} \\ x_{33} \end{bmatrix} = \begin{bmatrix} 0 \\ 0 \\ 0 \end{bmatrix}$$

and

$$\mathbf{x}_3 = \begin{bmatrix} -c \\ 0 \\ c \end{bmatrix}$$

since $\mathbf{x}_1^T\mathbf{x}_2 = \mathbf{x}_1^T\mathbf{x}_3 = \mathbf{x}_2^T\mathbf{x}_3 = 0$, the eigenvectors $\mathbf{x}_1$, $\mathbf{x}_2$, and $\mathbf{x}_3$ are mutually orthogonal. ∎

Example 2.42   Find the eigenvalues and the associated set of mutually orthogonal eigenvectors for the matrix

$$A = \begin{bmatrix} 4 & 0 & -1 & 0 \\ 0 & 3 & 0 & 0 \\ -1 & 0 & 4 & 0 \\ 0 & 0 & 0 & 1 \end{bmatrix}$$

From Eq. (2.108),

$$|\lambda I - A| = \begin{vmatrix} (\lambda - 4) & 0 & 1 & 0 \\ 0 & (\lambda - 3) & 0 & 0 \\ 1 & 0 & (\lambda - 4) & 0 \\ 0 & 0 & 0 & (\lambda - 1) \end{vmatrix}$$

$$= (\lambda - 1)\big[(\lambda - 3)(\lambda - 4)^2 - (\lambda - 3)\big]$$

$$= (\lambda - 1)(\lambda - 3)\big[(\lambda - 4)^2 - 1\big] = 0$$

Thus $\lambda_1 = 1$, $\lambda_2 = 3$, $\lambda_3 = 3$, and $\lambda_4 = 5$. For $\lambda_1 = 1$,

$$(\lambda_1 I - A)\mathbf{x}_1 = \begin{bmatrix} -3 & 0 & 1 & 0 \\ 0 & -2 & 0 & 0 \\ 1 & 0 & -3 & 0 \\ 0 & 0 & 0 & 0 \end{bmatrix} \begin{bmatrix} x_1 \\ x_{12} \\ x_{13} \\ x_{14} \end{bmatrix} = \begin{bmatrix} 0 \\ 0 \\ 0 \\ 0 \end{bmatrix}$$

or

$$
\begin{aligned}
-3x_{11} \qquad\quad + x_{13} &= 0 \\
-2x_{12} \qquad\qquad &= 0 \\
x_{11}' \qquad\quad -3x_{13} &= 0
\end{aligned}
$$

and

$$\mathbf{x}_1 = \begin{bmatrix} 0 \\ 0 \\ 0 \\ a \end{bmatrix}$$

For $\lambda_2 = 3$,

$$(\lambda_2 I - A)\mathbf{x}_2 = \begin{bmatrix} -1 & 0 & 1 & 0 \\ 0 & 0 & 0 & 0 \\ 1 & 0 & -1 & 0 \\ 0 & 0 & 0 & 2 \end{bmatrix} \begin{bmatrix} x_{21} \\ x_{22} \\ x_{23} \\ x_{24} \end{bmatrix} = \begin{bmatrix} 0 \\ 0 \\ 0 \\ 0 \end{bmatrix}$$

or

$$
\begin{aligned}
-x_{21} + x_{23} &= 0 \\
x_{21} - x_{23} &= 0 \\
2x_{24} &= 0
\end{aligned}
$$

and

$$\mathbf{x}_2 = \begin{bmatrix} b \\ c \\ b \\ 0 \end{bmatrix}$$

Since $\lambda_2 = \lambda_3$, there exists an eigenvector $\mathbf{x}_3$ such that $\mathbf{x}_2^T\mathbf{x}_3 = 0$ and $(\lambda_3 I - A)\mathbf{x}_3 = \emptyset$. These two equations lead to

$$
\begin{aligned}
bx_{31} + cx_{32} + bx_{33} &= 0 \\
-x_{31} \qquad\quad + bx_{33} &= 0 \\
x_{31} \qquad\quad - x_{33} &= 0 \\
2x_{24} &= 0
\end{aligned}
$$

which leads to definition of $\mathbf{x}_2$ and $\mathbf{x}_3$ as

$$\mathbf{x}_2 = \begin{bmatrix} b \\ b \\ b \\ 0 \end{bmatrix}, \qquad \mathbf{x}_3 = \begin{bmatrix} b \\ -2b \\ b \\ 0 \end{bmatrix}$$

For $\lambda_4 = 5$,

$$(\lambda_4 I - A)\mathbf{x}_4 = \begin{bmatrix} 1 & 0 & 1 & 0 \\ 0 & 2 & 0 & 0 \\ 1 & 0 & 1 & 0 \\ 0 & 0 & 0 & 4 \end{bmatrix} \begin{bmatrix} x_{41} \\ x_{42} \\ x_{43} \\ x_{44} \end{bmatrix} = \begin{bmatrix} 0 \\ 0 \\ 0 \\ 0 \end{bmatrix}$$

or

$$\begin{aligned} x_{41} \phantom{+ x_{42}} + x_{43} &= 0 \\ 2x_{42} \phantom{+ x_{43}} &= 0 \\ x_{41} \phantom{+ x_{42}} + x_{43} &= 0 \\ 4x_{44} &= 0 \end{aligned}$$

and

$$\mathbf{x}_4 = \begin{bmatrix} d \\ 0 \\ -d \\ 0 \end{bmatrix}$$

Since $\mathbf{x}_i^T \mathbf{x}_j = 0$ for $i \neq j$ and $i, j = 1, 2, 3, 4$, the set of eigenvectors is mutually orthogonal. ∎

Examples 2.41 and 2.42 show that the set of eigenvectors corresponding to the eigenvalues for a symmetric matrix is not unique. In Example 2.42 the eigenvectors were defined by

$$\mathbf{x}_1 = \begin{bmatrix} 0 \\ 0 \\ 0 \\ a \end{bmatrix}, \qquad \mathbf{x}_2 = \begin{bmatrix} b \\ b \\ b \\ 0 \end{bmatrix}, \qquad \mathbf{x}_3 = \begin{bmatrix} b \\ -2b \\ b \\ 0 \end{bmatrix}, \qquad \mathbf{x}_4 = \begin{bmatrix} d \\ 0 \\ -d \\ 0 \end{bmatrix}$$

Since any real values for a, b, and d will satisfy these eigenvectors, there are an infinite number of sets of eigenvectors for the matrix A. A similar statement applies to symmetric matrices in general.

In the preceding section we were able to identify conditions under which a quadratic form $\mathbf{x}^T A \mathbf{x}$ could be determined to be positive definite, negative definite, or neither. We accomplished this by reducing the quadratic form to a sum of squares by

$$\mathbf{x}^T A \mathbf{x} = \sum_{i=1}^{n} \frac{|A_i|}{|A_{i-1}|} z_i^2 \tag{2.115}$$

A similar reduction can be accomplished through the use of eigenvalues. Let B be a matrix of order n with columns a mutually orthogonal set of eigenvectors for the symmetric nth order matrix A. To reduce $\mathbf{x}^T A \mathbf{x}$ to a sum of squares let

$$\mathbf{y} = B^{-1}\mathbf{x} \qquad (2.116)$$

or

$$\mathbf{x} = B\mathbf{y} \qquad (2.117)$$

Then

$$\mathbf{x}^T A \mathbf{x} = \mathbf{y}^T B^T A B \mathbf{y} \qquad (2.118)$$

Based upon Eq. (2.118), $\mathbf{x}^T A \mathbf{x}$ can be expressed as

$$\mathbf{x}^T A \mathbf{x} = \sum_{i=1}^{n} \lambda_i z_i^2 \qquad (2.119)$$

where λ_i, $i = 1, 2, \ldots, n$, are the eigenvalues for A. To demonstrate this result let μ_i, $i = 1, 2, \ldots, n$, be the eigenvectors for A. Then

$$B = \begin{bmatrix} \mu_1, \mu_2, \ldots, \mu_n \end{bmatrix} \qquad (2.120)$$

Now

$$AB = \begin{bmatrix} A\mu_1, A\mu_2, \ldots, A\mu_n \end{bmatrix}$$

where $A\mu_i$ is a column vector. Since μ_i is an eigenvector for A,

$$A\mu_i = \lambda_i \mu_i \qquad (2.121)$$

and

$$AB = \begin{bmatrix} \lambda_1 \mu_1, \lambda_2 \mu_2, \ldots, \lambda_n \mu_n \end{bmatrix} \qquad (2.122)$$

Thus

$$B^T A B = \begin{bmatrix} \mu_1^T \\ \mu_2^T \\ \vdots \\ \mu_n^T \end{bmatrix} \begin{bmatrix} \lambda_1 \mu_1, \lambda_2 \mu_2, \ldots, \lambda_n \mu_n \end{bmatrix}$$

$$= \begin{bmatrix} \lambda_1 \mu_1^T \mu_1 & 0 & 0 \\ 0 & \lambda_2 \mu_2^T \mu_2 & 0 \\ \vdots & \vdots & \vdots \\ 0 & 0 & \lambda_n \mu_n^T \mu_n \end{bmatrix} \qquad (2.123)$$

where μ_i^T is a row vector. It should be noted that $B^T A B$ is composed of elements $\lambda_i \mu_j^T \mu_i$. But since μ_j and μ_i are eigenvectors for A, they are orthogonal and $\mu_j^T \mu_i = 0$ for $i \neq j$ and $\mu_i^T \mu_i \neq 0$. Finally,

$$\mathbf{x}^T A \mathbf{x} = \mathbf{y}^T B^T A B \mathbf{y} = \sum_{i=1}^{n} \lambda_i \mu_i^T \mu_i y_i^2 = \sum_{i=1}^{n} \lambda_i z_i^2 \qquad (2.124)$$

letting $z_i = \sqrt{\mu_i^T \mu_i}\, y_i$.

From Eq. (2.124) it follows that for $\mathbf{x} \neq \emptyset$

(1) $\mathbf{x}^T A \mathbf{x}$ is positive definite if $\lambda_i > 0$, $i = 1, 2, \ldots, n$,
(2) $\mathbf{x}^T A \mathbf{x}$ is negative definite if $\lambda_i < 0$, $i = 1, 2, \ldots, n$,
(3) $\mathbf{x}^T A \mathbf{x}$ is positive semidefinite if $\lambda_i \geq 0$, $i = 1, 2, \ldots, n$ and $\lambda_i = 0$ for at least one but not all i,
(4) $\mathbf{x}^T A \mathbf{x}$ is negative semidefinite if $\lambda_i \leq 0$, $i = 1, 2, \ldots, n$ and $\lambda_i = 0$ for at least one but not all i,
(5) $\mathbf{x}^T A \mathbf{x}$ is indefinite if $\lambda_i < 0$ for some i and $\lambda_j > 0$ for some j, $i, j = 1, 2, \ldots, n$.

Example 2.43   Show that the quadratic form defined by the matrix A is indefinite using the eigenvalue test

$$A = \begin{bmatrix} -4 & 0 & 0 \\ 0 & -1 & 2 \\ 0 & 2 & -2 \end{bmatrix}$$

The eigenvalues for A are defined by

$$|\lambda I - A| = \begin{vmatrix} (\lambda + 4) & 0 & 0 \\ 0 & (\lambda + 1) & -2 \\ 0 & -2 & (\lambda + 2) \end{vmatrix}$$

$$= (\lambda + 4)(\lambda + 1)(\lambda + 2) - 4(\lambda + 4) = (\lambda + 4)\big[(\lambda + 1)(\lambda + 2) - 4\big]$$

The eigenvalues for A are then

$$\lambda_1 = -4, \qquad \lambda_2 = \frac{-3 - \sqrt{17}}{2}, \qquad \lambda_3 = \frac{-3 + \sqrt{17}}{2}$$

Since $\lambda_1 < 0$, $\lambda_2 < 0$, $\lambda_3 > 0$, the quadratic form $\mathbf{x}^T A \mathbf{x}$ is indefinite. ∎

The eigenvalue test is completely conclusive in identifying the definiteness of a quadratic form. In the preceding section the leading principal minor test provided necessary and sufficient conditions for positive and negative definiteness but failed to lead to a conclusion if $|A_i| = 0$ for any i. When $|A_i| = 0$ for some i, the quadratic form could be positive, negative semidefinite, or indefinite. By examining the eigenvalues of A, however, we are able to determine semidefiniteness or indefiniteness in all cases of their occurrence. Thus if the analyst is interested only in whether the quadratic form is positive definite or negative definite, the leading principle minor test is adequate and may be preferred because of its simplicity. If specification of definiteness of a quadratic form is to be determined, whether definite, semidefinite or indefinite, the analyst may wish to use the eigenvalue test directly or apply the eigenvalue test if the leading principal minor test fails to lead to a conclusion.

SUMMARY

The purpose of this chapter was to introduce the reader to the elementary concepts of matrices, vectors, vector spaces, convex spaces, and quadratic forms. The elements of matrices, vectors, and quadratic forms will be used in Chapters 3 and 4. Vector spaces and convex spaces are important foundations of mathematical programming and will be referred to further in Chapter 7. Each concept presented has been accompanied by an interpretive discussion and illustrated by example. The application of the topics treated to practical problem solution has been demonstrated to a limited extent.

In this chapter, as in those which follow, we have not attempted to approach the subject matter in a rigorous theorem–proof manner. For a more rigorous and exhaustive discussion of matrices and linear algebra the reader should see the references at the end of this chapter.

PROBLEMS

1. Find the sum $A + B$ and products AB and BA, where

$$A = \begin{bmatrix} 4 & 1 & 3 \\ 2 & 0 & 0 \\ 1 & 2 & 1 \end{bmatrix}, \qquad B = \begin{bmatrix} 0 & 1 & 8 \\ 2 & 0 & 4 \\ 1 & 0 & 1 \end{bmatrix}$$

2. Let

$$A = \begin{bmatrix} 1 & 4 & 2 \\ 3 & 1 & 4 \\ 2 & 1 & 6 \end{bmatrix}, \qquad B = \begin{bmatrix} 1 \\ 4 \\ 1 \end{bmatrix}, \qquad C = \begin{bmatrix} 2 & 2 \\ 4 & 1 \\ 0 & 1 \end{bmatrix}$$

Evaluate those products AB, BA, AC, CA, BC, and CB which are defined.

3. Evaluate the determinants of the matrices in Problem 1.

4. Using the cofactor method evaluate the determinants of the following matrices:

$$A = \begin{bmatrix} 1 & 0 & 4 & 1 \\ 2 & 8 & 2 & 2 \\ 3 & 1 & 0 & 0 \\ 0 & 0 & 1 & 1 \end{bmatrix}, \qquad B = \begin{bmatrix} 1 & 2 & 1 & 1 \\ 3 & 6 & 4 & 5 \\ 2 & 2 & 2 & 2 \\ 8 & 5 & 2 & 3 \end{bmatrix}$$

5. By counterexample show that $|A \pm B|$ is not necessarily equal to $|A| \pm |B|$.

6. Find the inverse of each of the matrices in Problem 1.
7. Find the inverse of each nonsingular matrix in Problem 4.
8. Determine the length of the following vectors:

$$\mathbf{x}_1 = \begin{bmatrix} 0 \\ 1 \\ 4 \end{bmatrix}, \qquad \mathbf{x}_2 = \begin{bmatrix} 0 \\ 1 \\ 2 \\ 5 \end{bmatrix}, \qquad \mathbf{x}_3 = \begin{bmatrix} 1 \\ 2 \\ 8 \\ 7 \\ 7 \end{bmatrix}$$

9. Given the following vectors, find the distance between $\mathbf{x}_1$ and $\mathbf{x}_2$ and between $\mathbf{x}_3$ and $\mathbf{x}_4$:

$$\mathbf{x}_1 = \begin{bmatrix} 3 \\ 2 \\ 1 \end{bmatrix}, \qquad \mathbf{x}_2 = \begin{bmatrix} 1 \\ 1 \\ 0 \end{bmatrix}, \qquad \mathbf{x}_3 = \begin{bmatrix} 1 \\ 4 \\ 6 \\ 3 \end{bmatrix}, \qquad \mathbf{x}_4 = \begin{bmatrix} 1 \\ 7 \\ 7 \\ 9 \end{bmatrix}$$

10. In Problem 9 are $\mathbf{x}_1$ and $\mathbf{x}_2$ orthogonal?
11. Determine whether or not the following vectors form a mutually orthogonal set:

$$\mathbf{x}_1 = \begin{bmatrix} 1 \\ 0 \\ -1 \end{bmatrix}, \qquad \mathbf{x}_2 = \begin{bmatrix} 0 \\ 4 \\ 0 \end{bmatrix}, \qquad \mathbf{x}_3 = \begin{bmatrix} -4 \\ 0 \\ 4 \end{bmatrix}$$

12. Determine whether or not the following vectors form a mutually orthogonal set:

$$\mathbf{x}_1 = \begin{bmatrix} -1 \\ 1 \\ -1 \\ 1 \end{bmatrix}, \qquad \mathbf{x}_2 = \begin{bmatrix} 1 \\ 1 \\ -1 \\ -1 \end{bmatrix}, \qquad \mathbf{x}_3 = \begin{bmatrix} -1 \\ 1 \\ 1 \\ -1 \end{bmatrix}, \qquad \mathbf{x}_4 = \begin{bmatrix} 1 \\ 1 \\ 1 \\ 1 \end{bmatrix}$$

13. Determine whether or not the vectors in Problem 11 are linearly independent.
14. Determine whether or not the vectors $\mathbf{x}_1$, $\mathbf{x}_2$, and $\mathbf{x}_3$ are linearly independent:

$$\mathbf{x}_1 = \begin{bmatrix} 9 \\ 0 \\ 2 \end{bmatrix}, \qquad \mathbf{x}_2 = \begin{bmatrix} 1 \\ 1 \\ 0 \end{bmatrix}, \qquad \mathbf{x}_3 = \begin{bmatrix} 2 \\ 0 \\ 3 \end{bmatrix}$$

15. Determine whether or not the vectors $\mathbf{x}_1$, $\mathbf{x}_2$, $\mathbf{x}_3$, and $\mathbf{x}_4$ are linearly independent:

$$\mathbf{x}_1 = \begin{bmatrix} 4 \\ 0 \\ 2 \\ 0 \end{bmatrix}, \qquad \mathbf{x}_2 = \begin{bmatrix} 0 \\ -1 \\ 0 \\ 0 \end{bmatrix}, \qquad \mathbf{x}_3 = \begin{bmatrix} 2 \\ 0 \\ 3 \\ 0 \end{bmatrix}, \qquad \mathbf{x}_4 = \begin{bmatrix} 0 \\ 0 \\ 0 \\ 4 \end{bmatrix}$$

16. Do the vectors in Problem 15 form a mutually orthogonal set?
17. The space χ_3 includes all vectors $\mathbf{x}$ such that

$$\mathbf{x} = \begin{bmatrix} a \\ 0 \\ b \end{bmatrix}$$

where a and b are any real numbers. Is χ_3 a vector space?
18. The space χ_4 includes all vectors $\mathbf{x}$ such that

$$\mathbf{x} = \begin{bmatrix} a \\ b \\ c \\ d \end{bmatrix}$$

where a, b, c, and d are any real numbers such that $b \neq 0$. Is χ_4 a vector space?

19. Define the space spanned by the vectors

$$\mathbf{x}_1 = \begin{bmatrix} 2 \\ 3 \\ 1 \end{bmatrix}, \qquad \mathbf{x}_2 = \begin{bmatrix} 0 \\ 0 \\ 1 \end{bmatrix}$$

20. Define the space spanned by the vectors

$$\mathbf{x}_1 = \begin{bmatrix} 2 \\ 0 \\ 0 \\ 2 \end{bmatrix}, \qquad \mathbf{x}_2 = \begin{bmatrix} 0 \\ 3 \\ 3 \\ 0 \end{bmatrix}$$

21. Do the vectors in Problem 19 span 3-dimensional Euclidean space?
22. Do the vectors in Problem 20 span 4-dimensional Euclidean space?
23. Do the vectors in Problem 12 span 4-dimensional Euclidean space?
24. Are the vectors in Problem 12 a basis for 4-dimensional Euclidean space?
25. Using the rank method determine the number of vectors in the set in Problem 11 which are linearly independent.
26. Using the rank method determine the number of vectors in the set in Problem 12 which are linearly independent.
27. Using the rank method determine the number of vectors in the set in Problem 15 which are linearly independent.
28. Let $\mathbf{x}_1, \mathbf{x}_2, \ldots, \mathbf{x}_{n-1}$ be a set of mutually orthogonal n-dimensional nonzero vectors. If $\mathbf{y}_1$ and $\mathbf{y}_2$ are nonzero n-dimensional vectors which are both orthogonal to $\mathbf{x}_1$, $\mathbf{x}_2, \ldots, \mathbf{x}_{n-1}$, show that $\mathbf{y}_2$ is a scalar multiple of $\mathbf{y}_1$.
29. Show that any set of m n-dimensional vectors, $m < n$, spans a subspace of n-dimensional Euclidean space.
30. Do the vectors $\mathbf{x}_1$, $\mathbf{x}_2$, and $\mathbf{x}_3$ span 2-dimensional Euclidean space?

$$\mathbf{x}_1 = \begin{bmatrix} 0 \\ 1 \end{bmatrix}, \qquad \mathbf{x}_2 = \begin{bmatrix} 2 \\ 2 \end{bmatrix}, \qquad \mathbf{x}_3 = \begin{bmatrix} 3 \\ 2 \end{bmatrix}$$

31. In Problem 30 are $\mathbf{x}_1$ and $\mathbf{x}_2$ a basis for 2-dimensional Euclidean space?
32. Are the following vectors a basis for 4-dimensional Euclidean space?

$$\mathbf{x}_1 = \begin{bmatrix} 3 \\ 1 \\ 2 \\ 0 \end{bmatrix}, \quad \mathbf{x}_2 = \begin{bmatrix} 2 \\ 1 \\ 1 \\ 0 \end{bmatrix}, \quad \mathbf{x}_3 = \begin{bmatrix} 1 \\ 1 \\ 1 \\ 0 \end{bmatrix}, \quad \mathbf{x}_4 = \begin{bmatrix} 0 \\ 0 \\ 0 \\ 1 \end{bmatrix}$$

33. Let $\mathbf{y} = A\mathbf{x}$. Is the transformation one-to-one if

$$A = \begin{bmatrix} 1 & 0 & 2 \\ 0 & 2 & 0 \\ 2 & 0 & 1 \end{bmatrix}$$

34. Given the following transformation matrices, which define one-to-one transformations?

$$A = \begin{bmatrix} 2 & 1 & 1 & 1 \\ 0 & 1 & 2 & 4 \\ 0 & 1 & 5 & 1 \\ 2 & 2 & 1 & 0 \end{bmatrix}, \quad B = \begin{bmatrix} 0 & 0 & 1 & 2 \\ 1 & 1 & 1 & 1 \\ 0 & 1 & 4 & 2 \end{bmatrix}$$

$$C = \begin{bmatrix} 1 & 1 \\ 0 & 1 \\ 3 & 2 \end{bmatrix}, \quad D = \begin{bmatrix} 4 & 2 & 1 \\ 1 & 3 & 1 \\ 9 & 7 & 3 \end{bmatrix}$$

35. In Problem 34 define the vector space generated by each transformation matrix by defining those vectors which span the space.

36. For the transformation matrices given in Problem 34 define the dimension of the vectors generated and the subspace of Euclidean space to which the generated vectors are restricted.

37. Find the values of x_1, x_2, and x_3 which satisfy the following system of simultaneous linear equations:

$$
\begin{aligned}
x_1 \quad\quad + 2x_3 &= 1 \\
2x_2 \quad\quad &= 1 \\
2x_1 \quad\quad + x_3 &= 1
\end{aligned}
$$

38. Solve the following system of simultaneous linear equations:

$$
\begin{aligned}
2x_1 + x_2 + x_3 + x_4 &= 4 \\
x_2 + 2x_3 + 4x_4 &= 3 \\
x_2 + 5x_3 + x_4 &= 2 \\
2x_1 + 2x_2 + x_3 \quad &= 1
\end{aligned}
$$

39. Find the solution to the following system of simultaneous linear equations if it exists:

$$
\begin{aligned}
x_1 + 3x_2 + 4x_3 &= 2 \\
3x_1 + 9x_2 + 12x_3 &= 6 \\
18x_1 + 54x_2 + 72x_3 &= 36
\end{aligned}
$$

If a unique solution does not exist, determine whether no solution exists or an infinite number of solutions exist.

40. How many solutions exist for the set of simultaneous linear equations

$$A\mathbf{x} = \mathbf{b}$$

where A is as defined in Problem 34 and

$$
\mathbf{b} = \begin{bmatrix} 1 \\ 0 \\ 0 \\ 2 \end{bmatrix}
$$

41. How many solutions exist for the set of simultaneous linear equations

$$D\mathbf{x} = \mathbf{b}$$

where D is as defined in Problem 34 and

$$
\mathbf{b} = \begin{bmatrix} 2 \\ 1 \\ 2 \end{bmatrix}
$$

42. Let

$$
\mathbf{x}_1 = \begin{bmatrix} 2 \\ 1 \\ 3 \end{bmatrix}, \qquad \mathbf{x}_2 = \begin{bmatrix} 3 \\ 1 \\ 4 \end{bmatrix}
$$

Graphically define all convex combinations of $\mathbf{x}_1$ and $\mathbf{x}_2$.

43. Let

$$
\mathbf{x}_1 = \begin{bmatrix} 2 \\ 1 \\ 3 \end{bmatrix}, \qquad \mathbf{x}_2 = \begin{bmatrix} 4 \\ 1 \\ 4 \end{bmatrix}, \qquad \mathbf{x}_3 = \begin{bmatrix} 0 \\ 0 \\ 8 \end{bmatrix}
$$

Graphically define all convex combinations of $\mathbf{x}_1$, $\mathbf{x}_2$, and $\mathbf{x}_3$. Is the space defined a vector space?

44. Can a convex space ever be a vector space? Give an example.

45. Graph the convex space defined by the half-spaces

$$x_1 + x_2 \leqslant 20$$
$$x_1 + x_2 \geqslant 4$$
$$x_1 \geqslant 0$$
$$x_2 \geqslant 0$$

46. Graph the convex space defined by

$$x_1 + x_2 + x_3 \leqslant 30$$
$$x_1 \qquad + x_3 \geqslant 10$$
$$x_2 + x_3 \geqslant 10$$
$$x_1 + x_2 \qquad \geqslant 10$$
$$x_1 \geqslant 0$$
$$x_2 \geqslant 0$$
$$x_3 \geqslant 0$$

47. Determine whether the space defined by

$$x_1 + x_2 \geqslant 15$$
$$3x_1 + x_2 \leqslant 6$$
$$x_2 \geqslant 0$$

is convex.

48. Define the extreme points of the convex space in (a) Problem 45, (b) Problem 46.

49. Solve the following linear programming problems:

(a)

$$4x_1 + x_2 = \max$$

s.t.

$$x_1 + 3x_2 \leqslant 100$$
$$x_1, x_2 \geqslant 0$$

(b)

$$2x_1 + x_2 + 4x_3 = \max$$

s.t.
$$4x_1 + 5x_2 + 10x_3 \leqslant 100$$
$$10x_1 + 4x_2 + 40x_3 \leqslant 200$$
$$x_1, x_2, x_3 \geqslant 0$$

(c)

$$3x_1 + 3x_2 + 3x_3 = \min$$

s.t.
$$x_1 + x_2 + x_3 \leqslant 30$$
$$x_1 + x_2 \qquad \geqslant 10$$
$$x_1 \qquad + x_3 \geqslant 10$$
$$x_2 + x_3 \geqslant 10$$
$$x_1, x_2, x_3 \geqslant 0$$

(d)

$$3x_1 + 2x_2 + R_3 + x_4 = \min$$

s.t.

$$
\begin{aligned}
x_1 + x_2 + x_3 &\geqslant 20 \\
x_1 + x_3 + x_4 &\geqslant 20 \\
x_1 + x_2 + x_3 + x_4 &\leqslant 100 \\
x_1, x_2, x_3, x_4 &\geqslant 0
\end{aligned}
$$

50. Define the matrices of the following quadratic forms:
  (a) $\mathbf{x}^T A \mathbf{x} = 2x_1^2 + x_1 x_2 + x_2^2$;
  (b) $\mathbf{x}^T A \mathbf{x} = x_1^2 + x_2^2 + x_3^2 + x_4^2$;
  (c) $\mathbf{x}^T A \mathbf{x} = 2x_1^2 + x_2^2 + 3x_3^2 + 4x_1 x_3$;
  (d) $\mathbf{x}^T A \mathbf{x} = 2x_1 x_2 + 2x_1 x_3 + x_2^2 + 4x_2 x_3$;
  (e) $\mathbf{x}^T A \mathbf{x} = 4x_1^2 + 2x_2^2 + 4x_3^2 + x_1 x_3$.
51. Determine whether any of the quadratic forms in Problem 51 is positive definite or negative definite using the leading principal minor test.
52. Determine whether or not the following quadratic forms are positive definite, negative definite, or indefinite using the leading principal minor test:
  (a) $q = x_1^2 + 2x_1 x_2 + 2x_2^2 + 3x_3^2$;
  (b) $q = 4x_1^2 - x_2^2 + 4x_1 x_3 + 3x_3^2$;
  (c) $q = 9x_1^2 + x_2^2 + 4x_1 x_3 + 3x_3^2$.
53. Express each of the quadratic forms in Problem 52 as a sum of squares.
54. Find the eigenvalues of each of the following symmetric matrices:

$$
A = \begin{bmatrix} 1 & 0 & 2 \\ 0 & 2 & 3 \\ 2 & 3 & 1 \end{bmatrix}, \qquad
B = \begin{bmatrix} 2 & 0 & 0 & 3 \\ 0 & 1 & 0 & 0 \\ 0 & 0 & 4 & 0 \\ 3 & 0 & 0 & 3 \end{bmatrix}
$$

$$
C = \begin{bmatrix} 9 & 0 & 2 \\ 0 & 1 & 0 \\ 2 & 0 & 3 \end{bmatrix}, \qquad
D = \begin{bmatrix} 4 & 0 & 2 \\ 0 & -1 & 0 \\ 2 & 0 & 3 \end{bmatrix}
$$

55. Find a set of eigenvectors for each of the matrices in Problem 54 and show that each set is mutually orthogonal.
56. Using the eigenvalue test identify the definiteness of each quadratic form in Problem 50.
57. Using the eigenvalue test identify the definiteness of each quadratic form in Problem 52.

Suggested Further Reading

1. Draper, N. R., and Smith, H. (1967). "Applied Regression Analysis." Wiley, New York.
2. Franklin, J. N. (1968). "Matrix Theory." Prentice-Hall, Englewood Cliffs, New Jersey.
3. Grayhill, F. A. (1961). "Introduction to Linear Statistical Models," Vol. 1. McGraw-Hill, New York.
4. Gue, R. L., and Thomas, M. E. (1968). "Mathematical Methods in Operations Research." Macmillan, New York.
5. Hadley, G. (1961). "Linear Algebra." Addison-Wesley, Reading, Massachusetts.
6. Hohn, F. E. (1958). "Elementary Matrix Algebra." Macmillan, New York.
7. Kemeny, J. G., and Snell, J. L. (1960). "Finite Markov Chains." Van Nostrand, New York.

8. Kemeny, J. G., Mirkil, H., Snell, J. L., and Thompson, G. L. (1960). "Finite Mathematical Structures." Prentice-Hall, Englewood Cliffs, New Jersey.

9. Lancaster, P. (1969). "Theory of Matrices." Academic Press, New York.

10. Perlis, S. (1952). "Theory of Matrices." Addison-Wesley, Reading, Massachusetts.

11. Schmidt, J. W. (1974). "Mathematical Foundations for Management Science and Systems Analysis." Academic Press, New York.

12. Searle, S. R. (1971). "Linear Models." Wiley, New York.

13. Teichroew, D. (1964). "An Introduction to Management Science, Deterministic Models." Wiley, New York.

14. Yefimov, N. V. (1964). "Quadratic Forms and Matrices." Academic Press, New York.

Chapter 3 | Fundamental Concepts of Classical Optimization

INTRODUCTION

Prior to embarking on an investigation of the principles and techniques of classical optimization theory, it is worthwhile to first ensure that the student has an appreciation for the fundamental concepts which provide a basis for interpreting and characterizing optimization problems. In this text, attention is focused on certain mathematical relationships which represent the performance of a system and the restrictions to which this performance must conform. The mathematical relationship which represents the performance of a particular system is referred to as the *objective function*, and the mathematical restrictions imposed on the system's performance function are referred to as *constraints* (or restraints). Collectively, the objective function and constraint relationships represent a traditional mathematical model of the system.

Optimization problems have as their goal an attempt to establish a set of values for the model variables which yield the best (or optimal) value for the model's objective function. This best performance takes one of two characters: minimization (for example, of a measure of system cost) or maximization (for example, of a measure of system profit). One of these two characteristics of system performance is then the optimizing "objective."

It is frequently useful to think of the variables in an optimization problem as "activities" to be undertaken in a particular system's program of "things we can do." The values of these variables then represent "levels" (or "intensities") to which these activities are brought in an attempt to optimize the total performance of the system. Further, the constraints on

124

the system may be viewed as resource limitations on the system's performance, with each variable (activity) consuming a certain quantity of each of the available resources. Optimization problems may then be thought of as mathematical representations of the program of activities for a particular system; the resource availabilities and resource consumption characteristics of the activities comprise the program.

The mathematical relationships representing these programs, and the optimal-values of the variables comprising such programs, exhibit certain characteristics which will be addressed in the remainder of this chapter. What must be remembered is that the following descriptive characteristics, although presented in a mathematical or geometrical context, must in actual practice be interpreted in the context of the physical or socioeconomic system from which a particular mathematical model takes its form. The purpose here is to provide a fundamental, general basis from which such interpretations can arise.

EXTREME POINTS

Let us assume that we have defined an objective function, $f(x_1, \ldots, x_n)$, which represents a system performance measure in terms of a set of activities $(x_1, \ldots, x_n)$. If there are no restrictions on the choice of values to be assigned to these activities, then we have an "unconstrained" optimization problem. However, if there exist definable restrictions on the interactions of these activities, and/or their consumption of available resources, then we have a "constrained" optimization problem. Such constraints may take one of the following two forms:

$$g_i(x_1, \ldots, x_n) = b_i \quad \text{(an equality constraint)}$$

or

$$g_k(x_1, \ldots, x_n) \leqslant b_k \quad \text{(an inequality constraint)}$$

or

$$g_j(x_1, \ldots, x_n) \geqslant b_j \quad \text{(an inequality constraint)}$$

In subsequent chapters, the principles and techniques of classical optimization theory employed in finding optimum solutions to both constrained and unconstrained problems will be discussed. In these discussions methods will be described for isolating the extreme points of an objective function. Let us examine $f(\mathbf{x})$ in a neighborhood of $\mathbf{x}^*$ of radius $\epsilon > 0$. That is, we will examine the behavior of $f(\mathbf{x})$ at all points defined by $\mathbf{x}^* + \mathbf{h}$ for which $|\mathbf{h}| \leqslant \epsilon$ and for which the function is defined. If there exists an $\epsilon > 0$

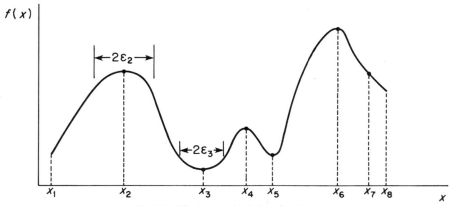

Fig. 3.1 Maxima and minima for $f(x)$.

such that

$$f(\mathbf{x}^*) \geqslant f(\mathbf{x}^* + \mathbf{h}) \tag{3.1}$$

or

$$f(\mathbf{x}^*) \leqslant f(\mathbf{x}^* + \mathbf{h}) \tag{3.2}$$

for all $\mathbf{h}$ such that $|\mathbf{h}| \leqslant \epsilon$, then $\mathbf{x}^*$ is an *extreme point* for $f(\mathbf{x})$. That is, $f(\mathbf{x}^*)$ is either greater than or equal to $f(\mathbf{x})$ for all $\mathbf{x}$ in an ϵ neighborhood of $\mathbf{x}^*$ or is less than or equal to $f(\mathbf{x})$ for all $\mathbf{x}$ in an ϵ neighborhood of $\mathbf{x}^*$. If all of the points in the ϵ neighborhood of $\mathbf{x}^*$ lie in the domain of definition of $f(\mathbf{x})$, then $\mathbf{x}^*$ is called an *interior extreme point*. For example, consider the function of a single variable shown in Fig. 3.1, where $f(\mathbf{x})$ is defined for $x_1 \leqslant x \leqslant x_8$. The points x_2, x_3, x_4, x_5, and x_6 are interior extreme points for $f(x)$. In each case we can choose an $\epsilon_i > 0$ such that $x_i + \delta_i(\delta_i$ being either positive or negative) is a point in the domain of $f(x)$ for $|\delta_i| < \epsilon_i$ and such that $f(x_i) \geqslant f(x_i + \delta_i)$ or $f(x_i) \leqslant f(x_i + \delta_i)$). On the other hand, x_7 is not an interior extreme point for $f(x)$ since $f(x_7 + \delta_7) > f(x_7)$ for all $\delta_7 < 0$ and $f(x_7 + \delta_7) < f(x_7)$ for all $\delta_7 > 0$ That is, there is no ϵ neighborhood of x_7 such the either Eq. (3.1) or (3.2) are satisfied.

Now consider the points x_1 and x_8 in Fig. 3.1. Every ϵ neighborhood of points about x_1 and x_8 includes points for which $f(x)$ is defined and points for which $f(x)$ is not defined. Specifically, $f(x_1 + \delta)$ is defined for $\delta \geqslant 0$ but not for $\delta < 0$. Similarly, $f(x_8 + \delta)$ is defined for $\delta \leqslant 0$ but not for $\delta > 0$. However, x_1 and x_8 are still extreme points for $f(x)$ (although not interior extreme points) since we can define an ϵ neighborhood of radius $\epsilon_1 > 0$ and $\epsilon_8 > 0$, respectively, such that $f(x_1) \leqslant f(x_1 + \delta_1)$ and $f(x_8) \leqslant f(x_8 + \delta_8)$ for all $|\delta_1| < \epsilon_1$ and $|\delta_8| < \epsilon_8$, where we consider only those points $x_1 + \delta_1$ and

$x_8 + \delta_8$ for which $f(x)$ is defined. While the points x_1 and x_8 are extreme points, they are not referred to as interior extreme points simply because they lie on the boundary of the domain of $f(x)$ rather than the interior of the domain. It can be shown that every boundary point for a continuous function is an extreme point.

If the domain of definition of $f(\mathbf{x})$ is unrestricted in the sense that $f(\mathbf{x})$ is defined for every vector $\mathbf{x}$, then the domain of definition is unbounded. In this case there are no boundary points for the domain and if the function possesses extreme points they are interior extreme points.

Extreme points can be used to define either a maximum (greatest) or a minimum (least) value of the objective function at a particular set of solution values for the variables identified in the mathematical model. There may exist, for a particular objection function, a number of extreme points. Obviously, not all of these will be *the* optimal solution to the particular problem at hand. A scheme for categorizing the extreme points of an objective function has been established, and is best described in the context of the following example. Consider the function of a single variable illustrated in Fig. 3.1. The values of $f(x)$ which represent extreme points of this function are labeled $x_1, x_2, x_3, x_4, x_5, x_6$, and x_8. Theoretically, we could arrive at all of these points as potential candidates for the maximum or minimum value of the function. Points x_2, x_4, and x_6 are candidates for the function's maximum, while points x_1, x_3, x_5, and x_8 are candidates for the function's minimum. Points x_2 and x_4 are referred to as *local maxima*, while the point x_6 is referred to as the *global maximum*, the distinction being that x_6 is *the* maximum value of the function while points x_2 and x_4 are maxima only in the local vincinity (or ϵ neighborhood) about them. Similarly, point x_3 is referred to as the *global minimum*, while points x_1, x_5, and x_8 are *local minima*.

When we are dealing with a constrained optimization problem these local and global extreme points are further classified as *feasible*—meaning that the extreme point in question satisfies all constraints—or as *infeasible* —meaning that the extreme point in question does not satisfy all constraints. The feasible extreme points for a constrained optimization problem are alternatively referred to as *relative local optima* or as *relative global optima*, indicating that these are extreme points of the function under investigation *relative to* a set of constraining relationships.

CONVEXITY AND CONCAVITY

Among the different types of functions which we will have occasion to examine, there exists a special class of functions, known as *convex functions*, that exhibit an important characteristic related to the identification of maxima and minima. This characteristic is termed *unimodality* and reflects the fact that the graph of these functions is characterized by a single peak or valley (i.e., one mode).

Functions of a Single Variable

A function $f(x)$ is said to be *convex* over some defined interval $a \leqslant x \leqslant b$ if for any two points x_1, x_2 in that interval, the following relation holds:

$$f[\lambda x_2 + (1 - \lambda)x_1] \leqslant \lambda f[x_2] + (1 - \lambda)f[x_1] \qquad (3.3)$$

where $0 \leqslant \lambda \leqslant 1$. In similar fashion, a function is said to be *concave* over some defined interval $a \leqslant x \leqslant b$ if for any two points x_1, x_2 in that interval, the following relation holds:

$$f[\lambda x_2 + (1 - \lambda)x_1] \geqslant \lambda f[x_2] + (1 - \lambda)f[x_1] \qquad (3.4)$$

where again $0 \leqslant \lambda \leqslant 1$.

These relationships may be interpreted in the following manner.

Convexity   A function is *convex* if a line segment drawn between any two points on its graph lies entirely on or above the graph. Note that if the line lies entirely above the graph except at the points a and b, the function is said to be *strictly* convex and the strict inequality holds for Eq. (3.3); see Fig. 3.2.

Concavity   A function is *concave* if a line segment drawn between any two points on its graph lies entirely on or below the graph. Again note that if the line lies entirely below the graph except at the points a and b, the function is said to be *strictly* concave and the strict inequality holds for Eq. (3.4); see Fig. 3.3.

The necessity of specifying an interval on x for which the function is defined as convex, concave, or neither convex nor concave may be represented by the function, $f(x) = x^3$. From an examination of the graph of this

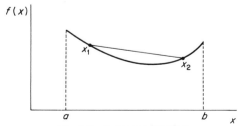

Fig. 3.2   A convex function.

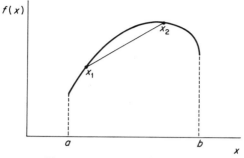

Fig. 3.3   A concave function.

function (see Fig. 3.4) we may note the following:

   (1)   Over the interval $(-1 \leqslant x < 0)$ the function may be classified as concave.
   (2)   Over the interval $(0 \leqslant x \leqslant 1)$ the function may be classified as convex.
   (3)   If the interval of definition is over $(-1 \leqslant x \leqslant 1)$, the function is neither convex nor concave.

Notice that the line $x = 0$ divides the graph into a convex region and

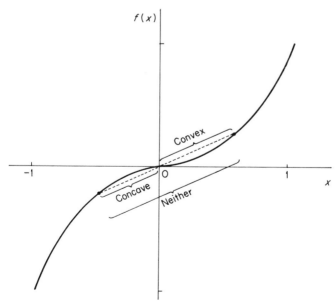

Fig. 3.4   Point of inflection at $x = 0$.

concave region. Points such as the point $(x = 0, f(x = 0))$ which exhibit this characteristic are termed *inflection points*.

There is one other important class of functions which deserves mention here. Note that if $f(x)$ were *linear*, then any two points on the straight-line graph of $f(x)$ would be connected by a line segment which lies *entirely on* the graph of $f(x)$. The question then arises, "Is $f(x)$ convex or concave?" The answer is *both*. For this reason linear functions may be termed *nonmodal*; the maximum and minimum values of such functions depend entirely on the interval of definition, or *region of feasibility*.

Function of More Than One Variable

The preceding definitions of convexity and concavity are readily generalized for functions of several variables. A function $f(\mathbf{x})$ is said to be convex over some convex space χ in n-dimensional space if for any two points $\mathbf{x}_1$ and $\mathbf{x}_2$ in χ the following relation holds:

$$f[\lambda \mathbf{x}_1 + (1 - \lambda)\mathbf{x}_2] \leqslant \lambda f[\mathbf{x}_1] + (1 - \lambda)f[\mathbf{x}_2] \tag{3.5}$$

where $0 \leqslant \lambda \leqslant 1$. Similarly, a function $f(\mathbf{x})$ is said to be concave over some convex space χ in n-dimentional space if for any two points $\mathbf{x}_1$ and $\mathbf{x}_2$ in χ the following relation holds:

$$f[\lambda \mathbf{x}_1 + (1 - \lambda)\mathbf{x}_2] \geqslant \lambda f[\mathbf{x}_1] + (1 - \lambda)f[\mathbf{x}_2] \tag{3.6}$$

where $0 \leqslant \lambda \leqslant 1$. The interpretation of these relationships is similar to that

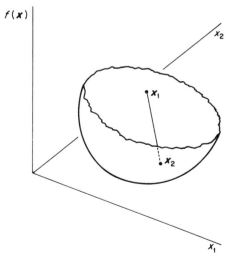

Fig. 3.5 A convex surface.

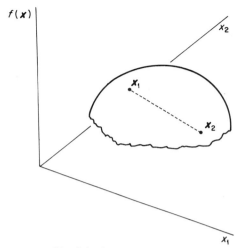

Fig. 3.6 A concave surface.

for the 1-dimensional case. A function $g = f(\mathbf{x})$ is a hypersurface in n-dimensional space. The function is convex if the line segment joining any two points $[\mathbf{x}_1, f(\mathbf{x}_1)]$ and $[\mathbf{x}_2, f(\mathbf{x}_2)]$ on the surface of $f(\mathbf{x})$ lies entirely on or above the surface, and concave if the line segment lies entirely on or below the surface; see Figs. 3.5, 3.6, and 3.7. Again, if the line segment lies strictly

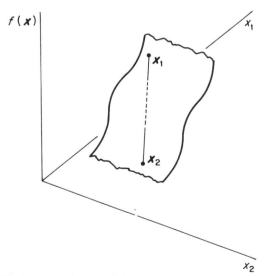

Fig. 3.7 A surface which is neither convex nor concave.

above or strictly below, then the corresponding strict inequality holds for relationships (3.5) or (3.6).

In general, convex functions and concave functions are both referred to under the general heading of *convex functions*. The difference being denoted, when necessary, by referring to convex functions as *convex upward*, and concave functions as *convex downward*.

The concepts of convexity and concavity play an important role in the identification of extreme points for continuous functions. Consider again the function shown in Fig. 3.1. The ϵ neighborhood of x_2, given as $\epsilon_2 > 0$, defines an interval of values for x for which the function $f(x)$ is concave. Similarly, the ϵ neighborhood, $\epsilon_3 > 0$ of x_3 defines an interval of values for x for which the function $f(x)$ is convex. The reader will note that x_4 and x_6 lie in intervals for which $f(x)$ is concave, while x_5 lies in an interval for which $f(x)$ is convex. Hence the interior extreme points for $f(x)$ lie in intervals for which the function is either convex or concave. In general if $\mathbf{x}^*$ is an interior extreme point for $f(\mathbf{x})$, then there exists an ϵ neighborhood about $\mathbf{x}^*$ for which $f(\mathbf{x})$ is either convex or concave. Depending upon the nature of the function and the interior extreme point $\mathbf{x}$ considered, the function may be strictly convex or strictly concave in an ϵ neighborhood of $\mathbf{x}^*$. However, neither strict concavity nor strict convexity in an ϵ neighborhood of $\mathbf{x}^*$ is necessary for the existence of an extreme point at $\mathbf{x}^*$ Consider, for example, a straight line with zero slope ($f(x) = a$). Every point on the line is an extreme point since every point satisfies the equality portion of Eqs. (3.1) and (3.2). In addition, this function is both convex and concave throughout its domain of definition since it satisfies the equality portions of Eqs. (3.3) and (3.4).

While every interior extreme point of a continuous function must lie in an ϵ neighborhood for which the function is either convex or concave, convexity does not necessarily imply the existence of an interior extreme point. For example consider the function $f(x) = e^{-x}$ for x on $(-\infty, \infty)$. This function is strictly convex but possesses no interior extreme point.

PROPERTIES OF CONVEX FUNCTIONS

(1)   The sum of convex (concave) functions is convex (concave).

(2)   The sum of convex (concave) functions is strictly convex (concave) if any one of the functions in the sum is strictly convex (concave).

(3)   A linear function $f(\mathbf{x}) = \mathbf{a}^T\mathbf{x}$ is both convex and concave since the defining inequalites hold as equalities.

(4)   If $f(x)$ is a convex function, and c is a constant, then (a) $c \cdot f(\mathbf{x})$ is convex if $c > 0$, (b) $c \cdot f(\mathbf{x})$ is concave if $c < 0$.

(5)   If $f(x)$ is a concave function, and d is a constant, then (a) $d \cdot f(\mathbf{x})$ is concave if $d > 0$, (b) $d \cdot f(\mathbf{x})$ is convex if $d < 0$.

CONVEXITY AND THE HESSIAN MATRIX

Having discussed the concept of convexity, the following question now remains: "How one decides whether a function is convex, concave, or neither in the ϵ neighborhood of a particular point $\mathbf{x}$?" Obviously, recourse to graphing the function in the ϵ neighborhood of the point of interest and then examining a myriad of lines applying relationships (3.5) and (3.6) would be impractical. Fortunately, information about the character of a continuous function in the neighborhood of any point can be obtained from the matrix of second partial derivatives (the Hessian matrix) of the function when evaluated at the point of interest.

If we have the function $f(x_1, \ldots, x_n)$, then its *Hessian matrix* (a matrix of second partial derivatives of $f(x_1, \ldots, x_n)$) is defined by

$$H_f(\mathbf{x}) = \begin{bmatrix} \dfrac{\partial^2 f}{\partial x_1 \, \partial x_1} & \cdots & \dfrac{\partial^2 f}{\partial x_1 \, \partial x_n} \\ \vdots & \ddots & \vdots \\ \dfrac{\partial^2 f}{\partial x_n \, \partial x_1} & \cdots & \dfrac{\partial^2 f}{\partial x_n \, \partial x_n} \end{bmatrix} \qquad (3.7)$$

When the Hessian matrix is evaluated at some point of interest $\mathbf{x}_0$, the character of the function $f(\mathbf{x})$ in the neighborhood of this point can be determined from the character of this quadratic form as follows:

(1)   If $H_f(\mathbf{x}_0)$ is positive definite, then $f(\mathbf{x})$ is convex in the neighborhood of $\mathbf{x}_0$.

(2)   If $H_f(\mathbf{x}_0)$ is negative definite, then $f(\mathbf{x})$ is concave in the neighborhood of $\mathbf{x}_0$.

(3)   If $H_f(\mathbf{x}_0)$ is indefinite, then the function is neither convex nor concave in the neighborhood of $\mathbf{x}_0$.

Further,

(4)   if $H_f(\mathbf{x})$ is positive definite for every $\mathbf{x}$, then the function is everywhere convex (e.g., unimodal).

(5)   if $H_f(\mathbf{x})$ is negative definite for every $\mathbf{x}$, then the function is everywhere concave (e.g., unimodal).

To illustrate these relationships, consider the following examples.

Example 3.1   Determine the character of the function

$$f(\mathbf{x}) = 2x_1^2 - 5x_1 + x_1 x_2 + x_2^2 - 4x_2$$

in the neighborhood of the point $\mathbf{x}_0 = \left[\begin{smallmatrix} 6/8 \\ 11/7 \end{smallmatrix}\right]$.

$$H_f(\mathbf{x}) = \begin{bmatrix} 4 & 1 \\ 1 & 2 \end{bmatrix} \rightarrow \text{positive definite for every } \mathbf{x}$$

Consequently, this function is everywhere convex. ∎

Example 3.2   Determine the character of the function

$$f(\mathbf{x}) = 12x_1 - x_1^3 + 6x_2 - x_2^2$$

in the neighborhood of the points $\mathbf{x}_0 = \left[\begin{smallmatrix} 2 \\ 3 \end{smallmatrix}\right]$ and $\mathbf{x}_1 = \left[\begin{smallmatrix} -2 \\ 3 \end{smallmatrix}\right]$.

$$H_f(\mathbf{x}) = \begin{bmatrix} -6x_1 & 0 \\ 0 & -2 \end{bmatrix}$$

$H_f(\mathbf{x}_0)$ is negative definite, so the function is concave in the neighborhood of $\mathbf{x}_0$. $H_f(\mathbf{x}_1)$ is indefinite, so the function is neither convex nor concave in the neighborhood of $\mathbf{x}_1$. ∎

THE CONCEPT OF SCHEEFFER, STOLZ, AND VAN DANTSHER

Later in this chapter, the necessary and sufficient conditions which must be satisfied for a particular point to be considered a local maximum (or minimum) of an objective function will be presented. Prior to the development of these conditions, Scheeffer, Stolz, and Van Dantsher devised methods for identifying a point as a maximum and minimum [4]. The essence of their approach to this determination will be presented here to reinforce the maximum and minimum value concept. It should be noted that recourse to such an approach continues to be used when the classical methods outlined in subsequent discussions fail to identify conclusively a particular point as a maximum or minimum.

Given that we have an objective function which we wish to optimize over an unconstrained set of activities, there are certain points on the surface of this function on which our attention must focus. These points are those which satisfy the condition that simultaneously the first partial derivatives of the objective function, with respect to each of its component variables, must vanish (e.g., must equal zero):

objective function: $f(x_1, \ldots, x_n)$

first-partial conditions: $\partial f / \partial x_k = 0, \qquad k = 1, \ldots, n$ (3.8)

The point (or points) which satisfy Eq. (3.8) are called *stationary points* of the objective function. Within the class of stationary points are found maxima, minima, and saddle points. A saddle point is a multivariate analog of a point of inflection for a function of a single variable. That is, a *saddle point* is a point at which $\partial f/\partial x_k = 0$, $k = 1, 2, \ldots, n$, but which is neither a maximum or a minimum. An example of a saddle point for a function of two variables is shown in Fig. 3.8. From among the stationary points, of particular interest are those points (if any) which represent the maximum or minimum value of the objective function, depending of course on the optimization goal. In general an objective function may possess several

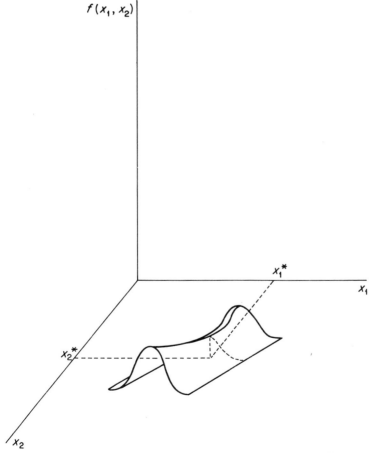

Fig. 3.8   Saddle point at x_1^*, x_2^* for the function $f(x_1, x_2)$.

stationary points. However, if the function of interest is strictly convex or strictly concave throughout its domain, then only one stationary point may exist. The stepwise procedure outlined below represents one approach to making this determination.

The basic idea on which such procedures are founded can be described as follows. If the stationary point we are attempting to classify is indeed a local optimum, then any movement away from this point, to some other point in the ϵ neighborhood of the first, will result in a less than optimal value of the objective function evaluated at this perturbed point. To clarify and expand this idea consider a modified first-order Taylor expansion of a function of three variables taken at a given stationary point $\mathbf{x}^*$:

$$f(\mathbf{x}^* + \mathbf{h}) - f(\mathbf{x}^*) \doteq h_1 \left. \frac{\partial f}{\partial x_1} \right|_{\mathbf{x}^* + \mathbf{h}} + h_2 \left. \frac{\partial f}{\partial x_2} \right|_{\mathbf{x}^* + \mathbf{h}} + h_3 \left. \frac{\partial f}{\partial x_3} \right|_{\mathbf{x}^* + \mathbf{h}} \quad (3.9)$$

where $\mathbf{h}$ is a vector of perturbations, or small movements, in the ϵ neighborhood of $\mathbf{x}^*$:

$$\mathbf{h} = \begin{bmatrix} h_1 \\ h_2 \\ h_3 \end{bmatrix}$$

Note that the sign of the sum of resultant terms on the right of the equality represents the direction of the incremental change from $f(\mathbf{x}^*)$ created by $\mathbf{h}$. However, since these first partial derivatives are evaluated at perturbed points and not at the stationary point, they may not necessarily vanish. Using this modified expansion as a basis, consider the following stepwise procedure for determining whether a stationary point is a maximum or a minimum:

Step 1:   Perturb one of the component variables, say x_p, by some value h_p away from its solution value, x_p^*.

Step 2:   Now perturb one of the remaining component variables, say x_i, a given number of times by various values of h_i which are each less than or equal to the absolute value of h_p. At each of these secondary perturbations record the sign of the following "test term":

$$\text{test term} = h_p \left. \frac{\partial f}{\partial x_p} \right|_{\substack{x_p^* + h_p \\ x_i^* + h_i}} + h_i \left. \frac{\partial f}{\partial x_i} \right|_{\substack{x_p^* + h_p \\ x_i^* + h_i}}. \quad (3.10)$$

Note: Any variable not perturbed by Step 1 or 2 remains at its solution value; therefore the term

$$h_k \left. \frac{\partial f}{\partial x_k} \right|_{\substack{x_k^* \\ x_p^* + h_p \\ x_i^* + h_i}} = 0 \quad (3.11)$$

since $h_k = 0$.

Step 3:   Repeat Step 2 until all component variables x_i, $i \neq p$, have been perturbed independently in this second stage.

Step 4:   Now return again to Step 1 and the original solution vector. Make the primary perturbation h_p with respect to a different component variable. Repeat Steps 2–4. This process is repeated until all component variables have been perturbed in Step 1 with succeeding secondary steps completed.

Once completed, a review is made of the record of signs for the test term denoted in Step 2. If all of these signs are positive, then the solution point is a minimum; and if all are negative, then the solution point is a maximum. In addition, note that if we observe alternating signs, we may conclude that the solution point is a saddle point. The procedure may be represented graphically as follows in Fig. 3.9.

Recalling that the partial derivatives $\partial f / \partial x_j|_{\mathbf{x}^* + \mathbf{h}}$ represent the slope of a line drawn tangent to the objective function surface at $x_j + h_j$, note the following relationship shown in Fig. 3.10 and Fig. 3.11. Notice that as $h_i \to 0$, its contribution to the test term also approaches zero and the test term becomes dominated by the primary perturbation and its corresponding partial derivative. Now we can better understand what Scheeffer and his contemporaries had in mind. Given that we are at some point on the surface of an objective function where the first partials vanish, if we move away from this point $\mathbf{x}^*$ to some other point $\mathbf{x}^* + \mathbf{h}$ in the ϵ neighborhood, then the value of our objective function will either strictly increase or strictly decrease if $\mathbf{x}^*$ is an extreme point. [Note the obvious exceptions:

(a) $\partial f / \partial x_p|_{\mathbf{x}^* + \mathbf{h}} = 0;$ (3.12)
(b) $h_j (\partial f / \partial x_p)|_{\mathbf{x}^* + \mathbf{h}} + h_k (\partial f / \partial x_i)|_{\mathbf{x}^* + \mathbf{h}} = 0.]$ (3.13)

In particular:

(1)   If all movements yield only additional positive values for $f(\mathbf{x})$, then $\mathbf{x}^*$ must be a minimum.

(2)   If all movements yield only additional negative values for $f(\mathbf{x})$, then $\mathbf{x}^*$ must be a maximum.

(3)   If some movements yield additional positive values and some additional negative values for $f(\mathbf{x})$, then we are neither at a maximum nor a minimum at $\mathbf{x}^*$, but rather a saddle point.

Scheffer's theory further states that if the minimum absolute value of the test term obtained for each $x_p + h_p$ (i.e., where $h_i = 0$) is zero then the order of the expansion is increased by one and a new test term is obtained from this order of the expansion. The entire procedure is then repeated until an expansion exists for which the minimum absolute value of the test term at each $x_p + h_p$ is not zero. The new test terms derived are applied with the same rationale.

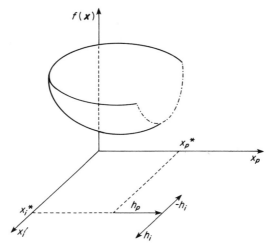

Fig. 3.9 Primary and secondary perturbations.

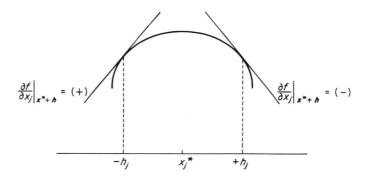

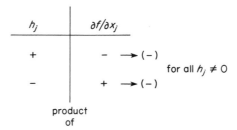

Fig. 3.10 The maximum case.

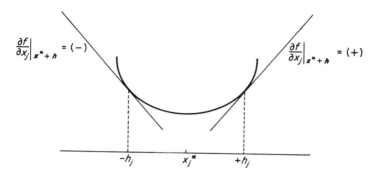

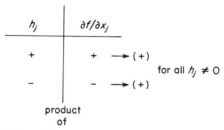

Fig. 3.11 The minimum case.

For example, if for every $x_p + h_p$ (where $h_i = 0$) in the first-order expansion the minimum absolute value of the test term had been zero, then we would have moved to the second order of the Taylor expansion. The new test term would have been

$$\frac{1}{2!}\left[h_1^2\frac{\partial^2 f}{\partial x_1^2} + h_2^2\frac{\partial^2 f}{\partial x_2^2} + h_3^2\frac{\partial^2 f}{\partial x_3^2}\right.$$
$$\left. + 2h_1 h_2\frac{\partial^2 f}{\partial x_1 \partial x_2} + 2h_1 h_3\frac{\partial^2 f}{\partial x_1 \partial x_3} + 2h_2 h_3\frac{\partial^2 f}{\partial x_2 \partial x_3}\right]\Bigg|_{x^*+h} \quad (3.14)$$

and the procedure would have been as before.

Example 3.3 Given that the stationary point of the function

$$f(\mathbf{x}) = 2x_1^2 - 4x_1 + x_2^2 - 6x_2$$

is $\mathbf{x}^* = \begin{bmatrix}1\\3\end{bmatrix}$, use Scheeffer's procedure to determine whether this is a minimizing point for the function.

Table 3.1

Summary of Scheeffer's Procedure for the Problem in Example 3.3

h_p	$\partial f/\partial x_1$	h_i	$\partial f/\partial x_2$	Test term
0.10000	0.40000	0.03333	0.06667	0.04222
0.10000	0.40000	0.03333	0.13333	0.04889
0.10000	0.40000	0.10000	0.20000	0.06000
0.10000	0.40000	− 0.03333	− 0.06667	0.04222
0.10000	0.40000	− 0.06667	− 0.13334	0.04889
0.10000	0.40000	− 0.10000	− 0.20000	0.06000
− 0.10000	− 0.40000	− 0.03333	− 0.06667	0.04222
− 0.10000	− 0.40000	− 0.06667	− 0.13334	0.04889
− 0.10000	− 0.40000	− 0.10000	− 0.20000	0.06000
− 0.10000	− 0.40000	0.03333	0.06667	0.04222
− 0.10000	− 0.40000	0.06667	0.13333	0.04889
− 0.10000	− 0.40000	0.10000	0.20000	0.06000
0.20000	0.80000	0.06667	0.13333	0.16889
0.20000	0.80000	0.13333	0.26667	0.19556
0.20000	0.80000	0.20000	0.40000	0.24000
0.20000	0.80000	− 0.06667	− 0.13334	0.16889
0.20000	0.80000	− 0.13333	− 2.26667	0.19556
0.20000	0.80000	− 0.20000	− 0.40000	0.24000
− 0.20000	− 0.80000	− 0.06667	− 0.13334	0.16889
− 0.20000	− 0.80000	− 0.013333	− 0.26667	0.19556
− 0.20000	− 0.80000	− 0.20000	− 0.40000	0.24000
− 0.20000	− 0.80000	0.06667	0.13333	0.16889
− 0.20000	− 0.80000	0.13333	0.26667	0.19556
− 0.20000	− 0.80000	0.20000	0.40000	0.24000
0.30000	1.20000	0.10000	0.20000	0.38000
0.30000	1.20000	0.20000	0.40000	0.44000
0.30000	1.20000	0.30000	0.60000	0.54000
0.30000	1.20000	− 0.10000	− 0.20000	0.38000
0.30000	1.20000	− 0.20000	− 0.40000	0.44000
0.30000	1.20000	− 0.30000	− 0.60000	0.54000
− 0.30000	− 1.20000	− 0.10000	− 0.20000	0.38000
− 0.30000	− 1.20000	− 0.20000	− 0.40000	0.44000
− 0.30000	− 1.20000	− 0.30000	− 0.60000	0.54000
− 0.30000	− 1.20000	0.10000	0.20000	0.38000
− 0.30000	− 1.20000	0.20000	0.40000	0.44000
− 0.30000	− 1.20000	0.30000	0.60000	0.54000

Let the primary perturbation be made first with respect to x_1 ($p = 1$) and the secondary perturbation with respect to x_2 ($i = 2$). For the sake of brevity, we will make relatively large perturbations that are few in number, yielding the results shown in Table 3.1

Note that the test term is positive in each instance. The reader should complete this example with the primary perturbation made with respect to

x_2 and the secondary made with respect to x_1. After noting again that all test term values are positive, the conclusion is that the point in question is indeed a minimizing point. ■

INDIRECT AND DIRECT METHODS OF OPTIMIZATION

The remainder of this and the next chapter is intended to provide an interpretive, as opposed to a theoretical, foundation for the methodologies and concepts of classical optimization theory. These methodologies are frequently referred to as *indirect methods of optimization*. They are termed *indirect* for the reason that the optimal value of the objective function and constituent problem variables are obtained in an indirect manner by satisfying certain specified "necessary and sufficient conditions" which must hold for *all* local optima of a particular objective function. In essence, these methodologies are not "directed" at obtaining *one* solution to the problem at hand; rather, they produce (theoretically) all potential candidates for optimizing solutions as a consequence of satisfying specified conditions which must hold for all optimizing solutions. A thorough understanding of these indirect methods of optimization is of importance in that they provide the foundation on which the modern *direct methods of optimization* rest.

In theory, the solution for any deterministic optimization problem can be obtained with the classical methods to be described in subsequent chapters. However, in practice the complexity of the mathematical relationships comprising a particular model, in terms of both the number of variables and constraints and the specific form of these relationships, frequently makes a manual solution by indirect methods impossible to obtain. This fact led to a need for the development of techniques which utilized the computational speed and capacity of a digital computer to overcome the difficulties inherent in the classical approach. The methodologies which sprang from this need are referred to as direct methods of optimization; "direct" in that their primary goal is to seek a particular solution to a specified problem in a direct and iterative fashion. Such techniques are often referred to as search procedures or sequential search procedures. In effect, these computer-oriented techniques are designed to obtain a local optimum for a specified objective function in a step-by-step manner, each step hopefully moving closer to the desired optimum.

As an example of one such direct method we shall discuss the method of steepest descent. The purpose of this example is to illustrate the general nature of direct optimization methods and, at the same time, show how this particular technique is related to classical optimization theory.

The Method of Steepest Descent

One fundamental concept serves as the foundation for this direct optimization technique. This concept requires an interpretation of the gradient vector of a function evaluated at a point in the domain of the function. The *gradient vector* is a vector of first partial derivatives of $f(\mathbf{x})$ with respect of each of the variables x_k, $k = 1, 2, \ldots, n$, and is given by

$$\nabla_{\mathbf{x}} f = \begin{bmatrix} \partial f / \partial x_1 \\ \partial f / \partial x_2 \\ \vdots \\ \partial f / \partial x_n \end{bmatrix} \tag{3.15}$$

The gradient vector $\nabla_{\mathbf{x}} f$ evaluated at the point $\mathbf{x}$ can be said to have the following properties with respect to its parent function $f(\mathbf{x})$:

(1)   It is normal to the function's contour line which passes through the specified point.

(2)   The gradient vector always points in a direction in which the function's value is increasing (e.g., conceptually, the gradient vector always points "uphill" on the function's surface).

(3)   The negative of the gradient vector, $-\nabla_{\mathbf{x}} f$, always points in a direction of decreasing function value.

These properties form the basis for a sequential search procedure which can be employed to find the minimizing point of a convex function. The goal of this iterative procedure is founded on a concept from classical optimization theory which requires that each component of the gradient vector must vanish (e.g., must equal zero) at the minimizing point of a convex function.

For purposes of this discussion, the specifics of the method of steepest descent will be suppressed in favor of employing an example problem to illustrate the essence of the procedure. (In chapter 4, a more thorough treatment will be given.)

Example 3.4   Find the minimum value of the unconstrained function

$$f(\mathbf{x}) = 2x_1^2 - 3x_1 - 4x_2 + x_2^2$$

In attempting to find the minimum of $f(\mathbf{x})$, one concern is to determine a direction of movement from any point on the surface of the function which will lead to a reduction in the value of the function. As already indicated, the negative gradient vector indicates the direction in which decreasing values of $f(\mathbf{x})$ will be found.

The negative gradient vector is given by

$$-\nabla_x f = \begin{bmatrix} -\partial f/\partial x_1 \\ -\partial f/\partial x_2 \end{bmatrix} = \begin{bmatrix} -4x_1 + 3 \\ -2x_2 + 4 \end{bmatrix}$$

A point must now be selected in the domain of the above function from which the search will begin. Let this point be denoted as x_0 and defined as

$$x_0 = \begin{bmatrix} 1 \\ 1 \end{bmatrix}$$

At this point, the negative gradient vector is evaluated and a direction for the search is defined. This direction coincides with the direction indicated by the resultant vector (see Fig. 3.12):

$$-\nabla_{x_0} f = \begin{bmatrix} -1 \\ 2 \end{bmatrix}$$

An attempt is now made to determine the step size (or length of travel) to be taken in this direction. This is accomplished by obtaining the minimum distance, in the direction indicated, at which one (or more) of the components of the gradient vector will vanish. Let L denote this distance, and let it be obtained by finding the minimum solution at which

$$\partial f/\partial x_1 = -4(1 - L) + 3 = 0$$

and

$$\partial f/\partial x_2 = -2(1 + 2L) + 4 = 0$$

From $\partial f/\partial x_1$, $L = 1/4$, and from $\partial f/\partial x_2$, $L = 1/2$; consequently, for a step size of $1/4$ in the direction indicated by $-\nabla_{x_0} f$ the first component of $-\nabla_x f$ will be driven to zero. The point at which this will occur is defined by

$$x_1 = x_0 + (L)(-\nabla_{x_0} f) = \begin{bmatrix} 1 \\ 1 \end{bmatrix} + \frac{1}{4}\begin{bmatrix} -1 \\ 2 \end{bmatrix} = \begin{bmatrix} \frac{3}{4} \\ \frac{3}{2} \end{bmatrix}$$

The above procedure is now repeated for this new point

$$-\nabla_{x_1} f = \begin{bmatrix} 0 \\ 1 \end{bmatrix}$$

Now $\partial f/\partial x_1$ is undefined in terms of L since this component is already zero. For $\partial f/\partial x_2$ we have

$$\partial f/\partial x_2 = -2(3/2 + L) + 4$$

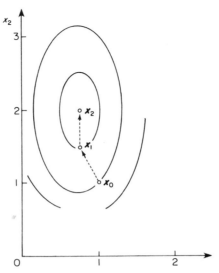

Fig. 3.12   An illustration of the method of steepest descent.

From $\partial f/\partial x_2$ we have $L = 1/2$. A new point is obtained,

$$
\mathbf{x}_2 =
\begin{bmatrix} \dfrac{3}{4} \\[2mm] \dfrac{3}{2} \end{bmatrix}
+ \frac{1}{2}
\begin{bmatrix} 0 \\ 1 \end{bmatrix}
=
\begin{bmatrix} \dfrac{3}{4} \\[2mm] 2 \end{bmatrix}
$$

and at this point both components of the gradient vector are found to vanish, indicating that this is the minimizing point. The resultant minimum value of $f(\mathbf{x})$ is found to be $-41/8$. The above procedure is illustrated graphically in Fig. 3.12. ∎

It is easily verified that the stationary point obtained from this function by the above method yields *the* minimum value of the objective function. By examining the matrix of second partial derivatives for this function, the Hessian matrix

$$
H_f(\mathbf{x}^*) =
\begin{bmatrix} 4 & 0 \\ 0 & 2 \end{bmatrix}
$$

it is observed to be positive definite for all $\mathbf{x}$. Consequently, this function is strictly convex and has but one stationary point. Therefore, the point obtained above is the only candidate for a minimizing point of this function. The fact that this point is a minimizing point could also have been established by a neighborhood search as described by Scheeffer, Stolz, and Van Dantscher.

As already mentioned, direct methods of optimization attempt to define the maximum or minimum of a function in a stepwise iterative fashion. The method of steepest descent is just one of many direct methods of optimization available to the analyst. Direct methods are most effective when the function to be optimized is unconstrained and possesses only one local maximum or minimum, which is then the global maximum or minimum. For a more complete discussion of direct methods of optimization, the reader should see Beveridge and Schechter [2] or Wilde and Beightler [7].

While direct methods of optimization have proven useful in the solution of many practical problems, the analyst should recognize several perplexing issues which may arise in their application. First, consider an unconstrained function $f(\mathbf{x})$ which possesses a single minimum (maximum) at $\mathbf{x}^*$. As a result of application of a direct method of optimization, a point $\mathbf{x}^0$ will be indicated as the value of $\mathbf{x}$ which minimizes (maximizes) $f(\mathbf{x})$. In most practical situations $\mathbf{x}^0 \neq \mathbf{x}^*$, although the distance between $\mathbf{x}^0$ and $\mathbf{x}^*$ may be sufficiently small that $f(\mathbf{x}^0) \simeq f(\mathbf{x}^*)$. That is, $\mathbf{x}^0$ may be an acceptable approximation to $\mathbf{x}^*$. However, this result cannot be guaranteed.

The second problem which must be recognized in the application of a direct method is that resulting when the function $f(\mathbf{x})$ possesses more than one local minimum (maximum). Suppose that $\mathbf{x}_1^*, \mathbf{x}_2^*, \ldots, \mathbf{x}_k^*$ are local minima (maxima) for $f(\mathbf{x})$. Application of a direct optimization technique will usually yield a point $\mathbf{x}^0$ such that $|f(\mathbf{x}_i^*) - f(\mathbf{x}^0)| \simeq 0$. However, $\mathbf{x}_i^*$ may not be a global optimum for $f(\mathbf{x})$, in which case $\mathbf{x}^0$ may be an unacceptable solution. Where the function to be optimized possesses, or is suspected to possess, more than one local minimum (maximum), the analyst may wish to apply the direct method of optimization several times using a different starting point at each application. Suppose a direct method is applied k times, where a different starting point for the search is chosen at each application, and yields the solution $\mathbf{x}_i^0$, $i = 1, 2, \ldots, k$. If $|\mathbf{x}_i^0 - \mathbf{x}_j^0| = 0$ and $|f(\mathbf{x}_i^0) - f(\mathbf{x}_j^0)| = 0$ for all $i \neq j$, then we may be satisfied that $f(\mathbf{x})$ possesses only one minimum (maximum), and that the vector $\mathbf{x}_i^0$ such that $f(\mathbf{x}_i^0) \leq f(\mathbf{x}_j^0)$ for all $i \neq j$ may be taken as the global minimum (maximum). However, if $|\mathbf{x}_i^0 - \mathbf{x}_j^0|$ and/or $|f(\mathbf{x}_i^0) - f(\mathbf{x}_j^0)|$ are significantly greater than zero for at least some $i \neq j$, then the analyst might conclude that the function possesses several minima (maxima). In this case the minimizing (maximizing) vector $\mathbf{x}_i^0$ can be found as before, provided the region of all local minima (maxima) $\mathbf{x}_i^*$, $i = 1, 2, \ldots, k$, has been located by the indicated minima (maxima) $\mathbf{x}_i^0$. The problem in this case lies in the judicious choice of starting points and in repeating the application of the direct search procedure with sufficient frequency. However, there are no foolproof rules for either the choice of starting points or identification of the number of times the search should be applied.

Probably the most serious problem encountered in the application of direct optimization techniques arises when the function to be optimized is constrained. Most direct methods are designed to deal with unconstrained functions; they perform poorly when the search for an optimum moves to a point near, or on, a boundary represented by a constraint. At this point, most direct procedures break down in that they are unable to define a direction which will lead the search along, or away from, the boundary (or constraint) toward the optimum of the constrained function.

The difficulties associated with direct methods of optimization just discussed do not arise when the indirect method can be applied. The indirect method of optimization is more often referred to as the classical method of optimization. The indirect or classical method offers the analyst a tool for identifying all local maxima and minima for both constrained and unconstrained continuous functions. In defining maxima and minima for unconstrained functions, the first step is to define the stationary points for the objective function as defined in Eq. (3.8). That is, the vector x^* satisfying Eq. (3.8) must be identified. In some cases closed-form solutions for x^* cannot be obtained, and it is usually in such instances that the analyst resorts to direct methods as already discussed. Computational difficulties also arise when attempting to optimize a constrained function through the classical method, but direct methods offer little relief in this case, as we have already mentioned. In this case the analyst may refer to a body of techniques called mathematical programming procedures. One such procedure, linear programming, was discussed briefly in chapter 2, and a more complete treatment is given in chapter 7.

In the remainder of this chapter we shall deal with the classical method of optimization of continuous unconstrained functions. In chapter 4 we shall discuss the extension of these methods to constrained functions.

INDIRECT METHODS OF OPTIMIZATION

The Necessary and Sufficient Conditions for an Unconstrained Maximum or Minimum

Although *necessary* and *sufficient* mean, in fact, what one might suppose they mean when applied to certain conditions which must be met in finding the maxim and minima of objective functions, let us discuss them briefly to make certain that the supposition is correct.

To begin, consider a simple Venn diagram containing the sets A, B as shown in Fig. 3.13. By saying that A is a *necessary* condition for B, we say that nothing is a case of B without being a case of A. By saying that B is a

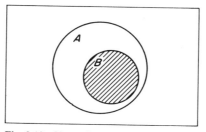

Fig. 3.13   Venn diagram for sets A and B.

sufficient condition for A, we mean that anything which is a case of B is a case of A.

For example, "Being at least thirty years old is a necessary but *not* a sufficient condition for being a United States Senator. Eating a pint of arsenic is a sufficient but *not* a necessary condition for dying" (From Barker [1]).

Functions of a Single Variable

Let the continuous function $f(x)$ be defined for $a \leqslant x \leqslant b$ and have a relative maximum or minimum at $x^* = c$, where $a < c < b$. If the derivative $f'(x)$ exists as a finite number at $x^* = c$, then

$$f'(c) = 0 \tag{3.16}$$

Equation (3.16) is the *necessary condition* for a maximum or minimum at $x = c$. We will demonstrate the proof that defines a relative minimum at $x^* = c$. The proof for a relative maximum follows a similar reasoning. For a relative minimum

$$f(c) \leqslant f(c + h) \tag{3.17}$$

for sufficiently small $|h| > 0$. We further hypothesize that

$$f'(c) = \lim_{h \to 0} \frac{f(c + h) - f(c)}{h} \tag{3.18}$$

exists and is a finite number, namely, zero. Taking the ratio whose limit is $f'(c)$, for h very small, we have the following,

$$\frac{f(c + h) - f(c)}{h} \geqslant 0 \qquad \text{if} \quad h > 0 \tag{3.19}$$

$$\frac{f(c + h) - f(c)}{h} \leqslant 0 \qquad \text{if} \quad h < 0 \tag{3.20}$$

since in both cases the numerator is either positive or zero. Therefore, if $h \to 0$ through positive values, we have

$$f'(c) \geqslant 0 \tag{3.21}$$

and if $h \to 0$ through negative values, we have

$$f'(c) \leqslant 0 \tag{3.22}$$

Now, since we have assumed that the derivative exists, we must have the same limit in both instances. That is,

$$0 \leqslant f'(c) \leqslant 0 \tag{3.23}$$

Obviously, this can only happen when

$$f'(c) = 0 \tag{3.24}$$

Thus the necessary condition for the continuous differentiable function $f(x)$ to have a relative maximum or minimum at $x^* = c$ $(a < c < b)$ is that the first derivative of $f(x)$ evaluated at $x^* = c$ must vanish:

$$f'(x)|_{x^* = c} = 0 \tag{3.25}$$

It should be noted that $f'(x^*) = 0$ does not necessarily imply that x^* is either a local maximum or a local minimum. In fact x^* may be a point of inflection. However, if $f(x)$ is continuous and differentiable at x^*, then x^* can be neither a maximum nor a minimum if $f'(x^*) \neq 0$. Hence the condition $f'(x^*) = 0$ defines one or more values of x^* at which $f(x)$ *may* achieve a local maximum or local minimum but does not imply that every, or even any, point x^* is a local maximum or minimum.

The sufficient conditions for the existence of a local maximum or minimum at a point x^* allow the analyst to determine the nature (minimum, maximum, or point of inflection) of the point x^*, where $f'(x^*) = 0$. Let $f(x)$ be a continuous function for which $f^i(x^*)$ exists for $i = 1$, $2, \ldots, n$. If

$$f'(x^*) = f^2(x^*) = \cdots = f^{(n-1)}(x^*) = 0 \tag{3.26}$$

and

$$f^n(x^*) \neq 0 \tag{3.27}$$

then

(1) if n *is* even and $f^n(x^*) > 0$, x^* is a local minimum,
(2) if n is even and $f^n(x^*) < 0$, x^* is a local maximum, and
(3) if n is odd, x^* is a point of inflection.

The condition that $f'(x^*) = 0$ and those given in 1, 2 and 3 above are *sufficient* for identification of x^* as a local maximum, local minimum, or a

point of inflection. The sufficient conditions are inconclusive if and only if
$f^i(x^*) = 0$ for $i = 1, 2, \ldots, n$ and $f^i(x^*)$ is undefined for $i > n$.

Proof of the sufficient condition proceeds as follows. By assumption we have

$$f'(x^*) = f^2(x^*) = \cdots f^{(n-1)}(x^*) = 0 \qquad (3.28)$$

Recalling the Taylor series expansion and letting $x_0 = x^*$, $x = x^* + h$, and
$x_1 = x^* + \theta h$, we then are left with

$$f(x^* + h) - f(x^*) = f^{(n)}(x^*)\frac{h^n}{n!} + f^{(n+1)}(x^* + \theta h)\frac{h^{n+1}}{(n+1)!} \qquad (3.29)$$

where $0 < \theta < 1$.

Further, we may reason that with h very small ($\simeq 0$)

$$R_n(x, h, \theta) = \frac{f^{(n+1)}(x_0 + \theta h)}{(n+1)!} h^{n+1} \simeq 0. \qquad (3.30)$$

We then have that the sign of $f(x^* + h) - f(x^*)$ is determined by the sign of

$$\frac{f^{(n)}(x^*)h^n}{n!} \qquad (3.31)$$

(a) If $f''(x^*) > 0$, then if n is even, $h^n > 0$ regardless of the sign of h
(i.e., $h > 0$ or $h < 0$). We may then conclude that $f''(x^*)h^n/n! > 0$ implies

$$f(x^* + h) - f(x) > 0 \qquad (3.32)$$

and x^* is a local minimum.

(b) If $f''(x^*) < 0$, then if n is even, again $h^n > 0$ regardless of the sign
of h, and $f''(x^*)h^n/n! < 0$ implies

$$f(x^* + h) - f(x^*) < 0 \qquad (3.33)$$

and x^* is a local maximum.

Note that if n happens to be odd then h^n will change sign depending on the
sign of h. We would then conclude that $x^* = c$ is not an extreme point but
rather a point of inflection.

Example 3.5 Find the stationary points for the function $f(x) = x^2 - 4x + 7$ and determine whether each is a local maximum, local minimum, or a point of inflection.

The necessary conditions for a local minimum or maximum yield

$$\frac{df}{dx} = 2x - 4 = 0, \qquad 2x = 4$$

and

$$x^* = 2$$

Since

$$\frac{d^2f}{dx^2} = 2 > 0$$

$x^* = 2$ is a local minimum for $f(x)$. Since $x^* = 2$ is the only stationary point for $f(x)$, it is a global minimum. ■

Example 3.6 Find the stationary points for the function $f(x) = x^5$ and determine whether each is a local maximum, local minimum, or a point of inflection.

The necessary conditions for a local maximum or minimum lead to

$$\frac{df}{dx} = 5x^4 = 0 \qquad \text{and} \qquad x^* = 0$$

From the sufficient conditions,

$$\frac{d^2f}{dx^2} = 20x^3 \bigg|_{x^*=0} = 0, \qquad \frac{d^3f}{dx^3} = 60x^2 \bigg|_{x^*=0} = 0$$

$$\frac{d^4f}{dx^4} = 120x \bigg|_{x^*=0} = 0, \qquad \frac{d^5f}{dx^5} = 120$$

Since $n = 5$, $x^* = 0$ is a point of inflection. ■

Functions of More Than One Variable

A necessary condition for a continuous, twice-differentiable function $f(\mathbf{x})$ to have an extreme point at $\mathbf{x}^*$ is

$$\frac{\partial f}{\partial x_i} \bigg|_{\mathbf{x}^*} = 0, \qquad i = 1, 2, \ldots, n \tag{3.34}$$

The proof is as follows for the case of a minimum at $\mathbf{x}^*$. From the definition of a minimum, $f(\mathbf{x}^*)$ is a minimum if for all suitably small $\mathbf{h}$, $f(\mathbf{x}^* + \mathbf{h}) - f(\mathbf{x}^*) > 0$. The proof now proceeds by contradiction for the minimum case; a similar reasoning holds for the maximum case. In establishing a contradiction we will assume that Eq. (3.34) does not hold at $\mathbf{x}^*$ for some i and show that this contradicts the proposition that $\mathbf{x}^*$ is local minimum. In particular let us assume that

$$\frac{\partial f}{\partial x_p} \bigg|_{\mathbf{x}^*} \neq 0 \tag{3.35}$$

and then demonstrate that this contradicts the proposition that $\mathbf{x}^*$ is a minimum. The contradiction comes about by showing that there exist vectors $\mathbf{h}_1$ and $\mathbf{h}_2$ such that for all $|\mathbf{h}_1| < \epsilon$ and $|\mathbf{h}_2| < \epsilon$ we have

$$f(\mathbf{x}^* + \mathbf{h}_1) - f(\mathbf{x}^*) < 0 \tag{3.36}$$

and

$$f(\mathbf{x}^* + \mathbf{h}_2) - f(\mathbf{x}^*) > 0 \tag{3.37}$$

which implies that $\mathbf{x}^*$ is not an extreme point. As we know, for $\mathbf{x}^*$ to be an extreme point, $f(\mathbf{x}^* + \mathbf{h}) - f(\mathbf{x}^*)$ *must* be of the same sign for all $\mathbf{x}^* + \mathbf{h}$ in an ϵ neighborhood of $\mathbf{x}^*$, where $|\mathbf{h}| < \epsilon$. From the first-order Taylor series expansion we have

$$f(\mathbf{x}^* + \mathbf{h}) - f(\mathbf{x}^*) = \nabla_x f(\mathbf{x}^*)\mathbf{h} + R_1(\mathbf{x}^*, \mathbf{h}, \theta) \tag{3.38}$$

Now let

$$\mathbf{h} = (0, 0, \ldots, h_p, 0, \ldots, 0), \tag{3.39}$$

That is, all elements of $\mathbf{h}$ are zero except the pth element, which is h_p. This yields

$$f(\mathbf{x}^* + \mathbf{h}) - f(\mathbf{x}^*) = \left.\frac{\partial f}{\partial x_p}\right|_{\mathbf{x}^*} h_p + R_1(\mathbf{x}^*, \mathbf{h}, \theta) \tag{3.40}$$

If h_p is small, then $R_1(\mathbf{x}^*, \mathbf{h}, \theta) \simeq 0$, and

$$f(\mathbf{x}^* + \mathbf{h}) - f(\mathbf{x}^*) \simeq \left.\frac{\partial f}{\partial x_p}\right|_{\mathbf{x}^*} h_p. \tag{3.41}$$

Now, if as assumed $\partial f / \partial x_p|_{\mathbf{x}^*} \neq 0$, then either

$$\left.\frac{\partial f}{\partial x_p}\right|_{\mathbf{x}^*} < 0 \tag{3.42}$$

or

$$\left.\frac{\partial f}{\partial x_p}\right|_{\mathbf{x}^*} > 0 \tag{3.43}$$

If

$$\left.\frac{\partial f}{\partial x_p}\right|_{\mathbf{x}^*} > 0$$

then either $h_p > 0$ and $f(\mathbf{x}^* + \mathbf{h}) - f(\mathbf{x}^*) > 0$ or $h_p < 0$ and $f(\mathbf{x}^* + \mathbf{h}) - f(\mathbf{x}^*) < 0$. If

$$\left.\frac{\partial f}{\partial x_r}\right|_{\mathbf{x}^*} < 0$$

then if $h_p > 0$, then $f(\mathbf{x^*} + \mathbf{h}) - f(\mathbf{x^*}) < 0$; or if $h_p < 0$, then $f(\mathbf{x^*} + \mathbf{h}) - f(\mathbf{x^*}) > 0$. In either case we contradict the proposition that $\mathbf{x^*}$ is an extreme point. We may therefore conclude that for $\mathbf{x^*}$ to be an extreme point, $\partial f / \partial x_i|_{\mathbf{x^*}} = 0$ for all x_i, $i = 1, \ldots, n$.

A sufficient condition for $f(\mathbf{x})$ to have a local minimum at $\mathbf{x^*}$, where

$$\left.\frac{\partial f}{\partial x_i}\right|_{\mathbf{x^*}} = 0, \qquad i = 1, 2, \ldots, n \tag{3.44}$$

is that the matrix of second partial derviatives of $f(\mathbf{x})$ (i.e., the Hessian matrix) evaluated at $\mathbf{x^*}$ be positive definite. Further, a sufficient condition for $f(\mathbf{x})$ to have a local maximum at $\mathbf{x^*}$ satisfying Eq. (3.44) is that the Hessian evaluated at $\mathbf{x^*}$ be negative definite.

From Taylor's mean-value theorem for functions of several variables,

$$f(\mathbf{x^*} + \mathbf{h}) - f(\mathbf{x^*}) = \frac{1}{2} \sum_{i=1}^{n} \sum_{j=1}^{n} h_i h_j \left.\frac{\partial^2 f}{\partial x_i \, \partial x_j}\right|_{\mathbf{x^*}} + R_2(\mathbf{x^*}, \mathbf{h}, \theta) \tag{3.45}$$

where $\mathbf{x^*} + \mathbf{h} = \mathbf{x}$, $\mathbf{x^*} = \mathbf{x}_0$, $h_k = (x_k - x_k^*)$, and $\mathbf{x}_1 = \mathbf{x^*} + \theta\mathbf{h}$, $0 < \theta < 1$, in the expression for Taylor's mean-value theorem in Chapter 1. Once again, if $\mathbf{h}$ is very small, then $R_2(\mathbf{x^*}, \mathbf{h}, \theta) \simeq 0$ and

$$f(\mathbf{x^*} + \mathbf{h}) - f(\mathbf{x^*}) \simeq \frac{1}{2} \sum_{i=1}^{n} \sum_{j=1}^{n} h_i h_j \left.\frac{\partial^2 f}{\partial x_i \, \partial x_j}\right|_{\mathbf{x^*}}$$

The right-hand side of this equation includes the Hessian matrix of second partial derivatives by noting that

$$\sum_{i=1}^{n} \sum_{j=1}^{n} h_i h_j \left.\frac{\partial^2 f}{\partial x_i \, \partial x_j}\right|_{\mathbf{x^*}} = \mathbf{h}^{\mathrm{T}} \mathbf{H}_f(\mathbf{x^*}) \mathbf{h} \tag{3.46}$$

where

$$\mathbf{h} = \begin{bmatrix} h_1 \\ h_2 \\ \vdots \\ h_n \end{bmatrix} \tag{3.47}$$

We may then write

$$f(\mathbf{x^*} + \mathbf{h}) - f(\mathbf{x^*}) \simeq \tfrac{1}{2} \mathbf{h}^{\mathrm{T}} \mathbf{H}_f(\mathbf{x^*}) \mathbf{h} \tag{3.48}$$

and the sign of $f(\mathbf{x^*} + \mathbf{h}) - f(\mathbf{x^*})$ will be determined by the sign of $\frac{1}{2} \mathbf{h}^{\mathrm{T}} \mathbf{H}_f(\mathbf{x^*}) \mathbf{h}$. By recognizing the right-hand side of this equation as a quadratic form (see Chapter 2), we need only show that $\mathbf{h}^{\mathrm{T}} \mathbf{H}_f(\mathbf{x^*}) \mathbf{h}$ is a positive definite quadratic form for a local minimum at $\mathbf{x^*}$ ($\mathbf{h}^{\mathrm{T}} \mathbf{H}_f(\mathbf{x^*}) \mathbf{h}$ is negative definite for a local maximum). That is, since for a positive definite quadratic form $h^T H_f(x^*)h > 0$, positive definiteness implies $f(x^* + h) - f(x^*) > 0$ and x^* is a local minimum. In a similar fashion negative definiteness of $h^T H_f(x^*)h$ implies that x^* is a local maximum. Finally, note the equivalence of the following statements:

(1) x^* is a local minimum (local maximum):
(2) $f(x^* + h) - f(x^*) > 0 \, (< 0)$ for $|h|$ suitably small;
(3) $\frac{1}{2} h^T H_f(x^*)h > 0 \, (< 0)$ for $|h|$ suitably small;
(4) $H_f(x^*)$ is positive definite (negative definite).

If the quadratic form $h^T H_f(x^*)h$ is indefinite, the point x^* is a saddle point. In the case of a semidefinite form, $h^T H_f(x^*)h$, the problem of determining the nature of x^* is more complex. When $h^T H_f(x^*)h$ is semidefinite, the method of Scheeffer, Stolz, and Van Dantsher may be applied.

The reader will recall that the leading principal minor and eigenvalue tests presented in Chapter 2 may be used to determine whether a quadratic form is positive or negative definite. The procedure for identifying the maxima or minima of an unconstrained continuous function of several variables is summarized in the next section.

Example 3.7   The time to produce a part on a specific machine is given as a function of the machine's speed (V) and feed rate (f). This function is

$$T(V, f) = \frac{C_1}{Vf} + C_2 V^2 + C_3 f$$

where C_1, C_2, and C_3 are known, nonnegative constants. What values of f and v will lead to producing a part in a minimum time?

Taking first partial derivatives of $T(V, f)$ yields

$$\frac{\partial T}{\partial V} = -\frac{C_1}{V^2 f} + 2C_2 V = 0 \qquad \text{or} \quad V^3 = \frac{C_1}{2C_2 f}$$

$$\frac{\partial T}{\partial f} = -\frac{C_1}{Vf^2} + C_3 = 0 \qquad \text{or} \quad V = \frac{C_1}{C_3 f^2}$$

Substitution of the expression for V obtained from the second equation into the first yields

$$\left(\frac{C_1}{C_3 f^2}\right)^3 = \left(\frac{C_1}{2C_2 f}\right) \qquad \text{or} \quad f^5 = \frac{2C_1^2 C_2}{C_3^3}.$$

Consequently,

$$f^* = \left(\frac{2C_1^2 C_2}{C_3^3}\right)^{1/5} \qquad \text{and} \qquad V^* = \left[\frac{C_1 C_3}{(2C_2)^2}\right]^{1/5}$$

To determine whether this solution is in fact a minimum, we form the Hessian matrix

$$H_T(V, f) = \begin{bmatrix} \dfrac{2C_1}{V^3 f} + 2C_2 & \dfrac{C_1}{V^2 f^2} \\ \dfrac{C_1}{V^2 f^2} & \dfrac{2C_1}{V f^3} \end{bmatrix}_{V^*, f^*}$$

Evaluating the Hessian matrix using V^* and f^*, we determine that it is positive definite, and consequently the solution for V^* and f^* obtained above is a minimum. ∎

Procedure for Finding Maxima and Minima

(1) Using the necessary conditions, set the first partial derivatives of $f(\mathbf{x})$ equal to zero:

$$\frac{\partial f}{\partial x_i} = 0 \qquad \text{for} \quad x_i, i = 1, \ldots, n \tag{3.49}$$

Solve these n equations simultaneously and obtain the solution vector (or vectors) $\mathbf{x}^*$. Any solution obtained here is a stationary point and is then a *potential* candidate for an extreme point. We know now that all extreme points are solutions to these n equations, but that not all solutions to these equations are extreme points.

(2) Using the sufficient conditions, take the second partial derivatives of the objective function, $f(\mathbf{x})$, and evaluate $(\partial^2 f / \partial x_i \, \partial x_j)|_{\mathbf{x}^*}$, $i, j = 1, 2, \ldots, n$.

(3) For each solution $\mathbf{x}^*$ determine whether $\mathbf{H}_f(\mathbf{x}^*)$ is positive definite, negative definite, or neither by applying either the leading principal minor or eigenvalue tests. All points $\mathbf{x}^*$ for which $\mathbf{H}_f(\mathbf{x}^*)$ is positive definite are local minima. All points $\mathbf{x}^*$ for which $\mathbf{H}_f(\mathbf{x}^*)$ is negative definite are local maxima. All points $\mathbf{x}^*$ for which $\mathbf{H}_f(\mathbf{x}^*)$ is indefinite are saddle points. The test is inconclusive for all points $\mathbf{x}^*$ for which $\mathbf{H}_f(\mathbf{x}^*)$ is semidefinite.

If the test in Step 3 results in a semidefinite form, then *no* conclusions can be drawn unless the remainder term is exactly equal to zero. For a more detailed discussion of this occurrence see Hancock's *Theory of Maxima and Minima* [4]. For all practical purposes, if a semidefinite Hessian is encountered, we may accept that the test as inconclusive in defining whether $\mathbf{x}^*$ is a minimizing or maximizing solution point. What may be the case is that a number of points in an ϵ neighborhood of $\mathbf{x}^*$ have the same value for $f(\mathbf{x})$ as for $\mathbf{x}^*$. That is, $f(\mathbf{x}^* + \mathbf{h}) = f(\mathbf{x}^*)$ for $\mathbf{h} \to 0$. This is analogous to a flat spot on the surface of $f(\mathbf{x})$ in the neighborhood of $\mathbf{x}^*$.

To verify this, a neighborhood search using Scheeffer's procedure may be attempted.

In many cases the analyst may find that the function under study possesses several local minima $x_1, x_2, \ldots, x_k$, and several local maxima, $x^*_{k+1} \ x^*_{k+2}, \ldots, x^*_m$. If these points are identified through the classical method, they are interior extreme points for $f(x)$. The global minimum and the global maximum for an unconstrained continuous function exists either at an interior extreme point or cannot be defined. The latter case results when the function $f(x)$ achieves its global minimum (maximum) as one or more elements of x increase or decrease without limit. Thus to identify the global minimum and maximum for $f(x)$, $f(x)$ may be evaluated at $f(x_i^*)$, $i = 1, 2, \ldots, m$. Selecting the extreme points x_j^* and x_l^* such that

$$f(x_j^*) \leqslant f(x_i^*), \qquad i = 1, 2, \ldots, m \tag{3.50}$$

and

$$f(x^*_l) \geqslant f(x^*_i), \qquad i = 1, 2, \ldots, m \tag{3.51}$$

indicates that x_j^* yields the least value of $f(x)$ and x_l^* yields the greatest value of $f(x)$ at least from among the extreme points. The function $f(x)$ is now examined as one or more elements of x increase or decrease without limit. If for any such combination of increasing or decreasing values of the elements of x

$$\lim_{|x| \to \infty} f(x) < f(x_j^*) \tag{3.52}$$

then x_j^* is not a global minimum, and the global minimum for $f(x)$ cannot be defined. Similarly, if for any combinations of increasing or decreasing values of the elements of x

$$\lim_{|x| \to \infty} f(x) > f(x_l^*) \tag{3.53}$$

then x_l^* is not a global maximum for $f(x)$ and the global maximum cannot be defined.

If a situation such as those represented in Eq. (3.52) or (3.53) occurs in practice, the analyst has probably either incorrectly formulated the objective function to be optimized or has failed to recognize one or more constraints on the problem. For example, suppose a model representing profit on operations has been developed and is a function of the variables advertising expenditures and average inventory level. If profit increases to its maximum as advertising expenditures go to infinity, the solution is obviously infeasible. In this case either the model does not recognize the effect of diminishing return on advertising expenditures or the analyst has failed to realize the limitation on available capital for advertising, which should have been expressed in the form of a constraint on the problem.

Example 3.8   Determine the minimum for

$$f(\mathbf{x}) = 30x_1^2 + 15x_2^2 - 62.5x_1 - 20x_2$$

From the necessary conditions for an interior extreme point

$$\frac{\partial f}{\partial x_1} = 60x_1 - 62.5, \qquad \frac{\partial f}{\partial x_2} = 30x_2 - 20$$

Solving for $\mathbf{x}^*$, we have $x_1^* = 625/600$, $x_2^* = 20/30$. The Hessian matrix evaluated at $\mathbf{x}^*$ is given by

$$\mathbf{H}_f(\mathbf{x}^*) = \begin{bmatrix} 60 & 0 \\ 0 & 30 \end{bmatrix}$$

Using the leading principal minor test, the determinants of the leading principal minors $\mathbf{H}_1$ and $\mathbf{H}_2$ are $|\mathbf{H}_1| = 60$, $|\mathbf{H}_2| = 1,800$, and $\mathbf{H}_f(\mathbf{x}^*)$ is positive definite. Thus

$$\mathbf{x}^* = \begin{bmatrix} x_1^* \\ x_2^* \end{bmatrix} = \begin{bmatrix} 625/600 \\ 2/3 \end{bmatrix}$$

is a minimum for $f(\mathbf{x})$. ∎

Convexity and the Sufficient Conditions

Let $f(x)$ be a continuous function of a single variable. We may classify $f(x)$ as a convex function if for any x in the domain of $f(x)$,

$$\frac{d^2f}{dx^2} \geqslant 0 \tag{3.54}$$

We may further state that if the strict inequality holds, i.e.,

$$\frac{d^2f}{dx^2} > 0 \tag{3.55}$$

then $f(x)$ is strictly convex. Similarly, we may classify $f(x)$ as a concave function if for any x in the domain of $f(x)$,

$$\frac{d^2f}{dx^2} \leqslant 0 \tag{3.56}$$

Again, we may further state that if the strict inequality holds,

$$\frac{d^2f}{dx^2} < 0 \tag{3.57}$$

then $f(x)$ is strictly concave (see Fig. 3.14).

Similar conclusions may be drawn concerning continuous functions of

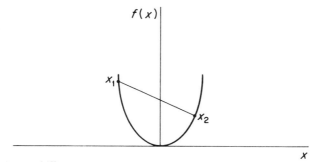

Fig. 3.14   A 1-dimensional convex function.

several variables. If $f(\mathbf{x})$ is a continuous function, then $f(\mathbf{x})$ is strictly convex throughout its domain of definition if $\mathbf{H}_f(\mathbf{x})$ is positive definite for all $\mathbf{x}$ in the domain of $f(\mathbf{x})$ and strictly concave if $\mathbf{H}_f(\mathbf{x})$ is negative definite for all $\mathbf{x}$ in the domain of $f(\mathbf{x})$ (see Fig. 3.15). Unconstrained functions which are strictly convex or strictly concave are particularly easy to deal with in the context of classical optimization. A strictly convex (concave) function may possess at most one stationary point. If this point is a local minimum (maximum), then it is also a global minimum (maximum).

Example 3.9   A farmer has offered to give you a rectangular section of his roadside property measuring 250,000 square feet. However, you must fence in your property using his fencing. If he charges you $5.50 for each linear foot of fencing, what dimension will you define for your property so as to minimize the cost you must incur for enclosing the property with a fence?

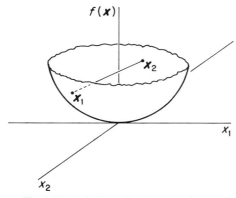

Fig. 3.15   A 2-dimensional convex function.

Let l be the length of the property and w the width of the property. The objective is then to minimize fencing cost $C(w,l)$ given by

$$C(w,l) = \$5.50(2l + 2w) = 11.0(l + w)$$

subject to the condition that

$$lw = 250,000$$

Writing l in terms of w using the above condition,

$$l = 250,000/w$$

and substituting into the objective function yields

$$C(w) = 11.0\left(\frac{250,000}{w} + w \right).$$

The stationary point of $C(w)$ with respect to w is found by

$$\frac{dC(w)}{dw} = -11\left(\frac{250,000}{w^2} \right) + 11 = 0$$

and consequently $w^* = \pm\sqrt{250,000} = \pm 500$ feet. Since a negative value is infeasible, we assume that the potential optimal width is 500 feet. Again, using the specified condition $lw = 250,000$, we find, substituting the value for w^*, that the optimal length l is also 500 feet. To ensure that this is a minimizing solution, we find

$$\frac{d^2C(w)}{dw^2} = 22\left(\frac{250,000}{w^3} \right)$$

and note that for any positive value of w this will be positive; consequently we have a minimizing solution. The total cost of fencing is

$$C(500,500) = 11.0(500 + 500) = \$11,000.$$

It should be noted that the same conclusion would have been reached if we had made the substitution in terms of l. ∎

Example 3.10   Show that $f(x) = x^2$ is strictly convex. Since

$$\frac{d^2f}{dx^2} = 2 > 0$$

for all x, $f(x)$ is strictly convex. ∎

Example 3.11   Show that

$$f(\mathbf{x}) = x_1^2 + x_2^2$$

is strictly convex.

Taking second partial derivatives, we have

$$\frac{\partial^2 f}{\partial x_2^2} = 2, \qquad \frac{\partial^2 f}{\partial x_1^2} = 2, \qquad \frac{\partial^2 f}{\partial x_1 \, \partial x_2} = \frac{\partial^2 f}{\partial x_2 \, \partial x_1} = 0$$

The Hessian matrix is then given by

$$\mathbf{H}_f(\mathbf{x}) = \begin{bmatrix} 2 & 0 \\ 0 & 2 \end{bmatrix}$$

Applying the leading principal minor test, $|H_1| = 2$, $|H_2| = 4$, and $f(\mathbf{x})$ is positive definite for all $\mathbf{x}$ and therefore strictly convex. ∎

Example 3.12 A product is to be purchased from a vendor and stored in a warehouse. This product is used at a constant rate and annual consumption is 10,000 units per year. It is fixed policy never to run short of the item and the vendor has promised immediate delivery of whatever is ordered. It costs $25 to place an order, and each unit that is ordered has a purchase price of $2. The warehousing cost is $0.25 per unit per year based on the average number of units in the warehouse. How many units should be ordered at one time and how many orders should be placed in one year? Let demand R be 10,000 units, order cost S be $25, holding cost K be $0.25, purchase price C be $2, order quantity be Q, number of orders be $R/Q = n$, and assume that total annual inventorying cost is given by the relationship

$$C(Q) = CR + S(R/Q) + K(Q/2)$$

From the necessary condition for the existence of an extreme point

$$\frac{dC(Q)}{dQ} = -\frac{SR}{Q^2} + \frac{K}{2} = 0 \qquad \text{and} \qquad Q^* = \sqrt{\frac{2SR}{K}}$$

Neglecting the negative root as infeasible,

$$Q^* = 1414.2 \text{ units}, \qquad n = R/Q^* = 7.07$$

Further, since $d^2C(Q)/dQ^2 = 2(SR/Q^3)$, $d^2C(Q)/dQ^2$ is greater than zero for every nonnegative Q, $C(Q)$ is strictly convex for $Q > 0$. Consequently, Q^* is the global minimum. ∎

Example 3.13 A company manufactures a product which it guarantees for a period of T years. If the product fails within the guarantee period the company must replace it at a cost of C_r. The cost of producing the item with a mean life u is $C_t u$. The probability that the unit fails during the guarantee period if it has a mean life u is given by P_f, where

$$P_f = \int_{-\infty}^{10(T-u)} \frac{1}{\sqrt{2\pi}} e^{-z^2/2} dz$$

and the total expected cost of production and replacement is given by $C_T(u)$, where

$$C_T(u) = C_t u + C_r \int_{-\infty}^{10(T-u)} \frac{1}{\sqrt{2\pi}} e^{-z^2/2} dz$$

Find the mean life u which will minimize total expected cost of manufacture and replacement.

From the necessary condition for the existence of an interior extreme point

$$\frac{d}{du} C_T(u^*) = 0$$

or

$$\frac{d}{du} C_T(u^*) = C_t - \frac{10C_r}{\sqrt{2\pi}} e^{-50(T-u^*)^2} = 0$$

Solving for u^* yields

$$u^* = T \pm \sqrt{-\frac{1}{50} \ln\left(\frac{C_t\sqrt{2\pi}}{10C_r}\right)}$$

For the sufficient conditions we have

$$\frac{d^2}{du^2} C_T(u^*) = -\frac{1000\, C_r(T - u^*)}{\sqrt{2\pi}} e^{-50(T-u^*)^2}$$

For

$$u^* = T - \sqrt{-\frac{1}{50} \ln\left(\frac{C_t\sqrt{2\pi}}{10C_r}\right)}$$

$(d^2/du^2)C_T(u^*) < 0$ and we have a local maximum.

$$u^* = T + \sqrt{-\frac{1}{50} \ln\left(\frac{C_t\sqrt{2\pi}}{10C_r}\right)}$$

$(d^2/du^2)C_T(u^*) > 0$ and we have a local minimum and the desired solution if $0 < C_t\sqrt{2\pi}/(10C_r) < 1$. If $C_t\sqrt{2\pi}/(10C_r) > 1$, the solution is composed of real and imaginary parts and hence is infeasible. ∎

PROBLEMS

1. Given the function: $f(x) = x + \cos x$ defined over the interval $0 \leqslant x \leqslant 2\pi$, where in this interval is the function convex, concave, neither convex nor concave?
2. In the region $0 \leqslant x_1 \leqslant 2$, $0 \leqslant x_2 \leqslant 2\pi$, where is the function $f(\mathbf{x}) = x_1^2 - \sin x_2$ convex, concave, neither convex nor concave?

3. Minimize $f(\mathbf{x}) = 3(x_1 - 4)^2 + 2(x_2 - 3)^2$.

4. Maximize $f(\mathbf{x}) = 4x_1 + 3x_2 - x_2^2 - 4x_1^2$.

5. Minimize $f(\mathbf{x}) = x_1^2 + 2x_1x_2 - 4x_3 + x_2x_3^2$.

6. Maximize $f(\mathbf{x}) = 2x_1 + 4x_2 - 3x_1x_2 - x_1^2 - 2x_2^2$.

7. Find and classify two stationary points of the following function:

$$f(\mathbf{x}) = -x_1^3 + 3x_1 + 84x_2 - 6x_2^2$$

8. Three oil fields are located according to a rectangular coordinate system. Each field produces an equal quantity of crude oil. A pipeline is to be laid from each field to a centrally located refinery. If the oil fields are located at $(0, 0)$, $(10, 5)$, $(8, 16)$, where should the refinery be located so that the total Euclidean distance $(\sum_{i=1}^{3}[(x - a_i)^2 + (y - b_i)^2]^{1/2})$ from the oil fields to the refinery is a minimum?

9. Considering the previous problem, what would be the location of the refinery if the objective was to minimize the total squared Euclidean distance $(\sum_{i=1}^{3}[(x - a_i)^2 + (y - b_i)^2])$ between the refinery and each oil field?

10. A seismic mapping vessel has obtained data points which describe the elevation contours of a harbor on the eastern coast of the United States. The following function has been synthesized from this data, and is proported to accurately describe the terrain beneath the harbor's waters:

$$f(\mathbf{x}) = 0.1x_2^3 - 0.2x_2^2 - 0.5x_1^2 + 0.04x_1x_2 + 0.03x_2 + 0.01x_1 - 0.5$$

where x_1 and x_2 are measured in miles due east and due north, respectively, from the center of the harbor. The harbor can be approximated in shape by a circle of 2 miles in radius with its center directly east of the harbor port, and the mouth of the harbor directly north of its center.

(a) Where are the deepest and highest points on the harbor's floor?

(b) The mouth of the harbor is one mile wide; where is the deepest point in the harbor's mouth and how deep is it? How deep is the harbor at its port?

(c) In what range of variation in x_1 and x_2 is the harbor convex, concave?

(d) Use Scheeffer's method to describe the floor of the harbor in a 0.5-mile neighborhood about its highest point and lowest point.

(e) Use the Hessian matrix to describe the floor of the harbor in a 0.5-mile neighborhood about the stationary points which are found by analysing the above function.

(f) Is there an island in the harbor?

11. Find and classify the stationary points of the function

$$f(x) = x^4 - 2x^3 + 7x$$

12. Describe the function

$$f(x) = (b/a)(a - x)^n$$

over the interval $0 \leqslant x \leqslant a$ when (a) n = 1, (b) n = 2, (c) n = 3, (d) n = 1/2 (e) n = -1, (f) n - 2.

13. The average cost of placing an order for a product or component is $72.00. The average cost for carrying one component in inventory for one year is $1.81. The forecast annual demand is 1, 128 units.

(a) Determine the economic purchased lot size for this part.

(b) What is the total annual variable cost and the unit annual variable cost of purchasing this part in economic lot sizes?

(c) Suppose you can manufacture this same component in your own plant at a rate of 3,133 units per year. If the setup cost is equal to your order cost, what is the economic manufactured lot size?

14. In reference to part (a) of the previous problem, the supplier has asked you to consider purchasing this item in lots of 500 units rather than in the lot size determined. If you do so, he will reduce his per unit price. Your carrying charges are 25% of the material cost. How much must the supplier reduce his price per unit so that your costs remain the same as they were for the lot size determined?

15. A company purchases subassemblies in lots of size L. Lots are labeled according to the mean life of the subassemblies included, either u_1 or u_2, where $u_2 > u_1$. To determine the proper categorization a sample of n items is drawn from each receipt lot, the life of each subassembly in the sample x_i, $i = 1, 2, \ldots, n$, is measured, and the sample mean life given by

$$\bar{x} = \frac{1}{n} \sum_{i=1}^{n} x_i$$

is computed. If $\bar{x}$ is less than a criterion U, the company assumes the mean subassembly life is u_1 and is u_2 if $\bar{x} \geqslant U$. The probability that the mean life of a subassembly lot is u_1 is p and is $(1 - p)$ for lots with mean life u_2. If the company categorizes a lot as having a mean u_1 when it actually has a mean u_2, a cost C_1 is incurred, and a cost C_2 occurs if the company categorizes the lot as having mean u_2 when it actually has a mean u_1. The expected cost of erroneous categorization $C_T(U)$ is given by

$$C_T(U) = C_1(1 - p) \int_{-\infty}^{\sqrt{n}(U - u_2)/\sigma} \frac{1}{\sqrt{2\pi}} e^{-z^2/2} \, dz + C_2 p \int_{\sqrt{n}(U - u_1)/\sigma}^{\infty} \frac{1}{\sqrt{2\pi}} e^{-z^2/2} \, dz$$

Find the value of U which will minimize the expected total cost of erroneous categorization if $u_2 = 5$, $u_1 = 1$, $\sigma = 0.30$, $C_1 = \$3.00$, $C_2 = \$10.00$, $p = 0.40$, $n = 10$.

16. The cost of fuel to run a vehicle is given by $C_1 k v^2$, where v is its speed in miles per hour (mi/hr) and k is a constant with dimension hr/mi^2. In addition, there is a fixed cost of C_2 per hour. Find the speed which will minimize cost per mile of operation if $k > 0$, $C_1 > 0$, $C_2 > 0$. The cost per mile of operation $C_T(v)$ is given by

$$C_T(v) = \frac{C_1 k v^2 + C_2}{v} = C_1 k v + \frac{C_2}{v} .$$

17. The cost of producing x units of product per month is given by $2x^2 + 80x + 50$, and the sale price per unit is $(100 - x)$. What should the monthly production rate be to maximize profit? Monthly profit $P(x)$ is given by

$$P(x) = x(100 - x) - (2x^2 + 80x + 50)$$

18. The demand for a certain product is constant and continuous with rate λ units per year and units of product are demanded one at a time. An inventory is maintained to meet this demand. At uniform intervals of time the inventory is replenished in lots of size q. If a unit of product is demanded when there is nothing on hand (stock out) the order for that unit is back ordered. Back orders are filled immediately upon replenishment of the inventory. Hence, if s units have been back ordered at the time of inventory replenishment, the inventory level after filling the back orders is $q - s$. The cost of carrying one unit in inventory for one year is C_I. The cost of a back order is composed of a fixed cost C_b and a cost C_β which is proportional to the duration of the back order. Each time the inventory is replenished a fixed cost C_0 arises. The annual cost $C_T(q, s)$ of operating the

inventory system, is given by

$$C_T(q,s) = \frac{C_0\lambda}{q} + \frac{C_1(q-s)^2}{2q} + \frac{C_b\lambda s}{q} + \frac{C_\beta s^2}{2q}$$

Find the values of q and s which will minimize the annual cost of operating the inventory system.

19. Annual demand for a particular product is dependent upon the annual investment in advertising. In particular, if x_1 is the advertising investment in dollars, then annual product demand $d(x_1)$ is given by

$$d(x_1) = ax_1/(x_1 + 1)$$

The selling price of each unit is p and the purchase cost of one unit is C_1. The cost of carrying one unit in inventory for one year is C_2. Inventory is stocked at the beginning of each year. If x_2 units are purchased at the beginning of the year and x_1 is invested in advertising, the annual profit can be estimated by

$$P(x) = (p - C_1)x_2 - x_1 - C_2x_2^2(x_1 + 1)/2ax_1$$

Find the advertising expenditure and initial inventory level which will maximize annual profit.

20. The *mode* of a continuous random variable is defined as the value of the random variable at which its probability density function is a maximum. Find the mode of the random variable x if its probability density function is defined by

(a)

$$f(x) = \frac{\lambda^\alpha}{(a-1)!} e^{a-1} e^{-\lambda x}, \qquad 0 < x < \infty, \quad \lambda > 0, \quad \alpha > 1,$$

(b)

$$f(x) = \frac{\Gamma(n+1/2)}{\sqrt{n\pi}\,\Gamma(n/2)}\left(1 + \frac{x^2}{n}\right)^{-(n+1)/2}, \qquad \infty < x < \infty, \quad n \geqslant 1.$$

21. An equation of the form

$$y = b_0 + b_1 x$$

is to be fit to an experimentally obtained set of data. There are n observed sets of data on x and y. That is, if x_i is the ith observed value of the independent variable x, then y_i is the corresponding observed value of the dependent variable y. The values of b_0 and b_1 are to be defined such that

$$\sum_{i=1}^{n} (y_i - b_0 - b_1 x_i)^2 = \min$$

Derive expressions for calculations of b_0 and b_1.

22. An air traffic controller has two aircraft on his radar scope, A and B, both flying level and at the same altitude. Aircraft A is flying along the straight line given by $x_1 + y_1 = 10$ and B along the straight line $3x_2 + y_2 = 10$. At time zero A is at the point $(-40, 50)$ and B is at $(-20, 70)$ as shown in Fig. 3.16. A is flying at 550 nautical miles per hour and B at 615 nautical miles per hour. At what point in time will the aircraft be closest to one another? If aircraft must maintain a separation distance of 5 nautical miles, will the separation standard be violated if the aircraft continue their flight paths? By how much must the velocity of B be changed at time zero so that the aircraft will not violate the 5-mile separation standard if current flight paths are maintained?

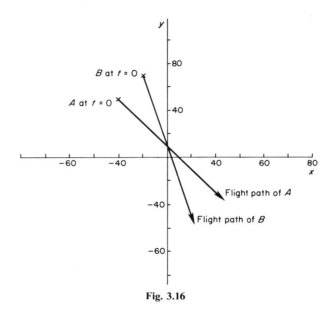

Fig. 3.16

Suggested Further Reading

1. Barker, S. F. (1965). "The Elements of Logic," McGraw-Hill, New York.
2. Beveridge, G. S. G., and Schechter, R. S. (1970). "Optimization: Theory and Practice," McGraw-Hill, New York.
3. Cooper, L. and Steinberg, D. (1970). "Introduction to Methods of Optimization," Saunders, Philadelphia, Pennsylvania.
4. Hancock, H., (1960). "Theory of Maxima and Minima," Dover, New York.
5. Klaf, A. A., (1956), "Calculus Refresher for Technical Men," Dover, New York.
6. Thompson, S. P. (1969). "Calculus Made Easy," Macmillan, New York.
7. Wilde, D. J., and Beightler, C. S. (1967). "Foundations of Optimization's." Prentice-Hall, Englewood Cliffs, New Jersey.
8. Zahradnik, R. L. (1971). "Theory and Techniques of Optimization," Barnes & Noble, New York.

Chapter 4 | Classical Optimization Theory For Constrained Functions

INTRODUCTION

In Chapter 3 methods were presented for determining the values of a set of variables which will maximize or minimize some continuous function of those variables, where it was assumed that the value of each variable could take on any real value. In many practical problems this assumption is unrealistically generous. To illustrate, consider an inventory problem in which we are concerned with identification of the optimal order quantities q_i, $i = 1, \ldots, m$, for m raw materials. If we assume that raw materials cannot be returned to the supplier once they have been received, inspected, and accepted by the purchaser, then the feasible values of q_i are restricted to nonnegative real numbers. However, the solution procedures presented in Chapter 3 could conceivably lead to optimal values of q_i, q_i^* such that $q_i^* < 0$ for one or more i. Obviously such a solution is without practical meaning.

In the constrained optimization problem we are concerned with finding the vector $\mathbf{x}^*$ which minimizes or maximizes $f(\mathbf{x})$ so that $\mathbf{x}^*$ does not violate any of the constraints on the problem. Any vector $\mathbf{x}$ which satisfies all of the constraints imposed on the problem is said to be a *feasible solution*. If the problem is unconstrained, then any solution $\mathbf{x}$ is feasible. The set of values $\mathbf{x}$ which satisfies all of the constraints simultaneously defines the *space of feasible solutions* for the problem and is sometimes referred to simply as the *solution space*.

As illustrated in several of the examples in Chapter 3, it is ocassionally possible to obtain the optimal feasible solution to a constrained problem

without specifically accounting for the constraints in the solution procedure. That is, the optimal solution is the same whether we account for the
constraints in the solution procedure or not. When the optimal solution for
the unconstrained problem is also a feasible solution for the constrained
problem, then the constraints are said to be *inactive* in that they do not
affect the optimal solution to the problem. When the optimal solution to
the unconstrained problem is infeasible for the constrained problem, then
at least some of the constraints are *active* or *binding*. In any constrained
optimization problem the resulting optimal solution may be such that some
of the constraints are active while others are inactive. For example, suppose
we wish to minimize $f(\mathbf{x}) = (x_1 - 7)^2 + (x_2 - 7)^2$ so that

$$x_1 + x_2 \leqslant 10$$
$$x_1 \geqslant 0$$
$$x_2 \geqslant 0$$

where $\mathbf{x}$ is a 2-dimensional vector. If the minimizing vector $\mathbf{x}^*$ is $[5 \quad 5]^T$,
then the first constraint is active since it is satisfied as an equality at $\mathbf{x}^*$.
However, the constraints $x_1 \geqslant 0$, $x_2 \geqslant 0$ are inactive since they are satisfied
as inequalities at $\mathbf{x}^*$. If the optimal solution to this problem were $\mathbf{x}^*$
$= [10 \quad 0]^T$, then the first and third constraints would be active at $\mathbf{x}^*$, while
the second constraint would be inactive. If $\mathbf{x}^* = [0 \quad 0]$, then the first
constraint would be inactive at $\mathbf{x}^*$, while the second and third constraints
would be active. If $\mathbf{x}^* = [2 \quad 2]^T$, then none of the constraints are active.
For the set of constraints defined in this example, there is no point $\mathbf{x}$ for
which all of the constraints are active.

Among a set of constraints there may be one or more which are
redundant. Suppose that two constraints are given by $g_1(\mathbf{x}) \leqslant b_1$ and
$g_2(\mathbf{x}) \leqslant b_2$. If every vector $\mathbf{x}$ which satisfies the first constraint also satisfies
the second constraint, then the second constraint is redundant or superflu-
ous. In general, if any set of constraints contains a constraint $g_i(\mathbf{x}) \leqslant b_i$
such that $g_i(\mathbf{x}) \leqslant b_i$ can be omitted from the set without changing the space
of feasible solutions for the problem, then that constraint is said to be
redundant. For example, consider the set of constraints given by

(1) $x_1 + x_2 \leqslant 30$
(2) $x_1 + x_2 \leqslant 60$
(3) $x_1 - x_2 \geqslant 50$
(4) $x_1 \geqslant 0$
(5) $x_2 \geqslant 0$

These constraints are shown graphically in Fig. 4.1, where the space of
feasible solutions is defined by the space C. The second constraint is
redundant since every solution which satisfies the first constraint automati-

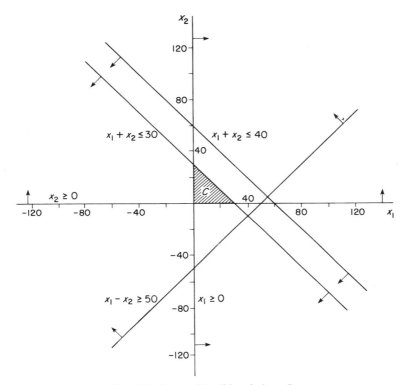

Fig. 4.1 Space of feasible solutions C.

cally satisfies the second although the converse is not true. Hence we can drop the second constraint without changing the space of feasible solutions for the problem. In addition, every solution which satisfies constraints (1), (4), and (5) also satisfies the third constraint. Hence the third constraint is also redundant and may be eliminated without altering the space of feasible solutions.

In this chapter we shall present indirect methods for determining the vector x^* which optimizes the continuous function $f(x)$ subject to a set of constraints. While these techniques are conceptually simple to interpret, they are computationally tedious to apply. For this reason, it is often useful first to solve the problem ignoring the constraints. If the unconstrained solution does not violate any of the constraints, then the problem is solved. However, if the unconstrained solution is infeasible in that it violates one or more of the constraints, then the techniques developed in this chapter should be applied. The following example illustrates a case where the methods presented in Chapter 3 yield both a feasible and an infeasible solution to the constrained problem.

Example 4.1 A company manufactures one of its products on a continuous basis. One of the raw materials used in the manufacturing process is to be purchased in lots of size q. The production rate ψ for the process is 10,000 units per year and one unit of raw material is required for each unit of final product. The cost C_1 of carrying one unit of raw material for one year is $50.00. The purchase price C_P for each unit of raw material is $150.00, and a cost C_0 of handling of $100.00 is added for each shipment and is independent of the size of the shipment. The total cost of purchasing, handling, and inventory per year for lots of size q is given by C_T where

$$C_T(q) = (1/2)C_1 q + C_0(\psi/q) + C_p\psi \qquad (4.1)$$

if the total amount purchased is ψ each year. Using the techniques presented in Chapter 3, find the optimal order quantity q^*. If the storage capacity for the raw material is W_C, determine whether the optimal order quantity derived is feasible if (a) $W_C = 300$, (b) $W_C = 150$.

The unconstrained optimization problem is given by

$$C_T(q) = \min$$

while the constrained problem is defined by

$$C_T(q) = \min$$
$$\text{s.t.}$$
$$0 \leqslant q \leqslant W_C$$

where

$$C_T(q) = (1/2)C_T q + C_0(\psi/q) + C_p\psi$$

For the unconstrained problem the value of q which minimizes $C_T(q)$ must satisfy the relationship

$$\frac{d}{dq} C_T(q) = 0 = \frac{C_1}{2} - \frac{C_0\psi}{q^2} \qquad (4.2)$$

Hence

$$q^* = \sqrt{2C_0\psi/C_1} \qquad (4.3)$$

and since $(d^2/dq^2)f(q^*) > 0$, $q^* = 200$ is a local minimum. For case (a) this solution is feasible since $q^* < 300$. However, in case (b) $q^* > 150$ and is therefore infeasible. Hence the methods presented in Chapter 3 are appropriate if $W_C = 300$ but are inappropriate for $W_C = 150$. ∎

The constrained optimization problem may be formulated as

$$f(\mathbf{x}) = \min \, (\max)$$

s.t.

$$g_i(\mathbf{x}) \leqslant 0, \qquad i = 1, 2, \ldots, k \qquad\qquad (4.4)$$

$$g\,(\mathbf{x}) = 0, \qquad i = k+1, k+2, \ldots, m$$

where $\mathbf{x}$ is an n-dimensional vector of variables and $g_i(\mathbf{x}) \leqslant 0$, $g_j(\mathbf{x}) = 0$, $i = 1, 2, \ldots, k$, $j = k+1, k+2, \ldots, m$ are a set of constraints which the minimizing (maximizing) vector $\mathbf{x}^*$ must satisfy. Frequently constraints are logically expressed in the form $h(\mathbf{x}) \geqslant b$. However, the formulation given in Eq. (4.4) still applies if we set $g(\mathbf{x}) = -h(\mathbf{x}) + b$, yielding the constraint $g(\mathbf{x}) \leqslant 0$. In some cases all of the constraints for the problem will be in the form $g(\mathbf{x}) \leqslant 0$. In rare cases all of the constraints will be in the form of equalities. Hence, the problem in Example 4.1 would be expressed as

$$\min f(q) = (1/2)C_1 q + C_0(\psi/q) + C_P\psi$$

s.t.

$$q - W_C \leqslant 0 \qquad\qquad (4.5)$$

$$-q \leqslant 0$$

In the next section of this chapter we shall present methods for solving the optimization problem defined by

$$f(\mathbf{x}) = \min\,(\max)$$

s.t.

$$g_1(\mathbf{x}) = 0$$

$$g_2(\mathbf{x}) = 0$$

$$\vdots \qquad\qquad (4.6)$$

$$g_m(\mathbf{x}) = 0$$

As we have mentioned, formulation of most practical problems will rarely lead to a set of constraints all of which are expressed as equalities. However, in the section of this chapter which deals with inequality constraints, we shall show that inequality constraints can be modified so that they may be expressed equivalently in the form of equality constraints. Thus the expression for the constrained optimization problem given in Eq. (4.6) may be thought of as a general formulation of the problem, since all constrained problems may ultimately be expressed in this form. Hence, the methods presented in the next section can be applied to the solution of a constrained optimization problem, where the constraints are expressed either as inequalities, equalities or both.

As we have noted, the classical techniques for solution of the constrained optimization problem are computationally tedious, and for this reason it is often worthwhile to first solve the problem as though it were unconstrained. If this solution satisfies the constraint set, then the solution is both optimal and feasible and hence the desired solution. If the unconstrained solution is not feasible, then the techniques presented in the next three sections may be applied. When some or all of the constraints are expressed in the form of equalities, the solution to the unconstrained problem usually will prove infeasible. In the case where some of the constraints are defined as equalities while others are given as inequalities, the analyst may wish initially to ignore the inequality constraints only. Once again if the optimum achieved is feasible, it is the desired solution.

OPTIMIZATION SUBJECT TO EQUALITY CONSTRAINTS

The problem addressed here is that defined in Eq. (4.6). Three alternative approaches to the solution of this problem will be presented and differ only with respect to the computational procedure applied.

The Method of Direct Elimination

The problem defined in Eq. (4.6) consists of the minimization or maximization of a function of n variables $f(\mathbf{x})$ subject to constraints expressed in the form of a set of m equations involving the same n variables. If $m > n$, the problem is overconstrained and has no solution unless at least $m - n$ constraints are redundant. In the latter case the problem is incorrectly formulated in that one or more constraints are unnecesary, since the restrictions they impose are implied by other constraints. Henceforth, we will assume no redundancy among the constraints. If $m = n$, the solution to the problem is the solution of the system of equations defined by the constraint set. If $m < n$, then there is an infinite number of feasible solutions satisfying the constraint set, and we wish to determine that feasible solution which minimizes or maximizes the function $f(\mathbf{x})$. (It should be noted that no solution exists if the constraint set includes contradictory constraints such as $x_1 + x_2 = 5$ and $x_1 + x_2 = 10$.)

In the remainder of our discussion we shall assume that $m < n$. The constraints defined by $g_i(\mathbf{x}) = 0$, $i = 1, 2, \ldots, m$, imply that once the values of $n - m$ of the n variables are defined, the values of the remaining m are given by the constraints. We have, then, complete freedom in choosing the values of only $n - m$ of the variables.

We may change the constrained optimization problem to an unconstrained optimization problem by solving for m of the variables in terms of the remaining $n - m$ using the m constraint equations $g_i(\mathbf{x}) = 0$, $i = 1$, $2, \ldots, m$. Let

$$x_i = \psi_i(x_{m+1}, x_{m+2}, \ldots, x_n), \qquad i = 1, 2, \ldots, m \qquad (4.7)$$

Then

$$f(\mathbf{x}) = f(\psi_1, \psi_2, \ldots, \psi_m, x_{m+1}, x_{m+2}, \ldots, x_n) \qquad (4.8)$$

Since $f(\psi_1, \psi_2, \ldots, \psi_m, x_{m+1}, x_{m+2}, \ldots, x_n)$ is a function of the variables $x_{m+1}, x_{m+2}, \ldots, x_n$ only, the problem is reduced to optimization of the constraint-free function defined in Eq. (4.8). Since the constraints have been removed, we may apply the techniques presented in Chapter 3 for optimization of unconstrained functions of several variables.

Example 4.2   A research and development organization wishes to conduct an experiment in which two ingredients, A and B, are to be used. If x_1 and x_2 are the number of units of A and B used, respectively, then the cost of the experiment is given by

$$C(\mathbf{x}) = C_1 x_1^2 + C_2 x_2 \qquad (4.9)$$

A total of k units are to be used for the experiment. That is,

$$x_1 + x_2 = k \qquad (4.10)$$

Since x_1 and x_2 must be nonnegative we have the additional constraints $x_1 \geqslant 0$ and $x_2 \geqslant 0$. How many units of A and B should be used in the experiment to minimize total cost if

$$C_1 = \$100.00, \qquad C_2 = \$1000.00, \qquad k = 20$$

To find the minimum cost allocation of ingredients for the experiment, we will ignore the constraints $x_1 \geqslant 0$ and $x_2 \geqslant 0$ for the present. If the optimal solution resulting is feasible, then these constraints have no effect and will require no further consideration. Solving for x_2 in terms of x_1 yields

$$x_2 = k - x_1 \qquad (4.11)$$

Substituting the expression for x_2 in Eq. (4.9), we have

$$C(x_1) = C_1 x_1^2 + C_2(k - x_1) \qquad (4.12)$$

and the problem is reduced to the optimization of an unconstrained function of one variable. The minimizing value of x_1 must satisfy the relationship given by

$$\frac{d}{dx_1} C(x_1) = 2C_1 x_1 - C_2 = 0 \qquad (4.13)$$

or

$$x_1^* = C_2/2C_1 \qquad (4.14)$$

Since

$$\frac{d^2}{dx_1^2} C(x_1) = 2C_1 > 0 \tag{4.15}$$

for $C_1 > 0$, $x_1^* = C_2/(2C_1)$ minimizes $C(x_1)$ and $x_2^* = k - [C_2/(2C_1)]$. Thus

$$x_1^* = 5, \qquad x_2^* = 15$$

is the optimal solution for the constrained optimization problem, since this solution satisfies all of the constraints on the problem including $x_1 \geqslant 0$ and $x_2 \geqslant 0$. ∎

Example 4.3   A retailer sells four products. He has found that annual profit is a function of the size of the initial inventory x_j, $j = 1, 2, 3, 4$, of each product and can be expressed as

$$P(\mathbf{x}) = \sum_{j=1}^{4} \left(a_j x_j^2 + b_j x_j \right) + 100,000 \tag{4.16}$$

where x_j is measured in gallons and

$$a_1 = -5, \qquad a_2 = -2, \qquad a_3 = -6, \qquad a_4 = -2$$
$$b_1 = 10000, \qquad b_2 = 8000, \qquad b_3 = 3600, \qquad b_4 = 4800$$

x_j is the initial inventory level of product j and the cost of carrying this inventory is projected to be $(1/2)C_{1j}x_j$, where

$$C_{11} = \$25.00, \qquad C_{12} = \$20.00, \qquad C_{13} = \$30.00 \qquad C_{14} = \$22.00$$

Available storage space is 10,000 square feet. Each unit of product line j requires s_j square feet for storage, where $s_1 = 4$, $s_2 = 4$, $s_3 = 5$, $s_4 = 5$. The company wishes to utilize all of its warehouse space and is willing to invest \$27,000 in inventory. Hence

$$\sum_{j=1}^{4} (1/2)C_{1j}x_j = 27,000 \tag{4.17}$$

$$\sum_{j=1}^{4} s_j x_j = 10,000 \tag{4.18}$$

where

$$x_j \geqslant 0, \qquad j = 1, 2, 3, 4$$

Determine the initial inventory levels x_j, $j = 1, 2, 3, 4$, which will maximize annual profit.

As in the preceding example we will initially ignore the nonnegativity constraint $x_j \geqslant 0, j = 1, 2, 3, 4$. Solving Eq. (4.17) for x_1 yields

$$x_1 = \frac{27{,}000 - 0.50(C_{12}x_2 + C_{13}x_3 + C_{14}x_4)}{0.50C_{11}}$$

$$= 2160 - 0.80x_2 - 1.20x_3 - 0.88x_4 \qquad (4.19)$$

Solving Eq. (4.18) for x_2 yields

$$x_2 = \frac{10{,}000 - s_1 x_1 - s_2 x_3 - s_4 x_4}{s_2}$$

$$= 2500 - x_1 - 1.25x_3 - 1.25x_4 \qquad (4.20)$$

Thus x_1 and x_2 may be expressed in terms of x_3 and x_4 as follows:

$$x_1 = 800 - x_3 + 0.60x_4 \qquad (4.21)$$

$$x_2 = 1700 - 0.25x_3 - 1.85x_4 \qquad (4.22)$$

and $P(\mathbf{x})$ is given by

$$P(\mathbf{x}) = -5(800 - x_3 + 0.60x_4)^2 + 10{,}000(800 - x_3 + 0.6x_4)$$

$$- 2(1700 - 0.25x_3 - 1.85x_4)^2 + 8000(1700 - 0.25x_3 - 1.85x_4)$$

$$- 6x_3^2 + 3600x_3 - 2x_4^2 + 4800x_4 \qquad (4.23)$$

$P(\mathbf{x})$ is now a function of the two variables x_3 and x_4. Applying the methods presented in Chapter 3, we have

$$\frac{\partial}{\partial x_3} P(\mathbf{x}) = 1300 - 22.25x_3 + 4.15x_4 = 0 \qquad (4.24)$$

$$\frac{\partial}{\partial x_4} P(\mathbf{x}) = 3780 + 4.15x_3 - 21.29x_4 = 0 \qquad (4.25)$$

which yields

$$x_3^* = 95.00, \qquad x_4^* = 196.1$$

From Eqs. (4.21) and (4.22),

$$x_1^* = 822.6, \qquad x_2^* = 1313.5$$

To determine whether the solution given maximizes $P(\mathbf{x})$, we take second partial derivatives with respect to x_3 and x_4.

$$\frac{\partial^2}{\partial x_3^2} P(\mathbf{x}) = -22.25, \qquad \frac{\partial^2}{\partial x_4^2} P(\mathbf{x}) = -21.29, \qquad \frac{\partial^2}{\partial x_3 \partial x_4} P(\mathbf{x}) = 4.15$$

and the Hessian matrix is given by

$$H = \begin{bmatrix} -22.25 & 4.15 \\ 4.15 & -21.29 \end{bmatrix}$$

The first and second leading principal minors are then -22.25 and 456.48, respectively. Since $H_1 < 0$ and $H_2 > 0$, the solution

$$\mathbf{x}^* = (822.6, 1313.5, 95.0, 196.1)$$

yields a maximum for $P(\mathbf{x})$ subject to the constraints specified and the maximum profit, including $x_j \geqslant 0, j = 1, 2, 3, 4$, is $\$13,052,334.14$. ■

The method of direct elimination is attractive because of its simplicity, provided the set of constraint equations can be solved to eliminate m variables. However, this technique is applicable only when there exists a nonsingular $(m \times m)$ maxtrix of first partial derivatives $(\partial / \partial x_j) g_i(\mathbf{x}^*)$ for some choice of variables x_j. As we shall see, this restriction applies to each of the techniques we shall present in this chapter.

The Method of Indirect Elimination

The method of direct elimination requires the solution of the m constraint equations for m of the decision variables in terms of the remaining $n - m$ variables followed by development of the function

$$f(\psi_1, \psi_2, \ldots, \psi_m, x_{m+1}, x_{m+2}, \ldots, x_n),$$

where

$$x_i = \psi_i(x_{m+1}, x_{m+2}, \ldots, x_n), \qquad i = 1, 2, \ldots, m \qquad (4.26)$$

Unless the constraint set $g_i(\mathbf{x}) = 0, i = 1, 2, \ldots, m$, yields a simple solution $\psi_i(x_{m+1}, x_{m+2}, \ldots, x_n)$ for x_i, the direct elimination procedure can be quite cumbersome and impractical. Resolution of the problem can be somewhat simplified through the method of indirect elimination. The method of indirect elimination will be presented without proof. For a derivation of the technique the reader should see Beveridge and Schechter [2] or Schmidt [7].

Let

$$f_j(\mathbf{x}) = \frac{\partial}{\partial x_j} f(\mathbf{x}), \qquad j = 1, 2, \ldots, n \qquad (4.27)$$

$$g_{i_j}(\mathbf{x}) = \frac{\partial}{\partial x_j} g_i(\mathbf{x}), \qquad i = 1, 2, \ldots, m, \quad j = 1, 2, \ldots, n \qquad (4.28)$$

where $f(\mathbf{x})$ and $g_i(\mathbf{x})$, $i = 1\ 2, \ldots, m$, are continuous and differentiable.

Further, let

$$J_j(\mathbf{x}) = \begin{bmatrix} f_j(\mathbf{x}) & f_1(\mathbf{x}) & f_2(\mathbf{x}) & \cdots & f_m(\mathbf{x}) \\ g_{1_j}(\mathbf{x}) & g_{1_1}(\mathbf{x}) & g_{1_2}(\mathbf{x}) & \cdots & g_{1_m}(\mathbf{x}) \\ g_{2_j}(\mathbf{x}) & g_{2_1}(\mathbf{x}) & g_{2_2}(\mathbf{x}) & \cdots & g_{2_m}(\mathbf{x}) \\ \vdots & \vdots & \vdots & & \vdots \\ g_{m_j}(\mathbf{x}) & g_{m_1}(\mathbf{x}) & g_{m_2}(\mathbf{x}) & \cdots & g_{m_m}(\mathbf{x}) \end{bmatrix} \qquad (4.29)$$

where $j = m + 1, m + 2, \ldots, n$, and

$$G(\mathbf{x}) = \begin{bmatrix} g_{1_1}(\mathbf{x}) & g_{1_2}(\mathbf{x}) & \cdots & g_{1_m}(\mathbf{x}) \\ g_{2_1}(\mathbf{x}) & g_{2_2}(\mathbf{x}) & \cdots & g_{2_m}(\mathbf{x}) \\ \vdots & \vdots & & \vdots \\ g_{m_1}(\mathbf{x}) & g_{m_2}(\mathbf{x}) & \cdots & g_{m_m}(\mathbf{x}) \end{bmatrix} \qquad (4.30)$$

If $\mathbf{x}^*$ is an extreme point for $f(\mathbf{x})$ satisfying the constraint set $g_i(\mathbf{x}) = 0$, $i = 1, 2, \ldots, m$, then

$$|J_j(\mathbf{x}^*)| = 0, \qquad j = m + 1, m + 2, \ldots, n \qquad (4.31)$$

if

$$|G(\mathbf{x}^*)| \neq 0 \qquad (4.32)$$

Equations (4.31) and (4.32) are the necessary conditions for the existence of an extreme point at $\mathbf{x}^*$. The values of $\mathbf{x}^*$ are those derived from the set of $n - m$ equations in Eq. (4.31) and the m constraints $g_i(\mathbf{x}) = 0$, $i = 1$, $2, \ldots, m$. That is, we have a set of n equations in n variables. To illustrate application of the method of indirect elimination let us reconsider the problem given in Example 4.3.

Example 4.4   Solve the problem in Example 4.3 using the method of indirect elimination.

From Example 4.3 we have

$$f(\mathbf{x}) = \sum_{j=1}^{4} \left(a_j x_j^2 + b_j x_j \right) + 100,000 \qquad (4.33)$$

and

$$g_1(\mathbf{x}) = \sum_{j=1}^{4} (1/2) C_{1j} x_j - 27{,}000 = 0 \qquad (4.34)$$

$$g_2(\mathbf{x}) = \sum_{j=1}^{4} s_j x_j - 10{,}000 = 0 \qquad (4.35)$$

Now

$$f_j(\mathbf{x}) = 2a_j x_j + b_j, \qquad j = 1, 2, 3, 4 \qquad (4.36)$$

$$g_{1_j}(\mathbf{x}) = (1/2) C_{1j}, \qquad j = 1, 2, 3, 4 \qquad (4.37)$$

$$g_{2_j}(\mathbf{x}) = s_j, \qquad j = 1, 2, 3, 4 \qquad (4.38)$$

and

$$J_3(\mathbf{x}) = \begin{bmatrix} -12x_3 + 3600 & -10x_1 + 10{,}000 & -4x_2 + 8000 \\ 15.00 & 12.50 & 10.00 \\ 5.00 & 4.00 & 4.00 \end{bmatrix} \qquad (4.39)$$

$$J_4(\mathbf{x}) = \begin{bmatrix} -4x_4 + 4800 & -10\,x_1 + 10{,}000 & -4x_2 + 8000 \\ 11.00 & 12.50 & 10.00 \\ 5.00 & 4.00 & 4.00 \end{bmatrix} \qquad (4.40)$$

$$G(\mathbf{x}) = \begin{bmatrix} 12.50 & 10.00 \\ 4.00 & 4.00 \end{bmatrix} \qquad (4.41)$$

Since $|G(\mathbf{x})| = 10.00$, the condition in Eq. (4.32) holds for all x and therefore $\mathbf{x}^*$. From

$$|J_3(\mathbf{x}^*)| = 0, \qquad |J_4(\mathbf{x}^*)| = 0$$

we have

$$100x_1 + 10x_2 - 120x_3 \qquad = 84{,}000 \qquad (4.42)$$

$$-60x_1 + 74x_2 \qquad -40x_4 = 40{,}000 \qquad (4.43)$$

The constraints $g_i(\mathbf{x}) = 0$, $i = 1, 2$, yield

$$12.5x_1 + 10.0x_2 + 15.0x_3 + 11.0x_4 = 27{,}000 \qquad (4.44)$$

$$4x_1 + \quad 4x_2 + \quad 5x_3 + \quad 5x_4 = 10{,}000 \qquad (4.45)$$

From Eqs. (4.42)–(4.45) we have

$$
\begin{bmatrix}
100 & 10 & -120 & 0 \\
-60 & 74 & 0 & -40 \\
12.5 & 10 & 15 & 11 \\
4 & 4 & 5 & 5
\end{bmatrix}
\begin{bmatrix}
x_1 \\ x_2 \\ x_3 \\ x_4
\end{bmatrix}
=
\begin{bmatrix}
84{,}000 \\ 40{,}000 \\ 27{,}000 \\ 10{,}000
\end{bmatrix}
$$

or $A\mathbf{x} = \mathbf{b}$. Solving for $\mathbf{x}$ yields

$$
\mathbf{x} =
\begin{bmatrix}
0.00412 & -0.00202 & 0.14371 & -0.33228 \\
0.00285 & 0.00924 & -0.00701 & 0.08938 \\
-0.00466 & -0.00091 & 0.11917 & -0.26945 \\
-0.00091 & -0.00487 & -0.22853 & 0.66377
\end{bmatrix}
\begin{bmatrix}
84{,}000 \\ 40{,}000 \\ 27{,}000 \\ 10{,}000
\end{bmatrix}
$$

or $\mathbf{x} = A^{-1}\mathbf{b}$ and

$$
\mathbf{x} =
\begin{bmatrix}
822.6 \\ 1313.5 \\ 95.0 \\ 196.1
\end{bmatrix}
\quad \blacksquare
$$

Situations may occur where $|G(\mathbf{x}^*)| = 0$ based upon the definition of $G(\mathbf{x})$ in Eq. (4.30). Recall that $G(\mathbf{x})$ is the matrix of first partial derivatives of $g_i(\mathbf{x})$, $i = 1, 2, \ldots, m$, with respect to the variables $x_1, x_2, \ldots, x_m$. Actually we may choose as elements for $G(\mathbf{x})$ the first partial derivatives of $g_i(\mathbf{x})$ $i = 1, 2, \ldots, m$, with respect to any m of the n variables x_i. To illustrate let

$$
F(\mathbf{x}) = \begin{bmatrix} f_1(\mathbf{x}) & f_2(\mathbf{x}) & \cdots & f_{k-1}(\mathbf{x}) & f_k(\mathbf{x}) & f_{k+1}(\mathbf{x}) & \cdots f_m(\mathbf{x}) \end{bmatrix}
$$

$$(4.46)$$

$$
\gamma_j(\mathbf{x}) =
\begin{bmatrix}
g_{1_j}(\mathbf{x}) \\
g_{2_j}(\mathbf{x}) \\
\vdots \\
g_{m_j}(\mathbf{x})
\end{bmatrix}
$$

$$(4.47)$$

Then from Eq. (4.29)

$$
J_j(\mathbf{x}) = \begin{bmatrix} f_j(\mathbf{x}) & F(\mathbf{x}) \\ \gamma_j(\mathbf{x}) & G(\mathbf{x}) \end{bmatrix},
\qquad j = m + 1, m + 2, \ldots, n
\qquad (4.48)
$$

Now suppose we that we choose to take partial derivatives of $g_i(\mathbf{x})$, $i = 1$, $2, \ldots, m$ with respect to $x_1, x_2, \ldots, x_{k-1}, x_h, x_{k+1}, \ldots, x_m$. That is, we replace $g_{i_k}(\mathbf{x})$ by $g_{i_h}(\mathbf{x})$, $i = 1, 2, \ldots, m$, where $h > m$. To accomplish this we replace $f_k(\mathbf{x})$ by $f_h(\mathbf{x})$ in Eq. (4.46) and $g_{i_k}(\mathbf{x})$, $i = 1, 2, \ldots, m$, in Eq. (4.30), yielding

$$G(\mathbf{x}) = \begin{bmatrix} g_{1_1}(\mathbf{x}) & g_{1_2}(\mathbf{x}) & \cdots & g_{1_{k-1}}(\mathbf{x}) & g_{1_h}(\mathbf{x}) & g_{1_{k+1}}(\mathbf{x}) & \cdots & g_{1_m}(\mathbf{x}) \\ g_{2_1}(\mathbf{x}) & g_{2_2}(\mathbf{x}) & \cdots & g_{2_{k-1}}(\mathbf{x}) & g_{2_h}(\mathbf{x}) & g_{2_{k+1}}(\mathbf{x}) & \cdots & g_{2_m}(\mathbf{x}) \\ \vdots & \vdots & & \vdots & \vdots & \vdots & & \vdots \\ g_{m_1}(\mathbf{x}) & g_{m_2}(\mathbf{x}) & \cdots & g_{m_{k-1}}(\mathbf{x}) & g_{m_h}(\mathbf{x}) & g_{m_{k+1}}(\mathbf{x}) & \cdots & g_{m_m}(\mathbf{x}) \end{bmatrix}$$

$$(4.49)$$

$$F(\mathbf{x}) = \begin{bmatrix} f_1(\mathbf{x}) & f_2(\mathbf{x}) & \cdots & f_{k-1}(\mathbf{x}) & f_h(\mathbf{x}) & f_{k+1}(\mathbf{x}) & \cdots & f_m(\mathbf{x}) \end{bmatrix}$$

$$(4.50)$$

$|J_j(\mathbf{x}^*)|$ is now evaluated for $j = k, m+1, m+2, \ldots, n$, where $j \neq h$.

In general $G(\mathbf{x})$ may be composed of elements which are the first partial derivatives of the constraints $g_i(\mathbf{x})$, $i = 1, 2, \ldots, m$, with respect to any m of the n variables, where the ith row of $G(\mathbf{x})$ is the first partial derivative of $g_i(\mathbf{x})$ with respect to the m variables chosen. From among all of the possible definitions of $G(\mathbf{x})$ some may be singular while others are nonsingular. However, for the solution procedure defined here we need find only one matrix $G(\mathbf{x})$ that is nonsingular. Once a nonsingular matrix $G(\mathbf{x})$ is defined $F(\mathbf{x})$ is defined such that the lth column of $J_j(\mathbf{x})$ consists of the first partial derivative of $f(\mathbf{x})$ and $g_i(\mathbf{x})$, $i = 1, 2, \ldots, m$, with respect to the same variable x_l. $|J_j(\mathbf{x})|$ is then evaluated with respect to each j such that $g_{i_j}(\mathbf{x})$, $i = 1, 2, \ldots, m$, is *not* contained in $G(\mathbf{x})$.

Example 4.5 In Example 4.3 suppose that no constraint is placed upon the investment in inventory. However, management has decided to allocate 6000 square feet to products 1 and 2 and 4000 square feet to product 3 and 4. Hence, the problem to be solved is to determine x_1, x_2, x_3, and x_4 such that

$$P(\mathbf{x}) = \sum_{j=1}^{4} (a_j x_j + b_j x_j)$$

is maximized subject to the constraints

$$s_1 x_1 + s_2 x_2 \qquad\qquad = 6{,}000 \qquad (4.51)$$

$$s_3 x_3 + s_4 x_4 = 4{,}000 \qquad (4.52)$$

where a_i, b_i, and s_i, $i = 1, 2, 3, 4$, are as defined in Example 4.3. Find the optimal values of x_1, x_2, x_3, x_4.

Let

$$g_1(\mathbf{x}) = s_1 x_1 + s_2 x_2 - 6000 = 0 \tag{4.53}$$

$$g_2(\mathbf{x}) = s_3 x_3 + s_4 x_4 - 4000 = 0 \tag{4.54}$$

If we let

$$G(\mathbf{x}) = \begin{bmatrix} g_{1_1}(\mathbf{x}) & g_{1_2}(\mathbf{x}) \\ g_{2_1}(\mathbf{x}) & g_{2_2}(\mathbf{x}) \end{bmatrix} \tag{4.55}$$

then $|G(\mathbf{x})| = 0$. Similarly, if we choose $G(\mathbf{x})$ as

$$G(\mathbf{x}) = \begin{bmatrix} g_{1_3}(\mathbf{x}) & g_{1_4}(\mathbf{x}) \\ g_{2_3}(\mathbf{x}) & g_{2_4}(\mathbf{x}) \end{bmatrix} \tag{4.56}$$

then $|G(\mathbf{x})| = 0$. However, if

$$G(\mathbf{x}) = \begin{bmatrix} g_{1_2}(\mathbf{x}) & g_{1_3}(\mathbf{x}) \\ g_{2_2}(\mathbf{x}) & g_{2_3}(\mathbf{x}) \end{bmatrix} \tag{4.57}$$

then $|G(\mathbf{x})| \neq 0$, although $G(\mathbf{x}^*)$ may prove to be singular once a solution is determined. For $G(\mathbf{x})$ as defined in Eq. (4.57)

$$F(\mathbf{x}) = \begin{bmatrix} f_2(\mathbf{x}) & f_3(\mathbf{x}) \end{bmatrix} \tag{4.58}$$

and $|J_j(\mathbf{x}^*)| = 0$ must be solved for $j = 1, 4$:

$$J_1(\mathbf{x}) = \begin{bmatrix} -10x_1 + 10,000 & -4x_2 + 8,000 & -6x_3 + 3,600 \\ 4 & 4 & 0 \\ 0 & 0 & 5 \end{bmatrix}$$

$$J_4(\mathbf{x}) = \begin{bmatrix} -4x_4 + 4,800 & -4x_2 + 8,000 & -6x_3 + 3,600 \\ 0 & 4 & 0 \\ 5 & 0 & 5 \end{bmatrix}$$

$|J_1(\mathbf{x})|$ and $|J_4(\mathbf{x})|$ yield the equations

$$-200x_1 + 80x_2 + 40,000 = 0, \qquad 120x_3 - 80x_4 + 24,000 = 0$$

and from the constraints,

$$4x_1 + 4x_2 - 6000 = 0, \qquad 5x_3 + 5x_4 - 4000 = 0$$

Hence

$$\begin{bmatrix} -200 & 80 & 0 & 0 \\ 0 & 0 & 120 & -80 \\ 4 & 4 & 0 & 0 \\ 0 & 0 & 5 & 5 \end{bmatrix} \begin{bmatrix} x_1 \\ x_2 \\ x_3 \\ x_4 \end{bmatrix} = \begin{bmatrix} -40,000 \\ -24,000 \\ 6,000 \\ 4,000 \end{bmatrix}$$

Solving for x^* we have

$$x_1^* = 571.43, \qquad x_2^* = 928.57, \qquad x_3^* = 200.00, \qquad x_4^* = 600.00$$

yielding an annual profit of \$12,425,714.29. ■

We have not presented sufficient conditions for the existence of an extreme point (local maximum or minimum) for the method of indirect elimination. While sufficient conditions exist, their application is computationally complex and beyond the scope of this text. For a discussion of the sufficient conditions, the reader should see Beveridge and Schechter [2]. Should several interior stationary points exist, the global minimum or maximum may be determined by evaluating $f(x)$ at each. In the following section we shall discuss a third alternative to the equality constrained optimization problem, wherein both necessary and sufficient conditions are presented.

At the outset of this discussion we pointed out that the methods of direct and indirect elimination perform the same function and are in essence identical. We will now show that the method of indirect elimination is indeed derived from the method of direct elimination. Given the function $f(x)$ and the constraints $g_i(x) = 0$, $i = 1, 2, \ldots, m$, where x is an n dimensional vector $(m < n)$, the first task was to solve for x_i, $i = 1, 2, \ldots, m$, in terms of x_j, $j = m + 1, m + 2, \ldots, n$, using the constraints. Thus, $f(x)$ is reduced from a constrained function in n variables to an unconstrained function in $n - m$ variables. Now

$$f_j(x) = \frac{\partial}{\partial x_j} f(x), \qquad j = m + 1, m + 2, \ldots, n \tag{4.59}$$

where

$$x_i = \psi_i(x_{m+1}, x_{m+2}, \ldots, x_n), \qquad i = 1, 2, \ldots, m \tag{4.60}$$

and

$$x = \begin{bmatrix} \psi_1 & \psi_2 & \cdots & \psi_m & x_{m+1} & \cdots & x_n \end{bmatrix} \tag{4.61}$$

Since $\psi_i(x_{m+1}, x_{m+2}, \ldots, x_n)$ is a function of x_j for $j = m + 1, m + 2, \ldots, n$, $f_j(x)$ is given by

$$f_j(x) = f_1(x) \frac{\partial \psi_1}{\partial x_j} + f_2(x) \frac{\partial \psi_2}{\partial x_j} + \cdots + f_m(x) \frac{\partial \psi_m}{\partial x_j} + f_j(x) \tag{4.62}$$

by the chain rule for differentiation. However, $\partial \psi_i / \partial x_j$, $i = 1, 2, \ldots, m$, can be expressed as

$$\frac{\partial \psi_i}{\partial x_j} = \frac{\begin{vmatrix} g_{1_1}(\mathbf{x}) & g_{1_2}(\mathbf{x}) & \cdots & g_{1_{i-1}}(\mathbf{x}) & g_{1_i}(\mathbf{x}) & g_{1_{i+1}}(\mathbf{x}) & \cdots & g_{1_m}(\mathbf{x}) \\ g_{2_1}(\mathbf{x}) & g_{2_2}(\mathbf{x}) & \cdots & g_{2_{i-1}}(\mathbf{x}) & g_{2_i}(\mathbf{x}) & g_{2_{i+1}}(\mathbf{x}) & \cdots & g_{2_m}(\mathbf{x}) \\ \vdots & \vdots & & \vdots & \vdots & \vdots & & \vdots \\ g_{m_1}(\mathbf{x}) & g_{m_2}(\mathbf{x}) & \cdots & g_{m_{i-1}}(\mathbf{x}) & g_{m_i}(\mathbf{x}) & g_{m_{i+1}}(\mathbf{x}) & \cdots & g_{m_m}(\mathbf{x}) \end{vmatrix}}{|G(\mathbf{x})|}$$

$$= \frac{|G_{ij}(\mathbf{x})|}{|G(\mathbf{x})|} \tag{4.63}$$

where $G_{ij}(\mathbf{x})$ is identical to $G(\mathbf{x})$ except that the ith column of $G(\mathbf{x})$ is replaced by the column vector with elements $g_{ij}(\mathbf{x})$, $i = 1, 2, \ldots, m$. Thus

$$f_j(\mathbf{x}) = \sum_{i=1}^{m} f_i(\mathbf{x}) \frac{|G_{ij}(\mathbf{x})|}{|G(\mathbf{x})|} + f_j(\mathbf{x})$$

$$= \frac{1}{|G(\mathbf{x})|} \left[\sum_{i=1}^{m} f_i(\mathbf{x}) |G_{ij}(\mathbf{x})| + f_j(\mathbf{x}) |G(\mathbf{x})| \right] \tag{4.64}$$

Having reduced $f(\mathbf{x})$ to a function of $n - m$ variables by elimination of x_1, $x_2, , \ldots, x_m$, if $\mathbf{x}^*$ is a stationary point for $f(\mathbf{x})$, then

$$f_j(\mathbf{x}^*) = 0, \qquad j = m + 1, m + 2, \ldots, n \tag{4.65}$$

or

$$\sum_{i=1}^{m} f_i(\mathbf{x}) |G_{ij}(\mathbf{x})| + f_j(\mathbf{x}) |G(\mathbf{x})| = 0, \qquad j = m + 1, m + 2, \ldots, n \tag{4.66}$$

since $G(\mathbf{x})$ is assumed to be nonsingular. Recalling the definition of $J_j(\mathbf{x})$ in Eq. (4.29) and defining $|J_j(\mathbf{x})|$ by the cofactor method using the first row of $J_j(\mathbf{x})$, we find that Eq. (4.66) is in fact $|J_j(\mathbf{x})|$. Since Eq. (4.65) must hold at a stationary point for $f(\mathbf{x})$, $\mathbf{x}^*$, and since Eq. (4.66) defines $|J_j(\mathbf{x})|$,

$$|J_j(\mathbf{x}^*)| = 0, \qquad j = m + 1, m + 2, \ldots, n$$

and we are led to the necessary conditions defined in Eq. (4.31). Hence the necessary conditions for an extreme point using the method of direct elimination lead to the necessary conditions for an extreme point for the method of indirect elimination. But Eq. (4.66) can be expressed as the determinant of the matrix $J_j(\mathbf{x})$, where $|J_j(\mathbf{x}^*)| = 0$, $j = m + 1, m + 2, \ldots, n$, is the necessary condition for existence of an extreme point at $\mathbf{x}^*$ for the method of indirect elimination.

The Method of Lagrange Multipliers

The third method presented for optimization subject to equality constraints is called the Lagrange multiplier technique and is integrally related to the two already presented. However, sufficient conditions for the existence of a maximum or minimum are more readily applied as a part of the Lagrange multiplier method than in the case of the indirect elimination method.

In applying the Lagrange multiplier method, the original problem statement given in Eq. (4.6) is transformed by forming the Lagrange function given by

$$L(\mathbf{x}, \boldsymbol{\lambda}) = f(\mathbf{x}) + \sum_{i=1}^{m} \lambda_i g_i(\mathbf{x}) \tag{4.67}$$

where λ_i, $i = 1, 2, \ldots, m$, are called Lagrange multipliers. If $|G(\mathbf{x}^*)| \neq 0$, then the vector $\mathbf{x}^*$ which minimizes or maximizes Eq. (4.67) is a minimum or maximum for the constrained optimization problem. However, to identify an extreme point $\mathbf{x}^*$, $L(\mathbf{x}, \boldsymbol{\lambda})$ must be differentiated with respect to both x_j, $j = 1, 2, \ldots, n$, and λ_i, $i = 1, 2, \ldots, m$. Hence, the Lagrange multiplier technique increases the dimensionality of the problem from one in n variables to one in $n + m$ variables. Differentiating $L(\mathbf{x}, \boldsymbol{\lambda})$ with respect to all x_j and λi we obtain the necessary conditions for an extreme point $\mathbf{x}^*$ given by

$$\frac{\partial}{\partial x_j} L(\mathbf{x}^*, \boldsymbol{\lambda}^*) = f_j(\mathbf{x}^*) + \sum_{i=1}^{m} \lambda_i g_{i_j}(\mathbf{x}^*) = 0, \qquad j = 1, 2, \ldots, n \tag{4.68}$$

$$\frac{\partial}{\partial \lambda_i} L(\mathbf{x}^*, \boldsymbol{\lambda}^*) = g_i(\mathbf{x}^*) = 0 \tag{4.69}$$

where

$$\lambda_i^* = - \frac{\begin{vmatrix} g_{1_1}(\mathbf{x}^*) & g_{1_2}(\mathbf{x}^*) & \cdots & g_{1_m}(\mathbf{x}^*) \\ g_{2_1}(\mathbf{x}^*) & g_{2_2}(\mathbf{x}^*) & \cdots & g_{2_m}(\mathbf{x}^*) \\ \vdots & \vdots & & \vdots \\ g_{i-1_1}(\mathbf{x}^*) & g_{i-1_2}(\mathbf{x}^*) & \cdots & g_{i-1_m}(\mathbf{x}^*) \\ f_1(\mathbf{x}^*) & f_2(\mathbf{x}^*) & \cdots & f_m(\mathbf{x}^*) \\ g_{i+1_1}(\mathbf{x}^*) & g_{i+1_2}(\mathbf{x}^*) & \cdots & g_{i+1_m}(\mathbf{x}^*) \\ \vdots & \vdots & & \vdots \\ g_{m_1}(\mathbf{x}^*) & g_{m_2}(\mathbf{x}^*) & \cdots & g_{m_m}(\mathbf{x}^*) \end{vmatrix}}{|G(\mathbf{x}^*)|}, \qquad i = 1, 2, \ldots, m \tag{4.70}$$

and $|G(\mathbf{x}^*)| \neq 0$.

Example 4.6   Let

$$f(\mathbf{x}) = x_1^2 + x_2^2 + x_3^2$$

Find the stationary values of x_1, x_2, and x_3 subject to the constraint

$$x_1 + x_2 + x_3 = 4$$

The Lagrange function for this problem is

$$L(\mathbf{x}, \boldsymbol{\lambda}) = x_1^2 + x_2^2 + x_3^2 + \lambda_1(x_1 + x_2 + x_3 - 4)$$

Taking first partial derivatives with respect to x_1, x_2, x_3, and λ_1 leads to

$$\frac{\partial}{\partial x_1} L(\mathbf{x}, \boldsymbol{\lambda}) = 2x_1 + \lambda_1 = 0$$

$$\frac{\partial}{\partial x_2} L(\mathbf{x}, \boldsymbol{\lambda}) = 2x_2 + \lambda_1 = 0$$

$$\frac{\partial}{\partial x_3} L(\mathbf{x}, \boldsymbol{\lambda}) = 2x_3 + \lambda_1 = 0$$

$$\frac{\partial}{\partial \lambda_1} L(\mathbf{x}, \boldsymbol{\lambda}) = x_1 + x_2 + x_3 - 4 = 0$$

From the first partials with respect to x_1, x_2, and x_3 we have

$$x_j = -\lambda_1/2, \qquad j = 1, 2, 3$$

Since $x_1 + x_2 + x_3 = 4$, we have

$$\lambda_1 = -8/3$$

and

$$x_j = 4/3, \qquad j = 1, 2, 3$$

For this problem $G(\mathbf{x})$ is a 1×1 matrix and

$$|G(\mathbf{x})| = g_{1_1}(\mathbf{x}) = 1$$

Hence, $|G(\mathbf{x}^*)| \neq 0$.   ∎

In the sections which follow we shall discuss three methods for determining whether a point satisfying the necessary conditions for a constrained extreme point is a relative minimum or a relative maximum. Following the presentation of these three approaches we shall discuss their relative strengths and weaknesses. A rigorous development of the sufficiency tests presented is beyond the scope of this text. For a more intensive treatment of these tests the reader should see Hancock [4] and Phipps [6].

The Generalized Sufficiency Test

Let $L(\mathbf{x}, \boldsymbol{\lambda})$ be as defined in Eq. (4.67) and let

$$L_{ij} = \frac{\partial^2}{\partial x_i \partial x_j} L(\mathbf{x}, \boldsymbol{\lambda}) \qquad (4.71)$$

$$g_{i_j} = \frac{\partial}{\partial x_j} g_i(\mathbf{x}) \qquad (4.72)$$

$$H_G(\mathbf{x}, \boldsymbol{\lambda}) = \begin{vmatrix} (L_{11} - \mu) & L_{12} & \cdots & L_{1n} & g_{1_1} & g_{2_1} & \cdots & g_{m_1} \\ L_{21} & (L_{22} - \mu) & \cdots & L_{2n} & g_{1_2} & g_{2_2} & \cdots & g_{m_2} \\ \vdots & \vdots & & \vdots & \vdots & \vdots & & \vdots \\ L_{n1} & L_{n2} & \cdots & (L_{nn} - \mu) & g_{1_n} & g_{2_n} & \cdots & g_{m_n} \\ g_{1_1} & g_{1_2} & \cdots & g_{1_n} & 0 & 0 & \cdots & 0 \\ g_{2_1} & g_{2_2} & \cdots & g_{2_n} & 0 & 0 & \cdots & 0 \\ \vdots & \vdots & & \vdots & \vdots & \vdots & & \vdots \\ g_{m_1} & g_{m_2} & \cdots & g_{m_n} & 0 & 0 & \cdots & 0 \end{vmatrix}$$

$$\qquad (4.73)$$

At $\mathbf{x}^*, \boldsymbol{\lambda}^*, |H_G(\mathbf{x}^*, \boldsymbol{\lambda}^*)| = 0$ yields a polynomial of order $n - m$ in μ:

(1) If the roots μ of $|H_G(\mathbf{x}^*, \boldsymbol{\lambda}^*)| = 0$ are all positive, then $\mathbf{x}^*, \boldsymbol{\lambda}^*$ is a relative minimum for $f(\mathbf{x})$ subject to the constraints $g_i(\mathbf{x}) = 0$, $i = 1, 2, \ldots, m$.

(2) If the roots μ of $|H_G(\mathbf{x}^*, \boldsymbol{\lambda}^*)| = 0$ are all negative then $\mathbf{x}^*, \boldsymbol{\lambda}^*$ is a relative maximum of $f(\mathbf{x})$ subject to the constraints $g_i(\mathbf{x}) = 0$, $i = 1, 2, \ldots, m$.

The Bordered Hessian (Phipps's) Test

The bordered Hessian test is little more than an alternative approach to the generalized sufficiency test. However, the computational effort required for the bordered Hessian test is usually less extensive than that for the generalized sufficiency test. For this reason the bordered Hessian test is more frequently used than the generalized test in determining whether a point $\mathbf{x}^*$ satisfying the necessary conditions for a constrained extreme point is either a minimum or a maximum for $f(\mathbf{x})$. The criterion matrix for this sufficiency test $H_B(\mathbf{x}, \boldsymbol{\lambda})$, called the *bordered Hessian matrix*, is defined by

$$
H_{\mathrm{B}}(\mathbf{x}, \boldsymbol{\lambda}) = \begin{vmatrix}
0 & 0 & \cdots & 0 & g_{1_1} & g_{1_2} & \cdots & g_{1_n} \\
0 & 0 & \cdots & 0 & g_{2_1} & g_{2_2} & \cdots & g_{2_n} \\
\vdots & \vdots & & \vdots & \vdots & \vdots & & \vdots \\
0 & 0 & \cdots & 0 & g_{m_1} & g_{m_2} & \cdots & g_{m_n} \\
g_{1_1} & g_{2_1} & \cdots & g_{m_1} & L_{11} & L_{12} & \cdots & L_{1n} \\
g_{1_2} & g_{2_2} & \cdots & g_{m_2} & L_{21} & L_{22} & \cdots & L_{2n} \\
\vdots & \vdots & & \vdots & \vdots & \vdots & & \vdots \\
g_{1_n} & g_{2_n} & \cdots & g_{m_n} & L_{n1} & L_{n2} & \cdots & L_{nn}
\end{vmatrix}
\tag{4.74}
$$

where g_{i_j} and L_{ij} are as defined in Eq. (4.71) and (4.72). If $|H_{\mathrm{B}_i}|$ is the ith leading principal minor of $H_{\mathrm{B}}(\mathbf{x}, \boldsymbol{\lambda})$ evaluated at the point $\mathbf{x}^*, \boldsymbol{\lambda}^*$ satisfying the necessary conditions for constrained extreme point, then

(1) $\mathbf{x}^*, \boldsymbol{\lambda}^*$ is a relative minimum if m is even and $|H_{\mathrm{B}_i}| > 0$, $i = 2m + 1, 2m + 2, \ldots, n + m$,

(2) $\mathbf{x}^*, \boldsymbol{\lambda}^*$ is a relative minimum if m is odd and $|H_{\mathrm{B}_i}| < 0$, $i = 2m + 1$, $2m + 2, \ldots, n + m$,

(3) $\mathbf{x}^*, \boldsymbol{\lambda}^*$ is a relative maximum if m is even and $(-1)^i |H_{\mathrm{B}_i}| > 0$, $i = 2m + 1, 2m + 2, \ldots, n + m$,

(4) $\mathbf{x}^*, \boldsymbol{\lambda}^*$ is a relative maximum if m is odd and $(-1)^{i+1}|H_{\mathrm{B}_i}| > 0$, $i = 2m + 1, 2m + 2, \ldots, n + m$.

Thus to determine whether a point satisfying the necessary conditions for an extreme point is a relative minimum or a relative maximum the last $n - m$ leading principal minors of $H_{\mathrm{B}}(\mathbf{x}^*, \boldsymbol{\lambda}^*)$ must be evaluated.

Example 4.7 Determine whether the stationary point identified in Example 4.6 is a minimum or maximum for $f(\mathbf{x})$.

To identify the nature of the stationary point, we must evaluate all second partial derivatives of $L(\mathbf{x}, \boldsymbol{\lambda})$ with respect to each of the n variables:

$$
\frac{\partial^2}{\partial x_1^2} L(\mathbf{x}, \boldsymbol{\lambda}) = 2, \qquad \frac{\partial^2}{\partial x_2^2} L(\mathbf{x}, \boldsymbol{\lambda}) = 2, \qquad \frac{\partial^2}{\partial x_3^2} L(\mathbf{x}, \boldsymbol{\lambda}) = 2
$$

$$
\frac{\partial^2}{\partial x_i \, \partial x_j} L(\mathbf{x}, \boldsymbol{\lambda}) = 0 \qquad \text{for} \quad i \neq j
$$

Hence $H_B(x^*, \lambda^*)$ is given by

$$H_B(x^*, \lambda^*) = \begin{bmatrix} 0 & 1 & 1 & 1 \\ 1 & 2 & 0 & 0 \\ 1 & 0 & 2 & 0 \\ 1 & 0 & 0 & 2 \end{bmatrix}$$

Since $n - m = 2$, we must evaluate the last two leading principal minors of H_B:

$$|H_{B_3}| = -4, \qquad |H_{B_4}| = -8$$

Since m is odd and $|H_{B_3}| < 0$, $|H_{B_4}| < 0$, $x^* = [4/3 \quad 4/3 \quad 4/3]$ is a local minimum. ∎

Example 4.8 Solve the problem in Example 4.3 using the Lagrange multiplier technique.

The Lagrange function for this problem is given by

$$L(\mathbf{x}, \boldsymbol{\lambda}) = \sum_{j=1}^{4} \left(a_j x_j^2 + b_j x_j \right) + 100,000 + \lambda_1 \left(\sum_{j=1}^{4} (1/2) C_{1j} x_j - 27,000 \right)$$

$$+ \lambda_2 \left(\sum_{j=1}^{4} s_j x_j - 10,000 \right)$$

Taking first partial derivatives with respect to $x_1, x_2, x_3, x_4, \lambda_1$, and λ_2 leads to

$$\frac{\partial}{\partial x_j} L(\mathbf{x}, \boldsymbol{\lambda}) = 2a_j x_j + b_j + \lambda_1 (C_{1j}/2) + \lambda_2 s_j = 0, \qquad j = 1, 2, 3, 4 \quad (4.75)$$

$$\frac{\partial}{\partial \lambda_1} L(\mathbf{x}, \boldsymbol{\lambda}) = \left(\sum_{j=1}^{4} (1/2) C_{1j} x_j - 27,000 \right) = 0 \tag{4.76}$$

$$\frac{\partial}{\partial \lambda_2} L(\mathbf{x}, \boldsymbol{\lambda}) = \left(\sum_{j=1}^{4} s_j x_j - 10,000 \right) = 0 \tag{4.77}$$

From Eq. (4.75),

$$x_j = -\frac{\lambda_1 C_{1j}}{4a_j} - \frac{\lambda_2 s_j}{2a_j} - \frac{b_j}{2a_j}, \qquad j = 1, 2, 3, 4 \tag{4.78}$$

From Eq. (4.76),

$$\sum_{j=1}^{4} (1/2) C_{1j} x_j = \sum_{j=1}^{4} \frac{C_{1j}}{2} \left[-\frac{\lambda_1 C_{1j}}{4a_j} - \frac{\lambda_2 s_j}{2a_j} - \frac{b_j}{2a_j} \right]$$

$$= -\lambda_1 \sum_{j=1}^{4} \frac{C_{1j}^2}{8a_j} - \lambda_2 \sum_{j=1}^{4} \frac{C_{1j} s_j}{4a_j} - \sum_{j=1}^{4} \frac{C_{1j} b_j}{4a_j} = 27,000 \tag{4.79}$$

and

$$\lambda_1 = \frac{-27,000 - \lambda_2 \sum_{j=1}^{4} \left[C_{1j} s_j / (4a_j) \right] - \sum_{j=1}^{4} \left[C_{1j} b_j / (4a_j) \right]}{\sum_{j=1}^{4} \left[C_{1j}^2 / (8a_j) \right]} \tag{4.80}$$

Finally, from Eq. (4.77) we have

$$\sum_{j=1}^{4} s_j x_j = \sum_{j=1}^{4} s_j \left[\frac{-\lambda_1 C_{1j}}{4a_j} - \frac{\lambda_2 s_j}{2a_j} - \frac{b_j}{2a_j} \right]$$

$$= -\lambda_1 \sum_{j=1}^{4} \frac{C_{1j} s_j}{4a_j} - \lambda_2 \sum_{j=1}^{4} \frac{s_j^2}{2a_j} - \sum_{j=1}^{4} \frac{s_j b_j}{2a_j}$$

$$= 10,000 \tag{4.81}$$

and

$$\lambda_1 = \frac{-10,000 - \lambda_2 \sum_{j=1}^{4} \left[s_j^2/(2a_j) \right] - \sum_{j=1}^{4} \left[s_j b_j/(2a_j) \right]}{\sum_{j=1}^{4} \left[C_{1j} s_j/(4a_j) \right]} \tag{4.82}$$

Solving equations (4.80) and (4.82) for λ_2 yields

$$\lambda_2 = \frac{\begin{aligned}&-\left\{ 10,000 + \sum_{j=1}^{4} \left[s_j b_j/(2a_j) \right] \right\} \sum_{j=1}^{4} \left[C_{1j}^2/(8a_j) \right] \\ &+ \left\{ 27,000 + \sum_{j=1}^{4} \left[C_{1j} b_j/(4a_j) \right] \right\} \sum_{j=1}^{4} \left[C_{1j} s_j/(4a_j) \right]\end{aligned}}{\sum_{j=1}^{4} \left[s_j^2/(2a_j) \right] \sum_{j=1}^{4} \left[C_{1j}^2/(8a_j) \right] - \left\{ \sum_{j=1}^{4} \left[C_{1j} s_j/(4a_j) \right] \right\}^2} \tag{4.83}$$

For the values given for the parameters of the problem we have

$$\sum_{j=1}^{4} \frac{s_j b_j}{2a_j} = -19,500.00, \qquad \sum_{j=1}^{4} \frac{C_{1j}^2}{8a_j} = -89.625, \qquad \sum_{j=1}^{4} \frac{C_{1j} s_j}{4a_j} = -35.00$$

$$\sum_{j=1}^{4} \frac{C_{1j} b_j}{4a_j} = -50,200.00 \qquad \sum_{j=1}^{4} \frac{s_j^2}{2a_j} = -13.933$$

Hence

$$\lambda_2^* = -1,658.782, \qquad \lambda_1^* = 388.924$$

Finally

$$x_1^* = 822.6, \qquad x_2^* = 1313.5$$
$$x_3^* = 95.0, \qquad x_4^* = 196.1$$

To show that this solution maximizes annual profit we have

$$\frac{\partial^2}{\partial x_i^2} L(\mathbf{x}, \boldsymbol{\lambda}) = 2a_j, \qquad j = 1, 2, 3, 4$$

$$\frac{\partial^2}{\partial x_i \partial x_j} L(\mathbf{x}, \boldsymbol{\lambda}) = 0, \qquad i \neq j$$

$$g_{1_j}(\mathbf{x}) = (1/2) C_{1j}, \qquad j = 1, 2, 3, 4$$

$$g_{2_j}(\mathbf{x}) = s_j, \qquad j = 1, 2, 3, 4$$

and

$$H_B(\mathbf{x}^*, \boldsymbol{\lambda}^*) = \begin{bmatrix} 0.0 & 0.0 & 12.5 & 10.0 & 15.0 & 11.0 \\ 0.0 & 0.0 & 4.0 & 4.0 & 5.0 & 5.0 \\ 12.5 & 4.0 & -10.0 & 0.0 & 0.0 & 0.0 \\ 10.0 & 4.0 & 0.0 & -4.0 & 0.0 & 0.0 \\ 15.0 & 5.0 & 0.0 & 0.0 & -12.0 & 0.0 \\ 11.0 & 5.0 & 0.0 & 0.0 & 0.0 & -4.0 \end{bmatrix}$$

Examining the last $n - m = 2$ leading principal minors by the cofactor method yields

$$|H_{B_5}| = (12.5) \begin{vmatrix} 0.0 & 12.5 & 10.0 & 15.0 \\ 0.0 & 4.0 & 4.0 & 5.0 \\ 4.0 & 0.0 & -4.0 & 0.0 \\ 5.0 & 0.0 & 0.0 & -12.0 \end{vmatrix}$$

$$- (10.0) \begin{vmatrix} 0.0 & 12.5 & 10.0 & 15.0 \\ 0.0 & 4.0 & 4.0 & 5.0 \\ 4.0 & -10.0 & 0.0 & 0.0 \\ 5.0 & 0.0 & 0.0 & -12.0 \end{vmatrix}$$

$$+ (15.0) \begin{vmatrix} 0.0 & 12.5 & 10.0 & 15.0 \\ 0.0 & 4.0 & 4.0 & 5.0 \\ 4.0 & -10.0 & 0.0 & 0.0 \\ 4.0 & 0.0 & -4.0 & 0.0 \end{vmatrix}$$

$$= -2225.00$$

$$|H_{B_6}| = -(11.0) \begin{vmatrix} 0.0 & 12.5 & 10.0 & 15.0 & 11.0 \\ 0.0 & 4.0 & 4.0 & 5.0 & 5.0 \\ 4.0 & -10.0 & 0.0 & 0.0 & 0.0 \\ 4.0 & 0.0 & -4.0 & 0.0 & 0.0 \\ 5.0 & 0.0 & 0.0 & -12.0 & 0.0 \end{vmatrix}$$

$$+ (5.0) \begin{vmatrix} 0.0 & 12.5 & 10.0 & 15.0 & 11.0 \\ 0.0 & 4.0 & 4.0 & 5.0 & 5.0 \\ 12.5 & -10.0 & 0.0 & 0.0 & 0.0 \\ 10.0 & 0.0 & -4.0 & 0.0 & 0.0 \\ 15.0 & 0.0 & 0.0 & -12.0 & 0.0 \end{vmatrix}$$

$$+ (-4.0)|H_{B_5}|$$

$$= 45{,}648$$

Since m is even and $|H_{B_5}| < 0$, $|H_{B_6}| > 0$, the solution $\mathbf{x}^*$ is a maximum for the function. ∎

The Carathéodory–Phipps Test

Another quadratic form associated with the Lagrange function $L(\mathbf{x}, \boldsymbol{\lambda})$ may be developed in the following alternative manner. Recall that the objective function $f(\mathbf{x})$ was expanded in a Taylor series to form

$$f(\mathbf{x}^* + \mathbf{h}) - f(\mathbf{x}^*) \doteq \nabla_{\mathbf{x}} f(\mathbf{x}^*)\mathbf{h} + (1/2)\mathbf{h}^{\mathrm{T}} H_f(\mathbf{x}^*)\mathbf{h}$$

Similarly, the constraints may be expanded as

$$g_i(\mathbf{x}^* + \mathbf{h}) - g_i(\mathbf{x}^*) \doteq \nabla_{\mathbf{x}} g_i(\mathbf{x}^*)\mathbf{h} + (1/2)\mathbf{h}^{\mathrm{T}} H_i(\mathbf{x}^*)\mathbf{h}, \qquad i = 1, \dots, m$$

By now appending, with Langrange multipliers, the expanded constraint equations to the expanded objective function and rearranging terms, the following relationship is obtained:

$$f(\mathbf{x}^* + \mathbf{h}) - f(\mathbf{x}^*)$$

$$= \nabla_{\mathbf{x}}\left[f(\mathbf{x}^*) - \sum_{i=1}^{m} \lambda_i g_i(\mathbf{x}^*) \right]\mathbf{h} + (1/2)\mathbf{h}^{\mathrm{T}}\left[H_f(\mathbf{x}^*) + \sum_{i=1}^{m} \lambda_i H_i(\mathbf{x}^*) \right]\mathbf{h}$$

It should be observed that the linear terms are precisely $\nabla_{\mathbf{x}} L(\mathbf{x}, \boldsymbol{\lambda})$, which in the Langrangian form is required to vanish as a necessary condition. Let

$$H_L(\mathbf{x}^*) = H_f(\mathbf{x}^*) + \sum_{i=1}^{m} \lambda_i H_i(\mathbf{x}^*)$$

$H_L(\mathbf{x}^*)$ can be used as a sufficiency test. If $H_L(\mathbf{x}^*)$ is positive definite at the point $(\mathbf{x}^*, \boldsymbol{\lambda}^*)$, then the solution may be classified as a relative minimum and is a relative maximum if $H_L(\mathbf{x}^*)$ is negative definite.

Consider an alternate approach to this formulation. Rather than carry the λ_1 through the development as unknown quantities, assume that a solution to the necessary conditions has been obtained. By evaluating the Lagrange function at a particular $\boldsymbol{\lambda}^*$ the following modified form is obtained:

$$L(\mathbf{x}, \boldsymbol{\lambda}^*) = f_\lambda(\mathbf{x}) = f(\mathbf{x}) + \sum_{i=1}^{m} \lambda_i^* g_i(\mathbf{x}) \qquad (4.84)$$

which returns to a function of n rather than $n + m$ variables. At the particular solution $\mathbf{x}^*$, as before, the term $\nabla_{\mathbf{x}} f_\lambda(\mathbf{x}^*)$ must still vanish, and also

$$f_\lambda(\mathbf{x}^* + \mathbf{h}) - f_\lambda(\mathbf{x}^*) \doteq (1/2)\mathbf{h}^{\mathrm{T}} H_\lambda(\mathbf{x}^*)\mathbf{h} \qquad (4.85)$$

$H_\lambda(\mathbf{x}^*)$ can be applied with the same rationale as $H_L(\mathbf{x}^*)$ in classifying a stationary point. There are some advantages to viewing the sufficiency test in this light. The most important of these is that $f_\lambda(\mathbf{x})$ may now be interpreted as a *transformed objective function*, for which the necessary conditions yield a solution which must satisfy the constraints. An important computational advantage may arise if one or more of the variables, say x_p, should disappear in forming $f_\lambda(\mathbf{x})$. This may be viewed as *direct elimination* of x_p precipitated by appending the subsidiary conditions to $f(\mathbf{x})$. If this should occur, then the quadratic form becomes

$$\mathbf{h}^{\mathrm{T}} H_\lambda(\mathbf{x}^*)\mathbf{h} = \sum_{\substack{i=1 \\ i \neq p}}^{n} \sum_{\substack{j=1 \\ j \neq p}}^{n} h_i h_j \frac{\partial f_\lambda^2(\mathbf{x})}{\partial x_i\, \partial x_j}\Bigg|_{\mathbf{x}^*} \qquad (4.86)$$

The following examples are intended to illustrate important aspects of the tests previously described as well as to demonstrate their strengths and weaknesses.

Example 4.9

$$f(\mathbf{x}) = x_1^2 + 2x_1 + 2x_1x_2 + 3x_2 + 2x_2^2 = \min$$

s.t.

$$g(\mathbf{x}) = x_1^2 - x_2 - 1 = 0$$

The Lagrange function is

$$L(\mathbf{x}, \lambda) = x_1^2 + 2x_1 + 2x_1x_2 + 3x_2 + 2x_2^2 + \lambda(x_1^2 - x_2 - 1)$$

The necessary conditions yields one solution to be

$$\mathbf{x}^* = \begin{bmatrix} -3/4 \\ -7/16 \end{bmatrix}, \qquad \lambda^* = -1/4. \quad \blacksquare$$

This example may be used to demonstrate a major weakness of the Hessian sufficiency test as well as introduce the concept of a transformed objective function. It is apparent from the development of the Hessian matrix that its ability to indicate a constrained extreme point is predicated on the fact that a point generated by the necessary conditions is, in fact, a candidate for an extreme point on the surface defined by $f(\mathbf{x})$. That is, $\mathbf{x}^*$ must also satisfy $\nabla_{\mathbf{x}} f(\mathbf{x}) = 0$, which in the above example is obviously not the case. However, by forming the transformed surface $f_\lambda(\mathbf{x})$ from the Langrange function as

$$f_\lambda(\mathbf{x}) = 3x_1^2/4 + 2x + 2x_1x_2 + 3x_2 + x_2/4 + 2x_2^2 + 1/4$$

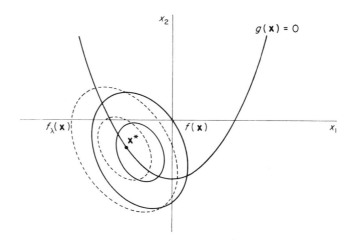

Fig. 4.2 The transformation from $f(\mathbf{x})$ to $f_\lambda(\mathbf{x})$.

it may be observed (Fig. 4.2) that $\mathbf{x}^*$ now satisfies $\nabla_x f_\lambda(\mathbf{x}) = 0$ as well as the constraint $g(\mathbf{x}) = 0$. The solution point $\mathbf{x}^*$ *must* then be a candidate for an extreme point on the surface defined by $f_\lambda(\mathbf{x})$. More often than not, this will not be the case for $f(\mathbf{x})$ alone. It is interesting to note that, even though the requirement for utilizing the Hessian was violated, if formed it would have indicated a minimum. To more fully emphasize the inappropriateness of the Hessian, and also the effect of a transformation from $f(\mathbf{x})$ to $f_\lambda(\mathbf{x})$, consider another example.

Example 4.10

$$f(\mathbf{x}) = 4x_1^2 - 2x_1 - 4x_2 - x_2^2 = \min$$
$$\text{s.t.}$$
$$g(\mathbf{x}) = x_2^2 - x_1 - 8 = 0$$

The Lagrange function is

$$L(\mathbf{x}, \lambda) = 4x_1^2 - 2x_1 - 4x_2 - x_2^2 + \lambda\left(x_2^2 - x_1 - 8\right)$$

The necessary conditions are resolved to yield the solution

$$\mathbf{x}^* = \begin{bmatrix} 2.9088 \\ 0.4611 \end{bmatrix}, \qquad \lambda^* = 1.688.$$

As before, the Hessian does not apply but it is of interest to note that it has an indefinite character. The transformed objective function for this problem appears as

$$f_\lambda(\mathbf{x}) = 4x_1^2 - 3.688x_1 - 4x_2 + 0.688x_2^2 - 13.5$$

By forming the matrix $H_\lambda(\mathbf{x}^*)$,

$$H_\lambda(\mathbf{x}^*) = \begin{bmatrix} 8 & 0 \\ 0 & 1.376 \end{bmatrix}$$

it is found that $\mathbf{x}^*$ is a relative minimum [i.e., $H_\lambda(\mathbf{x})$ is positive definite]. The transformation is seen to have converted the form of the objective function from one characterized by *hyperbolic contours*, namely, $f(\mathbf{x})$, to one characterized by *elliptic contours*, namely, $f_\lambda(\mathbf{x})$. ∎

Until now the Carathéodory–Phipps forms $H_L(\mathbf{x})$ and $H_\lambda(\mathbf{x})$ have been sufficient to characterize the indicated solution points as relative minima or maxima. The next example serves to indicate the case where these forms yield an inconclusive result.

Example 4.11

$$f(\mathbf{x}) = -x_1^3 + 3x_1 + 84x_2 - 6x_2^2 = \min$$
$$\text{s.t.}$$
$$g(\mathbf{x}) = x_1 + x_2 - 6 = 0$$

The Lagrange function is

$$L(\mathbf{x}, \lambda) = -x_1^3 + 3x_1 + 84x_2 - 6x_2^2 + \lambda(x_1 + x_2 - 6)$$

The necessary conditions lead to the two potential solutions

$$\mathbf{x}_1^* = \begin{bmatrix} -1 \\ 7 \end{bmatrix}, \quad \lambda_1^* = 0; \qquad \mathbf{x}_2^* = \begin{bmatrix} -3 \\ 9 \end{bmatrix}, \quad \lambda_2^* = 24$$

In an attempt to classify these candidates, the matrix $H_\lambda(\mathbf{x})$ is formed, giving

$$H_\lambda(\mathbf{x}) = \begin{bmatrix} -6x_1 & 0 \\ 0 & -12 \end{bmatrix}$$

Note that at both solution points, $H_\lambda(\mathbf{x})$ has an *indefinite* form; for example,

$$H_\lambda(\mathbf{x}_1^*) = \begin{vmatrix} 6 & 0 \\ 0 & -12 \end{vmatrix}, \qquad H_\lambda(\mathbf{x}_2^*) = \begin{vmatrix} 18 & 0 \\ 0 & -12 \end{vmatrix}$$

Extending the testing process to the generalized or the bordered Hessian tests, it would be found that $\mathbf{x}_2^*$ is, in fact, a relative minimum while $\mathbf{x}_1^*$ is a relative maximum.

the generalized test

the bordered Hessian

$$|H_G(\mathbf{x}, \lambda)| = \begin{vmatrix} (-6x_1 - \mu) & 0 & 1 \\ 0 & (-12 - \mu) & 1 \\ 1 & 1 & 0 \end{vmatrix} = 0, \quad |H_B(\mathbf{x}, \lambda)| = \begin{bmatrix} 0 & 1 & 1 \\ 1 & -6x_1 & 0 \\ 1 & 0 & -12 \end{bmatrix}$$

$\mu = -3$ at $\mathbf{x}_1^*$ negative definite at $\mathbf{x}_1^*$

$\mu = +3$ at $\mathbf{x}_2^*$ positive definite at $\mathbf{x}_2^*$ ∎

By examining the nature of the Carathéodory–Phipps test in light of the preceding discussion of the objective function transformation it becomes apparant that the conclusiveness of such a test is contingent on the fact that the solution points obtained from the necessary conditions are *extreme points on the surface defined by* $f_\lambda(\mathbf{x})$. Although this test is appropriate for such points, an indicated solution which fails to satisfy this test should *not* be disregarded as a candidate for a *relative* extreme point.

Returning to the generalized sufficiency test and bordered Hessian test previously outlined, it may be observed that these tests consider those points which are *relative extrema defined on the constraints*. In other words, these more general tests do, in fact, restrict consideration to perturbations $\mathbf{h}$ which must satisfy $\mathbf{g}(\mathbf{x}^* + \mathbf{h}) = 0$. Although this was assumed in the development of the Carathéodory–Phipps test, the test itself is insensitive to this restriction [i.e., $\mathbf{h}$ is not restricted by this test to satisfy $\mathbf{g}(\mathbf{x}^* + \mathbf{h}) = 0$]. This

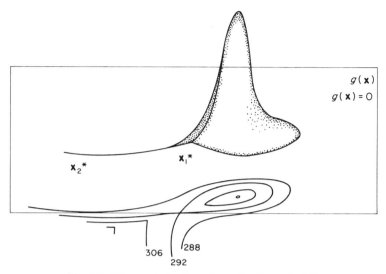

Fig. 4.3 The constrained maximum for Example 4.11.

point may be demonstrated more clearly by examining Fig. 4.3, which represents the indicated solutions to the immediately preceding example problem. The point x_1^* is seen to be a saddle point on the surface $f_\lambda(\mathbf{x})$ (therefore not an extreme point), while the point is a relative extreme point defined on the constraint.

Although the Carathéodory–Phipps test may fail to classify a solution point, it should be noted that the effort expended in obtaining the elements of the H_λ determinant are not wasted since the; correspond directly with the elements L_{ij} of the generalized and bordered Hessian tests.

It now remains to demonstrate, by one final example, the computational advantage mentioned in regard to using the alternative Carathéodory–Phipps form. Recall that by evaluating the Lagrangian at a particular λ^* and grouping like terms, one or more of the variables may disappear from $f_\lambda(\mathbf{x})$.

Example 4.12

$$f(\mathbf{x}) = x_1^2 + x_2^2 + x_3^2 = \min$$

s.t.

$$g(\mathbf{x}) = 4x_1 + x_2^2 + 2x_3 - 14 = 0$$

The Lagrange function is

$$L(\mathbf{x}, \lambda) = x_1^2 + x_2^2 + x_3^2 + \lambda(4x_1 + x_2^2 + 2x_3 - 14)$$

The necessary conditions give rise to the following three candidates as solution points:

$$\mathbf{x}_1^* = \begin{bmatrix} 2 \\ 2 \\ 1 \end{bmatrix}, \quad \lambda_1^* = -1; \qquad \mathbf{x}_2^* = \begin{bmatrix} 2 \\ -2 \\ 1 \end{bmatrix}, \quad \lambda_2^* = -1; \qquad \mathbf{x}_3^* = \begin{bmatrix} 2.8 \\ 0 \\ 1.4 \end{bmatrix},$$

$$\lambda_3^* = -1.4$$

$f_\lambda(\mathbf{x})$ is given by

$$f_\lambda(\mathbf{x}) = x_1^2 - 4x_1 + x_3^2 - 2x_3 + 14$$

for $\mathbf{x}_1^*$ and $\mathbf{x}_2^*$. Note that x_2 has disappeared (through evaluation with λ_1^* and λ_2^*). By forming $H_L(\mathbf{x})$ one would find that it has the semidefinite form

$$H_L(\mathbf{x}) = \begin{bmatrix} 2 & 0 & 0 \\ 0 & 0 & 0 \\ 0 & 0 & 2 \end{bmatrix}$$

However, observe that by forming $H_\lambda(\mathbf{x})$, as indicated previously, a positive definite result is obtained:

$$H_L(\mathbf{x}) = \begin{bmatrix} 2 & 0 \\ 0 & 2 \end{bmatrix}$$

The $H_L(\mathbf{x})$ test has given an inconclusive result, while the alternative $H_\lambda(\mathbf{x})$ has given a conclusive positive definite result, indicating that $\mathbf{x}_1^*$ and $\mathbf{x}_2^*$ are relative minima. The result obtained from $H_\lambda(\mathbf{x})$ is borne out by the generalized test, which also indicates $\mathbf{x}_1^*$ and $\mathbf{x}_2^*$ as relative minima since

$$\begin{vmatrix} (2-\mu) & 0 & 0 & 4 \\ 0 & (0-\mu) & 0 & 2x_2 \\ 0 & 0 & (2-\mu) & 2 \\ 4 & 2x_2 & 2 & 0 \end{vmatrix} = 0$$

yields $\mu = 2$, $8/9$, respectively. The alternative approach is not available when attempting to characterize $\mathbf{x}_3^*$, since none of the variables disappear when forming $f_\lambda(\mathbf{x})$ by evaluating $L(\mathbf{x}, \lambda)$ at λ_3^*. In fact this point can only be classified conclusively by one of the more general forms, which indicate that it is a relative maximum. ∎

It should by now be apparent that the alternative approach to the Carathéodory–Phipps test has one major disadvantage—any computational advantage gained by evaluating lower-order determinants may easily be offset if there are more than a limited number of distinct solutions for λ^*. If there are more than a limited number, then forming $H_\lambda(\mathbf{x})$ may require more computation than would be required by forming the more general representations $H_L(\mathbf{x}), H_B(\mathbf{x}, \boldsymbol{\lambda})$ and the generalized test.

Discussion

The preceding rudimentary examples have been presented to illustrate some of the distinct strengths and weaknesses of the various sufficiency tests outlined. Having viewed these tests in such a light, an attempt is now made to classsify them. The bordered Hessian and generalized sufficiency tests rank as the *most powerful*, since they alone incorporate a requirement that the constraints be satisfied directly in evaluating the character of the solution points generated by satisfying the necessary conditions. These tests may then be thought of as *constrained surface tests.* Unfortunately, these tests are also the most difficult computationally (the bordered Hessian being the less difficult of the two) by virtue of the order of the determinants which characterize their form. The Carathéodory–Phipps tests rank next in their ability to yield a classification for the solution points. Although they are appropriate for any solution point indicated by satisfying the necessary

Table 4.1

Summary of Sufficiency Test Criteria

Character	Hessian or Carathéodory–Phipps test	Generalized test	Bordered Hessian
Positive definite (minimum)	All leading principal minors are positive	All characteristic roots μ are positive	All leading principal minors, beginning with order $2m + 1$, have the sign $(-1)^m$
Negative definite (maximum)	Leading principal minors alternate in sign with the first being less than zero	All characteristic roots are negative	All leading principal minors beginning with order $2m + 1$, have an alternating sign pattern beginning with the sign $(-1)^{m+1}$
Indefinite (neither maximum or minimum)	If none of the above apply and all leading principal minors are nonzero	At least one characteristic root is positive and at least one is negative	If none of the above apply and all leading principal minors beginning with order $2m + 1$ are nonzero

conditions and are computationally less difficult than the more general tests, they may not always yield a conclusive result. As has been shown, this is due to the fact that they are tests which regard a solution as a point on the surface $f_\lambda(\mathbf{x})$ without regard for the constraints directly. Last, and by far least powerful, is the Hessian. This test is only valid when the solution point indicated on $f_\lambda(\mathbf{x})$ is also a stationary point on the surface $f(\mathbf{x})$. Even if this be the case, this test is no better than the Carathéodory–Phipps form and consequently is hardly worth consideration in practice. See Table 4.1.

OPTIMIZATION SUBJECT TO INEQUALITY CONSTRAINTS

Consider now the problem of optimizing the objective function

$$f(\mathbf{x}) = f(x_1, x_2, \ldots, x_n)$$

s.t.

$$g_i(\mathbf{x}) \leqslant b_i \qquad \text{for} \quad i = 1, \ldots, k \tag{4.87}$$

$$g_j(\mathbf{x}) \geqslant b_j \qquad \text{for} \quad j = k+1, \ldots, m \tag{4.88}$$

These subsidiary conditions are "inequality" relationships which define not only feasible "boundary" points but also those feasible "interior" points which simultaneously satisfy the inequality relationships of (4.87) and (4.88); see Fig. 4.4.

Observe that the constraining relationships of (4.87) and (4.88) can be made consistent with one another, as regards the "sense" of their inequalities, in the following manner. Constraints (4.87) can be made consistent in form with constraints (4.88) by multiplying both sides of (4.87) by -1 as

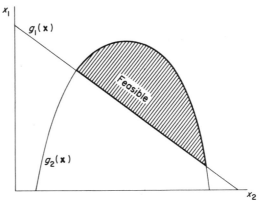

Fig. 4.4 Feasible boundary and interior points.

follows:

$$(-1)g_k(\mathbf{x}) \leqslant (-1)b_k \rightarrow -g_k(\mathbf{x}) \geqslant -b_k$$

This operation is termed *changing the sense of the inequality*. Similarly, the form of (4.88) can be altered to that of (4.87) by

$$(-1)g_j(\mathbf{x}) \geqslant (-1)b_j \rightarrow -g_j(\mathbf{x}) \leqslant -b_j$$

Now, being aware of this fact, we may write the inequality constrained optimization problem, without loss of generality, as

$$f(\mathbf{x}) = \min \text{ (max)}$$
$$\text{s.t.}$$
$$g_1(\mathbf{x}) - b_1 \leqslant 0$$
$$g_2(\mathbf{x}) - b_2 \leqslant 0 \qquad\qquad (4.89)$$
$$\vdots$$
$$g_m(\mathbf{x}) - b_m \leqslant 0$$

The constraint inequalities of (4.89) can be transformed into equality relationships by adding certain new variables to the problem, known as *slack variables*. These inequalities may now be written as equalities of the form

$$g_i(\mathbf{x}) + u_i^2 - b_i = 0, \qquad i = 1, \ldots, m$$

where the u_i are slack variables and are squared to insure that they will have a nonnegative effect on the constraints. It is apparent that the effect of the u must be nonnegative in order to convert the $\leqslant$ constraint to one of equality. Incorporating the slack variables as squared terms is a convenience; if we had not squared them, then we would have been forced to add an additional m constraints of the form

$$u_i \geqslant 0 \qquad \text{for} \quad i = 1, \ldots, m$$

to insure nonnegativity. We may now take the constraints defined by (4.89) and write them in a form suitable for solution by the Lagrange multiplier technique:

$$g_i(\mathbf{x}) + u_i^2 - b_i = 0 \qquad \text{for} \quad i = 1, \ldots, m \qquad\qquad (4.90)$$

or more conveniently for notational purposes,

$$g_i(\mathbf{x}, u_i, b_i) = 0 \qquad \text{for} \quad i = 1, \ldots, m \qquad\qquad (4.91)$$

The Lagrange function for the inequality constrained optimization problem appears as

$$L(\mathbf{x}, \boldsymbol{\lambda}, \mathbf{u}) = f(\mathbf{x}) + \sum_{i=1}^{m} \lambda_i g_i(\mathbf{x}, u_i, b_i)$$

$$= f(\mathbf{x}) + \sum_{i=1}^{m} \lambda_i \left[g_i(\mathbf{x}) + u_i^2 - b_i \right] \qquad (4.92)$$

The Kuhn–Tucker Conditions

We will now demonstrate the necessary and sufficient conditions which allow us to solve inequality constrained optimization problems. Let us assume that we have the problem

$$f(\mathbf{x}) = \min \ (\max)$$

s.t.

$$g_i(\mathbf{x}, u_i, b_i) = 0, \qquad i = 1, \ldots, m$$

As before, we may formulate this problem in the Lagrangian context as

$$L(\mathbf{x}, \boldsymbol{\lambda}, \mathbf{u}) = f(\mathbf{x}) + \sum_{i=1}^{m} \lambda_i g_i(\mathbf{x}, u_i, b_i) = \min \ (\max)$$

and obtain a solution by generating all stationary points of this Lagrange function. These stationary points may be obtained by solving the following simultaneous equations:

$$\frac{\partial L(\mathbf{x}, \boldsymbol{\lambda}, \mathbf{u})}{\partial x_j} = 0 = \frac{\partial f(\mathbf{x})}{\partial x_j} + \sum_{i=1}^{m} \lambda_i \frac{\partial g_i(\mathbf{x}, u_i, b_i)}{\partial x_j}, \qquad j = 1, \ldots, n \quad (4.93)$$

$$\frac{\partial L(\mathbf{x}, \boldsymbol{\lambda}, \mathbf{u})}{\partial \lambda_i} = 0 = g_i(\mathbf{x}, u_i, b_i) = g_i(\mathbf{x}) + u_i^2 - b_i, \qquad i = 1, \ldots, m \quad (4.94)$$

$$\frac{\partial L(\mathbf{x}, \boldsymbol{\lambda}, \mathbf{u})}{\partial u_i} = 0 = 2\lambda_i u_i, \qquad i = 1, \ldots, m \quad (4.95)$$

Observe that by multiplying (4.95) by $u_i/2$ we obtain

$$\lambda_i u_i^2 = 0$$

In addition, we may solve (4.94) in terms of u_i^2 as

$$u_i^2 = b_i - g_i(\mathbf{x})$$

Combining these relationships we obtain the m necessary conditions

$$\lambda_i \left[b_i - g_i(\mathbf{x}) \right] = 0 \qquad \text{for} \quad i = 1, \ldots, m \qquad (4.96)$$

These conditions are known as the *complementary slackness conditions*. The conditions of (4.96), together with those of (4.93) and (4.94) form the initial subset of necessary conditions for obtaining a local maximum of $f(\mathbf{x})$ under the defined constraints. There is, however, an additional necessary condition which must be met. This condition is that for a maximum of $f(\mathbf{x})$,

$$\lambda_i \leqslant 0 \qquad \text{for} \quad i = 1, \ldots, m \tag{4.97}$$

Let us examine this condition a bit further to establish its derivation as a necessary condition. Assume that we have satisfied the conditions of (4.93), (4.94), and (4.96), and that the solution point generated $(\mathbf{x}^*, \boldsymbol{\lambda}^*, \mathbf{u}^*)$ is indeed a relative maximum. From Eq. (4.92) we have

$$\frac{\partial f(\mathbf{x}^*)}{\partial b_i} = -\lambda_i \qquad \text{for } i = 1, \ldots, m$$

Our solution point then gives us a quantitative measure of the effect of variations in the constraint equations on the optimal value of the objective function.

Recall that from (4.95), at the optimal solution either $\lambda_i^* = 0$, or $u_i^* = 0$, or both equal zero must be the case. Let us assume that in this case some $u_i^* \neq 0$. This would imply that the constraint associated with u_i holds as a strict inequality. That is, if we relaxed this constraint and allowed b_i to increase by a small amount, then the extreme point solution would not be affected. If this be the case, then we may also observe that from our definition of the Lagrange multipliers, the following must be true:

$$\frac{\partial f(\mathbf{x}^*)}{\partial b_i} = -\lambda_i^* = 0$$

Alternatively, if we assume that at the optimal solution $\lambda_i^* \neq 0$, then u_i^* must vanish. We then have the constraint holding as a strict equality:

$$g_i(\mathbf{x}) = b_i$$

Let us take a contradictory view and assume in this case that $\lambda_i > 0$ and consequently $\partial f(\mathbf{x}^*)/\partial b_i < 0$. This would mean as b_i increases the objective function would in turn decrease. We are aware, however, that as b_i increases more feasible space is obtained and consequently—since we were previously restrained in obtaining a higher value for the objective function by the constraint—the optimal value of the objective function clearly cannot decrease. We then rightfully conclude that at the optimal solution to a maximization problem, $\lambda_i \leqslant 0$ for $i = 1, \ldots, m$ (see Figs. 4.5 and 4.6).

A similar reasoning prevails in developing the necessary conditions for an inequality constrained minimization problem. In this case the sense of the inequality associated with λ_i^* is reversed and we have for an inequality constrained minimum

$$\lambda_i \geqslant 0 \qquad \text{for} \quad i = 1, \ldots, m \tag{4.98}$$

Let us summarize the necessary conditions for an optimal solution to the inequality constrained optimization problem in Table 4.2.

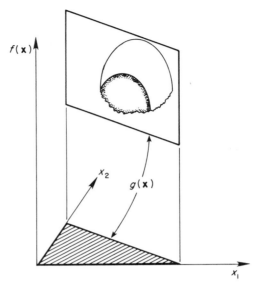

Fig. 4.5   The case where $\lambda_i < 0$, $u_i = 0$.

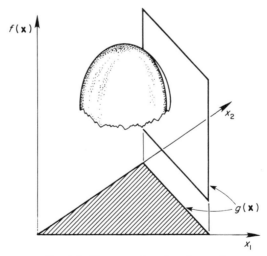

Fig. 4.6   The case where $\lambda_i = 0$, $u_i \neq 0$.

As regards the sufficiency of the above conditions, which are referred to as the Kuhn–Tucker conditions, let us demonstrate that if $f(\mathbf{x})$ is a strictly concave function and the constraints $g_i(\mathbf{x})$ for $i = 1, \ldots, m$ are convex, then the Kuhn–Tucker conditions are both necessary and sufficient. Recalling our definition of convex and concave functions, we may observe that if

Table 4.2

The Necessary Conditions for the Inequality Constrained
Optimization Problem

Maximum problem	Minimum problem
(a) $\lambda_i \leq 0, i = 1, \ldots, m$	(a) $\lambda_i \geq 0, i = 1, \ldots, m$

(b) $\dfrac{\partial L(\mathbf{x}^*, \boldsymbol{\lambda}^*, \mathbf{u}^*)}{\partial x_j} = 0, \quad j = 1, \ldots, n$

(c) $\lambda_i [g_i(\mathbf{x}^*) - b_i] = 0, \quad i = 1, \ldots, m$

(d) $g_i(\mathbf{x}^*) > b_i, \quad\quad\quad i = 1, \ldots, m$

$g_i(\mathbf{x})$ is convex and $\lambda_i \leq 0$, then their product $\lambda_i g_i(\mathbf{x})$ is concave. Given also that $f(\mathbf{x})$ is strictly concave, we then have that

$$f(\mathbf{x}) + \sum_{i=1}^{m} \lambda_i g_i(\mathbf{x}) \qquad (4.99)$$

is strictly concave.

In addition, since $\lambda_i u_i = 0$ and $\lambda_i b_i$ is a constant, we may conclude that if (4.99) is concave, then the Lagrange function $L(\mathbf{x}, \boldsymbol{\lambda}, \mathbf{u})$ is concave. We are aware that the necessary conditions require that $L(\mathbf{x}, \boldsymbol{\lambda}, \mathbf{u})$ have a stationary point in order for $f(\mathbf{x})$ to be maximized at $\mathbf{x}^*$. We also know that a strictly concave function is characterized by having *only one* stationary point; consequently the point $\mathbf{x}^*$ must be the relative maximum. We then have the case that the Kuhn–Tucker conditions are both necessary and sufficient. Note that a similar reasoning holds when minimizing a strictly convex function subject to convex constraints.

We should make a final point as regards the Kuhn–Tucker conditions. Recall that in our development of the Lagrange multiplier approach to equality constrained optimization problems, we required that at least one nonsingular matrix $G(\mathbf{x})$ could be formed from the system of constraint equations. A similar restriction holds for the inequality constrained case. That is, at least one nonsingular matrix $G(\mathbf{x})$ must be capable of being formed from the system of constraint equations which have been transformed to their equality form by the addition of the slack variables u_i^2. This is then an implicit necessary condition in the preceding development.

Example 4.13 Solution Procedure Consider the problem of finding a point on the circle of minimum radius, centered at the origin, which simultaneously satisfies the following inequality constraints:

$$g_1(x_1, x_2) = x_1 + x_2 \geq 1$$
$$g_2(x_1, x_2) = x_1 + 3x_2 \leq 6$$

Making $g_1(\mathbf{x})$ consistent with $g_2(\mathbf{x})$ by multiplying through by -1, we have

$$g_1(x_1, x_2) = -x_1 - x_2 \leqslant -1$$

By adding the slack variables we may now state the problem more formally as

$$f(\mathbf{x}) = x_1^2 + x_2^2 = \min$$

s.t.

$$-x_1 - x_2 + u_1^2 + 1 = 0$$
$$x_1 + 3x_2 + u_2^2 - 6 = 0$$

Continuing the solution procedure, we form the Lagrange function for this problem:

$$L(\mathbf{x}, \boldsymbol{\lambda}, \boldsymbol{\mu}) = x_1^2 + x_2^2 + \lambda_1\left(-x_1 - x_2 + u_1^2 + 1\right) + \lambda_2\left(x_1 + 3x_2 + u_2^2 - 6\right)$$

which allows us to treat the problem as unconstrained in the $n + 2m$ variables $x_j, j = 1, \ldots, n, u_i, \lambda_i, i = 1, \ldots, m$. We are now able to write the necessary conditions as follows:

$$\frac{\partial L}{\partial x_1} = 2x_1 - \lambda_1 + \lambda_2 = 0 \tag{4.100}$$

$$\frac{\partial L}{\partial x_2} = 2x_2 - \lambda_1 + 3\lambda_2 = 0 \tag{4.101}$$

$$\frac{\partial L}{\partial \lambda_1} = -x_1 - x_2 + u_1^2 + 1 = 0 \tag{4.102}$$

$$\frac{\partial L}{\partial \lambda_2} = x_1 + 3x_2 + u_2^2 - 6 = 0 \tag{4.103}$$

$$\frac{\partial L}{\partial u_1} = 2u_1\lambda_1 = 0 \tag{4.104}$$

$$\frac{\partial L}{\partial u_2} = 2u_2\lambda_2 = 0 \tag{4.105}$$

From our previous discussion, we recall that either $u_i = 0$, $\lambda_i = 0$, or both equal zero (for $i = 1, \ldots, m$) at the optimal solution. We should then be aware that there are 2^m possible cases which give rise to these conditions. It now remains to enumerate these potential outcomes until the appropriate solution is obtained. We have the distinct advantage, in this particular example, of knowing that once we find a case for which the minimum is indicated we may stop; since $f(\mathbf{x})$ is convex, this is the unique minimum solution.

Let us begin to enumerate the outcomes for u_i and λ_i attempting to find a solution.

Case I: [Conditions: $\lambda_1 = 0$, $\lambda_2 = 0$; u_1^2, $u_2^2 \geqslant 0$]   From (4.100) and (4.101) we have $x_1 = x_2 = 0$. However, in attempting to solve for (4.102) we have $u_1^2 = -1$, which violates the nonnegativity restriction on the u_i^2. We may then abandon this case as infeasible.

Case II: [Conditions: $u_1 = 0$, $u_2 = 0$; and for a minimum λ_1, $\lambda_2 \geqslant 0$] From (4.102) and (4.103) we have $x_1 = -3/2$, $x_2 = 5/2$. Substituting these values into (4.100) and (4.101) gives the solution for λ_1, λ_2:

$$\lambda_1 = -33/4, \qquad \lambda_2 = -21/4$$

This case is also abandoned since at the minimum we seek, the values for λ_1, λ_2 must be greater than or equal to zero.

Case III: [Conditions: $u_1 = 0$, $\lambda_2 = 0$; u_2, $\lambda_1 \geqslant 0$]   From (4.100), (4.101) and (4.102) we obtain the values for x_1 and x_2: $x_1 = x_2 = 1/2$. These same equations then also give that $\lambda_1 = 1$. Solving finally for u_2^2 in Eq. (4.103), we find that

$$u_2^2 = 4$$

and consequently that the optimal solution has been obtained and is

$$x_1 = x_2 = 1/2$$
$$u_1 = \lambda_2 = 0$$
$$\lambda_1 = 1$$
$$u_2^2 = 4$$

This solution is borne out in Fig 4.7. ■

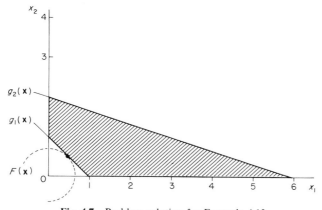

Fig. 4.7   Problem solution for Example 4.13.

A Remark on Inequality Constraints

Recalling the preceding example problem, observe that the first constraint held as a strict equality, while the second constraint held as a strict inequality at the optimal solution. Constraints which hold as strict equalities at the optimal solution are termed *tight* or *active* constraints, signifying that the solution is a boundary point of the feasible region restricted by that particular constraint. On the other hand, constraints which hold as strict inequalities at the optimum are termed *loose* or *inactive* constraints, signifying that the solution is an interior point in the feasible region defined by that particular constraint. It is then apparent that at the optimal solution, a constraint is readily detectable as tight or loose by whether its associated slack variable has a positive value or not. If the slack variable is positive, then the associated constraint must be loose. Conversely, if the slack variable is zero, then the associated constraint is tight. The slack variables can then be thought of as indicators of some distance between the solution point and their associated constraint.

Selecting Cases to Examine

The preceding example should give some insight into the existence of a strategy which can be employed in examining the various cases associated with an inequality constrained optimization problem. This strategy is based upon applying an interpretation of the values associated with the Lagrange multipliers and slack variables at a given solution to the necessary conditions. The strategy will be described in the context of an example problem; in general, it begins with solving the problem as if it were an unconstrained optimization problem (e.g., the case $\lambda_i = 0$, $i = 1, \ldots, m$).

Example 4.14   Solve the following problem:

$$f(\mathbf{x}) = x_1^2 - 5x_1 + 2x_2^2 - 4x_2 = \min$$

s.t.

$$x_1 + x_2 \leqslant 4$$
$$2x_1 - 3x_2 \leqslant 1$$

Forming the Lagrange function and then constructing the necessary conditions gives

$$2x_1 - 5 + \lambda_1 + 2\lambda_2 = 0$$
$$4x_2 - 4 + \lambda_1 - 3\lambda_2 = 0$$
$$x_1 + x_2 + u_1^2 - 4 = 0$$
$$2x_1 - 3x_2 + u_2^2 - 1 = 0$$
$$2\lambda_1 u_1 = 0$$
$$2\lambda_2 u_2 = 0$$

Beginning with Case I, $\lambda_1, \lambda_2 = 0$, the solution

$$\mathbf{x}^* = \begin{bmatrix} 2.5 \\ 1 \end{bmatrix}, \qquad u_1^2 = 0.5, \qquad u_2^2 = -1$$

is obtained.

Recall that assigning a value of zero to some λ_i in effect forces its associated constraint to be ignored in obtaining a solution to the problem at hand. In addition, the value obtained for some u_i^2 can be interpreted as indicating a distance between the solution point $\mathbf{x}^*$ and the constraint associated with u_i^2. If the value of u_i^2 is *negative* then the solution point is at a distance from the constraint in the *infeasible* region defined by that constraint.

The solution obtained for Case I lends itself to the following interpretation. Ignoring both constraints $(\lambda_1, \lambda_2 = 0)$ has generated a solution point which is interior to the region defined by the first constraint $(u_1^2 = 0.5)$, but which is outside the feasible region defined by the second constraint $(u_2^2 = -1)$. Apparently, ignoring the first constraint had no effect on generating a solution which would satisfy this constraint; however, ignoring the second constraint led to a solution which violated the constraint. Consequently, we cannot dismiss the effect of this constraint on obtaining a feasible solution. The next case to examine is then one in which the first constraint continues to be ignored but the second constraint is deemed active at the optimum solution.

For Case II, $\lambda_1 = 0$, $u_2 = 0$, the following solution is obtained:

$$\mathbf{x}^* = \begin{bmatrix} 77/34 \\ 20/17 \end{bmatrix}, \qquad u_1^2 = 19/34, \qquad \lambda_2 = 4/17$$

Case II yields a solution which satisfies the Kuhn–Tucker conditions (e.g., $\lambda_1, \lambda_2 \geqslant 0$; $u_1^2, u_2^2 \geqslant 0$) and is consequently a feasible candidate for the optimal solution to this problem. In fact, we need look no further, for that is the minimizing point. Observe that the effect of linear constraints on a constrained optimization problem does not change the "character" of the objective function, but rather only translates the location of the solution point. Since the first constraint does not restrict the solution to the unconstrained problem (Case I), it is of no use to consider the case $\lambda_2, u_1 = 0$. Also, since the objective function is strictly convex, forcing the solution point to move along the second constraint to the point where both constraints intersect (the case $u_1, u_2 = 0$) moves the solution away from the minimizing point of this function on the second constraint. It may then be concluded that the solution to Case II is the minimizing solution. ∎

Example 4.15 A chemical company makes two compounds, A and B. Each compound requires raw material I. The number of pounds of raw materials available for the next month production is 1000. Due to deterio-

206 4 Classical Optimization Theory for Constrained Functions

ration of raw materials, all of raw materials *I* available must be consumed in the production of compounds *A* and *B* during the next month. If x_1 and x_2 are the number of units of compounds *A* and *B*, respectively, produced during the next month, then total profit can be expressed by

$$\text{profit} = 3x_1 + 10x_2$$

the number of pounds of raw materials required for production of one unit of compounds *A* and *B* is given as follows:

	Compound	
Raw material	A	B
I	3	4

How many units of each compound should be produced during the coming month?

The problem may be formulated as

$$3x_1 + 10x_2 = \max$$
$$\text{s.t.}$$
$$3x_1 + 4x_2 = 1000$$
$$x_1, x_2, \geqslant 0$$

The Langrange function for this problem is given by

$$L(\mathbf{x}, \boldsymbol{\lambda}, \mathbf{u}) = 3x_1 + 10x_2 + \lambda_i(3x_1 + 4x_2 - 1000)$$
$$+ \lambda_2(x_1 - u_1^2) + \lambda_3(x_2 - u_2^2)$$

The necessary conditions for a stationary point are given by

$$\frac{\partial}{\partial x_1} L(\mathbf{x}, \boldsymbol{\lambda}, \mathbf{u}) = 3 + 3\lambda_1 + \lambda_2 \qquad = 0 \qquad (4.106)$$

$$\frac{\partial}{\partial x_2} L(\mathbf{x}, \boldsymbol{\lambda}, \mathbf{u}) = 10 + 4\lambda_1 + \lambda_3 \qquad = 0 \qquad (4.107)$$

$$\frac{\partial}{\partial \lambda_1} L(\mathbf{x}, \boldsymbol{\lambda}, \mathbf{u}) = 3x_1 + 4x_2 - 1000 = 0 \qquad (4.108)$$

$$\frac{\partial}{\partial \lambda_2} L(\mathbf{x}, \boldsymbol{\lambda}, \mathbf{u}) = x_1 - u_1^2 \qquad = 0 \qquad (4.109)$$

$$\frac{\partial}{\partial \lambda_3} L(\mathbf{x}, \boldsymbol{\lambda}, \mathbf{u}) = x_2 - u_2^2 \qquad = 0 \qquad (4.110)$$

$$\frac{\partial}{\partial u_1} L(\mathbf{x}, \boldsymbol{\lambda}, \mathbf{u}) = -2\lambda_2 u_1 \qquad = 0 \qquad (4.111)$$

$$\frac{\partial}{\partial u_2} L(\mathbf{x}, \boldsymbol{\lambda}, \mathbf{u}) = 2\lambda_3 u_2 \qquad = 0 \qquad (4.112)$$

Table 4.3

Possible Solutions for Example 4.15

λ_2	λ_3	λ_1	u_1	u_2	x_1	x_2	Comments
0	0	None	–	–	–	–	Infeasible
0	9	-1	$\sqrt{\dfrac{1000}{3}}$	0	$\dfrac{1000}{3}$	0	Feasible
$\dfrac{9}{2}$	0	$-\dfrac{5}{2}$	0	$\sqrt{250}$	0	250	Feasible
$\lambda_2 \neq 0$	$-6+\dfrac{4}{3}\lambda_2$	$-1-\dfrac{\lambda_2}{3}$	0	0	None	None	Infeasible

From Eqs. (4.111) and (4.112), λ_2 and λ_3 may be either zero or nonzero Table 4.3 gives solutions for each combination of λ_2 and λ_3.
Hence the two feasible solutions for the problem are given by

$$(\mathbf{x}^*,\boldsymbol{\lambda}^*,\mathbf{u}^*) = \begin{cases} (1000/3, & 0, & -1 & 0, & 9, & \sqrt{1000/3}, & 0) \\ (0, & 250, & -5/2, & 9/2, & 0, & 0, & \sqrt{250}) \end{cases}$$

The bordered Hessian matrix is given by

$$H_B(\mathbf{x},\boldsymbol{\lambda},\mathbf{u}) = \begin{bmatrix} 0 & 0 & 0 & 3 & 4 & 0 & 0 \\ 0 & 0 & 0 & 1 & 0 & -2u_1 & 0 \\ 0 & 0 & 0 & 0 & 1 & 0 & -2u_2 \\ 3 & 1 & 0 & 0 & 0 & 0 & 0 \\ 4 & 0 & 1 & 0 & 0 & 0 & 0 \\ 0 & -2u_1 & 0 & 0 & 0 & -2\lambda_2 & 0 \\ 0 & 0 & -2u_2 & 0 & 0 & 0 & -2\lambda_3 \end{bmatrix}$$

Since $m = 3$ and $n = 4$, the nature of the stationary points may be determined by evaluating $|H_{B_7}|$, which is given by

$$|H_{B_7}| = -72u_1^2\lambda_3 + u_2^2\lambda_2$$

For $(\mathbf{x}^*,\boldsymbol{\lambda}^*,\mathbf{u}^*) = (1000/3, 0, -1, 0, 9, \sqrt{1000/3}, 0)$, $|H_{B_7}| = -216{,}000$, and this point is a relative minimum. For $(\mathbf{x}^*,\boldsymbol{\lambda}^*,\mathbf{u}^*) = (0, 250, -5/2, 9/2, 0, 0, \sqrt{250})$, $|H_{B_7}| = 144{,}000$, and hence $x_1^* = 0$, $x_2^* = 250$ is the maximizing point for the problem. ∎

GENERAL REVIEW

It would be well here to pause and reflect a moment on the preceding development of optimization procedures to see whether we cannot detect some underlying trend in the evolution of these techniques. In fact, it takes only a moment to realize that we have been attempting, in the case of constrained problems, to work our way backward to solution procedures which will allow us to treat the problem at hand as an unconstrained optimization problem. We may then conclude that with each step forward, attempting to enhance our problem solving ability by encompassing additional types of problem contexts, we have used various mathematical techniques and procedures which allow us to consider these new problems as mere modifications of the unconstrained case. These procedures lead us to an eventual problem statement for which the techniques of unconstrained optimization apply. In other words, for each step forward we have taken, we have found a means whereby we may take a step backward and solve our new problem in the familiar surroundings of unconstrained optimization. This process may be viewed more precisely in the following representation of the progression of model classifications and solution approaches:

$$\begin{matrix} \text{unconstrained} \\ \text{optimization} \end{matrix} \leftarrow \text{Lagrange multipliers} \leftarrow \begin{matrix} \text{equality} \\ \text{constraints} \end{matrix} \leftarrow \begin{matrix} \text{slack} \\ \text{variables} \end{matrix} \leftarrow \begin{matrix} \text{inequality} \\ \text{constraints} \end{matrix}$$

PROBLEMS

1. Find the stationary vector $\mathbf{x}^*$ for the function

    $$f(\mathbf{x}) = x_1^2 + 2x_2^2 + 3x_3^2 + 2x_1 - x_2 - x_3$$
    s.t.
    $$x_1 + x_2 + x_3 = 0$$

    (a) by direct elimination,
    (b) by indirect elimination,
    (c) by the method of Lagrange multipliers.

    For parts (a) and (c), determine whether $\mathbf{x}^*$ is a minimum or maximum for $f(\mathbf{x})$.

2. Find the vector $\mathbf{x}^*$ which minimizes

    $$f(\mathbf{x}) = 2x_1^2 + x_2^2$$
    s.t.
    $$x_1 + x_2 = 1$$

    (a) by direct elimination,
    (b) by indirect elimination,
    (c) by the method of Lagrange multipliers.

3. Find the stationary point for

    $$f(\mathbf{x}) = 3x_1^3 + 2x_2^3 + x_3$$
    s.t.
    $$x_2 + x_3^2 = 0$$

    (a) by direct elimination,
    (b) by indirect elimination,
    (c) by the method of Lagrange multipliers.

4. Find and determine the nature (minimum or maximum) of the stationary points for

$$f(\mathbf{x}) = 2x_1 + x_2$$

s.t.

$$x_1 + x_2 = 5$$
$$x_1 - x_3^2 = 0$$
$$x_2 - x_4^2 = 0$$

   (a) by direct elimination,
   (b) by the method of Lagrange multipliers.
5. The number A to be divided into three parts, x_1, x_2, and x_3, $x_1 + x_2 + x_3 = A$. Find the values x_1, x_2, and x_3 such that their product $x_1 x_2 x_3$ is maximized.
6. A company manufactures closed cylindrical tanks. The volume of each tank is to be V, where $V = (\pi/4)D^2 L$; here D is the diameter of the top and bottom of the tank and L is its length. To minimize the cost of materials, the company would like to minimize the surface area A of the tanks, where $A = (\pi/2)D^2 + \pi DL$. Determine the values of D and L such that the surface area is minimized subject to the restriction that the volume of the tank is V.
7. A company maintains four service facilities. The service rate at the ith facility is μ_i and the rate of customer arrivals is α_i. The proportion of time the server is busy is given by α_i/μ_i. Hence, the proportion of time the server is busy can be increased if the customer arrival rate is increased. To increase the arrival rate at the ith facility by x_i requires an investment of $C_i x_i^2$ in promotional efforts. The company is willing to invest a total of I dollars in advertising. What investment should be made in advertising for each facility to maximize total utilization over all facilities?
8. Given the following data, solve Problem 7:

i	α_i	μ_i	C_i ($)	I
1	200	400	100	$4,000,000
2	400	600	200	
3	150	200	800	
4	500	600	300	

9. In Problem 7 suppose that the cost of idle time at the ith facility is C_{1i} per hour of idle time. Given the following data, find the optimal investment in advertising for each facility and the resulting increase in customer arrival rate if the cost of idle time is to be minimized subject to the investment constraint. Assuming 8 working hours per day and 200 working days per year, is the investment of $50,000 recovered in the first year in savings in idle time?

i	C_i ($)	C_{1i} ($/hr)	α_i (arrivals/hr)	μ_i (services/hr)
1	300	100	8	16
2	1000	600	10	20
3	700	400	12	24
4	700	300	6	18

$I = \$50,000.$

10. In Problem 9 suppose that the company wishes to determine the optimal investment in advertising to minimize the cost of idle time for the next year at the four service facilities. That is, no constraint is placed upon the total investment. If x_i is the increase in the arrival rate at facility i, then the net savings resulting from the investment in advertising is given by $S(\mathbf{x})$, where

$$S(\mathbf{x}) = \sum_{i=1}^{4} \left[\left(1 - \frac{\alpha_i + x_i}{\mu_i} \right) C_{1i} - C_i x_i^2 \right]$$

If the investment in advertising is such that $\alpha_i + x_i \geqslant \mu_i$, a state of instability will result at the ith facility. Hence, x_i is to be constrained so that

$$x_i \leqslant 0.99\mu_i - \alpha_i$$

Find the optimal investment in advertising for each facility.

11. A study is to be conducted to estimate the total value of property in a certain community. There are m classes of property (single-family residential, multifamily residential, commercial, industrial, etc.) in the community. A sample of n_i properties is to be selected at random from class i, $i = 1, 2, \ldots, m$, and the value of each property determined. The estimated mean value of property in class i is given by $\bar{x}_i$, where

$$\bar{x}_i = \frac{1}{n_i} \sum_{j=1}^{n_i} x_{ij}$$

and x_{ij} is the value of the jth property selected in class i. The standard deviation of property value in class i has been estimated to be σ_i. The standard deviation of property value is a measure of the variability of property value from one parcel to another. If $\bar{v}$ is the estimated mean value per parcel taken over all properties in the community, then

$$\bar{v} = \frac{1}{N} \sum_{i=1}^{m} M_i \bar{x}_i$$

where M_i is the total number of properties in class i and

$$N = \sum_{i=1}^{m} M_i$$

and the estimated total value of property in the community is $N\bar{v}$. Hence, the accuracy of the estimate of total value is dependent upon the accuracy of $\bar{v}$ as an estimate of the true mean property value per parcel in the community. A measure of the accuracy of the estimate $\bar{v}$ is the variance of $\bar{v}$ given by P:

$$P = \frac{1}{N^2} \sum_{i=1}^{m} M_i \frac{\sigma_i^2}{n_i}$$

That is, the smaller the value of P, the more accurate the estimate. The community would like the estimate of total value to be as accurate as possible but has a limited budget, T, for sampling. If C_i is the cost to appraise the value of a property in class i, then the budget limitation implies that

$$\sum_{i=1}^{m} C_i n_i = T$$

Determine the sample sizes n_i^*, $i = 1, 2, \ldots, m$, which will minimize P subject to the imposed budget limitations.

12. Given the problem situation in Problem 11, find the optimal sample sizes if cost is to be minimized subject to the restriction that the variance of $\bar{v}$ equals P'.

13. Given the following data, find the optimal solution for Problem 11:

i	M_i	σ_i ($)	c_i ($)	T ($)
1	4400	2,000	50	100,000
2	1200	16,000	200	
3	800	32,000	1,000	
4	200	4,800	100	
5	100	1,600	30	

14. Given the data in Problem 13 and $P' = 300$, solve Problem 12.
15. Solve Problem 11 if the cost of sampling is proportional to the square of the sample size. That is, the budget constraint is given by

$$\sum_{i=1}^{m} C_i n_i^2 = T$$

16. m service facilities are to be opened, where α_i and μ_i are the mean customer arrival and service rates, respectively, for facility i, $i = 1, 2, \ldots, m$. The cost of operating service facility i per unit of time at a rate μ_i (services/hr) is

$$C(\mu_i) = \frac{C_{1i}\alpha_i^2}{\mu_i(\mu_i - \alpha_i)} + \frac{C_{1i}\alpha_i}{\mu_i} + C_{2i}\mu_i, \qquad i = 1, 2, \ldots, m$$

where C_1 is the cost per unit of time spent by the customer in the system, and C_{2i} is the cost per unit of time for providing service at mean rate μ_i. Hence, the total cost of operating the m facilities per unit time at service rates μ_1 and μ_2 is

$$C(\mu_1, \mu_2) = \sum_{i=1}^{m} \left[\frac{C_{1i}\alpha_i^2}{\mu_i(\mu_i - \alpha_i)} + \frac{C_{1i}\alpha_i}{\mu_i} + C_{2i}\mu_i \right]$$

The cost of providing service per unit time at the facilities is to be limited to I dollars due to budget limitations. Hence,

$$\sum_{i=1}^{m} C_{2i}\mu_i = I$$

Find the optimal service rates at the m service facilities.

17. Solve Problem 16 given three facilities and the following data, where α_i is measured

i	α_i	C_{2i} ($)	C_{1i} ($)	I ($)
1	100	50	25	11,510
2	200	30	25	
3	50	10	25	

in customers per day and C_{1i} and C_{2i} are in dollars per day. Calculate the cost per day of the constrained optimal solution. What additional savings per day could be achieved if the constraint were removed?

18. Find the unconstrained optimal solution for Problem 17 using the gradient method. Let $r = 0.5$. Terminate the search when the reduction in the cost of service fails to exceed $50.00 on three successive iterations of the search.

19. A company distributes its products in two metropolitan areas located at coordinates (x_i, y_i), $i = 1, 2$. A warehouse is to be located at a point such that the two areas can be served at a minimum shipping cost. The demand in each area is given by d_i, $i = 1, 2$, and the annual cost of shipping from the warehouse location at (x_3, y_3) is given by

$$C(x_3, y_3) = \sum_{i=1}^{2} C_i d_i \left[(x_i - x_3)^2 + (y_i - y_3)^2 \right]$$

The following data is available, where d_i is in units per year and distances are measured in miles. Find the optimal warehouse location (x_3^*, y_3^*) using the gradient method. Terminate the search when the reduction in the annual cost of shipping fails to exceed $100.00 on three successive iterations of the search. Let the starting point for the search be $(42, 20)$.

i	c_i ($)	d_i	x_i	y_i
1	2.00	1000	4	8
2	3.00	4000	42	20

20. Minimize

$$f(\mathbf{x}) = x_1^2 + x_2^2 + 2x_1x_3 - 3x_1 - 4x_2 + x_3^2$$

s.t.

$$x_1 + x_2 = 4$$
$$x_1 - x_3 = 1$$

(a) by direct elimination,
(b) using the method of Lagrange multipliers.

21. Minimize

$$f(\mathbf{x}) = 30x_1 + 20x_2$$

s.t.

$$x_1 + x_2 \leqslant 8$$
$$6x_1 + 4x_2 \geqslant 12$$
$$5x_1 + 8x_2 = 20$$
$$x_1, x_2 \geqslant 0$$

(a) Solve this problem graphically. (Note that the gradient vector is constant.)
(b) Is the objective function convex?
(c) Solve using the method of Lagrange multipliers.
(d) Justify that the solution you obtain in (a) and (c) is indeed the minimum.

22. What are the cross-sectional dimensions of the strongest rectangular beam that can be cut from a round log which is 36 inches in diameter if the strength of the beam is proportional to its width and to the square of its depth?

23. We can improve the quality of signal received from a satellite by two methods: (1) increased power of signal; and (2) additional special data-processing time. Increasing power improves the signal by a factor of 0.2 per watt and special data processing improves the signal by 0.3 per minute. The cost of increasing power varies with the square of the watts times 0.175, and the cost of data processing varies with the square root of the number of minutes times 6. If the signal must be improved by at least a factor of 10, by how much power should the signal be increased and how many minutes of special processing should be used?

24. We have a rectangular piece of sheet metal 24 inches wide and 34 inches long. From this sheet, we are to remove equal square sections from each corner so that the sides may be bent upward to form a pan. How large should each of these sections be so that the volume of the resultant pan will be a maximum?

25. What are the dimensions and volume of the largest cylindrical tank that can be shipped by common carrier, if regulations prohibit the shipment of any tank the sum of whose length and circumference exceeds 10 feet?

26. We have a hoist mounted on one end of a 20-foot boom, the other end of which is to be fastened to a wall. We have 100 feet of cable, which is to be in one section or cut into two sections, to be used to add vertical support to the boom. Each section is to be connected to the wall above the boom and to the boom; the exact locations of these connection points are, as yet, undetermined. Where should these connection points be made so that the shear force on the boom at its wall connection is minimized?

27. We have three different kinds of machines (A, B, and C) on which a single product can be produced. The production cost incurred by operating each machine is a function of the number of units that it processes. If we let n_A be the number of units processed by A, n_B the number of units processed by B, and n_C the number of units processed by C, then the following table can be used to summarize the production costs incurred:

Machine	Operating cost ($/unit)
A	$0.5n_A^2 - 0.1n_A$
B	$10\sqrt{n_B} - 0.5n_B$
C	$n_C^2 - 0.75n_C$

How many units should be assigned to each machine if (a) 200 units of product are required, (b) 300 units of product are required, (c) 150 units of product are required?

28. Minimize

$$f(\mathbf{x}) = 2x_1^2 + 3x_2^2 + 4x_3^2 - 7x_1 - 6x_2 - 8x_3$$

s.t.

$$x_1 + x_2 \leq 4$$
$$x_2 - x_3 \leq 5$$

29. Minimize

$$f(\mathbf{x}) = 2x_1^2 + 3x_2^2 + 4x_3^2 - 8x_1 - 6x_2 + 8x_3$$

s.t.

$$x_1 + 2x_2 \leq 3$$
$$x_1 - x_3 \geq 2$$

30. Your firm plans to submit a bid for the design and construction of three chemical storage tanks. The company for which the tanks will be built has not completed its specifications, but you have been told that the production process will be set up to maximize profit. From preliminary information you know that mixture 1 contributes approximately $10 per gallon to profit, mixture 2 contributes approximately $8 per gallon, and mixture 3 contributes approximately $12 per gallon.

The production process itself begins in a blending tank, where ingredients for all three mixtures are originally combined. The capacity of this tank is 100,000 gallons. The contents of the blending tank are then run through a refining process. Each mixture is separated out in this process and has its volume reduced by a fixed percentage. The losses in volume, which are measured at the end of the refining stage, and time required to refine each mixture are given below. The total amount of time available for refining is 400 hours.

Mix	Loss in percent	Refining time per gallon (in hours)
#1	10	0.003
#2	15	0.004
#3	20	0.005

From the refining process each mixture is sequenced through an additive blender, which has a total of 400 hours available. The time required for each mixture to have additives blended is as follows:

Mix	Time to blend per gallon (in hours)
#1	0.008
#2	0.009
#3	0.004

The blending of additives adds virtually nothing to the volume of each mixture. The output from the blending process is then stored in the tanks you are planning to bid on.

In order for your firm to begin preliminary planning and design considerations, an estimate of each tank's capacity requirements (in gallons) is needed. How would you estimate these requirements?

Set this problem up as a mathematical model, defining all pertinent variables.

31. A company has developed the following total cost model for inventorying three products in its warehouse:

$$TC = \frac{20}{x_1} + 0.15x_1 + \frac{20}{x_2} + 0.05x_2 + \frac{45}{x_3} + 0.10x_3$$

However, there is a limitation on the amount of floor space available in the warehouse. This limitation is given by the following inequality relationship for these three products:

$$x_1 + x_2 + x_3 \leq 25$$

(a) What is the optimum inventory quantity of each product that can be stored in the warehouse?

(b) If the above constraint represents a limitation in square feet, how much would one additional square foot of warehouse space be worth?

(c) If the product associated with x_1 could be stacked two high, thereby reducing the square-foot requirement by 50%, what effect on the optimal solution would occur?

32. In Problem 31, what would be the solution if the following additional constraint is imposed (this constraint represents an upper limit on the amount of funds available for investment in inventory, given in hundreds of dollars)?

$$2x_1 + 3x_2 + x_3 \leq 40$$

What effect would there be on this new optimal solution if we could obtain an additional $500 for investment in inventory?

Suggested Further Reading

1. Bernholtz, B. (1964). A new derivation of the Kuhn-Tucker conditions. *Oper. Res.* **12**, No. 2.
2. Beveridge, G. S. G., and Schechter, R. S. (1970). "Optimization: Theory and Practice." McGraw-Hill, New York.
3. Gue, R. L., and Thomas, M. E. (1968). "Mathematical Methods in Operations Research." Macmillan, New York.
4. Hancock, H. (1960). "Theory of Maxima and Minima." Dover, New York.
5. Kuhn, H. W., and Tucker, A. W. (1951). Nonlinear programming. *Proc. Berkeley Symp. Math. Stat. Probab.*, 2nd. pp. 481–492.
6. Phipps, C. G. (1952). Maxima and minima under restraint. *Am. Math. Mon.* **59**, 230–235.
7. Schmidt, J. W. (1974). "Mathematical Foundations for Management Science and Systems Analysis." Academic Press, New York.
8. Teichroew, D. (1964). "An Introduction to Management Science: Deterministic Models." Wiley, New York.
9. Wilde, D. J., and Beightler, C. S. (1967). "Foundations of Optimization." Prentice-Hall, Englewood Cliffs, New Jersey.
10. Zangwill, W. I. (1969). "Nonlinear Programming." Prentice-Hall, Englewood Cliffs, New Jersey.

Chapter 5 | Finite Calculus

INTRODUCTION

Up to this point, our discussion of the analysis of systems through mathematical models and their manipulation has assumed that the associated variables are continuous. The performance of many practical systems, however, is influenced as much if not more by variables that are discrete. For example, inventory reorder points and replenishment quantities may be restricted to integer values, since it may not be possible to stock or order a partial unit. In a similar vein, decision variables such as the number of checkout counters at a supermarket, tellers at a bank, or seats on a commercial air carrier, the sample size for a quality control plan, the number of standby units provided for reliability improvement, and the size of a production run for a particular type of furniture would normally be treated as discrete variables.

The techniques already presented for the analysis of mathematical models that are functions of continuous variables are, in general, inappropriate for functions of discrete variables. Techniques appropriate for functions of continuous variables may provide approximate solutions when applied to functions of discrete variables, but this may be misleading.

The purpose of this chapter is to introduce the reader to functions of discrete variables and those methods appropriate for their analysis. To this end we will present the discrete analogs of differentiation and integration, methods for optimization of discrete functions and for the solution of difference equations, and the use of discrete methods for the approximation of continuous operations. While discrete variables need not be re-

216

stricted to integer values, we will restrict our attention to integer-valued variables since these are the most common in practice.

Perhaps the best method of characterizing a discrete variable is by contrasting its properties with those of continuous variables. If x is continuous throughout the finite interval (a, b), then x assumes an infinite number of values on that interval. In contrast, if x is discrete on the same interval, then x may assume only a finite number of values on that interval. For example, consider a parking lot with a capacity of 100 cars at which the temperature has been observed to vary between -10 and $105°F$. The number of cars n on the lot at any point in time must be one of the integers between 0 and 100 inclusive. Since n may assume only a finite number of values on any subinterval between 0 and 100, it is a discrete variable. However, temperature is continuous since it may assume an infinite number of values between -10 and $105°F$ or on any subinterval of nonzero width.

A function of a discrete variable may be either discrete or continuous on a subinterval of definition of the variable. For example, suppose that the number of sales per day x by a used car dealer is a discrete random variable. The probability mass function $p(x)$ of x is defined only for those values for which x is defined and is therefore discrete also. The cumulative distribution function $F(x)$ of x is defined as the probability that the number of sales is less than or equal to x, where $F(x)$ is defined for all x on the interval $(-\infty, \infty)$. Let int(x) be the integer part of x. That is,

$$\text{int}(2.5) = 2.$$

Now if we define $p(x)$ as

$$p(x) = \begin{cases} 0, & x = -\infty, \ldots, -2, -1 \\ \dfrac{\lambda^x}{x!} e^{-\lambda}, & x = 0, 1, 2, \ldots \end{cases} \tag{5.1}$$

where $\lambda > 0$, then $F(x)$ is given by

$$F(x) = \sum_{y=-\infty}^{\text{int}(x)} p(y), \qquad -\infty < x < \infty \tag{5.2}$$

Hence $F(x)$ is continuous on the open interval between adjacent integer values of x with points of discontinuity at integer values of x for $x = 0, 1, 2, \ldots$. The functions $p(x)$ and $F(x)$ are shown in Figs. 5.1 and 5.2, respectively.

More often than not functions of discrete variables are treated as discrete. In any case operations on functions of discrete variables such as the analogs of differentiation and integration are normally carried out at values for which the discrete variable is defined.

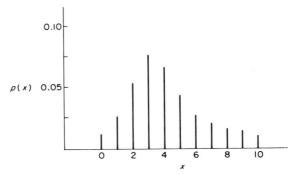

Fig. 5.1   Probability mass function of the discrete random variable x.

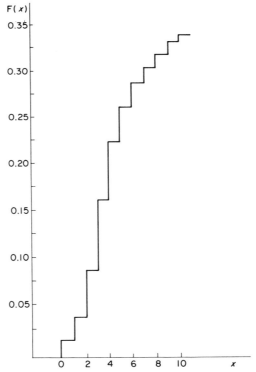

Fig. 5.2   Cumulative distribution function of the discrete random variable x.

THE DIFFERENCE

The discrete analog of differentiation is *differencing*. Recall that the derivative of $f(x)$ at the point x_0 was defined as

$$\frac{df(x_0)}{dx} = \lim_{\Delta x \to 0} \frac{f(x_0 + \Delta x) - f(x_0)}{\Delta x} \tag{5.3}$$

where $f(x)$ is assumed to be continuous on the open interval (a, b) including x_0. Now suppose that $f(x)$ is discrete and defined only at the points x_i, $i = 0, 1, 2, \ldots$, such that

$$x_{i+1} = x_i + \Delta x$$

The *divided difference* $Df(x_i)$ of $f(x)$ at x_i is defined as

$$Df(x_i) = \frac{f(x_{i+1}) - f(x_i)}{x_{i+1} - x_i} = \frac{f(x_i + \Delta x) - f(x_i)}{\Delta x} \tag{5.4}$$

Where x is integer valued, $\Delta x = 1$, $Df(x)$ is denoted $\Delta f(x)$ and is called the *simple difference*, where

$$\Delta f(x) = f(x + 1) - f(x) \tag{5.5}$$

Example 5.1   The function $f(x)$ is defined by

$$f(x) = x!, \qquad x = 0, 1, 2, \ldots$$

Find $\Delta f(x)$.

Since x is integer valued, $\Delta f(x)$ is given by Eq. (5.5) and

$$\Delta f(x) = (x + 1)! - x! = (x + 1)x! - x!$$

$$= x(x!), \qquad x = 0, 1, 2, \ldots \quad \blacksquare$$

Example 5.2   If $f(x)$ is given by

$$f(x) = \frac{1 - a^x}{1 - a}, \qquad x = 1, 2, 3, \ldots$$

find $\Delta f(x)$.

Since x is integer valued,

$$\Delta f(x) = f(x + 1) - f(x)$$

Thus

$$\Delta f(x) = \frac{1 - a^{x+1}}{1 - a} - \frac{1 - a^x}{1 - a} = \frac{a^x(1 - a)}{1 - a}$$

$$= a^x, \qquad x = 1, 2, 3, \ldots \quad \blacksquare$$

As in the case of the derivative of functions of continuous variables, special relationships exist for the difference of the sum, product, and ratio of functions of discrete variables. Specifically,

$$\Delta[h(x) + g(x)] = \Delta h(x) + \Delta g(x) \tag{5.6}$$

$$\Delta[h(x)g(x)] = h(x + 1)\,\Delta g(x) + g(x)\,\Delta h(x) \tag{5.7}$$

$$\Delta\left[\frac{h(x)}{g(x)}\right] = \frac{1}{g(x)g(x + 1)}\left[g(x)\,\Delta h(x) - h(x)\,\Delta g(x)\right] \tag{5.8}$$

where $g(x) \neq 0$ and $g(x + 1) \neq 0$ in Eq. (5.8). The expressions in Eqs. (5.6) to (5.8) find many useful applications. However, the difference of a function may often be defined with equal or greater ease through the basic definition of the differences in Eq. (5.5), even though the function may be expressed as the sum, product, or ratio of functions.

Example 5.3   Let

$$f(x) = \frac{(x - 1)(3x + 2)}{4x(x + 1)}, \qquad x = 1, 2, 3, \ldots.$$

Find $\Delta f(x)$ using (a) Eq. (5.5), (b) Eq. (5.8).
  For part (a)

$$\Delta f(x) = f(x + 1) - f(x)$$

$$= \frac{x(3x + 5)}{4(x + 1)(x + 2)} - \frac{(x - 1)(3x + 2)}{4x(x + 1)}$$

$$= \frac{1}{4(x + 1)}\left[\frac{x^2(3x + 5) - (x + 2)(x - 1)(3x + 2)}{x(x + 2)}\right]$$

$$= \frac{1}{x(x + 2)}$$

For part (b) let

$$h(x) = (x - 1)(3x + 2), \qquad g(x) = 4x(x + 1)$$

where

$$\Delta h(x) = x(3x + 5) - (x - 1)(3x + 2) = 6x + 2$$

$$\Delta g(x) = 4(x + 1)(x + 2) - 4x(x + 1) = 8(x + 1)$$

From Eq. (5.8),

$$\Delta f(x) = \frac{1}{16x(x+1)^2(x+2)}[8x(x+1)(3x+1) - 8(x-1)(x+1)(3x+2)]$$

$$= \frac{1}{2x(x+1)(x+2)}[x(3x+1) - (x-1)(3x+2)]$$

$$= \frac{2(x+1)}{2x(x+1)(x+2)} = \frac{1}{x(x+2)} \quad \blacksquare$$

Example 5.4 If

$$f(x) = 2^{x-1}(x^2 - 3x + 6)$$

define $\Delta f(x)$ using Eq. (5.7).

Let

$$h(x) = 2^{x-1}, \qquad g(x) = x^2 - 3x + 6$$

Then

$$\Delta h(x) = 2^x - 2^{x-1}$$

$$\Delta g(x) = (x+1)^2 - 3(x+1) + 6 - x^2 + 3x - 6 = 2(x-1)$$

From Eq. (5.7)

$$\Delta f(x) = 2(2^x)(x-1) + 2^{x-1}(x^2 - 3x + 6) = 2^{x-1}(x^2 + x + 2) \quad \blacksquare$$

HIGHER-ORDER DIFFERENCES

Higher-order differences are defined in a manner similar to that applied in the case of higher-order derivatives. The second divided difference of $f(x)$ at x_i is given by

$$\Delta^2 f(x_i) = \Delta f(x_{i+1}) - \Delta f(x_i) \tag{5.9}$$

In a similar manner, $\Delta^n f(x_i)$ is given by

$$\Delta^n f(x_i) = \Delta^{n-1} f(x_{i+1}) - \Delta^{n-1} f(x_i) \tag{5.10}$$

If we restrict our attention to integer-valued variables, we have

$$\Delta^n f(x) = \Delta^{n-1} f(x+1) - \Delta^{n-1} f(x) \tag{5.11}$$

or

$$\Delta^n f(x) = \sum_{i=0}^{n} (-1)^{n-i} \binom{n}{i} f(x+i) \tag{5.12}$$

Example 5.5   Evaluate the first, second, and third differences of $f(x)$ at $x = 1, 2, 3, 4$, where

$$f(x) = (2x - 1)^2$$

The first three differences of $f(x)$ are given by

$$\Delta f(x) = [2(x + 1) - 1]^2 - (2x - 1)^2 = 8x$$

$$\Delta^2 f(x) = \Delta[\Delta f(x)] = 8(x + 1) - 8x = 8$$

$$\Delta^3 f(x) = \Delta[\Delta^2 f(x)] = 8 - 8 = 0$$

The differences $\Delta f(x)$, $\Delta^2 f(x)$, and $\Delta^3 f(x)$ at $x = 1, 2, 3, 4$ are summarized in Table 5.1.   ∎

Rearrangement of the entries in Table 5.1 leads to a *difference table*, which, as we shall see, is often useful in numerical techniques for interpolation, differentiation, and integration. The general form of the difference tables is shown in Table 5.2. Using this table, higher-order differences are

Table 5.1

Evaluation of $\Delta f(x)$, $\Delta^2 f(x)$, and $\Delta^3 f(x)$ for Example 5.5

x	$f(x)$	$\Delta f(x)$	$\Delta^2 f(x)$	$\Delta^3 f(x)$
1	1	8	8	0
2	9	16	8	0
3	25	24	8	0
4	49	32	8	0

Table 5.2

Difference Table

x	$f(x)$	$\Delta f(x)$	$\Delta^2 f(x)$	$\Delta^3 f(x)$	$\Delta^4 f(x)$	$\Delta^5 f(x)$	$\Delta^6 f(x)$
x	$f(x)$						
		$\Delta f(x)$					
$x + 1$	$f(x + 1)$		$\Delta^2 f(x)$				
		$\Delta f(x + 1)$		$\Delta^3 f(x)$			
$x + 2$	$f(x + 2)$		$\Delta^2 f(x + 1)$		$\Delta^4 f(x)$		
		$\Delta f(x + 2)$		$\Delta^3 f(x + 1)$		$\Delta^5 f(x)$	
$x + 3$	$f(x + 3)$		$\Delta^2 f(x + 2)$		$\Delta^4 f(x + 1)$		$\Delta^6 f(x)$
		$\Delta f(x + 3)$		$\Delta^3 f(x + 2)$		$\Delta^5 f(x + 1)$	
$x + 4$	$f(x + 4)$		$\Delta^2 f(x + 3)$		$\Delta^4 f(x + 2)$		
		$\Delta f(x + 4)$		$\Delta^3 f(x + 3)$			
$x + 5$	$f(x + 5)$		$\Delta^2 f(x + 4)$				
		$\Delta f(x + 5)$					
$x + 6$	$f(x + 6)$						

Table 5.3

Difference Table for Example 5.6

x	$f(x)$	$\Delta f(x)$	$\Delta^2 f(x)$	$\Delta^3 f(x)$	$\Delta^4 f(x)$
4	625				
		$3125 - 625 = 2500$			
5	3125		$12,500 - 2500 = 10,000$		
		$15,625 - 3125 = 12,500$		$50,000 - 10,000 = 40,000$	
6	15625		$62,500 - 12,500 = 50,000$		$200,000 - 40,000 = -160,000$
		$78,125 - 15,625 = 62,500$		$250,000 - 50,000 = 200,000$	
7	78125		$312,500 - 62,500 = 250,000$		
		$390,625 - 78,125 = 312,500$			
8	390625				

evaluated successively, each stage building upon the previous stage using Eq. (5.11). This procedure is illustrated in the following example.

Example 5.6   Using a difference table, evalute $\Delta^4 f(x)$ at $x = 4$, where

$$f(x) = 5^x$$

To compute $\Delta^4 f(x)$ at $x = 4$, $f(x)$ must first be evaluated at $x = 4, 5, 6, 7, 8$. By applying Eq. (5.11) successively, we obtain the result in Table 5.3, where $\Delta^4 f(x) = 160,000$. ■

As the preceding discussion would suggest, difference tables are convenient in evaluating higher-order differences when $f(x)$ is defined in tabular form rather than functionally. This situation is particularly evident when observing physical phenomena, for which the value of $f(x)$ is observed and recorded for given values of x but the underlying functional relationship between $f(x)$ and x cannot be defined. Of course the procedure for evaluation of higher-order differences is identical to that in the case of functional definition of $f(x)$.

Example 5.7   Given the following table of values for $f(x)$, evaluate $\Delta^3 f(x)$ for $x = 0, 1, 2, 3$.

x	0	1	2	3	4	5	6
$f(x)$	1	3	5	9	12	8	4

The difference table for $f(x)$ is given in Table 5.4, where

$$\Delta^3 f(0) = 2, \qquad \Delta^3 f(1) = -3$$
$$\Delta^3 f(2) = -6, \qquad \Delta^3 f(3) = 7 ■$$

Table 5.4

Difference Table for Example 5.7

x	$f(x)$	$\Delta f(x)$	$\Delta^2 f(x)$	$\Delta^3 f(x)$
0	1			
		$3 - 1 = 2$		
1	3		$2 - 2 = 0$	
		$5 - 3 = 2$		$2 - 0 = 2$
2	5		$4 - 2 = 2$	
		$9 - 5 = 4$		$-1 - 2 = -3$
3	9		$3 - 4 = -1$	
		$12 - 9 = 3$		$-7 + 1 = -6$
4	12		$-4 - 3 = -7$	
		$8 - 12 = -4$		$0 + 7 = 7$
5	8		$-4 + 4 = 0$	
		$4 - 8 = -4$		
6	4			

Higher-order divided differences are defined in a slightly different manner than higher-order simple differences. If $D^n f(x_i)$ is the nth divided difference of $f(x)$ at x_i, then

$$D^n f(x_i) = \frac{D^{n-1}f(x_{i+1}) - D^{n-1}f(x_i)}{x_{i+n} - x_i} \tag{5.13}$$

As in the case of the simple difference, a difference table displaying successively higher-order divided differences is usually helpful in evaluating $D^n f(x_i)$. The application of the divided difference will be illustrated in our discussion of *numerical* methods for interpolation, differentiation, and integration.

THE ANTIDIFFERENCE AND SUMMATION OF SERIES

The reader will recall that the operational inverse of the derivative is the antiderivative. That is, if $F(x)$ is the antiderivative of $f(x)$, then

$$\frac{d}{dx} F(x) = f(x) \tag{5.14}$$

In the case of functions of discrete variables, the operational inverse of the difference is the antidifference. If $\Delta^{-1}f(x)$ is the antidifference of $f(x)$, then

$$\Delta\left[\Delta^{-1}f(x)\right] = f(x) \tag{5.15}$$

As the antiderivative is used to integrate the function $f(x)$, the antidifference performs the analogous discrete operation, summation. Thus for integers a and b,

$$\sum_{x=a}^{b} f(x) = \Delta^{-1}f(b+1) - \Delta^{-1}f(a) \tag{5.16}$$

To demonstrate the validity of Eq. (5.16), note that

$$\sum_{x=a}^{b} f(x) = \sum_{x=a}^{b} \Delta\left[\Delta^{-1}f(x)\right] \tag{5.17}$$

Since $\Delta[\Delta^{-1}f(x)] = \Delta^{-1}f(x+1) - \Delta^{-1}f(x)$, we have

$$\sum_{x=a}^{b} f(x) = \sum_{x=a}^{b} \left[\Delta^{-1}f(x+1) - \Delta^{-1}f(x)\right]$$

$$= \sum_{x=a}^{b} \Delta^{-1}f(x+1) - \sum_{x=a}^{b} \Delta^{-1}f(x)$$

$$= \Delta^{-1}f(b+1) + \sum_{x=a}^{b-1} \Delta^{-1}f(x+1) - \sum_{x=a+1}^{b} \Delta^{-1}f(x) - \Delta^{-1}f(a)$$

But

$$\sum_{x=a}^{b-1} \Delta^{-1}f(x+1) = \sum_{x=a+1}^{b} \Delta^{-1}f(x) \tag{5.18}$$

with the result given in Eq. (5.16).

As indicated in Eq. (5.16), finding the sum of the series $f(x)$ requires definition of the corresponding antidifference $\Delta^{-1}f(x)$. Table A of the Appendix gives $\Delta^{-1}f(x)$ for selected functions $f(x)$.

Example 5.8 Find (a) the sum of the integers from 0 to n, (b) the sum of the squares of the odd integers from 1 to n, (c) the sum of a^x from $x = 5$ to $x = n$.

For part (a),

$$f(x) = x$$

and from Table A of the Appendix,

$$\Delta^{-1}f(x) = \frac{x(x-1)}{2}$$

Thus

$$\sum_{x=0}^{n} x = \Delta^{-1}f(n+1) - \Delta^{-1}f(0) = \frac{n(n+1)}{2} - 0 = \frac{n(n+1)}{2}$$

In part (b),

$$f(x) = (2x-1)^2$$

From the antidifference table,

$$\Delta^{-1}f(x) = \frac{(x-1)\left[4(x-1)^2 - 1\right]}{3}$$

Therefore

$$\sum_{x=1}^{n} f(x) = \Delta^{-1}f(n+1) - \Delta^{-1}f(1)$$

and

$$\sum_{x=1}^{n} f(x) = \frac{n(4n^2 - 1)}{3} - 0 = \frac{n(4n^2 - 1)}{3}$$

For part (c),

$$f(x) = a^x, \qquad \Delta^{-1}f(x) = \frac{a^x - 1}{a - 1}$$

Hence

$$\sum_{x=5}^{n} f(x) = \sum_{x=5}^{n} a^x$$

$$= \Delta^{-1}f(n+1) - \Delta^{-1}f(5)$$

$$= \frac{a^{n+1}-1}{a-1} - \frac{a^5-1}{a-1} = \frac{1}{a-1}(a^{n+1}-a^5) \quad \blacksquare$$

As already indicated, evaluation of $\sum_{x=a}^{b} f(x)$ depends upon the ability of the analyst to identify the antidifference of $f(x)$. This may be a rather challenging task if an extensive antidifference table is not available. Similar situations arise when attempting to integrate a continuous function. In the latter case one often resorts to integration by parts. A similar approach may be taken in the case of summation. Specifically let $f(x)$, $h(x)$, and $g(x)$ be functions of the discrete variable x such that

$$f(x) = h(x)\Delta g(x) \tag{5.19}$$

The expression for the sum of $f(x)$ by parts from $x = a$ to $x = b$ is given by

$$\sum_{x=a}^{b} f(x) = h(b+1)g(b+1) - h(a)g(a) - \sum_{x=a}^{b} g(x+1)\Delta h(x) \tag{5.20}$$

where a and b are integers such that $a \leqslant b$. As in the case of integration by parts, application of Eq. (5.20) depends upon the choice of $h(x)$ and $g(x)$ such that the sum of $g(x+1)\Delta h(x)$ can be conveniently evaluated.

Example 5.9 Evaluate

$$\sum_{x=0}^{n} xa^x$$

using summation by parts, assuming $\Delta^{-1}(a^x) = (a^x - 1)/(a-1)$.

Let

$$h(x) = x, \qquad \Delta g(x) = a^x$$

Now

$$g(x) = \frac{a^x - 1}{a-1}, \qquad \Delta h(x) = 1$$

From Eq. (5.20),

$$\sum_{x=0}^{n} xa^x = h(n+1)g(n+1) - h(0)g(0) - \sum_{x=0}^{n} g(x+1)\Delta h(x)$$

$$= (n+1)\frac{a^{n+1}-1}{a-1} - (0) - \sum_{x=0}^{n} \frac{a^{x+1}-1}{a-1}$$

$$= (n+1)\frac{a^{n+1}-1}{a-1} - \frac{a}{a-1}\sum_{x=0}^{n} a^x + \sum_{x=0}^{n} \frac{1}{a-1}$$

But

$$\Delta^{-1}(a^x) = \frac{a^x - 1}{a - 1}, \qquad \Delta^{-1}\left(\frac{1}{a - 1}\right) = \frac{x}{a - 1}$$

and

$$\sum_{x=0}^{n} a^x = \frac{a^{n+1} - 1}{a - 1}, \qquad \sum_{x=0}^{n}\left(\frac{1}{a - 1}\right) = \frac{n + 1}{a - 1}$$

Therefore

$$\sum_{x=0}^{n} xa^x = (n + 1)\frac{a^{n+1} - 1}{a - 1} - \frac{a^{n+2} - a}{(a - 1)^2} + \frac{n + 1}{(a - 1)}$$

$$= \frac{a}{(a - 1)^2}\left[(n + 1)(a - 1)a^n - a^{n+1} + 1\right] \quad \blacksquare$$

Example 5.10   Evaluate

$$\sum_{x=1}^{n} \frac{x(x - 1)^2(x - 1)!}{2}$$

using summation by parts and assuming $\Delta^{-1}(x\,x!) = x!$.

Let

$$h(x) = \frac{x(x - 1)}{2}, \qquad \Delta g(x) = (x - 1)(x)!$$

Then

$$\Delta h(x) = x, \qquad g(x) = (x - 1)!$$

By Eq. (5.20),

$$\sum_{x=1}^{n} \frac{x(x - 1)^2(x - 1)!}{2} = \frac{n(n + 1)}{2}n! - (0) - \sum_{x=1}^{n} x\,x!$$

$$= \frac{n(n + 1)}{2}n! - \left[(n + 1)! - 1\right]$$

$$= \frac{(n - 2)(n + 1)!}{2} + 1 \quad \blacksquare$$

In the next section we shall treat the problem of finding the optimum of a function of a discrete variable using the difference. Many problems treated by the operations research analyst deal with optimization of functions which include the sum of a series. For example, suppose that $C(x)$ is given by

$$C(x) = \sum_{y=a(x)}^{b(x)} f(x, y) \tag{5.21}$$

where $x, y, a(x)$, and $b(x)$ are integer valued, $a(x) < b(x)$, and $a(x)$ and $b(x)$ are increasing integer functions of x. As we shall see in the next section, the minimum or maximum of $C(x)$ can be determined by differencing $C(x)$ with respect to x. $\Delta C(x)$ can be simply defined by

$$\Delta C(x) = \sum_{y=a(x+1)}^{b(x+1)} f(x+1, y) - \sum_{y=a(x)}^{b(x)} f(x, y) \qquad (5.22)$$

Frequently Eq. (5.22) is the simplest and most direct method for evaluating $\Delta C(x)$. However, application of Eq. (5.22) may be quite tedious, and the process may be simplified through an alternative expression for $\Delta C(x)$. Noting that

$$\sum_{y=a(x+1)}^{b(x+1)} f(x+1, y) = \sum_{y=a(x)}^{b(x)} f(x+1, y) - \sum_{y=a(x)}^{a(x+1)-1} f(x+1, y)$$

$$+ \sum_{y=b(x)+1}^{b(x+1)} f(x+1, y) \qquad (5.23)$$

we have

$$\Delta C(x) = \sum_{y=a(x)}^{b(x)} \left[f(x+1, y) - f(x, y) \right] - \sum_{y=a(x)}^{a(x+1)-1} f(x+1, y)$$

$$+ \sum_{y=b(x)+1}^{b(x+1)} f(x+1, y) \qquad (5.24)$$

Letting $\Delta_x f(x, y)$ denote the first difference of $f(x, y)$ with respect to x,

$$\Delta_x f(x, y) = f(x+1, y) - f(x, y) \qquad (5.25)$$

and

$$\Delta C(x) = \sum_{y=a(x)}^{b(x)} \Delta_x f(x, y) - \sum_{y=a(x)}^{a(x+1)-1} f(x+1, y) + \sum_{y=b(x)+1}^{b(x+1)} f(x+1, y)$$

$$(5.26)$$

If $a(x)$ and $b(x)$ are constants such that

$$a(x) = c, \qquad b(x) = d$$

then

$$\Delta C(x) = \sum_{y=c}^{d} \Delta_x f(x, y) \qquad (5.27)$$

Example 5.11   Let

$$C(x) = \sum_{y=1}^{n} (y^3 + x)$$

Find $\Delta C(x)$.

Since the limits of the sum are constants, $\Delta C(x)$ is defined as in Eq. (5.27) and

$$\Delta C(x) = \sum_{y=1}^{n} \Delta_x(y^3 + x)$$

$$= \sum_{y=1}^{n} \{[y^3 + (x+1)] - [y^3 + x]\} = \sum_{y=1}^{n} (1)$$

Now

$$\Delta^{-1}(1) = y \qquad \text{and} \qquad \Delta C(x) = (n+1) - 1 = n \quad \blacksquare$$

Example 5.12   If

$$C(x) = \sum_{y=x}^{x+n} (y - x)$$

find $\Delta C(x)$ (a) using Eq. (5.22), (b) using Eq. (5.26).

For part (a),

$$\Delta C(x) = \sum_{y=x+1}^{x+n+1} (y - x - 1) - \sum_{y=x}^{x+n} (y - x)$$

Now

$$\sum_{y=x+1}^{x+n+1} (y - x - 1) = \sum_{y=x+1}^{x+n+1} y - (x+1) \sum_{y=x+1}^{x+n+1} (1)$$

Since

$$\Delta^{-1}(y) = \frac{y(y-1)}{2}, \qquad \Delta^{-1}(1) = y$$

we have

$$\sum_{y=x+1}^{x+n+1} (y - x - 1)$$

$$= \left[\frac{(x+n+2)(x+n+1)}{2} - \frac{x(x+1)}{2} \right]$$

$$\qquad - (x+1)[(x+n+2) - (x+1)]$$

$$= \frac{n(n+1)}{2}$$

Further,

$$\sum_{y=x}^{x+n} (y-x) = \sum_{y=x}^{x+n} y - x \sum_{y=x}^{x+n} (1)$$

$$= \left[\frac{(x+n+1)(x+n)}{2} - \frac{x(x-1)}{2} \right] - x\big[(x+n+1) - x\big]$$

$$= \frac{n(n+1)}{2}$$

and

$$\Delta C(x) = \frac{n(n+1)}{2} - \frac{n(n+1)}{2} = 0$$

For part (b),

$$f(x, y) = (y - x)$$
$$f(x+1, y) = (y - x - 1)$$
$$\Delta_x f(x, y) = y - (x+1) - (y-x) = -1$$
$$a(x) = x, \qquad a(x+1) = x+1$$
$$b(x) = x + n, \qquad b(x+1) = x + n + 1$$

and

$$\Delta C(x) = - \sum_{y=x}^{x+n} (1) - \sum_{y=x}^{x} (y-x-1) + \sum_{y=x+n+1}^{x+n+1} (y-x-1)$$

Since

$$\Delta^{-1}(1) = y$$

$\Delta C(x)$ is given by

$$\Delta C(x) = -(x+n+1) + x - (x-x-1) + (x+n+1-x-1) = 0 \quad \blacksquare$$

Example 5.13   Find $\Delta C(x)$ using Eq. (5.26), where

$$C(x) = \sum_{y=x}^{x^2} (x+y)$$

Letting

$$a(x) = x, \qquad a(x+1) = x+1$$
$$b(x) = x^2, \qquad b(x+1) = (x+1)^2$$

and noting that

$$\Delta_x f(x, y) = \big[(x+1) + y\big] - (x+y) = 1$$
$$f(x+1, y) = x + y + 1$$

we have

$$C(x) = \sum_{y=x}^{x^2} (1) - \sum_{y=x}^{x} (x + y + 1) + \sum_{y=x^2+1}^{(x+1)^2} (x + y + 1)$$

Now

$$\sum_{y=x}^{x^2} (1) = (x^2 + 1) - x = x^2 - x + 1$$

$$\sum_{y=x}^{x} (x + y + 1) = 2x + 1$$

$$\sum_{y=x^2+1}^{(x+1)^2} (x + y + 1) = (x + 1) \sum_{y=x^2+1}^{(x+1)^2} (1) + \sum_{y=x^2+1}^{(x+1)^2} (y)$$

and

$$(x + 1) \sum_{y=x^2+1}^{(x+1)^2} (1) = (x + 1)\left\{ \left[(x + 1)^2 + 1 \right] - (x^2 + 1) \right\}$$

$$= 2x^2 + 3x + 1$$

Since

$$\Delta^{-1}(y) = \frac{y(y - 1)}{2}$$

we have

$$\sum_{y=x^2+1}^{(x+1)^2} (y) = \frac{(x + 1)^2 \left[(x + 1)^2 + 1 \right]}{2} - \frac{(x^2 + 1)x^2}{2}$$

$$= 2x^3 + 3x^2 + 3x + 1$$

and

$$\sum_{y=x^2+1}^{(x+1)^2} (x + y + 1) = (2x^2 + 3x + 1) + (2x^3 + 3x^2 + 3x + 1)$$

$$= 2x^3 + 5x^2 + 6x + 2$$

Therefore

$$\Delta C(x) = (x^2 - x + 1) - (2x + 1) + (2x^3 + 5x^2 + 6x + 2)$$

$$= 2x^3 + 6x^2 + 3x + 2 \quad \blacksquare$$

Example 5.14 Solve the problem in Example 5.13 by evaluating the sum and differencing the result.

From Example 5.13,

$$C(x) = \sum_{y=x}^{x^2} (x + y)$$

and

$$C(x) = x \sum_{y=x}^{x^2} (1) + \sum_{y=x}^{x^2} (y)$$

Since

$$\Delta^{-1}(1) = y, \qquad \Delta^{-1}(y) = \frac{y(y-1)}{2}$$

$C(x)$ is given by

$$C(x) = x\left[(x^2 + 1) - x\right] + \left[\frac{x^2(x^2 + 1)}{2} - \frac{x(x-1)}{2}\right]$$

$$= (1/2)\left[x^4 + 2x^3 - 2x^2 + 3x\right]$$

$\Delta C(x)$ is then given by

$$\Delta C(x) = (1/2)\left\{\left[(x+1)^4 + 2(x+1)^3 - 2(x+1)^2 + 3(x+1)\right]\right.$$

$$\left. - \left[x^4 + 2x^3 - 2x^2 + 3x\right]\right\}$$

$$= (1/2)(4x^3 + 12x^2 + 6x + 4)$$

$$= 2x^3 + 6x^2 + 3x + 2 \quad\blacksquare$$

Examples 5.11–5.14 illustrate three methods for differencing a function which includes the sum of a series. In summary these methods include

(1) evaluating of the sum and differencing the result,
(2) applying the basic definition of the difference to the sum [Eq. (5.22)],
(3) applying Eq. (5.26) or Eq. (5.27).

The most appropriate method will depend upon the function included in the summation.

OPTIMIZATION

In Chapters 3 and 4 the problem of finding the maxima or minima of functions of continuous variables was discussed in some detail. The problem of identifying the optima for functions of discrete variables is just as important to the operations research analyst. In the case of continuous

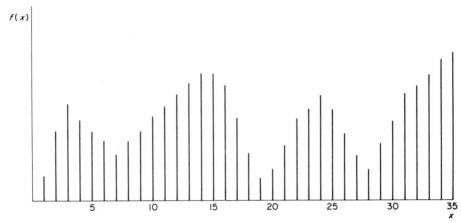

Fig. 5.3 Discrete function with several local minima and maxima.

functions we used the derivative to identify local minima and maxima. The difference is used in a similar manner for discrete functions.

As in the case of continuous functions, a discrete function may have several local minima and maxima, as shown in Fig. 5.3. In Fig. 5.3, on the closed interval $[1, 35]$ $f(x)$ has local minima at $x = 1, 7, 19, 28$ and local maxima at $x = 3, 14, 15, 24, 35$. We will define x^* as an extreme point for $f(x)$ on the closed interval $[a, b]$ if

$$f(x^*) \leqslant f(x), \qquad a \leqslant x \leqslant b \tag{5.28}$$

or

$$f(x^*) \geqslant f(x), \qquad a \geqslant x \geqslant b \tag{5.29}$$

For the case in Eq. (5.28), x^* is a minimum, and it is a maximum in Eq. (5.29).

In the case of functions of continuous variables we examined the neighborhood of a point x^* to determine whether or not x^* was an extreme point. Specifically, if x^* is an extreme point for $f(x)$, then x^* is a minimum if

$$f(x^*) \leqslant f(x^* \pm \epsilon), \qquad \epsilon \geqslant 0 \tag{5.30}$$

and is a maximum if

$$f(x^*) \geqslant f(x^* \pm \epsilon), \qquad \epsilon \geqslant 0 \tag{5.31}$$

In the case of discrete functions of integer-valued variables we cannot examine the behavior of $f(x)$ in an ϵ neighborhood of x^* since $f(x^* + \epsilon)$ is not defined for $0 < \epsilon < 1$. Hence we examine $f(x)$ at $x^* - 1$ and $x^* + 1$.

That is, if

$$f(x^* - 1) > f(x^*) < f(x^* + 1) \tag{5.32}$$

then x^* is a local minimum for $f(x)$, and it is a local maximum if

$$f(x^* - 1) < f(x^*) > f(x^* + 1) \tag{5.33}$$

From Eq. (5.32),

$$f(x^* + 1) - f(x^*) > 0 \tag{5.34}$$

and

$$f(x^*) - f(x^* - 1) < 0 \tag{5.35}$$

imply that x^* is a local minimum or

$$\Delta f(x^* - 1) < 0 < \Delta f(x^*) \tag{5.36}$$

In a similar manner, if x^* is a local maximum, then

$$f(x^* + 1) - f(x^*) < 0 \tag{5.37}$$

and

$$f(x^*) - f(x^* - 1) > 0 \tag{5.38}$$

or

$$\Delta f(x^* - 1) > 0 > \Delta f(x^*) \tag{5.39}$$

The reader should note that Eq. (5.36) is a necessary and sufficient condition for a local minimum at x^* and that Eq. (5.39) is necessary and sufficient for a local maximum at x^*.

If either or both of the inequalities in Eqs. (5.36) or (5.39) are changed to $\leqslant$ or $\geqslant$, respectively, the conditions given no longer indicate that x^* is necessarily an extreme point. This is illustrated in Figures 5.4–5.7. In Figs. 5.4 and 5.5 we have

$$\Delta f(x^* - 1) = 0 < \Delta f(x^*) \tag{5.40}$$

On the interval $[a, b]$ x^* would be considered a point of inflection for $f(x)$, as shown in Fig. 5.4, but would be considered a local minimum in the case of Fig. 5.5. In Figs. 5.6 and 5.7

$$\Delta f(x^* - 1) > 0 = \Delta f(x^*) \tag{5.41}$$

In Fig. 5.6 x^* is a point of inflection on the interval $[a, b]$, while x^* is a local maximum in Fig. 5.7. Thus if $\Delta f(x^* - 1) = 0$ or $\Delta f(x^*) = 0$, we are not in a position to determine whether or not x^* is an extreme point.

To generalize the condition for the existence of an extreme point at x^*, let $f(x)$ be a function of the integer valued variable x defined on the closed

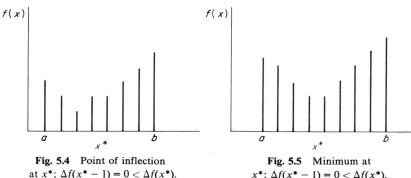

Fig. 5.4   Point of inflection
at x^*; $\Delta f(x^* - 1) = 0 < \Delta f(x^*)$.

Fig. 5.5   Minimum at
x^*; $\Delta f(x^* - 1) = 0 < \Delta f(x^*)$.

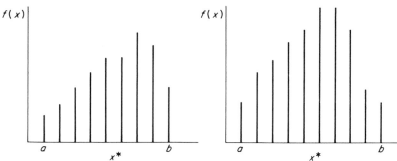

Fig. 5.6   Point of inflection
at x^*; $\Delta f(x^* - 1) > 0 = \Delta f(x^*)$.

Fig. 5.7   Maximum at
x^*; $\Delta f(x^* - 1) > 0 = \Delta f(x^*)$.

interval $[x^* - m, x^* + n]$, where m and n are integers:

(1)   If $\Delta f(x^* - 1) < 0 < \Delta f(x^*)$, x^* is a local minimum on $[x^* - m, x^* + n]$.

(2)   If $\Delta f(x^* - 1) > 0 > \Delta f(x^*)$, x^* is a local maximum on $[x^* - m, x^* + n]$.

(3)   If $\Delta f(x^* + i) = 0$, $i = -j + 1, \ldots, k - 1$, where $j \leqslant m, k \leqslant n$, and $\Delta f(x^* - j) \leqslant 0 \leqslant \Delta f(x^* + k)$, then x^* is a local minimum on $[x^* - m, x^* + n]$.

(4)   If $\Delta f(x^* + i) = 0$, $i = -j + 1, \ldots, k - 1$, where $j \leqslant m, k \leqslant n$, and $\Delta f(x^* - j) \geqslant 0 \geqslant f(x^* + k)$, then x^* is a local maximum on $[x^* - m, x^* + n]$.

Example 5.15   Find and identify the extreme points for

$$f(x) = x^2 + 4x - 7$$

where x is integer valued.

The first difference of $f(x)$ is given by

$$\Delta f(x) = \left[(x+1)^2 + 4(x+1) - 7\right] - \left[x^2 + 4x - 7\right] = 2x + 5$$

If $f(x)$ has a unique local maximum x^*, then

$$\Delta f(x^* - 1) > 0 > \Delta f(x^*)$$

and

$$2(x^* - 1) + 5 > 0 > 2x^* + 5$$

Now $2(x^* - 1) + 5 > 0$ implies $x^* > -3/2$ and $2x^* + 5 < 0$ implies x^* $< -5/2$. Since $x^* > -3/2$ and $x^* < -5/2$ are contradictory conditions, $f(x)$ does not possess an interior maximum.

If $f(x)$ has an interior minimum, then

$$\Delta f(x^* - 1) < 0 < \Delta f(x^*)$$

and

$$2(x^* - 1) + 5 < 0 < 2x^* + 5$$

$2(x^* - 1) + 5 < 0$ implies $x^* < -3/2$ and $2x^* + 5 > 0$ implies $x^* >$ $-5/2$. Hence x^* is that integer such that

$$-5/2 < x^* < -3/2$$

and $x^* = 2$ minimizes $f(x)$. ∎

Example 5.16 Find and identify the extreme points for $f(x)$, where

$$f(x) = (1/3)x^3 + x^2 + 4$$

The first difference of $f(x)$ is given by

$$\Delta f(x) = \left[(1/3)(x+1)^3 + (x+1)^2 + 4\right] - \left[(1/3)x^3 + x^2 + 4\right]$$

$$= (1/3)(3x^2 + 9x + 4)$$

If $f(x)$ possesses an interior maximum x^*, then

$$\Delta f(x - 1) > 0 > \Delta f(x^*)$$

or

$$(1/3)\left[3(x^* - 1)^2 + 9(x^* - 1) + 4\right] > 0 > (1/3)(3x^{*2} + 9x^* + 4)$$

Now

$$3(x^* - 1)^2 + 9(x^* - 1) + 4 > 0$$

implies $x < -1.46$ or $x^* > 0.46$. Further,

$$3x^{*2} + 9x^*_* + 4 < 0$$

implies $-2.46 < x^* < -0.54$. Hence the only permissible integer value of x^* is $x^* = -2$, which maximizes $f(x)$.

If $f(x)$ possesses an interior minimum, then
$$\Delta f(x^* - 1) < 0 < \Delta f(x^*)$$
or
$$(1/3)\left[3(x^* - 1)^2 + 9(x^* - 1) + 4\right] < 0 < (1/3)(3x^{*2} + 9x^* + 4)$$

Now
$$3(x^* - 1)^2 + 9(x^* - 1) + 4 < 0$$
implies $-1.46 < x^* < 0.46$ and
$$3x^{*2} + 9x^* + 4 > 0$$
implies $x^* < -2.46$ and $x^* > -0.54$. Hence $-0.54 < x^* < 0.46$ and $x^* = 0$ is the only permissible integer value of x^* and is the minimizing value for $f(x)$. ∎

Example 5.17   Find the value of x which maximizes the Poisson probabiltity mass function $p(x)$, where
$$p(x) = \frac{\lambda^x}{x!} e^{-\lambda}, \qquad x = 0, 1, 2, \ldots, \qquad \lambda > 0$$

The difference of $p(x)$ is given by
$$\Delta p(x) = \frac{\lambda^{x+1}}{(x + 1)!} e^{-\lambda} - \frac{\lambda^x}{x!} e^{-\lambda} = \frac{\lambda^x}{x!} e^{-\lambda}\left[\frac{\lambda}{x + 1} - 1\right]$$

If the maximum x^* for $p(x)$ is unique, then
$$\Delta p(x^* - 1) > 0 > \Delta p(x^*)$$

That is, x^* must satisfy
$$\frac{\lambda^{x^*-1}}{(x^* - 1)!} e^{-\lambda}\left[\frac{\lambda}{x^*} - 1\right] > 0 > \frac{\lambda^{x^*}}{x^*!} e^{-\lambda}\left[\frac{\lambda}{(x^* + 1)} - 1\right]$$

Multiplying throughout the inequality by $(x^* - 1)!/[\lambda^{x^*-1}e^{-\lambda}]$ yields
$$\left[\frac{\lambda}{x^*} - 1\right] > 0 > \frac{\lambda}{x^*}\left[\frac{\lambda}{(x^* + 1)} - 1\right]$$

Now
$$\frac{\lambda}{x^*} - 1 > 0$$
implies $x^* < \lambda$. Since $x^* \geqslant 0$ and $\lambda > 0$,
$$\frac{\lambda}{x^* + 1} - 1 < 0$$
implies $x^* + 1 > \lambda$. Therefore x^* is that integer which satisfies the

relationship

$$x^* < \lambda < x^* + 1$$

or x^* is the largest integer such that $x^* < \lambda$. If λ is an integer, then $x^* = \lambda$ or $x^* = \lambda - 1$. ∎

Example 5.18 A company has decided to use an attributes sampling plan for the purpose of quality control. The plan calls for the random selection and inspection of n units from each production lot. If the number of defects detected in the sample x exceeds the acceptance number c, the lot is rejected, and it is accepted otherwise. The sample size has already been determined and the cost of using such a quality control plan is a function of c and is given by

$$
\begin{aligned}
C(c) = C_I n + C_R L \Bigg[& p \sum_{x=c+1}^{n} \frac{(nq_1)^x}{x!} e^{-nq_1} \\
& + (1-p) \sum_{x=c+1}^{n} \frac{(nq_2)^x}{x!} e^{-nq_2} \Bigg] \\
+ C_A (L-n) \Bigg[& pq_1 \sum_{x=0}^{c} \frac{(nq_1)^x}{x!} e^{-nq_1} \\
& + (1-p)q_2 \sum_{x=0}^{c} \frac{(nq_2)^x}{x!} e^{-nq_2} \Bigg]
\end{aligned}
$$

where C_I is the unit inspection cost, C_R the unit cost of rejection, C_A the unit cost of accepting a defective unit, L the lot size, q_1 the proportion of defective units in acceptable lots, q_2 the proportion of defective units in unacceptable lots, where $q_2 > q_1$, and p the probability that the lot has proportion defective q_1. Find the acceptance number which will minimize $C(c)$.

The first difference of $C(c)$ is

$$
\begin{aligned}
\Delta C(c) = - C_R L \Bigg[& p \frac{(nq_1)^{c+1}}{(c+1)!} e^{-nq_1} + (1-p) \frac{(nq_2)^{c+1}}{(c+1)!} e^{-nq_2} \Bigg] \\
+ C_A (L-n) \Bigg[& pq_1 \frac{(nq_1)^{c+1}}{(c+1)!} e^{-nq_1} + (1-p)q_2 \frac{(nq_2)^{c+1}}{(c+1)!} e^{-nq_2} \Bigg]
\end{aligned}
$$

For a minimum at c^* we have

$$\Delta C(c^* - 1) < 0 < \Delta C(c^*)$$

Let

$$A_1 = q_1 C_A(L - n) - C_R L, \qquad A_2 = q_2 C_A(L - n) - C_R L$$

Then c^* must satisfy

$$A_1 p \frac{(nq_1)^{c^*}}{c^*!} e^{-nq_1} + A_2(1 - p) \frac{(nq_2)^{c^*}}{c^*!} e^{-nq_2}$$

$$< 0 < A_1 p \frac{(nq_1)^{c^*+1}}{(c^*+1)!} e^{-nq_1} + A_2(1 - p) \frac{(nq_2)^{c^*+1}}{(c^*+1)!} e^{-nq_2}$$

The left hand side of the inequality reduces to

$$\left(\frac{q_2}{q_1} \right)^{c^*} < - \frac{A_1 p}{A_2(1 - p)} e^{-n(q_1 - q_2)}$$

Taking natural logarithms of both sides,

$$c^* \ln(q_2/q_1) < \ln \left[\frac{C_R L - q_1 C_A(L - n)}{q_2 C_A(L - n) - C_R L} \right] + \ln \left(\frac{p}{1 - p} \right) + n(q_2 - q_1)$$

and

$$c^* < \frac{\ln \left[\dfrac{C_R L - q_1 C_A(L - n)}{q_2 C_A(L - n) - C_R L} \right] + \ln \left(\dfrac{p}{1 - p} \right) + m(q_2 - q_1)}{\ln(q_2/q_1)}$$

Following an argument similar to the above, $\Delta C(c)$ leads to

$$c^* > \frac{\ln \left[\dfrac{C_R L - q_1 C_A(L - n)}{q_2 C_A(L - n) - C_R L} \right] + \ln \left(\dfrac{p}{1 - p} \right) + n(q_2 - q_1)}{\ln(q_2/q_1)} - 1$$

Letting

$$\psi = \frac{\ln \left[\dfrac{C_R L - q_1 C_A(L - n)}{q_2 C_A(L - n) - C_R L} \right] + \ln \left(\dfrac{p}{1 - p} \right) + n(q_2 - q_1)}{\ln(q_2/q_1)}$$

c^* must satisfy the inequality

$$\psi - 1 < c^* < \psi$$

If ψ is an integer, then $c^* = \psi - 1$ or $c^* = \psi$. ∎

Example 5.19 In Example 5.18 find c^* if

$$p = 0.800, \qquad q_1 = 0.005, \qquad q_2 = 0.050, \qquad L = 10,000$$

$$n = 200, \qquad C_R = \$0.01, \qquad C_A = \$1.00$$

From Example 5.18,

$$\psi = \frac{\ln\left[\dfrac{C_R L - q_1 C_A(L-n)}{q_2 C_A(L-n) - C_R L}\right] + \ln\left(\dfrac{p}{1-p}\right) + n(q_2 - q_1)}{\ln(q_2/q_1)}$$

$$= \frac{\ln\left[\dfrac{(0.01)(10{,}000) - (0.005)(1.00)(10{,}000 - 200)}{(0.05)(1.00)(10{,}000 - 200) - (0.01)(10{,}000)}\right] + \ln\left(\dfrac{0.80}{0.20}\right) + 200(0.045)}{\ln(0.050/0.005)}$$

$$= 3.63$$

Since $\psi - 1 < c^* < \psi$, $c^* = 3$. ∎

Example 5.20   The cost $C(q)$ of operating an inventory system is given by

$$C(q) = C_0 \frac{\lambda}{q} + C_I \frac{q-1}{2}$$

where λ is the annual demand rate, q the order quantity, C_0 the order cost, and C_I the unit cost of carrying one unit of product in inventory for one year. Find the value of q which minimizes $C(q)$.

The first difference of $C(q)$ is given by

$$\Delta C(q) = \left[C_0 \frac{\lambda}{q+1} + \frac{C_I q}{2}\right] - \left[C_0 \frac{\lambda}{q} + \frac{C_I(q-1)}{2}\right] = -\frac{C_0 \lambda}{q(q+1)} + \frac{C_I}{2}$$

If q^* minimizes $C(q)$, then

$$\Delta C(q^* - 1) < 0 < \Delta C(q^*)$$

Now

$$-\frac{C_0 \lambda}{q^*(q^* - 1)} + \frac{C_I}{2} < 0 \quad \text{implies} \quad q^*(q^* - 1) < \frac{2 C_0 \lambda}{C_I}$$

and

$$-\frac{C_0 \lambda}{q^*(q^* + 1)} + \frac{C_I}{2} > 0 \quad \text{implies} \quad q^*(q^* + 1) > \frac{2 C_0 \lambda}{C_I}$$

Hence q^* is that integer satisfying the inequality

$$q^*(q^* - 1) < \frac{2 C_0 \lambda}{C_I} < q^*(q^* + 1) \quad ∎$$

Example 5.21   If

$$C_0 = \$100.00, \qquad C_I = \$200.00, \qquad \lambda = 2000$$

find the value of q which minimizes $C(q)$ in Example 5.20.

From Example 5.20,

$$2C_0\lambda/C_1 = 2000$$

The largest value of q^* such that

$$q^*(q^* - 1) < 2000$$

is $q^* = 45$. Since $q^*(q^* - 1) < 2000 < q^*(q^* + 1)$ for $q^* = 45$, this is the value of q which minimizes $C(q)$. ∎

NUMERICAL METHODS

Anyone who has used tables of trigonometric functions or cumulative distribution functions has encountered the problem of interpolation. Interpolation is also sometimes required when experimental data are available only for a specific series of values $[x, f(x)]$. In a similar vein the analyst may be interested in the derivative or integral of a tabulated function. In this section we shall present techniques which may be used for interpolation, differentiation, and integration of tabulated functions. While these techniques yield only approximations to the true result, they are nonetheless quite useful in practice.

Interpolation

Suppose that values of $f(x)$ are tabulated at $x_0, x_1, \ldots, x_n$ and that based upon this data we wish to determine the value of $f(x)$ at $x_i < x < x_{i+1}$, $i < n$. That is, we wish to approximate the value of $f(x)$ by interpolation between $f(x_i)$ and $f(x_{i+1})$. The values $x_0, x_1, \ldots, x_n$ need not be integer valued, and $(x_{i+1} - x_i)$ and $(x_{j+1} - x_j)$ need not be equal for $i \neq j$. In determining the interpolated value of $f(x)$ we first approximate the function $f(x)$ based upon its tabulated values. In this section the function used to approximate $f(x)$ will be a polynomial in all cases.

The simplest approximating function, and probably the most frequently used, is the straight line. If $\hat{f}(x)$ is the approximating function, then

$$\hat{f}(x) = a + bx \tag{5.42}$$

Suppose that the function to be approximated is as shown in Fig. 5.8 and that values of $f(x)$ are tabulated at $x_0, x_1, \ldots, x_n$. To approximate $f(x)$ by a linear function $\hat{f}(x)$, successive values of $f(x_i)$ are joined by a straight line, as in Fig. 5.8. That is, we attempt to define the slope b and y intercept a in Eq. (5.42) such that

$$f(x_i) = a + bx_i \tag{5.43}$$

$$f(x_{i+1}) = a + bx_{i+1} \tag{5.44}$$

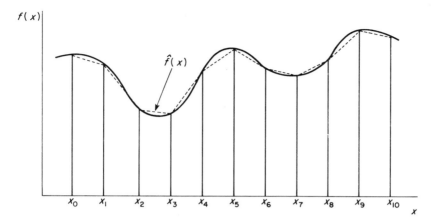

Fig. 5.8   Linear approximation for the function $f(x)$.

Solving Eqs. (5.43) and (5.44) for a and b we have

$$b = \frac{f(x_{i+1}) - f(x_i)}{x_{i+1} - x_k} = Df(x_i) \qquad (5.45)$$

$$a = f(x_i) - x_i Df(x_i) \qquad (5.46)$$

where $Df(x_i)$ is the first divided difference of $f(x)$ at x_i. Thus $\hat{f}(x)$ for $x_i < x < x_{i+1}$ is given by

$$\hat{f}(x) = f(x_i) - x_i Df(x_i) + x Df(x_i) = f(x_i) + (x - x_i) Df(x_i) \quad (5.47)$$

The value of $f(x)$ is then approximated by substituting x in Eq. (5.47).

Example 5.22   The following values have been recorded for the cumulative distribution function of the standard normal random variable.

i	0	1	2	3	4	5	6	7	8
x_i	− 2.0	− 1.5	− 1.0	− 0.5	0.0	0.5	1.0	1.5	2.0
$f(x_i)$	0.023	0.067	0.159	0.309	0.500	0.692	0.841	0.933	0.977

By linear interpolation find the value of $f(x)$ for $x = -1.75, -0.75, 0.25, 1.25$.

To determine $\hat{f}(x)$ for the values of x specified, $Df(x_i)$ must be computed for $i = 0, 1, \ldots, 7$. This is most conveniently accomplished by a divided difference table. A divided difference table is identical to a difference table except that differences are replaced by divided differences. The required divided difference table for this example is shown in Table 5.5.

Table 5.5

Divided Difference Table for Example 5.22

i	x_i	$f(x_i)$	$Df(x_i)$
0	-2.0	0.023	
			$\dfrac{0.067 - 0.023}{-1.5 + 2.0} = 0.088$
1	-1.5	0.067	
			$\dfrac{0.159 - 0.067}{-1.0 + 1.5} = 0.184$
2	-1.0	0.159	
			$\dfrac{0.309 - 0.159}{-0.5 + 1.0} = 0.300$
3	-0.5	0.309	
			$\dfrac{0.500 - 0.309}{0.0 + 0.5} = 0.382$
4	0.0	0.500	
			$\dfrac{0.692 - 0.500}{0.5 - 0.0} = 0.384$
5	0.5	0.692	
			$\dfrac{0.841 - 0.692}{1.0 - 0.5} = 0.298$
6	1.0	0.841	
			$\dfrac{0.933 - 0.841}{1.5 - 1.0} = 0.184$
7	1.5	0.933	

The solutions for the required interpolated values of $f(x)$ are summarized in Table 5.6, where Eq. (5.47) is used to compute $\hat{f}(x)$. The exact values of $f(x)$ are given by $f(x)$ in Table 5.6. ∎

In Example 5.22 linear interpolation led to reasonable approximations $\hat{f}(x)$ for $f(x)$. However, in cases where $x_{i+1} - x_i$ is relatively large or where

Table 5.6

Interpolated Values of $f(x)$ for Example 5.22

x	$\hat{f}(x)$	$f(x)$
-1.75	$\hat{f}(x) = f(x_0) + (-1.75 - x_0)\,Df(x_0)$	
	$= 0.023 + (-175 + 2.00)(0.088)$	
	$= 0.045$	0.040
-0.75	$\hat{f}(x) = f(x_2) + (-0.75 - x_2)\,Df(x_2)$	
	$= 0.159 + (-0.75 + 1.00)(0.300)$	
	$= 0.234$	0.227
0.25	$\hat{f}(x) = f(x_4) + (0.25 - x_4)\,Df(x_4)$	
	$= 0.500 + (0.25 - 0.00)(0.384)$	
	$= 0.596$	0.599
1.25	$\hat{f}(x) = f(x_6) + (1.25 - x_6)\,Df(x_6)$	
	$= 0.841 + (1.25 - 1.00)(0.184)$	
	$= 0.887$	0.894

the behavior of $f(x)$ is erratic, linear interpolation may yield a poor approximation for $f(x)$. In these cases a higher-order polynomial approximation for $f(x)$ will usually improve the accuracy of the interpolated values. To illustrate, suppose we wish to approximate $f(x)$ by a quadratic equation of the form

$$\hat{f}(x) = a + bx + cx^2 \tag{5.48}$$

The constants a, b, and c are defined such that

$$f(x_i) = a + bx_i + cx_i^2 \tag{5.49}$$

$$f(x_{i+1}) = a + bx_{i+1} + cx_{i+1}^2 \tag{5.50}$$

$$f(x_{i+2}) = a + bx_{i+2} + cx_{i+2}^2 \tag{5.51}$$

That is, the approximating quadratic equation is to pass through $f(x_i)$, $f(x_{i+1})$, and $f(x_{i+2})$. Solving for a, b, and c yields

$$a = f(x_i) - x_i\, Df(x_i) - x_i x_{i+1} D^2f(x_i) \tag{5.52}$$

$$b = Df(x_i) - (x_{i+1} + x_i) D^2f(x_i) \tag{5.53}$$

$$c = D^2f(x_i) \tag{5.54}$$

where $D^2f(x_i)$ is the second divided difference defined by

$$D^2f(x_i) = \frac{Df(x_{i+1}) - Df(x_i)}{x_{i+2} - x_i} \tag{5.55}$$

Hence if $x_i < x < x_{i+2}$,

$$\hat{f}(x) = f(x_i) + (x - x_i) Df(x_i) + (x - x_i)(x - x_{i+1}) D^2f(x_i) \tag{5.56}$$

Example 5.23 $\sin(x)$ has been recorded for the values of x (in radians) shown in the following table.

i	0	1	2	3	4	5	6	7	8	9	10	11
x	0.00	0.05	0.20	0.50	0.70	0.80	0.90	1.00	1.05	1.20	1.40	1.60
$f(x)$	0.00	0.05	0.20	0.48	0.64	0.72	0.78	0.84	0.87	0.93	0.99	1.00

Using quadratic interpolation, estimate $\sin(x)$ for $x = 0.10, 0.60, 0.85, 1.02, 1.30$.

To estimate $\sin(x)$ for the values of x given, we apply Eq. (5.56). Again a divided difference table is convenient for computing $Df(x)$ and $D^2f(x)$, and these computations are summarized in Table 5.7. The calculations necessary for determining the interpolated values of $\sin(x)$ are shown in Table 5.8, where $\hat{f}(x)$ and $f(x)$ are the interpolated and true values of $\sin(x)$ for each value of x. ■

Table 5.7

Divided Difference Table for Example 5.22

i	x_i	$f(x_i)$	$Df(x_i)$	$D^2f(x_i)$
0	0.00	0.00		
			$\dfrac{0.05 - 0.00}{0.05 - 0.00} = 1.00$	
1	0.05	0.05		$\dfrac{1.00 - 1.00}{0.20 - 0.00} = 0.00$
			$\dfrac{0.20 - 0.05}{0.20 - 0.05} = 1.00$	
2	0.20	0.20		$\dfrac{0.93 - 1.00}{0.50 - 0.05} = -0.16$
			$\dfrac{0.48 - 0.20}{0.50 - 0.20} = 0.93$	
3	0.50	0.48		$\dfrac{0.80 - 0.93}{0.70 - 0.20} = -0.26$
			$\dfrac{0.64 - 0.48}{0.70 - 0.50} = 0.80$	
4	0.70	0.64		$\dfrac{0.80 - 0.80}{0.80 - 0.50} = 0.00$
			$\dfrac{0.72 - 0.64}{0.80 - 0.70} = 0.80$	
5	0.80	0.72		$\dfrac{0.60 - 0.80}{0.90 - 0.70} = -1.00$
			$\dfrac{0.78 - 0.72}{0.90 - 0.80} = 0.60$	
6	0.90	0.78		$\dfrac{0.60 - 0.60}{1.00 - 0.80} = 0.00$
			$\dfrac{0.84 - 0.78}{1.00 - 0.90} = 0.60$	
7	1.00	0.84		$\dfrac{0.60 - 0.60}{1.05 - 0.90} = 0.00$
			$\dfrac{0.87 - 0.84}{1.05 - 1.00} = 0.60$	
8	1.05	0.87		$\dfrac{0.40 - 0.60}{1.20 - 1.00} = -1.00$
			$\dfrac{0.93 - 0.87}{1.20 - 1.05} = 0.40$	
9	1.20	0.93		$\dfrac{0.30 - 0.40}{1.40 - 1.05} = -0.29$
			$\dfrac{0.99 - 0.93}{1.40 - 1.20} = 0.30$	
10	1.40	0.99		$\dfrac{0.05 - 0.30}{1.60 - 1.20} = -0.63$
			$\dfrac{1.00 - 0.99}{1.60 - 1.40} = 0.05$	
11	1.60	1.00		

Equations (5.47) and (5.56) may be generalized to an nth-degree polynomial through Newton's divided difference formula, given by

$$f(x) = f(x_i) + \sum_{j=0}^{n-1} \left[\prod_{k=i}^{j+i} (x - x_k) \right] D^{j+1}f(x_i) \qquad (5.57)$$

Table 5.8

Interpolated Values for sin(x) in Example 5.23

x	$\hat{f}(x)$	$f(x)$
0.10	$\hat{f}(x) = f(x_1) + (x - x_1)\,Df(x_1) + (x - x_1)(x - x_2)\,D^2f(x_1)$ $= 0.05 + (0.10 - 0.05)(1.00) + (0.10 - 0.05)(0.10 - 0.20)(-1.16)$ $= 0.11$	
		0.10
0.60	$\hat{f}(x) = f(x_3) + (x - x_3)\,Df(x_3) + (x - x_3)(x - x_4)\,D^2f(x_3)$ $= 0.48 + (0.60 - 0.50)(0.80) + (0.60 - 0.50)(0.60 - 0.70)(0.00)$ $= 0.56$	
		0.56
0.85	$\hat{f}(x) = f(x_5) + (x - x_5)\,Df(x_5) + (x - x_5)(x - x_6)\,D^2f(x_5)$ $= .72 + (0.85 - 0.80)(0.60) + (.085 - 0.80)(0.85 - 0.90)(0.00)$ $= 0.75$	
		0.75
1.02	$\hat{f}(x) = f(x_7) + (x - x_7)\,Df(x_7) + (x - x_7)(x - x_8)\,D^2f(x_7)$ $= 0.84 + (1.02 - 1.00)(0.60) + (1.02 - 1.00)(1.02 - 1.05)(-1.00)$ $= 0.85$	
		0.85
1.30	$\hat{f}(x) = f(x_9) + (x - x_9)\,Df(x_9) + (x - x_9)(x - x_{10})\,D^2f(x_9)$ $= 0.93 + (1.30 - 1.20)(0.30) + (1.30 - 1.20)(1.30 - 1.40)(-0.63)$ $= 0.97$	
		0.96

where

$$\prod_{k=i}^{j+i} (x - x_k) = (x - x_i)(x - x_{i+1}) \cdots (x - x_{i+j}) \qquad (5.58)$$

and $D^kf(x_i)$ is the kth divided difference of $f(x)$ evaluated at x_i and is defined by

$$D^kf(x_i) = \frac{D^{k-1}f(x_{i+1}) - D^{k-1}f(x_i)}{x_{i+k} - x_i} \qquad (5.59)$$

If $x_{i+1} - x_i = \Delta x$ for all i, then $D^kf(x_i)$ can be expressed by

$$D^kf(x_i) = \frac{1}{k!\,(\Delta x)^k} \sum_{j=0}^{k} (-1)^{k-j} \binom{k}{j} f(x_i + \Delta x) \qquad (5.60)$$

where

$$\binom{k}{j} = \frac{k!}{j!\,(k - j)!} \qquad (5.61)$$

As illustrated in Examples 5.22 and 5.23 it is usually convenient to calculate $D^kf(x_i)$ using a divided difference table.

Differentiation

The basis for numberical differentiation is similar to that for interpolation. That is, we start with an approximation $\hat{f}(x)$ to $f(x)$ and differentiate the result. Starting with Newton's divided difference formula, Eq. (5.57) and differentiating with respect to x, we have

$$\hat{f}'(x) = \sum_{j=0}^{n-1} \frac{d}{dx}\left[\prod_{k=i}^{j+i}(x - x_k)\right] D^{j+1}f(x_i) \tag{5.62}$$

Now

$$\frac{d}{dx}\prod_{k=i}^{j+i}(x - x_k) = 1, \qquad j = 0$$

$$= \prod_{k=i+1}^{j+i}(x - x_k) + (x - x_i)\prod_{k=i+2}^{j+i}(x - x_k)$$

$$+ \prod_{l=i}^{i+1}(x - x_l)\prod_{k=i+3}^{j+i}(x - x_k) + \prod_{l=i}^{i+2}(x - x_l)\prod_{k=i+4}^{j+i}(x - x_k) + \cdots$$

$$+ \prod_{k=i}^{j+i-1}(x - x_k), \qquad j > 0$$

or

$$\frac{d}{dx}\prod_{k=i}^{j+i}(x - x_k) = 1, \qquad j = 0$$

$$= \sum_{l=i}^{j+i}\prod_{\substack{k=i \\ k \neq l}}^{j+i}(x - x_k) \tag{5.63}$$

Thus $\hat{f}'(x)$ is given by

$$\hat{f}'(x) = Df(x_i) + \sum_{j=1}^{n-1}\left[\sum_{l=i}^{j+i}\prod_{\substack{k=i \\ k \neq l}}^{j+i}(x - x_k)\right] D^{j+1}f(x_i) \tag{5.64}$$

where $n > 1$. If $n = 1$

$$\hat{f}'(x) = Df(x_i) \tag{5.65}$$

Example 5.24 Given the data in Example 5.22, estimate $f'(x)$ at $x = 1.75, -0.75, 0.25$ using Eq. (5.64) and $n = 3$.

For $n = 3$,

$$\hat{f}'(x) = Df(x_i) + \left[(x - x_{i+1}) + (x - x_i)\right] D^2f(x_i)$$

$$+ \left[(x - x_{i+1})(x - x_{i+2}) + (x - x_i)(x - x_{i+2})\right.$$

$$\left. + (x - x_i)(x - x_{i+1})\right] D^3f(x_i)$$

The divided difference table for this problem is given in Table 5.9, and the calculations required for $\hat{f}'(x)$ are summarized in Table 5.10, where $f'(x)$ is the actual value of the derivative at x. ∎

Table 5.9

Table 5.9

Divided Difference Table for Example 5.24

i	x_i	$f(x_i)$	$Df(x_i)$	$D^2f(x_i)$	$D^3f(x_i)$
0	− 2.0	0.023			
			0.088		
1	− 1.5	0.067		$\dfrac{0.184 - 0.088}{-1.0 + 2.0} = 0.096$	
			0.184		$\dfrac{0.116 - 0.096}{-0.5 + 2.0} = 0.013$
2	− 1.0	0.159		$\dfrac{0.300 - 0.184}{-0.5 + 1.5} = 0.116$	
			0.300		$\dfrac{0.082 - 0.116}{0.0 + 1.5} = -0.023$
3	− 0.5	0.309		$\dfrac{0.382 - 0.300}{0.0 + 1.0} = 0.082$	
			0.382		$\dfrac{0.002 - 0.082}{0.5 + 1.0} = -0.053$
4	0.0	0.500		$\dfrac{0.384 - 0.382}{0.5 + 0.5} = 0.002$	
			0.384		$\dfrac{-0.086 - 0.002}{1.0 + 0.5} = -0.059$
5	0.5	0.692		$\dfrac{0.298 - 0.384}{1.0 - 0.0} = -0.086$	
			0.298		$\dfrac{-0.114 + 0.086}{1.5 - 0.0} = -0.019$
6	1.0	0.841		$\dfrac{0.184 - 0.298}{1.5 - 0.5} = -0.114$	
			0.184		
7	1.5	0.933			

Integration

As in the case of numerical differentiation, numerical integration is performed by operating on a functional approximation to the tabular function. In this case the operation is integration. That is, $\hat{f}(x)$ is an approximation for $f(x)$; then $\int_a^b f(x)\, dx$ is approximated by $\int_a^b \hat{f}(x)\, dx$. If $a = x_0$ and $b = x_m$, then

$$\int_{x_0}^{x_m} \hat{f}(x)\, dx = \sum_{l=0}^{m-1} \int_{x_l}^{x_{l+1}} \hat{f}(x)\, dx \qquad (5.66)$$

Approximating $f(x)$ by Eq. (5.57), we have

$$\int_{x_0}^{x_m} \hat{f}(x)\, dx = \sum_{l=0}^{m-1} \int_{x_l}^{x_{l+1}} \left\{ f(x_l) + \sum_{j=0}^{n-1} \left[\prod_{k=i}^{j+l} (x - x_k) \right] D^{j+1} f(x_i) \right\} dx$$

$$(5.67)$$

Table 5.10

Estimated Derivative of $f(x)$ for Example 5.24

x	$\hat{f}'(x)$	$f(x)$
-1.75	$\hat{f}'(x) = Df(x_0) + [(x - x_1) + (x - x_0)]\,D^2f(x_0) + [(x - x_1)(x - x_2) + (x - x_0)(x - x_2)$ $\quad + (x - x_0)(x - x_1)]\,D^3f(x_0)$ $= 0.088 + [(-1.75 + 1.50) + (-1.75 + 2.00)](0.096) + [(-1.75 + 1.50)(-1.75 + 1.00)$ $\quad + (-1.75 + 2.00)(-1.75 + 1.00) + (-1.75 + 2.00)(-1.75 + 1.50)](0.013)$ $= 0.087$	0.086
-0.75	$\hat{f}'(x) = Df(x_2) + [(x - x_3) + (x - x_2)]\,D^2f(x_2) + [(x - x_3)(x - x_4) + (x - x_2)(x - x_4)$ $\quad + (x - x_2)(x - x_3)]\,D^3f(x_2)$ $= 0.300 + [(-0.75 + 0.50) + (-0.75 + 1.00)](0.082) + [(-0.75 + 0.50)(-0.75 - 0.00)$ $\quad + (-0.75 + 1.00)(-0.75 - 0.00) + (-0.75 + 1.00)(-0.75 + 0.50)](-0.053)$ $= 0.303$	0.301
0.25	$\hat{f}'(x) = Df(x_4) + [(x - x_5) + (x - x_4)]\,D^2f(x_4) + [(x - x_5)(x - x_6) + (x - x_4)(x - x_6)$ $\quad + (x - x_4)(x - x_5)]\,D^3f(x_4)$ $= 0.384 + [(0.25 - 0.50) + (0.25 - 0.0)](-0.086) + [(0.25 - 0.50)(0.25 - 1.00)$ $\quad + (0.25 - 0.00)(0.25 - 1.00) + (0.25 - 0.00)(0.25 - 0.50)](-0.019)$ $= 0.385$	0.387

or

$$\int_a^b \hat{f}(x)\,dx = \sum_{i=0}^{m-1}(x_{i+1} - x_i)f(x_i)$$

$$+ \sum_{i=0}^{m-1}\sum_{j=0}^{n-1}D^{j+1}f(x_i)\int_{x_i}^{x_{i+1}}\left[\prod_{k=i}^{j+i}(x - x_k)\right]dx \quad (5.68)$$

When $n = 1$, Eq. (5.68) leads to the trapezoidal rule for numerical integration given by

$$\int_a^b \hat{f}(x)\,dx = \sum_{i=0}^{m-1}(x_{i+1} - x_i)f(x_i) + \sum_{i=0}^{m-1}Df(x_i)\int_{x_i}^{x_{i+1}}(x - x_k)\,dx$$

$$= \sum_{l=0}^{m-1}\left[(x_{i+1} - x_i)f(x_i) + \frac{(x_{i+1} - x_i)^2}{2}Df(x_i)\right] \quad (5.69)$$

Noting that

$$Df(x_i) = \frac{f(x_{i+1}) - f(x_i)}{x_{i+1} - x_k}$$

it follows that

$$\int_{x_0}^{x_m}\hat{f}(x)\,dx = \sum_{i=0}^{m-1}\left\{(x_{i+1} - x_i)f(x_i) + \frac{(x_{i+1} - x_i)}{2}[f(x_{i+1}) - f(x_i)]\right\}$$

$$= \sum_{i=0}^{m-1}\frac{(x_{i+1} - x_i)}{2}[f(x_i) + f(x_{i+1})] \quad (5.70)$$

If $(x_{i+1} - x_i) = \Delta x$ for all i,

$$\int_{x_0}^{x_m}\hat{f}(x)\,dx = \frac{\Delta x}{2}\sum_{i=0}^{m-1}[f(x_i) + f(x_{i+1})]$$

$$= \frac{\Delta x}{2}\left[f(x_0) + 2\sum_{i=1}^{m-1}f(x_i) + f(x_m)\right] \quad (5.71)$$

When $n = 2$ and m is even, the resulting expression for the approximate integral is called Simpson's rule. For $(x_{i+1} - x_i) = \Delta x$, Simpson's rule is

$$\int_{x_0}^{x_m}\hat{f}(x)\,dx = \frac{\Delta x}{3}[f(x_0) + 4f(x_1) + 2f(x_2) + 4f(x_3) + \cdots$$

$$+ 2f(x_{m-2}) + 4f(x_{m-1}) + f(x_m)] \quad (5.72)$$

Example 5.25   Tabular values of the function e^{-x} are given as follows:

i	0	1	2	3	4	5	6
x_i	0.00	0.50	1.00	1.50	2.00	2.50	3.00
$f(x_i)$	1.000	0.607	0.368	0.223	0.135	0.082	0.050

Using the trapazoidal rule, approximate $\int_0^3 e^{-x}\,dx$.
Since $(x_{i+1} - x_i) = 0.50$ for all i, we apply Eq. (5.71) and

$$\int_0^3 \hat{f}(x)\,dx = \frac{0.50}{2}\left[1.000 + 2(0.607 + 0.368 + 0.223\right.$$

$$\left. + 0.135 + 0.082) + 0.050\right] = 0.970$$

The true value of $\int_0^3 e^{-x}\,dx$ is 0.950.   ■

Example 5.26   The probability density function of the gamma random variable is defined as

$$f(x) = \frac{\lambda^n}{\Gamma(n)}\,x^{n-1}e^{-\lambda x}, \qquad 0 < x < \infty$$

Tabular values of $f(x)$ are given in the following table, where $\lambda = 3.0$ and $n = 5.0$. Using Simpson's rule, find $\int_0^a f(x)\,dx$ for $a = 1.20, 1.80, 2.40$.

i	0	1	2	3	4	5	6	7	8
x_i	0.00	0.30	0.60	0.90	1.20	1.50	1.80	2.10	2.40
$f(x_i)$	0.000	0.033	0.217	0.447	0.574	0.570	0.480	0.362	0.251

For this problem $\Delta x = (x_{i+1} - x_i) = 0.30$ for all i. For $a = 1.20$,

$$\int_0^a \hat{f}(x)\,dx = \frac{\Delta x}{3}\left[f(x_0) + 4f(x_1) + 2f(x_2) + 4f(x_3) + f(x_4)\right]$$

$$= \frac{0.30}{3}\left[0.000 + 4(0.033) + 2(0.217)\right.$$

$$\left. + 4(0.447) + 0.574\right] = 0.293$$

For $a = 1.80$,

$$\int_0^a \hat{f}(x) \, dx = \frac{\Delta x}{3} \left[f(x_0) + 4f(x_1) + 2f(x_2) + 4f(x_3) \right.$$

$$+ 2f(x_4) + 4f(x_5) + f(x_6) \big]$$

$$= \frac{0.30}{3} \left[0.000 + 4(0.033) + 2(0.217) + 4(0.447) \right.$$

$$+ 2(0.574) + 4(0.570) + 0.480 \big]$$

$$= 0.626$$

Finally, for $a = 2.40$,

$$\int_0^a \hat{f}(x) \, dx = \frac{\Delta x}{3} \left[0.000 + 4(0.033) + 2(0.217) + 4(0.447) + 2(0.574) \right.$$

$$+ 4(0.570) + 2(0.480) + 4(0.362) + 0.251 \big]$$

$$= 0.844$$

The true values for $\int_0^a f(x) \, dx$ are as follows:

$$\int_0^{1.20} f(x) \, dx = 0.294, \qquad \int_0^{1.80} f(x) \, dx = 0.627, \qquad \int_0^{2.40} f(x) \, dx = 0.844 \quad \blacksquare$$

SUMMARY

This chapter has been devoted to a discussion of techniques useful in the analysis of functions of a discrete variable. As we have pointed out, the difference and antidifference operators play a role with respect to discrete functions analogous to that of the derivative and antiderivative in the case of continuous functions. In operations research the difference operator probably is most widely used in problems dealing with the optimization of discrete functions, while the antidifference has important applications in determining the sum of a series. The numerical techniques for interpolation, differentiation, and integration have important applications when the underlying function $f(x)$ describing the behavior of a system is unknown, but can be observed for specific values of x. In addition numerical differentiation and particularly numerical integration are quite useful when the function can be defined analytically, but analytic differentiation or integration cannot be readily accomplished, if at all.

PROBLEMS

1. Find $\Delta f(x)$, where

   (a) $f(x) = (1/2)x(x - 1)$,
   (b) $f(x) = [(1/2)x(x + 1)]^2$,
   (c) $f(x) = (x + 1)x(2x - 1)(3x - 2)$.

   In all cases x is integer valued.

2. Find $\Delta f(x)$, where

   (a) $f(x) = 4x + 3$,
   (b) $f(x) = x^2 + 6$,
   (c) $f(x) = 1/(x + 2)$,
   (d) $f(x) = x^2 - 2x + 1$.

   In all cases $x = 1, 2, \ldots, n$ and $f(x) = 0$ for $x < 1$ and $x > n$.

3. Find $\Delta f(x)$, where

   (a) $f(x) = x^2 + 4x + 5$,
   (b) $f(x) = x^3 + 3x^2 + 4$,
   (c) $f(x) = x/(x + 1)$.

   In all cases $x = 0, 1, 2, \ldots, n$, $f(x) = 3$ for $x = -1, -2, \ldots$, and $f(x) = 0$ for $x > n$.

4. Show that

   (a) $\Delta[cf(x)] = c \, \Delta f(x)$,
   (b) $\Delta[c/f(x)] = -c \, \Delta f(x)/[f(x)f(x + 1)]$.

5. Show that

$$\Delta\left[\sin\left(\frac{x\theta}{2} \right) \sin\left(\frac{x\theta - \theta}{2} \right) \operatorname{cosec}\left(\frac{\theta}{2} \right) \right] = \sin(x\theta)$$

6. If

$$x^{(n)} = x(x - 1)(x - 2) \cdots (x - n + 1)$$

   and

$$x^{[n]} = x(x + 1)(x + 2) \cdots (x + n - 1)$$

   Show that

   (a) $\Delta x^{(n)} = nx^{(n-1)}$,
   (b) $\Delta(1/x^{[n]}) = -n/x^{[n+1]}$.

7. Let $f(x) = (a + bx)^{(n)}$, where

$$(a + bx)^{(n)} = [a + bx][a + b(x - 1)][a + b(x - 2)] \cdots [a + b(x - n + 1)]$$

   Show that

$$\Delta f(x) = bn(a + bx)^{(n - 1)}$$

8. Let

$$f(x) = \begin{cases} 0, & x = -(n + 1), -(n + 2) \\ -x^2, & x = -n, -(n - 1), \ldots, 0 \\ x^2, & x = 1, 2, \ldots, n \\ 0, & x = n + 1, n + 2, \ldots \end{cases}$$

   Find $\Delta f(x)$.

9. Find $\Delta f(x)$ if

$$f(x) = \frac{2^x}{x+2} - \frac{1}{2}, \qquad x = 1, 2, \ldots$$

10. If $F(x)$ is the cumulative distribution function of the integer-valued random variable x, then its probability mass function $q(x)$ is given by

$$q(x) = \Delta F(x)$$

Find the probability mass function associated with each of the following cumulative distribution functions:

(a) $F(x) = x(x+1)(2x+1)/n(n+1)(2n+1)$, $x = 1, 2, \ldots, n$;
(b) $F(x) = (1 - p^x)/(1 - p^n)$, $x = 1, 2, \ldots, n$.

11. Let

$$f(x) = x^2 - 2x + 1$$

where $x = 0, 1/2, 1, 3/2, 2, \ldots$. Find the first divided difference of $f(x)$.

12. If

$$f(x) = ae^x, \qquad x = 1, 3, 5, \ldots$$

find the first divided difference of $f(x)$.

13. The following values of the function $f(x)$ have been recorded:

i	0	1	2	3	4	5	6
x_i	1	5	7	8	12	17	25
$f(x_i)$	3	27	51	66	146	127	89

Find the first divided difference of $f(x)$, $Df(x_i)$, for $i = 0, 1, \ldots, 5$.

14. Show that

$$Df(x_i) = \frac{\begin{vmatrix} f(x_i) & f(x_{i+1}) \\ 1 & 1 \end{vmatrix}}{\begin{vmatrix} x_i & x_{i+1} \\ 1 & 1 \end{vmatrix}}$$

15. Show that

$$D^2 f(x_i) = \frac{\begin{vmatrix} f(x_i) & f(x_{i+1}) & f(x_{i+2}) \\ x_i & x_{i+1} & x_{i+2} \\ 1 & 1 & 1 \end{vmatrix}}{\begin{vmatrix} x_i^2 & x_{i+1}^2 & x_{i+2}^2 \\ x_i & x_{i+1} & x_{i+2} \\ 1 & 1 & 1 \end{vmatrix}}$$

16. Derive the expression in Eq. (5.8).
17. Derive the expression in Eq. (5.9).
18. Define $\Delta^2 f(x)$ for each function in Problem 1.
19. Find $\Delta^2 f(x)$ and $\Delta^3 f(x)$, where

(a) $f(x) = x/(x+1)$,
(b) $f(x) = 1/(x+2)$,
(c) $f(x) = x^3 + 3x^2 + 4$,

for $x = 1, 2, 3, \ldots$.

20. For the functions in Problem 19 evaluate $\Delta^2 f(x)$ and $\Delta^3 f(x)$ for $x = 1, 2, 3, 4$.

21. Find $\Delta^2 f(x)$ and $\Delta^3 f(x)$ for the functions in Problem 6.

22. Evaluate $D^2 f(x)$ and $D^3 f(x)$ for the function defined in Problem 13.

23. Define the sum of the following series:

(a) $\sum_{x=0}^{b} x^4$;

(b) $\sum_{x=a}^{b} \{1/[x(x+1)]\}$;

(c) $\sum_{x=0}^{b} \{x/[(x+1)!]\}$;

(d) $\sum_{x=1}^{8} (2x-1)^3$;

(e) $\sum_{x=5}^{9} \{(x^2 + x - 1)/[(x+2)!]\}$.

24. Show that

$$\sum_{x=0}^{n} x k^x = k \frac{d}{dk} \sum_{x=0}^{n} k^x$$

and

$$\sum_{x=0}^{n} x(x-1)k^x = k^2 \frac{d^2}{dk^2} \sum_{x=0}^{n} k^x$$

25. Using the expressions in Problem 24, find

(a) $\sum_{x=0}^{n} x k^x$,

(b) $\sum_{x=0}^{n} x(x-1)k^x$,

(c) $\sum_{x=0}^{n} x^2 k^2$.

26. The probability mass function of the geometric random variable is defined by

$$q(x) = p(1-p)^{x-1}, \qquad x = 1, 2, \ldots$$

where $0 < p < 1$. The mean μ and variance σ^2 of x are defined by

$$\mu = \sum_{x=1}^{\infty} xq(x), \qquad \sigma^2 = \sum_{x=1}^{\infty} (x - \mu)^2 q(x)$$

Find μ and σ^2.

27. If $q(x)$ is the probability mass function of the random variable x, $x = 0, 1, 2, \ldots$, then the cumulative distribution function is given by $F(x)$, where

$$F(x) = \sum_{y=0}^{x} q(y)$$

If

$$q(x) = \frac{(1-p)p^x}{1 - p^{n+1}}, \qquad x = 0, 1, 2, \ldots, n$$

find $F(x)$.

28. Find the mean and variance of the random variable in Problem 27 (see Problem 26).

29. The probability mass function of the random variable x is given by

$$q(x) = \frac{2x}{n(n+1)}, \qquad x = 0, 1, 2, \ldots, n$$

(a) Find the cumulative distribution function for x (see Problem 27).

(b) Find the mean of x (see Problem 26).

(c) Find the variance of x (see Problem 26).

30. The probability mass function of the rectangular random variable is given by

$$q(x) = \frac{1}{b - a + 1}, \qquad x = a, a+1, \ldots, b$$

where a and b are integers and $a < b$. Find

(a) the cumulative distribution function for x (see Problem 27),

(b) the mean of x (see Problem 26),

(c) the variance of x (see Problem 26).

31. Derive an expression for $\Delta C(x)$, where

$$C(x) = \sum_{y=a(x)}^{b} f(x, y)$$

for x and y integer valued.

32. Derive an expression for $\Delta C(x)$, where

$$C(x) = \sum_{y=a}^{b(x)} f(x, y)$$

for x and y integer valued.

33. Using Eq. (5.27), find the first difference of the expressions in Problem 23.

34. Using Eq. (5.26), find the first difference of

(a) $\sum_{y=x}^{x+n}(y - x^2)$,

(b) $\sum_{y=x}^{x^2}(y^2 + x)$,

(c) $\sum_{y=x}^{x+n}(y\, y! - x\, x!)$

for x and y integer valued and $x \geqslant 0$.

35. If

$$C(x) = \sum_{y=a(x)}^{b(x)} \sum_{z=g(x, y)}^{h(x, y)} f(x, y, z)$$

where x, y, z, $a(x)$, $b(x)$, $g(x, y)$, and $h(x, y)$ are integer valued and $a(x) < b(x)$ and $g(x, y) < h(x, y)$, show that

$$\Delta C(x) = \sum_{y=a(x)}^{b(x)} \sum_{z=g(x, y)}^{h(x, y)} \Delta_x f(x, y, z)$$

$$+ \sum_{y=a(x)}^{b(x)} \left[\sum_{z=h(x, y)+1}^{h(x+1, y)} f(x+1, y, z) - \sum_{z=g(x, y)}^{g(x+1, y)-1} f(x+1, y, z) \right]$$

$$+ \sum_{y=b(x)+1}^{b(x+1)} \sum_{z=g(x+1, y)}^{h(x+1, y)} f(x+1, y, z) - \sum_{y=a(x)}^{a(x+1)-1} \sum_{z=g(x+1, y)}^{h(x+1, y)} f(x+1, y, z)$$

36. Find and identify the extreme points of

(a) $f(x) = 6x^4 - 8x^3$, $x = 0, \pm 1, \pm 2, \ldots$,

(b) $f(x) = 2x^3 - 6x^2 + 1$, $x = 0, \pm 1, \pm 2, \ldots$,

(c) $f(x) = \{5!/[x!(5 - x)!]\}(0.8)^x(0.2)^{5-x}$, $x = 0, 1, 2, 3, 4, 5$,

(d) $f(x) = (1/4)x^4 - 2x^2$, $x = 0, \pm 1, \pm 2, \ldots$.

37. The mode of a discrete random variable x is that value of x at which its probability mass function assumes its maximum. Find the mode of the random variables with the following probability mass functions:

(a) $q(x) = 1/(b - a + 1)$, $x = a, a + 1, \ldots, b$;

(b) $q(x) = \binom{n}{x}p^x(1 - p)^{n-x}$, $x = 0, 1, 2, \ldots, n$;

(c) $q(x) = \binom{x-1}{r-1}p^r(1 - p)^{x-r}$, $x = r, r + 1, r + 2, \ldots$;

(d) $q(x) = p(1 - p)^{x-1}$, $x = 1, 2, 3, \ldots$.

38. The annual cost of maintaining a production line is given by

$$C(n) = C_L n + \frac{\lambda}{n\mu + \lambda} C_P + \frac{n\lambda\mu}{n\mu + \lambda} C_D$$

where C_D is the fixed cost of a system failure, C_P the time dependent cost of a system failure, C_L the annual cost of a maintenance man, λ the mean system failure rate, n the maintenance crew size, and $n\mu$ the repair rate. Find the value of n which minimizes $C(n)$.

39. In Problem 38 let
$$C_D = \$14.00, \qquad C_P = \$800,000, \qquad C_1 = \$10,000$$
$$\lambda = 100, \qquad \mu = 1000$$

Find the value n which minimizes $C(n)$.

40. The cost of operating an attributes acceptance sampling quality control system is given by

$$C(c) = C_I n + (L - n)\left[\frac{C_a}{n + a + z} \sum_{x=0}^{c} (x+1)\binom{n+a+x}{a} \right.$$
$$\left. + C_r \sum_{x=c+1}^{n} \binom{n+a-x}{a} \right] / \binom{n+a+1}{n}$$

where C_I is the unit inspection cost, C_a the cost of an accepted unit which is defective, C_r the cost of a rejected unit, L the lot size, n the sample size, and c the acceptance number. Find the value of c which minimizes $C(c)$.

41. In Problem 40, if
$$C_I = \$250.00, \qquad C_a = \$25.00, \qquad C_r = \$2.00$$
$$L = 10,000, \qquad n = 70$$

find the value of c which minimizes $C(c)$.

42. The cost of producing x units of product per month is $2x^2 + 8x + 50$, and the sale price per unit is $(100 - x)$. What should the monthly production rate be to maximize profit, where monthly profit is given by

$$P(x) = x(100 - x) - (2x^2 + 80x + 50)$$

43. In Problem 18 of Chapter 3 find the order quantity q which minimizes the total cost of operating the inventory system.

44. The purchase price of a piece of equipment is C_p and it costs C_k to operate and maintain the equipment during the kth year of its life. If i is the interest rate on capital borrowed to finance the equipment, then the fixed annual cost of the equipment is $F(r)$, where

$$F(r) = \left(\frac{i}{1+i} \right) \frac{(1+i)^r}{(1+i)^r - 1} \left[C_p + \sum_{k=1}^{r} \frac{1}{(1+i)^{k-1}} C_k \right]$$

and r is the number of years until the equipment is replaced. Find the value of r which will minimize the fixed annual cost of equipment.

45. In Problem 44 let
$$i = 0.10, \qquad C_p = \$50,000, \qquad C_k = \$20,000 + \$2000(k - 1)$$

Find the optimal value of r.

46. Given the following tabulation of $f(x)$, estimate $f(x)$ at $x = 3, 5, 7, 9$ using a quadratic approximating function:

i	0	1	2	3	4	5	6	7	8	9
x_i	0	2	4	6	8	10	12	14	16	18
$f(x_i)$	1	-7	33	217	641	1401	2593	4313	6657	9721

47. Solve Problem 46 using a cubic approximation function.
48. For the function tabulated in Problem 46 estimate the derivative of $f(x)$ at $x = 3, 5, 7, 9$, where a quadratic function is used to approximate $f(x)$.
49. For the function tabulated in Problem 46 estimate $\int_0^9 f(x)\, dx$ using (a) the trapezoidal rule, (b) Simpson's rule.
50. The probability density function of the normal random variable with mean μ and variance σ^2 is given by

$$f(x) = \frac{1}{\sigma\sqrt{2\pi}}\, e^{-(x-u)^2/(2\sigma^2)}, \qquad -\infty < x < \infty$$

Let $\mu = 5$, $\sigma = 1$. By tabulating $f(x)$ at $x = 1.0, 1.5, 2.0, 2.5, 3.0, 3.5, 4.0, 4.5, 5.0, 5.5, 6.0$, find $F(x)$ at $x = 3.0, 4.0, 5.0, 6.0$ using Simpson's rule, where

$$F(x) = \int_{1.0}^{x} f(x)\, dx$$

51. Given the cost function in Problem 45, develop a quadratic approximation for $F(r)$ by tabulating $F(r)$ for $r = 1, 4, 7, 10, 13, 16, 19, 22, 25$. Based upon this approximation, estimate the values of $F(5)$, $F(6)$, $F(20)$, $F(23)$, and compare these estimates with the corresponding true values of $F(r)$.

Suggested Further Reading

1. Beckenbach, E. F., ed. (1956). "Modern Mathematics for the Engineer." McGraw-Hill, New York.
2. Boole, G. (1960). "A Treatise on the Calculus of Finite Differences." Dover, New York.
3. Gelfond, A. O. (1961). "The Solution of Equations in Integers." Freeman, San Francisco, California.
4. Giffin, W. C. (1971). "Introduction to Operations Engineering." Irwin, Homewood, Illinois.
5. Giffin, W. C. (1975). "Transform Techniques for Probability Modeling." Academic Press, New York.
6. Goldberg, S. (1958). "Difference Equations." Wiley (Interscience), New York.
7. Jolley, L. B. W. (1961). "Summation of Series." Dover, New York.
8. Jordan, C. (1950). "Calculus of Finite Differences." Chelsea, Bronx, New York.
9. Miller, K. S. (1960). "An Introduction to the Calculus of Finite Differences and Difference Equations." Holt, New York.
10. Richardson, C. H. (1954). "An Introduction to the Calculus of Finite Differences." Van Nostrand, Princeton, New Jersey.
11. Sasieni, M., Yaspan, A., and Friedman, L. (1959). "Operations Research; Methods and Problems." Wiley, New York.
12. Schmidt, J. W. (1974). "Mathematical Foundations for Management Science and Systems Analysis." Academic Press, New York.
13. Wagner, H. M. (1969). "Principles of Operations Research with Applications to Managerial Decisions." Prentice-Hall, Englewood Cliffs, New Jersey.
14. Wylie, C. R. (1960). "Advanced Engineering Mathematics." McGraw-Hill, New York.

Chapter 6 | Operational Methods

INTRODUCTION

This chapter deals with transform methods frequently employed in the development and analysis of system models. As the application of a transform involves an operation on a function, these techniques are usually referred to as operational methods. In a sense the solution of a problem through the application of a transform may be thought of as an indirect procedure, but nonetheless reduces the complexity involved in obtaining the solution.

The transform methods presented here are appropriate for the analysis of functions of continuous and discrete variables. While most of the continuous and discrete transforms presented may be used for the same purpose, each finds widespread use in operations research, and the reader should be familiar with each.

The continuous transforms treated are the *Fourier*, *Laplace*, and *Mellin* transforms and the *characteristic* and *moment generating* functions. The most widely used in operations research as well as engineering and the physical sciences is the Laplace transform primarily because extensive tables of Laplace transform pairs are readily available. The Laplace transform finds its most frequent use in the solution of differential equations. The Mellin transform is particularly useful in dealing with the product or ratio of random variables, while the characteristic and moment generating functions are useful in problems concerned with the sum of random variables. All of the continuous transforms are based on the Fourier transform, and all may be used to find moments about the origin.

The discrete transforms discussed in this chapter are the *geometric* and

Z transforms and the *characteristic* and *moment generating* functions. The geometric and Z transforms find much the same application. They are useful in solving difference equations and in determining the distribution of the sum of random variables. When the geometric transform is applied to a probability mass function, it is sometimes referred to as the probability generating function. The characteristic and moment generating functions play the same role with respect to discrete random variables as they do in the case of continuous random variables. All of the discrete transforms may be used to identify moments about the origin.

All of the transforms presented in this chapter are termed *linear*. That is, if $T[f_1(t)]$ and $T[f_2(t)]$ are the transforms of $f_1(t)$ and $f_2(t)$, then the transform T is linear if

$$T[f_1(t) \pm f_2(t)] = T[f_1(t)] \pm T[f_2(t)]$$

In some cases the transform of a function may not exist. For example, the Fourier transform of the function $f(t)$ exists if and only if $\int_{-\infty}^{\infty} |f(t)| \, dt$ converges, where $f(t)$ must be continuous at all but a finite number of points t. However, if the transform of a function exists, then it is unique. That is, if $f_1(t)$ and $f_2(t)$ are such that

$$T[f_1(t)] = T[f_2(t)]$$

then $f_1(t) = f_2(t)$ at least at all but a finite number of points t. The converse is also true. If $f_1(t) = f_2(t)$, then $T[f_1(t)] = T[f_2(t)]$. Thus $f(t)$ and $T[f(t)]$ form a unique *transform pair*.

In using transforms for such purposes as the solution of differential or difference equations or defining the distribution of a function of random variables, the solution usually rests upon the ability of the analyst to identify the function $f(t)$ associated with the transform $T[f(t)]$. The inverse of $T[f(t)]$, that is, $f(t)$ and sometimes denoted $T^{-1}[f(t)]$, can be determined analytically. However, analytic inversion usually requires integration in the complex plane, and the process can prove to be a tedious undertaking. For this reason tables of transform pairs are more frequently applied to the inversion process, rendering it a simple look-up process. Tables of Laplace, geometric, and Z transform pairs are given in the Appendix. Tables of characteristic and moment generating functions and Mellin transform pairs are given in Tables 6.1, 6.2, and 6.3.

CONTINUOUS TRANSFORMS

In this section we shall discuss several continuous transforms that have proven useful in solving problems commonly encountered by the operations research analyst. The transforms treated include the Fourier and

Laplace transforms, the characteristic and moment generating functions, and the Mellin transform. While all of these transforms are related to the Fourier transform and often may be used interchangeably, each appears in the literature on operations research and should be familiar to the reader. The transform techniques discussed here have application in solving differential and integral equations, finding the moments of a continuous random variable, and identifying the distribution of functions of continuous random variables. Each of these applications will be illustrated by example throughout the discussion.

Fourier Transform

The basis for the continuous transforms wi.ich will be discussed in this chapter is the *Fourier transform*. If $f(t)$ is a function of t, then the Fourier transform of $f(t)$ is given by

$$F_t(u) = \int_{-\infty}^{\infty} f(t)e^{-iut}\,dt \tag{6.1}$$

where $i = \sqrt{-1}$. However, $F_t(u)$ exists if and only if $f(t)$ has a finite number of discontinuities and is absolutely integrable on the interval $(-\infty, \infty)$. That is,

$$\int_{-\infty}^{\infty} |f(t)|\,dt < \infty \tag{6.2}$$

$F_t(u)$ and $f(t)$ form a unique transform pair in that $f(t)$ uniquely defines $F_t(u)$ and $F_t(u)$ uniquely defines $f(t)$. Thus given $F_t(u)$, we may define $f(t)$ by

$$f(t) = \frac{1}{2\pi} \int_{-\infty}^{\infty} F_t(u)e^{iut}\,du \tag{6.3}$$

That is, $f(t)$ is the inverse transform of $F_t(u)$ and will sometimes be denoted $F_t^{-1}(u)$.

In many of the problems we shall discuss, the solution to the problem is first to find $F_t(u)$ for some unknown function $f(t)$ and having determined $F_t(u)$, then to define the corresponding function $f(t)$. Once $F_t(u)$ is obtained we could apply Eq. (6.3) to the task of determining $f(t)$. However, since Eq. (6.3) requires integration in the complex plane, this approach may prove tedious. This difficulty can often be overcome by consulting a table of Fourier transform pairs.

Example 6.1   Find the Fourier transform of $f(t)$, where

$$\text{(a)} \quad f(t) = \frac{1}{\sqrt{2\pi}} e^{-t^2/2}$$

$$\text{(b)} \quad f(t) = \begin{cases} e^t, & -\infty < t \le 0 \\ e^{-t}, & 0 < t < \infty \end{cases}$$

For part (a),

$$F_t(u) = \int_{-\infty}^{\infty} \frac{1}{\sqrt{2\pi}} e^{-t^2/2} e^{-iut} \, dt$$

Now $-(\frac{1}{2} t^2 + iut)$ may be expressed as

$$-\frac{t^2}{2} - iut = -\frac{t^2 + 2iut}{2} = -\frac{(t + iu)^2}{2} - \frac{u^2}{2}$$

since $i^2 = -1$. Therefore

$$F_t(u) = e^{-u^2/2} \int_{-\infty}^{\infty} \frac{1}{\sqrt{2\pi}} e^{-(t+iu)^2/2} \, dt = e^{-u^2/2}$$

For part (b),

$$F_t(u) = \int_{-\infty}^{0} e^t e^{-iut} \, dt + \int_{0}^{\infty} e^{-t} e^{-iut} \, dt$$

$$= \int_{-\infty}^{0} e^{(1-iu)t} \, dt + \int_{0}^{\infty} e^{-(1+iu)t} \, dt$$

$$= \frac{1}{1 - iu} + \frac{1}{1 + iu} = \frac{2}{(1 - iu)(1 + iu)} \quad \blacksquare$$

Moments

One of the common uses of transforms is in determining the *moments* of a function about zero. This application is particularly evident in dealing with probabilistic systems, for which the first and second moments are used to define the mean and variance of a random variable. The third and fourth moments are used to determine the skewness and kurtosis of the distribution of the random variable. If the nth moment m_n of the function $f(t)$ exists, then

$$m_n = \frac{1}{(-i)^n} \frac{d^n}{du^n} F_t(u)|_{u=0} \tag{6.4}$$

The validity of Eq. (6.4) is easily demonstrated. If the nth moment of $f(t)$

exists, then

$$m_n = \int_{-\infty}^{\infty} t^n f(t) \, dt \tag{6.5}$$

From Eq. (6.4),

$$\frac{d^n}{du^n} F_t(u) = \frac{d^n}{du^n} \int_{-\infty}^{\infty} f(t) e^{-iut} \, dt = \int_{-\infty}^{\infty} f(t) \left[\frac{d^n}{du^n} e^{-iut} \right] dt$$

$$= \int_{-\infty}^{\infty} (-it)^n f(t) e^{-iut} \, dt = (-i)^n \int_{-\infty}^{\infty} t^n f(t) e^{-iut} \, dt \tag{6.6}$$

and

$$\frac{d^n}{du^n} F_t(u)\Big|_{\mu=0} = (-i)^n \int_{-\infty}^{\infty} t^n f(t) e^{-iut} \, dt \Big|_{\mu=0}$$

$$= (-i)^n \int_{-\infty}^{\infty} t^n f(t) \, dt = (-i)^n m_n \tag{6.7}$$

Division of Eq. (6.7) by $(-1)^n$ yields Eq. (6.5), and the proof is complete. The reader should note that although $F_t(u)$ may be defined, some or all of the moments of $f(t)$ may not exist, since $\int_{-\infty}^{\infty} t^n f(t) e^{-iut} \, dt$ may not converge for some $n > 0$.

Example 6.2   The probability density function of the gamma random variable t is given by

$$f(t) = \begin{cases} 0, & t < 0 \\ \dfrac{\lambda^n}{\Gamma(n)} t^{n-1} e^{-\lambda t}, & 0 < t < \infty \end{cases}$$

Find the Fourier transform of $f(t)$ and determine mean m_1 and variance σ^2 of t, where

$$\sigma^2 = m_2 - m_1^2 \tag{6.8}$$

The Fourier transform of $f(t)$ is given by

$$Ft(u) = \int_{-\infty}^{0} (0) e^{-iut} \, dt + \int_{0}^{\infty} \frac{\lambda^n}{\Gamma(n)} t^{n-1} e^{-\lambda t} e^{-iut} \, dt$$

$$= \int_{0}^{\infty} \frac{\lambda^n}{\Gamma(n)} t^{n-1} e^{-(\lambda + iu)t} \, dt$$

$$= \frac{\lambda^n}{\Gamma(n)} \int_{0}^{\infty} t^{n-1} e^{-(\lambda + iu)t} \, dt = \left(\frac{\lambda}{\lambda + iu} \right)^n$$

The first and second derivatives of $F_t(u)$ are

$$\frac{d}{du} F_t(u) = - \frac{in\lambda^n}{(\lambda + iu)^{n+1}}, \qquad \frac{d^2}{du^2} F_t(u) = \frac{i^2 n(n + 1)\lambda^n}{(\lambda + iu)^{n+2}}$$

and

$$\frac{d}{du} F_t(u)\big|_{\mu=0} = -\frac{in}{\lambda}, \qquad \frac{d^2}{du^2} F_t(u)\big|_{\mu=0} = \frac{i^2 n(n+1)}{\lambda^2}$$

Therefore

$$m_1 = \frac{n}{\lambda}, \qquad m_2 = \frac{n(n+1)}{\lambda^2}$$

and

$$\sigma^2 = \frac{n(n+1)}{\lambda^2} - \frac{n^2}{\lambda^2} = \frac{n}{\lambda^2} \quad \blacksquare$$

Example 6.3   Let

$$f(t) = \begin{cases} 0, & -\infty < t < 0 \\ c, & -0 < t < \infty \end{cases}$$

Show that the moments of $f(t)$ do not exist.
    $F_t(u)$ is given by

$$F_t(u) = \int_{-\infty}^{\infty} (0)e^{-iut}\, dt + \int_0^{\infty} ce^{-iut}\, dt = c\int_0^{\infty} e^{-iut}\, dt = \frac{c}{iu}$$

Now

$$\frac{d}{du} F_t(u) = -\frac{ic}{(iu)^2}$$

Since

$$-\frac{ic}{(iu)^2}\bigg|_{\mu=0} \to \infty$$

m_1 does not exist. In general,

$$\frac{d^n}{du^n} F_t(u) = \frac{(-i)^n c\, n!}{(iu)^n} \qquad \text{and} \qquad \frac{d^n}{du^n} F_t(u)\big|_{\mu=0} \to \infty$$

Thus none of the moments of $f(t)$ exist.   ■

Convolution

In probabilistic modeling the analyst is often faced with finding the distribution of a function of one or more random variables. The most commonly encountered case involves the sum of random variables. For example, consider the problem of determining the time t a traveler spends between arriving at an air terminal and boarding the aircraft. We may break t into two parts. Let t_1 be the time between arrival at the terminal and the completion of ticketing and baggage checking, and let t_2 be the time spent waiting to board his/her flight after ticketing and baggage checking. Then

$$t = t_1 + t_2 \tag{6.9}$$

If $g(t_1)$ and $h(t_2)$ are the probability density functions of t_1 and t_2 and $f(t)$ is the probability density function of t, then

$$f(t) = \int_0^t g(t_1)h(t - t_1)\, dt_1 \tag{6.10}$$

The limits of integration are 0 and t, since t_1 and t_2 may not be negative but also may not exceed t. If the random variables t_1 and t_2 may assume values on the interval $(-\infty, \infty)$, then $f(t)$ is expressed by

$$f(t) = \int_{-\infty}^{\infty} g(t_1)h(t - t_1)\, dt_1 \tag{6.11}$$

While $f(t)$ often may be defined without difficulty by direct application of Eqs. (6.10) or (6.11), the task is sometimes a tedious one and can be simplified through the use of transforms. Specifically, if $F_t(u)$, $F_{t_1}(u)$, and $F_{t_2}(u)$ are the Fourier transforms of $f(t)$, $g(t_1)$, and $h(t_2)$, respectively, then

$$F_t(u) = F_{t_1}(u)F_{t_2}(u) \tag{6.12}$$

and $f(t)$ is defined by $F_t^{-1}(u)$.

Example 6.4 Let t_1 and t_2 be the monthly profits resulting from the sale of two products. If t_1 and t_2 are normally distributed random variables with probability density functions

$$g_j(t_j) = \frac{1}{\sigma_j\sqrt{2\pi}}\, e^{-(t_j - m_j)^2/(2\sigma_j^2)}, \qquad -\infty < t_j < \infty, \quad j = 1, 2$$

find the probability density function of total monthly profit.

Let

$$t = t_1 + t_2$$

Then by Eq. (6.12),

$$F_t(u) = F_{t_1}(u)F_{t_2}(u)$$

Now

$$F_{t_j}(u) = \int_{-\infty}^{\infty} g_j(t_j)e^{-iut_j}\, dt = \int_{-\infty}^{\infty} \frac{1}{\sigma_j\sqrt{2\pi}}\, e^{-(t_j - m_j)^2/(2\sigma_j^2)}e^{-iut_j}\, dt$$

Considering the exponent of e,

$$-iut_j - \frac{(t_j - m_j)^2}{2\sigma_j^2} = -\frac{t_j^2 - 2(m_j - \sigma_j^2 iu)t_j + m_j^2}{2\sigma_j^2}$$

$$= -\frac{[t_j - (m_j - iu\sigma_j^2)]^2}{2\sigma_j^2} - \left[ium_j + \frac{u^2\sigma_j^2}{2} \right]$$

Thus

$$F_{t_j}(u) = e^{-[ium_j + (u^2\sigma_j^2/2)]} \int_{-\infty}^{\infty} \frac{1}{\sigma_j\sqrt{2\pi}} e^{-[t_j - (m_j - iu\sigma_j^2)]^2/(2\sigma_j^2)} \, dt_j$$

$$= e^{-[ium_j + (u^2\sigma_j^2/2)]}$$

and

$$F_t(u) = e^{-[ium_1 + (u^2\sigma_1^2/2)]} e^{-[ium_2 + (u^2\sigma_2^2/2)]}$$

$$= e^{-[iu(m_1 + m_2) + (u^2/2)(\sigma_1^2 + \sigma_2^2)]}$$

Since $F_t(u)$ has the general form

$$F_t(u) = e^{-[iu\alpha + (u^2/2)\beta]}$$

which is the same as the form for $F_{t_j}(u)$ and $F_{t_j}(u)$, t is normally distributed with mean $m_1 + m_2$, variance $\sigma_1^2 + \sigma_2^2$, and probability density function

$$f(t) = \frac{1}{\sqrt{\sigma_1^2 + \sigma_2^2}\,\sqrt{2\pi}} e^{-[t - (m_1 + m_2)]^2/[2(\sigma_1^2 + \sigma_2^2)]}, \quad -\infty < t < \infty \quad \blacksquare$$

Example 6.5 The weekly costs of operation of two production lines are t_1 and t_2. These costs have probability density functions given by

$$f_j(t_j) = \begin{cases} 0, & -\infty < t_j < 0 \\ \lambda_j e^{-\lambda_j t_j}, & 0 < t_j < \infty \end{cases}$$

where $\lambda_j > 0$, $j = 1, 2$. Find the probability density function of the total weekly cost $t = t_1 + t_2$

(a) using Fourier transforms,
(b) using the convolution formula in Eq. (6.10).

For part (a), $F_{t_j}(u)$ is given by

$$F_{t_j}(u) = \int_{-\infty}^{0} (0)e^{iut_j}\,dt_j + \int_{0}^{\infty}\lambda_j e^{-\lambda_j t_j}e^{-iut_j}\,dt$$

$$= \int_{0}^{\infty}\lambda_j e^{-(\lambda_j + iu)t_j}\,dt = \frac{\lambda_j}{\lambda_j + iu}, \qquad j = 1, 2$$

Hence if $t = t_1 + t_2$, then

$$F_t(u) = \frac{\lambda_1 \lambda_2}{(\lambda_1 + iu)(\lambda_2 + iu)}$$

$$= \frac{\lambda_1}{\lambda_1 - \lambda_2}\left[\frac{\lambda_2}{\lambda_2 + iu}\right] - \frac{\lambda_2}{\lambda_1 - \lambda_2}\left[\frac{\lambda_1}{\lambda_1 + iu}\right]$$

$$= \frac{\lambda_1 \lambda_2}{\lambda_1 - \lambda_2}\left[\frac{1}{\lambda_2 + iu} - \frac{1}{\lambda_1 + iu}\right]$$

If $F_t^{-1}(u)$ is the inverse of $F_t(u)$, then the probability density function of t ($g(t)$) is

$$g(t) = \frac{\lambda_1 \lambda_2}{\lambda_1 - \lambda_2}\left[F_t^{-1}\left(\frac{1}{\lambda_2 + iu}\right) - F_t^{-1}\left(\frac{1}{\lambda_1 + iu}\right)\right]$$

and

$$F_t^{-1}\left(\frac{1}{\lambda_j + iu}\right) = e^{-\lambda_j t}$$

Therefore

$$g(t) = \frac{\lambda_1 \lambda_2}{\lambda_1 - \lambda_2}\left[e^{-\lambda_2 t} - e^{-\lambda_1 t}\right]$$

In part (b),

$$g(t) = \int_{0}^{t} f_1(t_1)f_2(t - t_1)\,dt_1$$

$$= \int_{0}^{t}\lambda_1\lambda_2 e^{-\lambda_1 t_1}e^{-\lambda_2(t - t_1)}\,dt_1$$

$$= \lambda_1\lambda_2 e^{-\lambda_2 t}\int_{0}^{t}e^{-(\lambda_1 - \lambda_2)t_1}\,dt_1$$

$$= \lambda_1\lambda_2 e^{-\lambda_2 t}\left[\frac{1 - e^{-(\lambda_1 - \lambda_2)t}}{\lambda_1 - \lambda_2}\right] = \frac{\lambda_1\lambda_2}{\lambda_1 - \lambda_2}\left[e^{-\lambda_2 t} - e^{-\lambda_1 t}\right] \quad \blacksquare$$

Laplace Transform

The Laplace transform, like the other continuous transforms discussed in the chapter, is a derivative of the Fourier transform. It is used with greater frequency than the Fourier transform, particularly in solving differential equations. As we mentioned in the preceding section, the Fourier transform of $f(t)$ exists if $f(t)$ is absolutely integrable on $(-\infty, \infty)$. However, the operations research analyst is often forced to deal with functions which do not satisfy this requirement. One need only consider the polynomials to illustrate this point.

The Laplace transform possesses properties which guarantee its existence under conditions less restrictive than those of the Fourier transform. The *two-sided* Laplace transform of $f(t)$ is defined by

$$\mathcal{L}[f(t)] = L(s) = \int_{-\infty}^{\infty} f(t)e^{-st}\, dt \qquad (6.13)$$

where

$$s = \sigma + iw \qquad (6.14)$$

Hence, the Laplace transform is actually the Fourier transform of $f(t)e^{-\sigma t}$. More often than not the variable t is restricted to nonnegative values for most practical problems. For this reason the *one-sided* Laplace transform is that most commonly encountered in practice and is given by

$$\mathcal{L}[f(t)] = L(s) = \int_{0}^{\infty} f(t)e^{-st}\, dt \qquad (6.15)$$

where s is as defined in Eq. (6.14).

The Laplace transform of $f(t)$ may be shown to exist if $f(t)$ is continuous at all but a finite number of points on every interval $[0, a]$ and if

$$\lim_{t\to\infty} [f(t)e^{-\sigma t}] = 0 \qquad (6.16)$$

for $\sigma > b$, where b is a real number.

Example 6.6 Show that the one-sided Laplace transform of t^n exists, where n is a positive integer, and derive the transform of t^n.

From Eq. (6.16), $\mathcal{L}[t^n]$ exists if t^n is continuous for every finite closed interval $[0, a]$ and if $\lim_{t\to\infty}[t^n e^{-\sigma t}] = 0$ for $\sigma > b$. That t^n is continuous for all $t > 0$ can be shown without difficulty. Now noting that

$$e^{-\sigma t} = 1 \Big/ \left[\sum_{k=0}^{\infty} \frac{(\sigma t)^k}{k!} \right]$$

we have

$$\lim_{t\to\infty}\left[t^n e^{-\sigma t}\right] = \lim_{t\to\infty}\left\{t^n \bigg/ \left[\sum_{k=0}^{\infty}\frac{(\sigma t)^k}{k!}\right]\right\}$$

$$= \lim_{t\to\infty}\left[1\bigg/\left(\sum_{k=0}^{n}\frac{\sigma^k}{k!\,t^{n-k}} + \sum_{k=n+1}^{\infty}\frac{\sigma^k t^{k-n}}{k!}\right)\right]$$

$$= 1\bigg/\lim_{t\to\infty}\left(\sum_{k=0}^{n}\frac{\sigma^k}{k!\,t^{n-k}} + \sum_{k=n+1}^{\infty}\frac{\sigma^k t^{k-n}}{k!}\right)$$

by Eq. (1.22). But

$$\lim_{t\to\infty}\left[\sum_{k=0}^{n}\frac{a^k}{k!\,t^{n-k}}\right] = \frac{\sigma^n}{n!}$$

for all $\sigma < \infty$ and

$$\lim_{t\to\infty}\left[\sum_{k=n+1}^{n}\frac{\sigma^k t^{k-n}}{k!}\right] = \infty$$

Hence

$$\lim_{t\to\infty}\left[t^n e^{-\sigma t}\right] = \frac{1}{\infty} = 0$$

for all real σ and $\mathcal{L}[t^n]$ exists.

To define $\mathcal{L}[t^n]$, $L(s)$, we have

$$L(s) = \int_0^{\infty} t^n e^{-st}\,dt = \frac{n!}{s^{n+1}} \quad\blacksquare$$

Example 6.7 The Laplace transform of $g(t)$ is given by $G(s)$:

$$f(t) = e^{at}g(t)$$

Show that the one-sided Laplace transform of $f(t)$, $L(s)$, is defined by

$$L(s) = G(s - a)$$

From the definition of the one-sided Laplace transform

$$L(s) = \int_0^{\infty} e^{at}g(t)e^{-st}\,dt = \int_0^{\infty} g(t)e^{-(s-a)t}\,dt$$

since

$$\int_0^{\infty} g(t)e^{-st}\,dt = G(s) \tag{6.17}$$

we have

$$L(s) = G(s - a)$$

by replacing s by $s - a$ in Eq. (6.17). $\blacksquare$

As in the case of all transforms, the usefulness of the Laplace transform often depends upon the ability of the analyst to determine the function $f(t)$ once the transform $L(s)$ is defined. This can be accomplished, frequently with difficulty, through the appropriate inversion formula or by consulting a table of Laplace transforms. The inversion formula for determining $f(t)$ given the one-sided Laplace transform $L(s)$ is

$$f(t) = \frac{1}{2\pi i} \int_{a-i\infty}^{a+i\infty} L(s)e^{st}\, ds \tag{6.18}$$

where a is a constant chosen so that the singularities of $L(s)$ lie to the left of the line joining $a - i\infty$ and $a + i\infty$. As in the case of the Fourier transform, the inversion relationship in Eq. (6.18) requires integration in the complex plane. An abbreviated table of Laplace transforms is given in Table B of the Appendix.

Moments

The moments of a function $f(t)$ may be obtained, if they exist, from the associated Laplace transform as follows:

$$m_n = \frac{1}{(-1)^n} \frac{d^n}{ds^n} L(s) \Big|_{s=0} \tag{6.19}$$

Example 6.8 The probability density function of the chi-square random variable t is given by

$$f(t) = \frac{1}{2^{n/2}\Gamma(n/2)}\, t^{(n/2)-1}e^{-t/2}, \quad 0 < t < \infty$$

Find the mean and variance of t using the Laplace transform.

From Example 6.2 the mean of t is given by m_1 and the variance σ^2 by

$$\sigma^2 = m_2 - m_1^2$$

The Laplace transform of $f(t)$ is

$$L(s) = \int_0^\infty \frac{1}{2^{n/2}\Gamma(n/2)}\, t^{(n/2)-1}e^{-t/2}e^{-st}\, dt$$

$$= \frac{1}{2^{n/2}\Gamma(n/2)} \int_0^\infty t^{(n/2)-1}e^{-(1/2+s)t}\, dt$$

$$= \frac{1}{2^{n/2}\Gamma(n/2)} \frac{\Gamma(n/2)}{((2s+1)/2)^{n/2}} = \frac{1}{(1+2s)^{n/2}}$$

Now from Eq. (6.19),

$$m_1 = - \left. \frac{d}{ds} L(s) \right|_{s=0} = -\left[-n(1 + 2s)^{-(n+2)/2} \big|_{s=0} \right] = n$$

and

$$m_2 = \left. \frac{d^2}{ds^2} L(s) \right|_{s=0} = n(n + 2)(1 + 2s)^{-(n+4)/2} \big|_{s=0} = n(n + 2)$$

Hence

$$\sigma^2 = n(n + 2) - n^2 = 2n \quad \blacksquare$$

Partial Fraction Expansion

As already mentioned, the solution to many problems for which transforms are used lies in recognition of the inverse of the transform. While transform tables are helpful in this regard, they normally include only a limited number of transform pairs. When the transform of concern is not included in a transform table but is a ratio of polynomials in the transform variable, it may sometimes be expressed as a linear combination of simpler transforms each of which is included in the table.

Like the Fourier and other transforms discussed here the Laplace transform is a linear operator in the sense that if

$$f(t) = c_1 g_1(t) + c_2 g_2(t) \tag{6.20}$$

then

$$\mathcal{L}[f(t)] = c_1 \mathcal{L}[g_1(t)] + c_2 \mathcal{L}[g_2(t)] \tag{6.21}$$

Now suppose we seek the inverse of the Laplace transform $\mathcal{L}[f(t)]$, are unable to locate it in a table of transform pairs, but can express $\mathcal{L}[f(t)]$ as

$$\mathcal{L}[f(t)] = \sum_{i=1}^{n} c_i \mathcal{L}[g_i(t)] \tag{6.22}$$

where the inverse of $\mathcal{L}[g_i(t)]$, $g_i(t)$, can be determined, $i = 1, 2, \ldots, n$. Then

$$f(t) = \sum_{i=1}^{n} c_i g_i(t) \tag{6.23}$$

It is not at all uncommon to find a Laplace transform expressed as a ratio of polynomials in s. That is,

$$L(s) = \frac{A(s)}{B(s)} \tag{6.24}$$

where $A(s)$ and $B(s)$ are polynomials in s and $A(s)$ is of degree less than

$B(s)$. When $B(s)$ can be factored into the product of linear terms in s, $L(s)$ can be expressed as the sum of terms for which the denominator of each term is one of the factors of $B(s)$. For example, consider

$$L(s) = \frac{s^2 + 1}{s^3 - s} \qquad (6.25)$$

Factoring the denominator we have

$$L(s) = \frac{s^2 + 1}{s(s + 1)(s - 1)} = -\frac{1}{s} + \frac{1}{s + 1} + \frac{1}{s - 1} \qquad (6.26)$$

While $L(s)$, as given in Eq. (6.25), may not be found in a table of Laplace transforms, each of the terms in Eq. (6.26) is likely to appear. In this case, consulting Table B of the Appendix, we have

$$\mathcal{L}^{-1}\left(\frac{1}{s}\right) = 1, \qquad \mathcal{L}^{-1}\left(\frac{1}{s + 1}\right) = e^{-t}, \qquad \mathcal{L}^{-1}\left(\frac{1}{s - 1}\right) = e^t$$

and

$$\mathcal{L}^{-1}\left(\frac{s^2 + 1}{s^3 - s}\right) = f(t) = -1 + e^{-t} + e^t$$

The technique used here for expressing $L(s)$ as defined in Eq. (6.24) as a linear combination of simpler terms is called *partial fraction expansion*. Assume $L(s)$ is as defined in Eq. (6.24) and that $B(s)$ is given by

$$B(s) = (s - a_1)^{n_1}(s - a_2)^{n_2}(s - a_3)^{n_3} \cdots (s - a_m)^{n_m} \qquad (6.27)$$

Then $L(s)$ may be expressed as

$$L(s) = \sum_{i=1}^{n_1} \frac{c_{1i}}{(s - a_1)^i} + \sum_{i=2}^{n_2} \frac{c_{2i}}{(s - a_2)^i} + \cdots$$
$$+ \sum_{i=1}^{n_j} \frac{c_{ji}}{(s - a_j)^i} + \cdots + \sum_{i=1}^{n_m} \frac{c_{mi}}{(s - a_m)^i} \qquad (6.28)$$

where

$$c_{ji} = \frac{1}{(n_j - i)!} \lim_{s \to a_j} \frac{d^{n_j - i}}{ds^{n_j - i}} (s - a_j)^{n_j} L(s) \qquad (6.29)$$

for $i = 1, 2, \ldots, n_j - 1$ and $j = 1, 2, \ldots, m$. For $i = n_j$

$$c_{jn_j} = \lim_{s \to a_j} (s - a_j)^{n_j} L(s) \qquad (6.30)$$

Example 6.9   Let

$$L(s) = \frac{s^2 + 1}{(s - 1)(s + 1)(s - 2)}$$

Using partial fraction expansion, find $f(t)$.
From Eq. (6.28), $L(s)$ may be expressed by

$$L(s) = \frac{c_{11}}{(s - 1)} + \frac{c_{21}}{(s + 1)} + \frac{c_{31}}{(s - 2)}$$

Now

$$c_{11} = \lim_{s \to 1} (s - 1)L(s) = \lim_{s \to 1} \left[\frac{s^2 + 1}{(s + 1)(s - 2)} \right] = -1$$

$$c_{21} = \lim_{s \to -1} (s + 1)L(s) = \lim_{s \to -1} \left[\frac{s^2 + 1}{(s - 1)(s - 2)} \right] = \frac{1}{3}$$

$$c_{31} = \lim_{s \to 2} (s - 2)L(s) = \lim_{s \to 2} \left[\frac{s^2 + 1}{(s - 1)(s + 1)} \right] = \frac{5}{3}$$

and

$$L(s) = - \frac{1}{(s - 1)} + \frac{1}{3(s + 1)} + \frac{5}{3(s - 2)}$$

From Table B of the Appendix,

$$\mathcal{L}^{-1}\left[\frac{1}{s - 1} \right] = e^t, \qquad \mathcal{L}^{-1}\left[\frac{1}{s + 1} \right] = e^{-t}, \qquad \mathcal{L}^{-1}\left[\frac{1}{s - 2} \right] = e^{2t}$$

and

$$f(t) = -e^t + (1/3)e^{-t} + (5/3)e^{2t}   \blacksquare$$

Example 6.10   Let

$$L(s) = \frac{1}{(s - 1)(s + 2)^3}$$

Using partial fraction expansion, find $f(t)$.
From Eq. (6.28)

$$L(s) = \frac{c_{11}}{(s - 1)} + \frac{c_{21}}{(s + 2)} + \frac{c_{22}}{(s + 2)^2} + \frac{c_{23}}{(s + 2)^3}$$

and from Eqs. (6.29) and (6.30),

$$c_{11} = \lim_{s \to 1} (s - 1)L(s) = \lim_{s \to 1} \frac{1}{(s + 2)^3} = \frac{1}{27}$$

$$c_{23} = \lim_{s \to -2} (s + 2)^3 L(s) = \lim_{s \to -2} \frac{1}{(s - 1)} = -\frac{1}{3}$$

$$c_{22} = \frac{1}{1!} \lim_{s \to -2} \frac{d}{ds} (s + 2)^3 L(s)$$

$$= \frac{1}{1!} \lim_{s \to -2} \frac{d}{ds} \left(\frac{1}{s - 1} \right) = \lim_{s \to -2} \left[-\frac{1}{(s - 1)^2} \right] = -\frac{1}{9}$$

$$c_{21} = \frac{1}{2!} \lim_{s \to -2} \frac{d^2}{ds^2} (s + 2)^3 L(s)$$

$$= \frac{1}{2!} \lim_{s \to -2} \frac{d^2}{ds^2} \left(\frac{1}{s - 1} \right) = \frac{1}{2} \lim_{s \to -2} \left[\frac{2}{(s - 1)^3} \right] = -\frac{1}{27}$$

and

$$L(s) = \frac{1}{27(s - 1)} - \frac{1}{27(s + 2)} - \frac{1}{9(s + 2)^2} - \frac{1}{3(s + 2)^3}$$

Hence

$$f(t) = \frac{1}{27} \mathcal{L}^{-1} \left(\frac{1}{s - 1} \right) - \frac{1}{27} \mathcal{L}^{-1} \left(\frac{1}{s + 2} \right)$$

$$- \frac{1}{9} \mathcal{L}^{-1} \left[\frac{1}{(s + 2)^2} \right] - \frac{1}{3} \mathcal{L}^{-1} \left[\frac{1}{(s + 2)^3} \right]$$

$$= (1/27)e^t - (1/27)e^{-2t} - (1/9)te^{-2t} - (1/6)t^2e^{-2t} \quad \blacksquare$$

Example 6.11 If

$$L(s) = \frac{s^3}{(s + 1)^2(s - 1)^3}$$

find $f(t)$ using partial fraction expansion.
From Eq. (6.28),

$$L(s) = \frac{c_{11}}{(s + 1)} + \frac{c_{12}}{(s + 1)^2} + \frac{c_{21}}{(s - 1)} + \frac{c_{22}}{(s - 1)^2} + \frac{c_{23}}{(s - 1)^3}$$

and from Eqs. (6.29) and (6.30)

$$c_{12} = \lim_{s \to -1} (s + 1)^2 L(s) = \lim_{s \to -1} \left[\frac{s^3}{(s - 1)^3} \right] = \frac{1}{8}$$

$$c_{11} = \lim_{s \to -1} \frac{d}{ds} (s + 1)^2 L(s)$$

$$= \lim_{s \to -1} \frac{d}{ds} \left[\frac{s^3}{(s - 1)^3} \right] = \lim_{s \to -1} \left[-\frac{3s^2}{(s - 1)^4} \right] = -\frac{3}{16}$$

$$c_{23} = \lim_{s \to 1} (s - 1)^3 L(s) = \lim_{s \to 1} \left[\frac{s^3}{(s + 1)^2} \right] = \frac{1}{4}$$

$$c_{22} = \lim_{s \to 1} \frac{d}{ds} (s - 1)^3 L(s)$$

$$= \lim_{s \to 1} \frac{d}{ds} \left[\frac{s^3}{(s + 1)^2} \right] = \lim_{s \to 1} \left[s^2 \frac{(s + 3)}{(s + 1)^3} \right] = \frac{1}{2}$$

$$c_{21} = \frac{1}{2!} \lim_{s \to 1} \frac{d^2}{ds^2} (s - 1)^3 L(s)$$

$$= \frac{1}{2!} \lim_{s \to 1} \frac{d^2}{ds^2} \left[\frac{s^3}{(s + 1)^2} \right] = \frac{1}{2!} \lim_{s \to 1} \left[\frac{6s}{(s + 1)^4} \right] = \frac{3}{16}$$

and

$$L(s) = -\frac{3}{16(s + 1)} + \frac{1}{8(s + 1)^2} + \frac{3}{16(s - 1)} + \frac{1}{2(s - 1)^2} + \frac{1}{4(s - 1)^3}$$

or

$$f(t) = -\frac{3}{16} \mathcal{L}^{-1} \left[\frac{1}{s + 1} \right] + \frac{1}{8} \mathcal{L}^{-1} \left[\frac{1}{(s + 1)^2} \right]$$

$$+ \frac{3}{16} \mathcal{L}^{-1} \left[\frac{1}{s - 1} \right] + \frac{1}{2} \mathcal{L}^{-1} \left[\frac{1}{(s - 1)^2} \right] + \frac{1}{4} \mathcal{L}^{-1} \left[\frac{1}{(s - 1)^3} \right]$$

$$= -(3/16)e^{-t} + (1/8)te^{-t} + (3/16)e^{t} + (1/2)te^{t} + (1/8)t^2e^{t} \quad \blacksquare$$

Convolution

If $g(t_1)$ and $h(t_2)$ are defined for $t_1, t_2 > 0$, then the convolution $f(t)$ of $g(t_1)$ and $h(t_2)$ is given by

$$f(t) = \int_0^t g(t_1) h(t - t_1) \, dt_1 \tag{6.31}$$

If $L_1(s)$ and $L_2(s)$ are the Laplace transforms of $g(t_1)$ and $h(t_2)$, then the Laplace transform of $f(t)$, $L(s)$ is

$$L(s) = L_1(s)L_2(s) \qquad (6.32)$$

As in the case of the Fourier transform, the relationship in Eq. (6.32) provides a means for determining the distribution of the sum of continuous random varlables.

Example 6.12   The probability density function of the gamma random variable x is given by

$$g(x) = \frac{\lambda^n}{\Gamma(n)} x^{n-1} e^{-\lambda x}, \qquad 0 < x < \infty$$

Find the probability density function of the sum of m independent gamma random variables, each with parameters $\lambda > 0$ and $n > 0$.

Let x_i be a gamma random variable with parameters λ and n, and let t_k represent the sum $\sum_{i=1}^{k} x_i$. If $f_k(t_k)$ is the probability density function of t_k, then for $k = 2$, $t_2 = x_1 + x_2$, and the probability density function of t_2 is given by

$$f_2(t_2) = \int_0^{t_2} g(x_1)g(t_2 - x_1)\, dx_1$$

If

$$L_2(s) = \mathcal{L}[\, f_2(t_2)]$$

then

$$L_2(s) = \mathcal{L}[\, g(x)]^2$$

For t_3 we have

$$f_3(t_3) = \int_0^{t_3} f_2(t_2)g(t_3 - t_2)\, dt_2$$

or

$$L_3(s) = \mathcal{L}[\, f_2(t_2)]\mathcal{L}[\, g(x)] = \mathcal{L}[\, g(x)]^3$$

Continuing in this manner,

$$L_m(s) = \mathcal{L}[\, g(x)]^m$$

Now from Table B of the Appendix

$$\mathcal{L}[\, g(x)] = \lambda^n \mathcal{L}\left[\frac{x^{n-1}}{\Gamma(n)} e^{-\lambda x}\right] = \frac{\lambda^n}{(s + \lambda)^n} = \left(1 + \frac{s}{\lambda}\right)^{-n}$$

and

$$\mathcal{L}[\, g(x)]^m = \left(1 + \frac{s}{\lambda}\right)^{-mn}$$

Again from Table B of the Appendix,

$$f_m(t_m) = \frac{\lambda^{mn}}{\Gamma(mn)} t_m^{mn-1} e^{-\lambda t_m}, \qquad 0 < t_m < \infty$$

and the sum of m independent identically distributed gamma random variables, each with parameters λ and n, is also gamma distributed with parameters λ and mn. ∎

Differential Equations

The Laplace transformation probably finds its most widespread application in the solution of linear ordinary differential equations with constant coefficients. If $f'(t)$ is the first derivative of $f(t)$, then

$$\mathcal{L}[f'(t)] = \int_0^\infty f'(t)e^{-st}\,dt \tag{6.33}$$

Letting

$$u = e^{-st}, \qquad du = f'(t)\,dt$$

and integrating by parts yields

$$\mathcal{L}[f'(t)] = f(t)e^{-st}\big|_0^\infty + s\int_0^\infty f(t)e^{-st}\,dt$$
$$= -f(0) + s\mathcal{L}[f(t)] = -f(0) + sL(s) \tag{6.34}$$

By a similar argument it can be shown that the Laplace transform of the nth derivative of $f(t)$ is defined by

$$[f^n(t)] = s^n L(s) - \sum_{j=1}^{n} s^{n-j} f^{j-1}(0) \tag{6.35}$$

Since the Laplace transform of the nth derivative of $f(t)$ can be expressed in terms of the Laplace transform of $f(t)$, the solution of many differential equations can be obtained with relative ease. As Eq. (6.35) indicates, the solution requires definition of $f^{j-1}(0)$, $j = 1, 2, \ldots, n$, called the boundary conditions for the problem.

Example 6.13   Solve the following differential equations using Laplace transforms:

(a) $2f(t) - 3f'(t) + f^2(t) = 0$, $f(0) = 1$, $f'(0) = 0$;
(b) $f(t) + f^2(t) - 2 = t^2$, $f(0) = f'(0) = 0$;
(c) $f'(t) + f^2(t) + \sin(t) = \cos(t)$, $f(0) = 0$, $f'(0) = 1$.

For part (a), the Laplace transform of the differential equation is given by

$$\mathcal{L}\left[2f(t) - 3f'(t) + f^2(t)\right]$$

$$= 2\mathcal{L}\left[f(t)\right] - 3\mathcal{L}\left[f'(t)\right] + \mathcal{L}\left[f^2(t)\right]$$

$$= 2L(s) - 3sL(s) + 3f(0) + s^2L(s) - sf(0) - f'(0)$$

$$= L(s)(s^2 - 3s + 2) + \left[f(0)(3 - s) - f'(0)\right] = 0$$

Thus

$$L(s) = \frac{s - 3}{(s - 1)(s - 2)}$$

By partial fraction expansion

$$L(s) = \frac{c_{11}}{(s - 1)} + \frac{c_{21}}{(s - 2)}$$

and

$$c_{11} = \lim_{s \to 1}(s - 1)L(s) = \lim_{s \to 1}\left[\frac{s - 3}{s - 2}\right] = 2$$

$$c_{21} = \lim_{s \to 2}(s - 2)L(s) = \lim_{s \to 2}\frac{s - 3}{s - 1} = -1$$

and

$$L(s) = \frac{2}{(s - 1)} - \frac{1}{(s - 2)}$$

or

$$f(t) = 2e^t - e^{2t}$$

To check this solution note that

$$f'(t) = 2e^t - 2e^{2t}, \qquad f^2(t) = 2e^t - 4e^{2t}$$

and

$$2f(t) - 3f'(t) + f^2(t) = (4e^t - 2e^{2t}) - (6e^t - 6e^{2t}) + (2e^t - 4e^{2t}) = 0$$

In part (b),

$$\mathcal{L}\left[f(t) + f^2(t) - 2\right] = \mathcal{L}\left[t^2\right]$$

Now

$$\mathcal{L}\left[f(t) + f^2(t) - 2\right] = L(s) + s^2L(s) - sf(0) - f'(0) - (2/s)$$

$$= L(s)(s^2 + 1) - \left[sf(0) + f'(0) + (2/s)\right]$$

and

$$\mathcal{L}[t^2] = \frac{2}{s^3}$$

Therefore

$$L(s)(s^2 + 1) = \frac{2}{s^3} + \frac{2}{s}$$

since $f(0) = f'(0) = 0$. Therefore

$$L(s) = \frac{2(s^2 + 1)}{s^3(s^2 + 1)} = \frac{2}{s^3}$$

and

$$f(t) = t^2$$

Again checking this solution

$$f^2(t) = 2 \quad \text{and} \quad f(t) + f^2(t) - 2 = t^2 + 2 - 2 = t^2$$

For part (c),

$$\mathcal{L}[f'(t) + f^2(t) + \sin(t)] = \mathcal{L}[\cos(t)]$$

and

$$\mathcal{L}[f'(t) + f^2(t) + \sin(t)] = [sL(s) - f(0)] + [s^2L(s) - sf(0) - f'(0)]$$

$$+ \frac{1}{s^2 + 1} = s(s + 1)L(s) + \frac{1}{s^2 + 1} - 1$$

$$\mathcal{L}[\cos(t)] = \frac{s}{s^2 + 1}$$

Therefore

$$s(s + 1)L(s) = \frac{s - 1}{s^2 + 1} + 1 = \frac{s(s + 1)}{s^2 + 1}$$

or

$$L(s) = \frac{1}{s^2 + 1}$$

and from Table B of the Appendix,

$$f(t) = \sin(t)$$

Checking this solution we have

$$f'(t) = \cos(t), \quad f^2(t) = -\sin(t)$$

and

$$f'(t) + f^2(t) + \sin(t) = \cos(t) - \sin(t) + \sin(t) = \cos(t) \quad \blacksquare$$

Example 6.14 Units arrive to a single channel service system one at a time. The time between successive arrivals is exponentially distributed with parameter $\lambda > 0$. Service time for arrivals is also exponentially distributed but with parameter $\mu > 0$, where $\lambda < \mu$. No waiting line is allowed for arriving customers. Hence the number of units in the system at any point in time may not exceed one. Let $P_i(t)$ be the probability that i units are in the system at time t, $i = 0, 1$. Thus

$$P_1(t) = 1 - P_0(t)$$

The behavior of the system can be described by the differential equation

$$\frac{\lambda + \mu}{\mu} P_0(t) + \frac{1}{\mu} P_0'(t) = 1$$

If the system is empty at $t = 0$, find $P_0(t)$ and $P_1(t)$.

The Laplace transform of the differential equation is

$$\frac{\lambda + \mu}{\mu} L(s) + \frac{1}{\mu} [sL(s) - P_0(0)] = \frac{1}{s}$$

where

$$L(s) = \mathcal{L}[P_0(t)]$$

Thus

$$L(s)\left(\frac{\lambda + \mu + s}{\mu}\right) = \frac{1}{s} + \frac{P_0(0)}{\mu}$$

Since the system is assumed to be empty at $t = 0$, $P_0(0) = 1$ and

$$L(s)\left(\frac{\lambda + \mu + s}{\mu}\right) = \frac{\mu + s}{s\mu}, \quad \text{or} \quad L(s) = \frac{\mu + s}{s(\lambda + \mu + s)}$$

From Table B of the Appendix,

$$P_0(t) = \frac{\mu + \lambda e^{-(\lambda + \mu)t}}{\lambda + \mu}$$

Since $P_1(t) = 1 - P_0(t)$,

$$P_1(t) = 1 - \frac{\mu + \lambda e^{-(\lambda + \mu)t}}{\lambda + \mu} = \frac{\lambda}{\lambda + \mu}\left[1 - e^{-(\lambda + \mu)t}\right] \quad \blacksquare$$

Integral and Integrodifferential Equations

The use of the Laplace transform in the solution of differential equations can be extended to the solution of integral equations and integrodifferential equations. An integral equation has the general form

$$f(t) = g(t) + \int_{a(t)}^{b(t)} h(x, t) f(x) \, dx \qquad (6.36)$$

where $g(t)$ and $h(x, t)$ are known functions and $f(t)$ is to be determined. An important class of integral equations is that in which the integral in Eq. (6.36) is a convolution. In this case the integral equation is given by

$$f(t) = g(t) + \int_0^t h(t - x) f(x) \, dx \qquad (6.37)$$

Applying the Laplace transform to the solution of (6.37) let

$$L_g(s) = \mathcal{L}[g(t)], \qquad L_h(s) = \mathcal{L}[h(t)], \qquad L_f(s) = \mathcal{L}[f(t)]$$

Then

$$L_f(s) = L_g(s) + L_f(s) L_h(s) \qquad (6.38)$$

or

$$L_f(s) = \frac{L_g(s)}{1 - L_h(s)} \qquad (6.39)$$

Example 6.15   The expected number of failures of a piece of equipment in the interval $(0, t)$ is given by the mean value function $m(t)$. If $f(t)$ is the probability density function of the time between successive failures, then

$$m(t) = \int_0^t f(x) \, dx + \int_0^t m(t - x) f(x) \, dx$$

Time until failure is exponentially distributed with probability density function

$$f(x) = \lambda e^{-\lambda x}, \qquad 0 < x < \infty$$

Define $m(t)$.

Let the Laplace transforms of $m(t)$ and $f(x)$ be defined by

$$L_m(s) = \mathcal{L}[m(t)], \qquad L_f(s) = \mathcal{L}[f(t)]$$

Now

$$\mathcal{L}\left[\int_0^t f(x) \, dx \right] = \frac{1}{s} L_f(s)$$

$$\mathcal{L}\left[\int_0^t m(t - x) f(x) \, dx \right] = L_m(s) L_f(s)$$

and

$$L_m(s) = \frac{L_f(s)}{s} + L_m(s) L_f(s)$$

or

$$L_m(s) = \frac{L_f(s)}{s[1 - L_f(s)]}$$

Now

$$L_f(s) = \frac{\lambda}{s + \lambda} \qquad \text{and} \qquad L_m(s) = \frac{\lambda}{s^2}$$

Therefore

$$m(t) = \lambda t \quad \blacksquare$$

An integrodifferential equation is one which contains both the integral and derivatives of the function to be determined. An example of such an equation is

$$f(t) = f'(t) + f^2(t) + \int_0^t f(x)\, dx$$

The Laplace transform can be applied to the solution for $f(t)$ in a manner similar to that in the case of differential and integral equations. Of course conditions for $f(t)$ and its derivatives at $t = 0$ must be defined, since the equation contains derivatives of $f(t)$.

Example 6.16   Given the equation

$$5f'(t) + \int_0^t f(x)\, dx = 10$$

determine $f(t)$ if $f(0) = 0$.

Taking Laplace transforms we have

$$\mathcal{L}[f'(t)] = sL(s) - f(0) = sL(s), \qquad \mathcal{L}\left[\int_0^t f(x)\,dx\right] = \frac{L(s)}{s}, \qquad \mathcal{L}[10] = \frac{10}{s}$$

and

$$5sL(s) + \frac{L(s)}{s} = \frac{10}{s}, \qquad L(s)\left(\frac{5s^2 + 1}{s}\right) = \frac{10}{s}$$

or

$$L(s) = \frac{10}{5s^2 + 1} = \frac{2}{s^2 + \frac{1}{5}}$$

Therefore

$$f(t) = 2\sqrt{5}\, \sin(t/\sqrt{5}) \quad \blacksquare$$

Example 6.17   A circuit consists of an inductance l, resistance R, and capacitance C, connected in series. An electromotive force V is applied at $t = 0$. The current $I(t)$ flowing at t may be determined by solving the following integrodifferential equation:

$$V = RI(t) + lI'(t) + \frac{1}{C}\int_0^t I(x)\,dx$$

If $I(0) = 0$, find $I(t)$.

Taking Laplace transforms we have

$$\mathcal{L}[I(t)] = L(s), \qquad \mathcal{L}[I'(t)] = sL(s) - I(0) = sL(s)$$

$$\mathcal{L}\left[\int_0^t I(x)\,dx\right] = \frac{L(s)}{s}, \qquad \mathcal{L}[V] = \frac{V}{s}$$

and

$$\frac{V}{s} = RL(s) + lsL(s) + \frac{L(s)}{Cs}$$

or

$$L(s) = V/\left[l\left(s^2 + \frac{R}{l} + s + \frac{1}{lC}\right)\right]$$

Since

$$s^2 + \frac{R}{l}s + \frac{1}{lC} = \left[s + \frac{R}{2l} - \sqrt{\frac{R^2}{4l^2} - \frac{1}{lC}}\right]\left[s + \frac{R}{2l} + \sqrt{\frac{R^2}{4l^2} - \frac{1}{lC}}\right]$$

$I(t)$ is given by

$$I(t) = \frac{V}{2l\sqrt{(R^2/4l^2) - (1/lC)}}\left[e^{-Rt/2l + t\sqrt{(R^2/4l^2) - (1/lC)}}\right.$$

$$\left. - e^{-Rt/2l - t\sqrt{(R^2/4l^2) - (1/lC)}}\right] \quad ∎$$

Characteristic Function

The characteristic function is a rather simple variation of the Fourier transform that has gained widespread use in probability theory. If x is a continuous random variable with probability density function $f(x)$, then the characteristic function $\phi_x(\mu)$ of x is

$$\phi_x(\mu) = \int_{-\infty}^{\infty} f(x)e^{i\mu x}\,dx \tag{6.40}$$

with inverse given by

$$f(x) = \phi_x^{-1}(\mu) = \frac{1}{2\pi}\int_{-\infty}^{\infty} \phi_x(\mu)e^{-i\mu x}\,d\mu \tag{6.41}$$

The reader will note that $f(x)$ as given in Eq. (6.41) is actually the Fourier transform of $\phi_x(\mu)$ multiplied by $1/(2\pi)$, while $\phi_x(\mu)$ is the inverse Fourier transform of $f(x)$ multiplied by 2π. Since for every probability density function $f(x)$,

$$\int_{-\infty}^{\infty} f(x)\,dx = 1 \tag{6.42}$$

$f(x)$ is absolutely integrable on $(-\infty, \infty)$, and the characteristic function of x always exists.

The expected value of a function $\psi(x)$ of the random variable x is given by

$$E[\psi(x)] = \int_{-\infty}^{\infty} \psi(x)f(x)\,dx \tag{6.43}$$

Letting

$$\psi(x) = e^{i\mu x}$$

the characteristic function of x may be thought of as the expected value of $e^{i\mu x}$. The characteristic function of a function of x, $\psi(x)$, may be defined in a similar manner as

$$\phi_{\psi(x)}(\mu) = E\left[e^{i\mu\psi(x)}\right] = \int_{-\infty}^{\infty} e^{i\mu\psi(x)}f(x)\,dx \tag{6.44}$$

Moments

As in the case of the Fourier and Laplace transforms, the moments of a random variable x can be obtained from its characteristic function; specifically,

$$m_n = \frac{1}{i^n}\frac{d^n}{d\mu^n}\,\phi_x(\mu)\big|_{\mu=0} = E(x^n) \tag{6.45}$$

if m_n exists.

Convolution

Let x_1 and x_2 be continuous random variables with probability density functions $g(x_1)$ and $h(x_2)$ and characteristic functions $\phi_{x_1}(\mu)$ and $\phi_{x_2}(\mu)$. If $x = x_1 + x_2$, then the probability density function of x, $f(x)$ is given by Eqs. (6.10) or (6.11), and the characteristic function of x is

$$\phi_x(\mu) = \phi_{x_1}(\mu)\phi_{x_2}(\mu) \tag{6.46}$$

The probability density function $f(x)$ of x is then defined by inverting $\phi_x(\mu)$ using a table of characteristic functions, such as that in Table 6.1, or Eq. (6.41). As with the Fourier and Laplace transforms, the inversion equation for $\phi_x(\mu)$ requires complex integration, which may prove quite tedious, and tables are often a convenient alternative in defining $\phi_x^{-1}(\mu)$.

Example 6.18   Let $x_1, x_2, \ldots, x_n$ be independent, identically distributed normal random variables each with mean zero and variance one. Using characteristic functions, show that

$$y = \sum_{j=1}^{n} x_j^2$$

is chi-square distributed.

First consider the random variable x_j^2. Since x_j is normally distributed with mean zero and unit variance, its probability density function is given by

$$f(x_j) = \frac{1}{\sqrt{2\pi}} e^{-x_j^2/2}, \qquad -\infty < x_j < \infty$$

We will first determine the characteristic function of x_j^2 and then the characteristic function of $\sum_{j=1}^{n} x_j^2$. The characteristic function of x_j^2 is given by

$$\phi_{x_j^2}(\mu) = \int_{-\infty}^{\infty} e^{i\mu x_j^2} f(x_j)\, dx_j$$

$$= \int_{-\infty}^{\infty} \frac{1}{\sqrt{2\pi}} e^{-(1-2i\mu)x_j^2/2}\, dx_j.$$

Letting $z = \sqrt{1-2i\mu}\, x_j$ we have

$$\phi_{x_j^2}(\mu) = (1-2i\mu)^{-1/2} \int_{-\infty}^{\infty} \frac{1}{\sqrt{2\pi}} e^{-z^2/2}\, dz = (1-2i\mu)^{-1/2}$$

Since $x_1, x_2, \ldots, x_n$ are independent and identically distributed

$$\phi_y(\mu) = \prod_{j=1}^{n} \phi_{x_j^2}(\mu) = (1-2i\mu)^{-n/2}$$

From Table 6.1, y is chi-square distributed with parameter n called the *degrees of freedom*. ∎

Example 6.19   Using the characteristic function of the Laplace random variable x, find its mean and variance if $\lambda = 1$.

From Table 6.1,

$$\phi_x(\mu) = \frac{e^{i\mu\beta}}{\mu^2 + 1}$$

Table 6.1

Properties of Some Important Continuous Random Variables

Random variable	Probability density function	Moment generating function	Characteristic function	Mean	Variance
Normal	$\dfrac{1}{\sigma\sqrt{2\pi}}\,e^{-(x-m)^2/(2\sigma^2)},\ -\infty < x < \infty$	$e^{[ms+(\sigma^2 s^2/2)]}$	$e^{[i\mu m-(\sigma^2\mu^2/2)]}$	m	σ^2
Exponential	$\lambda e^{-\lambda x},\ 0 < x < \infty$	$[1-(s/\lambda)]^{-1}$	$[1-(i\mu/\lambda)]^{-1}$	λ^{-1}	λ^{-2}
Gamma	$\dfrac{\lambda^n}{\Gamma(n)}\,x^{n-1}e^{-\lambda x},\ 0 < x < \infty$	$[1-(s/\lambda)]^{-n}$	$[1-(i\mu/\lambda)]^{-n}$	$n\lambda^{-1}$	$n\lambda^{-2}$
Chi-square	$\dfrac{1}{2^{n/2}\Gamma(n/2)}\,x^{(n/2)-1}e^{-x/2},\ 0 < x < \infty$	$(1-2s)^{-n/2}$	$(1-2i\mu)^{-n/2}$	n	$2n$
Uniform	$\dfrac{1}{b-a},\ a < x < b$	$\dfrac{e^{bs}-e^{as}}{s(b-a)}$	$\dfrac{e^{i\mu b}-e^{i\mu a}}{i\mu(b-a)}$	$\dfrac{a+b}{2}$	$\dfrac{(b-a)^2}{12}$
Laplace	$(\lambda/2)e^{-\lambda|x-\beta|},\ -\infty < x < \infty$	$\dfrac{\lambda^2 e^{\beta s}}{\lambda^2-s^2}$	$\dfrac{\lambda^2 e^{i\mu\beta}}{\lambda^2+\mu^2}$	β	$\dfrac{2}{\lambda^2}$

and from Eq. (6.45),

$$m_1 = \frac{1}{i} \frac{d}{d\mu} \phi_x(\mu)\big|_{\mu=0}$$

$$= \frac{1}{i} e^{i\mu\beta} \left[\frac{i\beta}{(\mu^2+1)} - \frac{2\mu}{(\mu^2+1)^2} \right]\bigg|_{\mu=0} = \beta$$

$$m_2 = \frac{1}{i^2} \frac{d^2}{d\mu^2} \phi_x(\mu)\big|_{\mu=0}$$

$$= \frac{1}{i^2} e^{i\mu\beta} \left[\frac{i^2\beta^2}{(\mu^2+1)} - \frac{4i\mu\beta}{(\mu^2+1)^2} + \frac{6\mu^2-2}{(\mu^2+1)^3} \right]\bigg|_{\mu=0} = \beta^2 + 2$$

since $i^2 = -1$. The variance of x, σ^2, is given by

$$\sigma^2 = m_2 - m_1^2 = \beta^2 + 2 - \beta^2 = 2$$

and the Laplace random variable has mean β and variance 2. ■

Moment Generating Function

The moment generating function bears a relationship to the Laplace transform similar to that between the characteristic function and the Fourier transform. That is, if $f(x)$ is the probability density function of x, then

$$M_x(s) = \int_{-\infty}^{\infty} e^{sx} f(x)\, dx = E(e^{sx}) \qquad (6.47)$$

Unlike the characteristic function, the moment generating function does not exist for every continuous random variable. Specifically, if $E(e^{sx})$ exists for all s on some interval containing zero, then the moment generating function exists. If $\psi(x)$ is a function of x, then the moment generating function of $\psi(x)$ is

$$M_{\psi(x)}(s) = \int_{-\infty}^{\infty} e^{s\psi(x)} f(x)\, dx \qquad (6.48)$$

As its name might imply, the principal use of the moment generating function is in defining the moments of a random variable if they exist. However, it is also applicable to the derivation of probability density functions of functions of random variables through Eq. (6.48) and convolution as discussed below.

Moments

If it exists, the nth central moment of the random variable x may be defined by

$$m_n = \frac{d^n}{ds^n} M_x(s)\big|_{s=0} = E(x^n) \tag{6.49}$$

Convolution

The moment generating function may be used in a manner identical to the Fourier and Laplace transforms and the characteristic function in defining the distribution of the sum of random variables. Let $x = x_1 + x_2$, where x_1 and x_2 are random variables defined on $(-\infty, \infty)$ with moment generating functions $M_{x_1}(s)$ and $M_{x_2}(s)$ and probability density functions $g(x_1)$ and $h(x_2)$. The probability density function of x is given in Eq. (6.11), and $M_x(s)$ is defined as

$$M_x(s) = M_{x_1}(s)M_{x_2}(s) \tag{6.50}$$

If x_1 and x_2 are restricted to values on $(0, \infty)$, then $f(x)$ is given by Eq. (6.31), but Eq. (6.50) still holds.

Example 6.20 If x is a continuous random variable with probability density function $f(x)$, $a < x < b$, show that $y = -x$ has probability density function $f(-y)$, $-b < y < -a$.
The moment generating function of y is

$$M_y(s) = \int_a^b e^{-sx}f(x)\,dx$$

Let $y = -x$. Then $x = -y$, $dx = -dy$, and

$$M_y(s) = -\int_{-a}^{-b} e^{sy}f(-y)\,dy, \quad \text{or} \quad M_y(s) = \int_{-b}^{-a} e^{sy}f(-y)\,dy$$

Hence the probability density function of y is $f(-y)$, $-b < y < -a$. ∎

Example 6.21 Annual income x_1 to a nonprofit organization is exponentially distributed with parameter λ. Annual cost of operation x_2 is also exponentially distributed with parameter λ. Using the moment generating function, determine the distribution of net annual income x where

$$x = x_1 - x_2$$

From Table 6.1,

$$M_{x_1}(s) = \left(1 - \frac{s}{\lambda}\right)^{-1}$$

For $M_{-x_2}(s)$ we have

$$M_{-x_2}(s) = E(e^{-sx_2}) = \int_0^\infty \lambda e^{-sx_2} e^{-\lambda x_2} dx_2$$

$$= \lambda \int_0^\infty e^{-x_2(s+\lambda)} dx_2 = \frac{\lambda}{s+\lambda} = \left(1 + \frac{s}{\lambda}\right)^{-1}$$

Thus since $x = x_1 + (-x_2)$,

$$M_x(s) = M_{x_1}(s)M_{-x_2}(s) = \left(1 - \frac{s}{\lambda}\right)^{-1}\left(1 + \frac{s}{\lambda}\right)^{-1} = \frac{\lambda^2}{\lambda^2 - s^2}$$

From Table 6.1, x has a Laplace distribution with mean zero and variance $2/\lambda^2$ and

$$f(x) = \frac{\lambda}{2} e^{-\lambda|x|}, \qquad -\infty < x < \infty \quad \blacksquare$$

Example 6.22 In Example 6.21 suppose that

$$x = \beta + x_1 - x_2$$

where $\beta > 0$. Find the probability density function of x.

From Example 6.21,

$$M_{-x_2}(s) = \frac{\lambda}{\lambda + s}$$

For $\beta + x_1$ we have

$$M_{\beta + x_1}(s) = \int_0^\infty e^{(\beta + x_1)s} \lambda e^{-\lambda x_1} dx_1$$

$$= e^{\beta s} \int_0^\infty \lambda e^{x_1 s} e^{-\lambda x_1} dx_1 = \frac{\lambda e^{\beta s}}{\lambda - s}$$

and

$$M_x(s) = \frac{\lambda^2 e^{\beta s}}{(\lambda^2 - s^2)}$$

From Table 6.1, x has the Laplace distribution with mean β, variance $2/\lambda^2$, and

$$f(x) = \frac{\lambda}{2} e^{-\lambda|x - \beta|}, \qquad -\infty < x < \infty \quad \blacksquare$$

Mellin Transform

The final continuous transform to be treated in this chapter is the Mellin transform. As indicated earlier the characteristic and moment generating functions find important applications in determining the distribution of the sum of random variables. The principal application of the Mellin transform is in determining the product and quotient of continuous random variables. Like the other continuous transforms presented here, the Mellin transform may also be used to compute the moments of a random variable.

The Mellin transform of $f(x)$ is defined by

$$F_{M_x}(s) = \int_0^\infty x^{s-1} f(x)\, dx \tag{6.51}$$

The transform may also be defined for $-\infty < x < \infty$, but we will restrict one attention to positive-valued variables. The inverse transform is

$$f(x) = \frac{1}{2\pi i} \lim_{b \to \infty} \int_{c-ib}^{c+ib} x^{-s} F_{M_x}(s)\, ds \tag{6.52}$$

From Eq. (6.51),

$$F_{M_x}(s) = E(x^{s-1}) \tag{6.53}$$

As in the case of the other continuous transforms, a table of transform pairs in the most convenient method for finding the inverse of $F_{M_x}(s)$.

An abbreviated version of such a table is given in Table 6.2.

Example 6.23   Derive the Mellin transform for the chi-square random variable.

The probability density function of the chi-square random variable is given by

$$f(x) = \frac{1}{2^{(n/2)} \Gamma(n/2)} x^{(n/2)-1} e^{-x/2},\ 0 < x < \infty$$

From Eq. (6.52),

$$F_{M_x}(s) = \frac{1}{2^{(n/2)} \Gamma(n/2)} \int_0^\infty x^{s+(n/2)-2} e^{-x/2}\, dx$$

$$= \frac{1}{2^{n/2} \Gamma(n/2)} \frac{\Gamma[s + (n/2) - 1]}{\left(\frac{1}{2}\right)^{s+(n/2)-1}}$$

$$= \frac{\Gamma[s + (n/2) - 1]}{2^{-s+1} \Gamma(n/2)} \qquad \blacksquare$$

Moments

The process of finding the nth moment of a random variable is somewhat simpler for the Mellin transform than for the continuous transforms discussed thus far. In particular,

$$m_n = F_{M_x}(n + 1) \tag{6.54}$$

Table 6.2 Mellin Transform Pairs: $F_{M_x}(s) = \int_0^\infty x^{s-1} f(x)\, dx$

Random variable	Probability density function	$F_{M_x}(s)$
λx		$\lambda^{s-1} F_{M_x}(s)$
x^λ		$F_{M_x}(\lambda s - \lambda + 1)$
$1/x$		$F_{M_x}(2-s)$
$x_1 x_2$		$F_{M_{x_1}}(s) F_{M_{x_2}}(s)$
x_1/x_2		$F_{M_{x_1}}(s) F_{M_{x_2}}(2-s)$
$x_1^{\lambda_1} x_2^{\lambda_2}$		$F_{M_{x_1}}(\lambda_1 s - \lambda_1 + 1) F_{M_{x_2}}(\lambda_2 s - \lambda_2 + 1)$
Exponential	$\lambda e^{-\lambda x},\ 0 < x < \infty$	$(1/\lambda)^{s-1} \Gamma(s)$
Gamma	$\dfrac{\lambda^n}{\Gamma(n)} x^{n-1} e^{-\lambda x},\ 0 < x < \infty$	$(1/\lambda)^{s-1} \dfrac{\Gamma(n+s-1)}{\Gamma(n)}$
Chi-square	$[2^{n/2}\Gamma(n/2)]^{-1} x^{(n/2)-1} e^{-x/2},\ 0 < x < \infty$	$(2)^{s-1}\Gamma[(n/2) + s - 1]/\Gamma(n/2)$
Uniform	$(b-a)^{-1},\ a < x < b$	$(b^s - a^s)/s(b-a)$
Beta	$\dfrac{\Gamma(a+b)}{\Gamma(a)\Gamma(b)} x^{a-1}(1-x)^{b-1},\ 0 < x < 1$	$\dfrac{\Gamma(a+b)\Gamma(a+s-1)}{\Gamma(a+b+s-1)\Gamma(a)}$
F	$\dfrac{\Gamma[(n_1+n_2)/2]}{\Gamma(n_1/2)\Gamma(n_2/2)} (n_1/n_2)^{n_1/2} \dfrac{x^{(n_1/2)-1}}{[1+(n_1/n_2)x]^{(n_1+n_2)/2}},\ 0 < x < \infty$	$\left(\dfrac{n_2}{n_1}\right)^{s-1} \dfrac{\Gamma[(n_1/2)+s-1]\Gamma[(n_2/2)-s+1]}{\Gamma(n_1/2)\Gamma(n_2/2)}$
Weibull	$(a/b^a)x^{a-1}e^{-(x/b)^a},\ 0 < x < \infty$	$b^{s-1}\Gamma[(s+a-1)/a]$
Ratio of i.i.d. exponentials	$1/(x+1)^2,\ 0 < x < \infty$	$\Gamma(s)\Gamma(2-s)$
Product of i.i.d. betas with $b = 1$	$-a^2 x^{a-1}\ln(x),\ 0 < x < 1$	$a^2/(a+s-1)^2$
Product of i.i.d. uniforms with $a = 0,\ b = 1$	$-\ln(x),\ 0 < x < 1$	$1/s^2$
Ratio of i.i.d. uniforms with $0 < a < b$	$\begin{cases} \dfrac{b^2 - a^2/x}{2(b-a)^2}, & a/b < x < 1 \\[2mm] \dfrac{b^2/x - a^2}{2(b-a)^2}, & 1 < x < b/a \end{cases}$	$\dfrac{(b^s - a^s)(b^{2-s} - a^{2-s})}{s(2-s)(b-a)^2}$

That is, the nth moment about zero is calculated simply by replacing s in the Mellin transform by $n + 1$. This property of the transform is demonstrated by noting that the Mellin transform of $f(x)$ is $E(x^{s-1})$. Replacing s by $n + 1$, we have $E(x^n)$, which is the nth moment about xero.

Example 6.24   Find the mean and variance of the beta random variable using the Mellin transform.

From Table 6.2,

$$F_{M_x}(s) = \frac{\Gamma(a + b)\Gamma(a + s - 1)}{\Gamma(a + b + s - 1)\Gamma(a)}$$

Evaluating $F_{M_x}(s)$ at $s = 2$, we have

$$m_1 = \frac{\Gamma(a + b)\Gamma(a + 1)}{\Gamma(a + b + 1)\Gamma(a)} = \frac{a}{a + b}$$

where $\Gamma(n + 1) = n\Gamma(n)$. The second moment about zero is

$$m_2 = F_{M_x}(3) = \frac{\Gamma(a + b)\Gamma(a + 2)}{\Gamma(a + b + 2)\Gamma(a)}$$

$$= \frac{(a + 1)a}{(a + b + 1)(a + b)}$$

and the variance σ^2 of the beta random variable is

$$\sigma^2 = m_2 - m_1^2 = \frac{(a + 1)a}{(a + b + 1)(a + b)} - \left(\frac{a}{a + b}\right)^2$$

$$= \frac{ab}{(a + b + 1)(a + b)^2} \quad \blacksquare$$

Example 6.25   The probability density function of the Maxwell random variable is given by

$$f(x) = \sqrt{\frac{2}{\pi}} \, \lambda^3 x^2 e^{-\lambda^2 x^2/2}, \qquad 0 < x < \infty$$

Derive the Mellin transform of x and find the mean and variance of x.
From Eq. (6.51),

$$F_{M_x}(s) = \int_0^\infty x^{s-1} f(x)\, dx = \sqrt{\frac{2}{\pi}} \, \lambda^3 \int_0^\infty x^{s+1} e^{-\lambda^2 x^2/2}\, dx$$

$$= \frac{2^{(s+1)/2}\Gamma[(s + 2)/2]}{\sqrt{\pi}\, \lambda^{s-1}}$$

The mean of x is

$$m_1 = F_{M_2}(2) = \frac{2^{3/2}}{\lambda \sqrt{\pi}}$$

For m_2 we have

$$m_2 = F_{M_x}(3) = \frac{2^{4/2}\Gamma(5/2)}{\sqrt{\pi}\,\lambda^2} = \frac{3}{\lambda^2}$$

and

$$\sigma^2 = m_2 - m_1^2, \qquad \sigma^2 = \frac{3}{\lambda^2} - \frac{8}{\pi\lambda^2} = \frac{1}{\lambda^2}\left(3 - \frac{8}{\pi}\right) \quad \blacksquare$$

Products and Ratios of Random Variables

The Mellin transform is unique among continuous transforms in that it is a particularly convenient technique for dealing with products or ratios of independent random variables. Let x_1 and x_2 be positive-valued continuous random variables with probability density functions $g(x_1)$ and $h(x_2)$, respectively. Let $x = x_1 x_2$ and let $f(x)$ be the probability density function of x. Then

$$f(x) = \int_0^\infty \frac{1}{x_2} g\left(\frac{x}{x_2}\right) h(x_2)\,dx_2 \tag{6.55}$$

and the Mellin transform $F_{M_x}(s)$ of $f(x)$ is given by

$$F_{M_x}(s) = F_{M_{x_1}}(s) F_{M_{x_2}}(s) \tag{6.56}$$

where $F_{M_{x_1}}(s)$ and $F_{M_{x_2}}(s)$ are the Mellin transforms of x_1 and x_2, respectively.

Now if we let $x = x_1/x_2$, then $f(x)$ is given by

$$f(x) = \int_0^\infty x_2 g(xx_2) h(x_2)\,dx_2 \tag{6.57}$$

and

$$F_{M_x}(s) = F_{M_{x_1}}(s) F_{M_{x_2}}(2 - s) \tag{6.58}$$

In a similar fashion, if $x = 1/x_1$, then

$$F_{M_x}(s) = F_{M_{x_1}}(2 - s) \tag{6.59}$$

Example 6.26 Let x_1 and x_2 be independent chi-square random variables with degrees of freedom (parameters) n_1 and n_2, respectively. If

$$x = \frac{x_1/n_1}{x_2/n_2} \tag{6.60}$$

show that x has an F distribution with n_1 and n_2 degrees of freedom using the Mellin transform.

The Mellin transform of x_i/n_i, $i = 1, 2$, is

$$F_{M_{x_i/n_i}}(s) = \int_0^\infty \left(\frac{x_i}{n_i}\right)^{s-1} \frac{1}{2^{n_i/2}\Gamma(n_i/2)} x_i^{(n_i/2)-1} e^{-x_i/2} \, dx_i$$

$$= \left(\frac{1}{n_i}\right)^{s-1} F_{M_{x_i}}(s)$$

$$= \left(\frac{2}{n_i}\right)^{s-1} \frac{\Gamma[(n_i/2) + s - 1]}{\Gamma(n_i/2)}$$

The Mellin transform of x as defined in Eq. (6.60) may be expressed by Eq. (6.58) or

$$F_{M_x}(s) = F_{M_{x_1/n_1}}(s) F_{M_{x_2/n_2}}(2 - s)$$

where

$$F_{M_{x_1/n_1}}(s) = \left(\frac{2}{n_1}\right)^{s-1} \frac{\Gamma[(n_1/2) + s - 1]}{\Gamma(n_1/2)}$$

and

$$F_{M_{x_2/n_2}}(2 - s) = \left(\frac{2}{n_2}\right)^{1-s} \frac{\Gamma[(n_2/2) - s + 1]}{\Gamma(n_2/2)}$$

Therefore

$$F_{M_x}(s) = \left(\frac{n_2}{n_1}\right)^{s-1} \frac{\Gamma[(n_1/2) + s - 1]\Gamma[(n_2/2) - s + 1]}{\Gamma(n_1/2)\Gamma(n_2/2)}$$

From Table 6.2, x is F distributed with parameters n_1 and n_2. ∎

Example 6.27 The random variable x_1 has a gamma distribution with parameters n and λ. If

$$x = \lambda x_1$$

show that x has a gamma distribution with parameters n and $\lambda = 1$.

From Table 6.2,

$$F_{M_{x_1}}(s) = \left(\frac{1}{\lambda}\right)^{s-1} \frac{\Gamma(n + s - 1)}{\Gamma(n)}$$

Also from Table 6.2,

$$F_{M_{\lambda x_1}}(s) = \lambda^{s-1} F_{M_{x_1}}(s), \qquad F_{M_{\lambda x_1}} = \frac{\Gamma(n + s - 1)}{\Gamma(n)}$$

Hence

$$f(x) = \frac{1}{\Gamma(n)} x^{n-1} e^{-x}, \qquad 0 < x < \infty$$

and x is gamma distributed with parameters n and $\lambda = 1$. ∎

DISCRETE TRANSFORMS

The role of transforms in the analysis of functions of discrete variables is similar to that in the case of continuous variables. In this section we shall present the Z and geometric transforms as well as extensions of the characteristic and moment generating functions to discrete random variables. The application of the Z and geometric transforms to the solution of difference equations, the discrete analog of differential equations, will be presented along with methods for determining the moments of discrete functions and the sum of independent discrete random variables. The applications of the characteristic and moment generating functions for discrete random variables are much the same as those presented for continuous random variables.

Geometric Transform

Let $f(x)$ be a function of the integer-valued variable x, $x = 0, 1, 2, \ldots$. The geometric transform of $f(x)$, if it exists, is

$$G[f(x)] = G_x(z) = \sum_{x=0}^{\infty} z^x f(x) \tag{6.61}$$

The geometric transform of $f(x)$ exists if $\sum_{x=0}^{\infty} z^x f(x)$ converges for all z on $(-1, 1)$. The series $\sum_{x=0}^{\infty} z^x f(x)$ can be shown to converge if $\sum_{x=0}^{\infty} f(x)$ converges as follows. Assume $\sum_{x=0}^{\infty} f(x)$ converges. Then for z on the interval $(-1, 1)$,

$$z^x f(x) \leqslant f(x) \tag{6.62}$$

for all x. Thus

$$\sum_{x=0}^{\infty} z^x f(x) \leqslant \sum_{x=0}^{\infty} f(x) \tag{6.63}$$

and if $\sum_{x=0}^{\infty} f(x)$ converges, $\sum_{x=0}^{\infty} z^x f(x)$ converges also.

Analytic definition of $f(x)$ given $G_x(z)$ is usually more easily obtained from the geometric transform than was the case with the continuous transforms presented in the preceding section. In particular, if $G_x(z)$ is the geometric transform of $f(x)$, then

$$f(x) = \frac{1}{x!} \frac{d^x}{dz^x} G_x(z)\big|_{z=0} \tag{6.64}$$

Although application of Eq. (6.64) is rather straightforward, it may prove tedious, and tables of geometric transform pairs may simplify the inversion process considerably. A short table of geometric transform pairs is given in Table C of the Appendix.

When $f(x)$ is the probability mass function (p.m.f.) of a discrete random variable, the geometric transform is often referred to as the *probability generating function*. Since $G_x(z)$ exists if $\sum_{x=0}^{\infty} f(x)$ converges, the geometric transform always exists for a discrete random variable as

$$\sum_{x=0}^{\infty} f(x) = 1 \tag{6.65}$$

if $f(x)$ is a probability mass function. Further, if $f(x)$ is a probability mass function, then the geometric transform is simply the expected value of z^x, or

$$G_x(z) = E(z^x) \tag{6.66}$$

Example 6.28 The Poisson random variable has the probability mass function given by

$$f(x) = \frac{\lambda^x}{x!} e^{-\lambda}, \qquad x = 0, 1, 2, \ldots$$

Find the geometric transform (probability generating function) of $f(x)$ and invert the transform to obtain $f(x)$.

From Eq. (6.61),

$$G_x(z) = \sum_{x=0}^{\infty} z^x f(x) = \sum_{x=0}^{\infty} z^x \frac{\lambda^x}{x!} e^{-\lambda}$$

Now

$$\sum_{x=0}^{\infty} \frac{a^x}{x!} = e^a$$

Hence

$$G_x(z) = e^{\lambda z} e^{-\lambda} = e^{-\lambda(1-z)}$$

To find the inverse of $G_x(z)$, we apply Eq. (6.64)

$$f(x) = \frac{1}{x!} \frac{d^x}{dz^x} G_x(z)\big|_{z=0}$$

The xth derivative of $G_x(z)$ with respect to z is

$$\frac{d^x}{dz^x} G_x(z) = \frac{d^x}{dz^x} \left[e^{-\lambda(1-z)} \right] = \lambda \frac{d^{x-1}}{dz^{x-1}} \left[e^{-\lambda(1-z)} \right]$$

$$= \lambda^x e^{-\lambda(1-z)}$$

at $z = 0$, $e^{-\lambda(1-z)} = e^{-\lambda}$ and

$$f(x) = \frac{\lambda^x}{x!} e^{-\lambda} \quad \blacksquare$$

Example 6.29   Show that

$$G(x^k) = z \frac{d}{dz} G(x^{k-1})$$

By definition of the geometric transform of x^{k-1},

$$G(x^{k-1}) = \sum_{x=0}^{\infty} x^{k-1} z^x$$

Now

$$\frac{d}{dz} G(x^{k-1}) = \frac{d}{dz} \sum_{x=0}^{\infty} x^{k-1} z^x = \sum_{x=0}^{\infty} x^{k-1} \frac{d}{dz} z^x = \sum_{x=0}^{\infty} x^k z^{x-1}$$

Multiplying by z yields

$$z \sum_{x=0}^{\infty} x^k z^{k-1} = \sum_{x=0}^{\infty} x^k z^x = G(x^k)$$

Thus

$$G(x^k) = z \frac{d}{dz} G(x^{k-1}) \quad \blacksquare$$

Example 6.30   Let

$$f(x) = \sum_{i=0}^{x} g(i) h(x - i)$$

Show that

$$G[f(x)] = G[g(x)] G[h(x)]$$

By definition of the geometric transform,

$$G[f(x)] = \sum_{x=0}^{\infty} z^x \sum_{i=0}^{\infty} g(i) h(x - i) = \sum_{x=0}^{\infty} \sum_{i=0}^{x} z^i g(i) z^{x-i} h(x - i)$$

Now consider the double sum

$$\sum_{i=0}^{\infty} \sum_{j=0}^{i} t(j)v(i-j) = \left[t(0)v(0) \right] + \left[t(0)v(1) + t(1)v(0) \right]$$

$$+ \left[t(0)v(2) + t(1)v(1) + t(2)v(0) \right]$$

$$+ \cdots + \left[t(0)v(i) + t(1)v(i-1) + \cdots \right.$$

$$+ \left. t(i)v(0) \right] + \cdots$$

$$= t(0) \sum_{k=0}^{\infty} v(k) + t(1) \sum_{k=0}^{\infty} v(k)$$

$$+ t(2) \sum_{k=0}^{\infty} v(k) + \cdots + t(i) \sum_{k=0}^{\infty} v(k) + \cdots$$

$$= \sum_{j=0}^{\infty} t(j) \sum_{i=j}^{\infty} v(i-j)$$

and

$$G[f(x)] = \sum_{i=0}^{\infty} z^i g(i) \sum_{x=i}^{\infty} z^{x-i} h(x-i) = \sum_{i=0}^{\infty} z^i g(i) \sum_{k=0}^{\infty} z^k h(k)$$

Therefore

$$G[f(x)] = G[g(x)]G[h(x)] \quad \blacksquare$$

Moments

The moments of $f(x)$ can be obtained from the geometric transform in a manner similar to that employed for the continuous transforms. However, the algebraic manipulation for moments of higher order is more complicated than was the case with continuous transforms. Recall that $G_x(z)$ is given by

$$G_x(z) = \sum_{x=0}^{\infty} z^x f(x)$$

Taking first derivatives of both sides with respect to z yields

$$\frac{d}{dz} G_x(z) = \sum_{x=0}^{\infty} xz^{x-1} f(x) \qquad (6.67)$$

Evaluating $G_x'(z)$ at $z = 1$ yields

$$G_x'(1) = \sum_{x=0}^{\infty} xf(x) \qquad (6.68)$$

or

$$m_1 = G'_x(1) \tag{6.69}$$

The second derivative of $G_x(z)$ at $z = 1$ is

$$G''_x(1) = \sum_{x=0}^{\infty} x(x-1)z^{x-2}f(x)|_{z=1} = \sum_{x=0}^{\infty} x(x-1)f(x)$$

$$= \sum_{x=0}^{\infty} x^2 f(x) - \sum_{x=0}^{\infty} xf(x) = m_2 - m_1 \tag{6.70}$$

Hence

$$m_2 = G''_x(1) + G'_x(1) \tag{6.71}$$

For the nth derivative of $G_x(z)$ at $z = 1$ we have

$$G_x^n(1) = \sum_{x=0}^{\infty} x(x-1)(x-2) \cdots (x-n+1)z^{x-n}f(x)|_{z=1}$$

$$= \sum_{x=0}^{\infty} x(x-1)(x-2) \cdots (x-n+1)f(x) \tag{6.72}$$

The right-hand side of Eq. (6.72) is called the nth factorial moment of $f(x)$ and is denoted by $m_{(n)}$. Let

$$x^{(n)} = x(x-1)(x-2) \cdots (x-n+1) = \frac{x!}{(x-n)!} \tag{6.73}$$

Then

$$m_{(n)} = \sum_{x=0}^{\infty} x^{(n)}f(x) \tag{6.74}$$

To define m_3 we have

$$m_{(3)} = G_x^3(1) = \sum_{x=0}^{\infty} x(x-1)(x-2)f(x) \tag{6.75}$$

or

$$m_{(3)} = \sum_{x=0}^{\infty} (x^3 - 3x^2 + 2x)f(x) = m_3 - 3m_2 + 2m_1 \tag{6.76}$$

and

$$m_3 = m_{(3)} + 3m_2 + 2m_1 = G_x^3(1) + 3G_x^2(1) + G'_x(1) \tag{6.77}$$

Higher-order moments may be calculated in a similar manner.

Example 6.31   The probability mass function of the Poisson random variable is defined by

$$f(x) = \frac{\lambda^x}{x!} e^{-\lambda}, \qquad x = 0, 1, 2, \ldots$$

Find the mean and variance of x.

From Eq. (6.69),

$$m_1 = G_x'(z)|_{z=1}$$

and from Table C of the Appendix,

$$G_x(z) = e^{-\lambda(1-z)}$$

Thus

$$G_x'(z) = \lambda e^{-\lambda(1-z)} \qquad \text{and} \qquad m_1 = \lambda$$

For the variance of x we must first define $m_{(2)}$.

$$m_{(2)} = G_x^2(z)|_{z=1} = \lambda^2 e^{-\lambda(1-z)}|_{z=1} = \lambda^2$$

and

$$m_2 = m_{(2)} + m_1 = \lambda(\lambda + 1)$$

The variance σ^2 of x is then

$$\sigma^2 = m_2 - m_1^2 = \lambda \qquad \blacksquare$$

Convolution

If x_1 and x_2 are independent, integer-valued discrete random variables, $x_i = 0, 1, 2, \ldots$, $i = 1, 2$, with probability mass functions $g(x_1)$ and $h(x_2)$ and geometric transforms $G_{x_1}(z)$ and $G_{x_2}(z)$, then the probability mass function of $x = x_1 + x_2$ is

$$f(x) = \sum_{x_1=0}^{x} g(x_1)h(x - x_1) \qquad (6.78)$$

and the geometric transform of $f(x)$ is

$$G_x(z) = G_{x_1}(z)G_{x_2}(z) \qquad (6.79)$$

where $x = 0, 1, 2, \ldots$. As with the other transforms already presented, Eq. (6.79) can be extended to the sum of an arbitrary number of independent random variables. That is, if $x = x_1 + x_2 + \cdots + x_n$, then

$$G_x(z) = \prod_{i=1}^{n} G_{x_i}(z) \qquad (6.80)$$

Example 6.32   The independent random variables $x_1, x_2, \ldots, x_n$ are Bernoulli distributed, each with parameter p. Show that $x_1 + x_2 + \cdots + x_n$ is binomially distributed with parameters p and n.

From Table C of the Appendix the geometric transform of the Bernoulli random variable is

$$G_x(z) = [pz + (1-p)]$$

If

$$x = x_1 + x_2 + \cdots + x_n$$

then

$$G_x(z) = [G_x(z)]^n$$

since each of the n random variables is Bernoulli distributed with parameter p. Hence

$$G_x(z) = [pz + (1-p)]^n$$

But from Table C this is the geometric transform of the binomial random variable, and x is binomially distributed with parameters p and n. ∎

Example 6.33   The random variables x_1 and x_2 are independent and geometrically distributed with parameters p_1 and p_2, respectively, where $0 < p_1, p_2 < 1$, and $x_i = 0, 1, 2, \ldots$, $i = 1, 2$. Using geometric transforms, find the distribution of $x_1 + x_2$.

From Table C of the Appendix the geometric transform of x_i is

$$G_{x_i}(z) = \frac{p_i}{1 - (1 - p_i)z}$$

If

$$x = x_1 + x_2$$

then

$$G_x(z) = \frac{p_1 p_2}{[1 - (1 - p_1)z][1 - (1 - p_2)z]}$$

The inverse of $G_x(z)$ is not given in Table C. However, by partial fraction expansion we have

$$c_{11} = \lim_{z \to 1/(1-p_1)} [1 - (1 - p_1)z] G_x(z)$$

$$= \lim_{z \to 1/(1-p_1)} \frac{p_1 p_2}{[1 - (1 - p_2)z]} = \frac{p_1 p_2 (1 - p_1)}{p_2 - p_1}$$

$$c_{21} = \lim_{z \to 1/(1-p_2)} [1 - (1 - p_2)z] G_x(z)$$

$$= \lim_{z \to 1/(1-p_2)} \frac{p_1 p_2}{[1 - (1 - p_1)z]} = \frac{p_1 p_2 (1 - p_2)}{p_1 - p_2}$$

and

$$G_x(z) = \frac{p_1 p_2 (1 - p_1)}{(p_2 - p_1)[1 - (1 - p_1)z]} + \frac{p_1 p_2 (1 - p_2)}{(p_1 - p_2)[1 - (1 - p_2)z]}$$

From Table C of the Appendix,

$$G_x^{-1}\left[\frac{1}{1 - (1 - p_i)z}\right] = (1 - p_i)^x$$

Thus

$$f(x) = \frac{p_1 p_2}{p_2 - p_1}(1 - p_1)^{x+1} + \frac{p_1 p_2}{p_1 - p_2}(1 - p_2)^{x+1}$$

$$= \frac{p_1 p_2}{p_1 - p_2}[(1 - p_2)^{x+1} - (1 - p_1)^{x+1}], \qquad x = 0, 1, 2, \ldots \quad \blacksquare$$

Difference Equations

The discrete analog of the differential equation is the difference equation. A difference equation relates $f(x)$ to first- or higher-order differences $\Delta^n f(x)$ over a defined range of values of x. As the geometric transform is a linear operator, it should not be surprising that is a useful tool in solving difference equations as the Laplace transform is in the case of differential equations.

Consider the difference equation given by

$$a_2 \Delta^2 f(x) + a_1 \Delta f(x) + a_0 f(x) = s(x), \qquad x = 0, 1, 2, \ldots \quad (6.81)$$

Applying the geometric transform to both sides of the equation, we have

$$a_2 \frac{(1 - z)^2 G_x(z) - (1 - 2z)f(0) - zf(1)}{z^2}$$
$$+ a_1 \frac{(1 - z)G_x(z) - f(0)}{z} + a_0 G_x(z) = G[s(x)] \qquad (6.82)$$

To determine the function $f(x)$ that satisfies Eq. (6.81), we first solve Eq. (6.82) for $G_x(z)$. The solution for $G_x(z)$ requires definition of the geometric transform of $s(x)$ and specification of $f(0)$ and $f(1)$. Once $G_x(z)$ is defined, $G_x^{-1}(z)$ yields the required solution for $f(x)$.

Example 6.34 Determine the function $f(x)$ which satisfies the difference equation

$$\Delta f(x) - 3f(x) = 0$$

if $f(0) = 2$.

The geometric transform of the difference equation is

$$G_x[\Delta f(x) - 3f(x)] = G_x[\Delta f(x)] - 3G_x[f(x)]$$
$$= (z^{-1} - 1)G_x(z) - 3G_x(z) - z^{-1}f(0)$$
$$= (z^{-1} - 4)G_x(z) - \frac{f(0)}{z}$$

where

$$G_x(z) = G[f(x)]$$

Hence

$$G_x(z) = \frac{2}{1 - 4z} \quad \text{and} \quad G_x^{-1}(z) = 2(4^x)$$

or

$$f(x) = 2(4^x), \qquad x = 0, 1, 2 \ldots \quad \blacksquare$$

Example 6.35   A single-channel queueing system serves units one at a time. The time required to service a unit is exponentially distributed with parameter μ. The time between successive arrivals is also exponentially distributed but with parameter λ, $\lambda < \mu$. If x is the steady-state number of units in the system, then the probability mass function $f(x)$ of x, satisfies the relationship

$$-\lambda \Delta f(x) + \mu \Delta f(x + 1) = 0, \qquad x = 0, 1, 2, \ldots$$

where

$$f(1) = \frac{\lambda}{\mu} f(0) \quad \text{and} \quad \sum_{x=0}^{\infty} f(x) = 1$$

Determine the probability mass function of x.

Let $G_x(z)$ be the geometric transform of $f(x)$. Taking the geometric transform of the difference equation yields

$$G[-\lambda \Delta f(x) + \mu \Delta f(x + 1)] = -\lambda G[\Delta f(x)] + \mu G[\Delta f(x + 1)]$$

Now from Table C of the Appendix,

$$G[\Delta f(x)] = \frac{(1 - z)G_x(z) - f(0)}{z}$$

and

$$G[\Delta f(x + 1)] = G[f(x + 2)] - G[f(x + 1)]$$
$$= \frac{G_x(z) - f(0) - zf(1)}{z^2} - \frac{G_x(z) - f(0)}{z}$$

Thus

$$G\left[-\lambda\Delta f(x) + \mu\Delta f(x+1)\right] = -\frac{\lambda(1-z)G_x(z) - \lambda f(0)}{z}$$

$$+ \frac{\mu G_x(z) - \mu f(0) - \mu z f(1)}{z^2} - \frac{\mu G_x(z) - \mu f(0)}{z}$$

Noting that $f(1) = (\lambda/\mu)f(0)$,

$$G\left[-\lambda\Delta f(x) + \mu\Delta f(x+1)\right] = (1/z^2)\left[-\lambda z(1-z)G_x(z) + \lambda z f(0) + \mu G_x(z)\right.$$

$$\left. - \mu f(0) - \lambda z f(0) - \mu z G_x(z) + \mu z f(0)\right]$$

$$= \frac{(1-z)}{z^2}\left[(\mu - \lambda z)G_x(z) - \mu f(0)\right] = 0$$

and for $G_x(z)$ we have

$$G_x(z) = \frac{\mu f(0)}{\mu - \lambda z} = \frac{f(0)}{1 - (\lambda/\mu)z}$$

Finally,

$$f(x) = f(0)\left(\frac{\lambda}{\mu}\right)^x$$

Since $\sum_{x=0}^{\infty} f(x) = 1$, we have

$$f(0) + \sum_{x=1}^{\infty} f(x) = f(0) + f(0)\sum_{x=1}^{\infty}\left(\frac{\lambda}{\mu}\right)^x$$

$$= f(0) + f(0)\left[\sum_{x=0}^{\infty}\left(\frac{\lambda}{\mu}\right)^x - 1\right]$$

Hence

$$f(0) = 1 - \frac{\lambda}{\mu} \qquad \text{and} \qquad f(x) = \left(\frac{\lambda}{\mu}\right)^x\left(1 - \frac{\lambda}{\mu}\right) \quad \blacksquare$$

Example 6.36   A sum of money $S(0)$ is invested at time 0 at an interest rate of i per time period. If $S(x)$ is the value of the investment at time period x, then $S(x)$ satisfies the difference equation

$$\Delta S(x) - iS(x) = 0$$

Express $S(x)$ in terms of $S(0)$.

The geometric transform of the difference equation is

$$G\left[\Delta S(x) - iS(x)\right] = \frac{(1-z)}{z}G_x(z) - \frac{S(0)}{z} - iG_x(z)$$

or

$$G_x(z)\left[\frac{(1-z)}{z} - i\right] = \frac{S(0)}{z} \quad \text{and} \quad G_x(\dot{z}) = \frac{S(0)}{1-(1+i)z}$$

From Table C of the Appendix,

$$S(x) = (1+i)^x S(0) \quad \blacksquare$$

Z Transform

The Z transform is closely related to the geometric transform; both find similar applications. The Z transform of $f(x)$ is defined as follows:

$$Z[f(x)] = Z_x(z) = \sum_{x=0}^{\infty} z^{-x} f(x) \tag{6.83}$$

$Z_x(z)$ exists if the series in Eq. (6.83) converges for $|z| > 1$. A table of Z transform pairs is given in Table D of the Appendix.

The Z transform of the convolution of the functions $g(x)$ and $h(x)$ is given by

$$Z_x(z) = Z[g(x)]Z[h(x)] \tag{6.84}$$

Central moments may be obtained from the Z transform in a manner similar to that for the geometric transform. Taking the first derivative of $Z_x(z)$ with respect to z yields

$$Z_x'(z) = \sum_{x=0}^{\infty} - xz^{-x-1}f(x) \tag{6.85}$$

Hence

$$m_1 = -Z_x'(1) \tag{6.86}$$

Further

$$Z_x^2(z) = \sum_{x=0}^{\infty} x(x+1)z^{-x-2}f(x) \tag{6.87}$$

Letting

$$x^{[n]} = x(x+1)\cdots(x+n-1) = \frac{(x+n-1)!}{(x-1)!} \tag{6.88}$$

we have

$$m_{[2]} = Z_x^2(1) \tag{6.89}$$

Continuing in this manner,

$$m_{[n]} = \sum_{x=0}^{\infty} x^{[n]} f(x) = (-1)^n Z_x^n(1) \qquad (6.90)$$

If x is a discrete random variable, then

$$m_1 = m_{[1]} = -Z_x'(1) \qquad (6.91)$$

$$m_2 = m_{[2]} - m_{[1]} = Z_x^2(1) + Z_x'(1) \qquad (6.92)$$

and

$$\sigma^2 = Z_x^2(1) + Z_x'(1) - [Z_x'(1)]^2 \qquad (6.93)$$

Example 6.37 Derive the Z transform of the binomial random variable and compute its mean and variance.

The probability mass function of the binomial random variable is

$$f(x) = \binom{n}{x} p^x (1-p)^{n-x}, \qquad x = 0, 1, 2, \ldots, n$$

From Eq. (6.83),

$$Z_x(z) = \sum_{x=0}^{n} z^{-x} \binom{n}{x} p^x (1-p)^{n-x}$$

$$= \sum_{x=0}^{n} \binom{n}{x} (z^{-1}p)^x (1-p)^{n-x} = [z^{-1}p + (1-p)]^n$$

From Eq. (6.91),

$$m_1 = -Z_x'(z)|_{z=1} = \frac{np}{z^2} [z^{-1}p + (1-p)]^{n-1}|_{z=1} = np$$

and from Eq. (6.89),

$$m_{[2]} = Z_x^2(z)|_{z=1}$$

$$= \frac{n(n-1)p^2}{z^4} [z^{-1}p + (1-p)]^{n-2} + \frac{2np}{z^3} [z^{-1}p + (1-p)]^{n-1}|_{z=1}$$

$$= np[(n-1)p + 2]$$

Hence

$$\sigma^2 = np[(n-1)p + 2] - np - (np)^2 = np(1-p) \qquad \blacksquare$$

Example 6.38 Solve the problem in Example 6.36 using the Z transform.

The Z transform of the difference equation in Example 6.36 is

$$Z[\Delta S(x) - iS(x)] = (z-1)Z_x(z) - zS(0) - iZ_x(z)$$

and

$$Z_x(z) = \frac{zS(0)}{z - (1 + i)}$$

Hence from Table D of the Appendix,

$$S(x) = (1 + i)^x S(0)   \blacksquare$$

Example 6.39   Given the difference equation

$$\Delta f(x) - (a - 1)f(x) - b = 0, \qquad x = 0, 1, 2, \ldots$$

define $f(x)$ in terms of $f(0)$, where a and b are constants and $a \neq 1$.
The Z transform of the difference equation is given by

$$Z[\Delta f(x) - (a - 1)f(x) - b] = (z - 1)Z_x(z) - zf(0)$$

$$- (a - 1)Z_x(z) - \frac{bz}{z - 1} = 0$$

Solving for $Z_x(z)$ yields

$$Z_x(x) = \frac{zf(0)}{(z - a)} + \frac{bz}{(z - 1)(z - a)}$$

By partial fraction expansion the second term becomes

$$\frac{bz}{(z - 1)(z - a)} = \frac{b}{(1 - a)(z - 1)} - \frac{ab}{(1 - a)(z - a)}$$

$$= \frac{b}{(1 - a)} \left[\frac{1}{(z - 1)} - \frac{a}{(z - a)} \right]$$

and

$$Z_x(z) = \frac{zf(0)}{(z - a)} + \frac{b}{(1 - a)} \left[\frac{1}{(z - 1)} - \frac{a}{(z - a)} \right]$$

From Table D of the Appendix,

$$Z^{-1} \left[\frac{z}{(z - a)} \right] = a^x$$

$$Z^{-1} \left[\frac{1}{(z - 1)} \right] = 1, \qquad x = 1, 2, \ldots$$

$$Z^{-1} \left[\frac{1}{(z - a)} \right] = a^{x-1}, \qquad x = 1, 2, \ldots$$

and

$$f(x) = f(0)a^x + \frac{b}{(1-a)}[1 - a^x]$$

$$= \left[f(0) - \frac{b}{(1-a)} \right] a^x + \frac{b}{1-a}, \qquad x = 1, 2, \ldots \quad \blacksquare$$

Characteristic Function

The characteristic function plays the same role in the case of discrete random variables as it does in the case of continuous random variables. If x is a discrete random variable with probability mass function $f(x)$, then the characteristic function of x is

$$\phi_x(\mu) = \sum_{x=-\infty}^{\infty} e^{i\mu x} f(x) \qquad (6.94)$$

and its inverse is given by

$$f(x) = \lim_{t \to \infty} \frac{1}{2t} \int_{-t}^{t} e^{-i\mu x} \phi_x(\mu)\, d\mu \qquad (6.95)$$

As in the case of continuous random variables, the characteristic function of a discrete random variable always exists. The characteristic functions of several important discrete random variables are given in Table 6.3. Equations (6.45) and (6.46) are applicable to discrete as well as continuous random variables in determining central moments and the characteristic function of the convolution of random variables, respectively.

Example 6.40   Daily sales x for a particular product have been found to have a geometric distribution with probability mass function

$$f(x) = p(1-p)^x, \qquad x = 0, 1, 2, \ldots$$

where $0 < p < 1$. Derive the characteristic function of x and compute the mean and variance of daily sales.

From Eq. (6.94),

$$\phi_x(\mu) = \sum_{x=0}^{\infty} e^{i\mu x} p(1-p)^x = p \sum_{x=0}^{\infty} \left[e^{i\mu}(1-p) \right]^x = \frac{p}{1 - (1-p)e^{i\mu}}$$

Table 6.3
Properties of Some Important Discrete Random Variables

Random variable	Probability mass function	Moment generating function	Characteristic function	Mean	Variance
Bernoulli	$p^x(1-p)^{1-x}, x=0,1$	$[pe^s+(1-p)]$	$[pe^{iu}+(1-p)]$	p	$p(1-p)$
Binomial	$\binom{n}{x}p^x(1-p)^{n-x}, x=0,1,\ldots,n$	$[pe^s+(1-p)]^n$	$[pe^{iu}+(1-p)]^n$	np	$np(1-p)$
Poisson	$\dfrac{\lambda^x}{x!}e^{-\lambda}, x=0,1,2,\ldots$	$e^{-\lambda(1-e^s)}$	$e^{-\lambda(1-e^{iu})}$	λ	λ
Geometric	$p(1-p)^x, x=0,1,2,\ldots$	$\left[\dfrac{p}{1-(1-p)e^s}\right]$	$\left[\dfrac{p}{1-(1-p)e^{iu}}\right]$	$\dfrac{1-p}{p}$	$\dfrac{1-p}{p^2}$
Geometric	$p(1-p)^{x-1}, x=1,2,3,\ldots$	$\left[\dfrac{pe^s}{1-(1-p)e^s}\right]$	$\left[\dfrac{pe^{iu}}{1-(1-p)e^{iu}}\right]$	$\dfrac{1}{p}$	$\dfrac{1-p}{p^2}$
Rectangular	$\dfrac{1}{b-a+1}, x=a,a+1,\ldots,b$	$\left[\dfrac{e^{(b+1)s}-e^{as}}{(b-a+1)(e^s-1)}\right]$	$\left[\dfrac{e^{(b+1)iu}-e^{aiu}}{(b-a+1)(e^{iu}-1)}\right]$	$\dfrac{a+b}{2}$	$\dfrac{(b+a)^2+2(b-a)}{12}$
Negative binomial	$\binom{n+x-1}{x}p^n(1-p)^x, x=n,n+1,\ldots$	$\left[\dfrac{pe^s}{1-(1-p)e^s}\right]^n$	$\left[\dfrac{pe^{iu}}{1-(1-p)e^{iu}}\right]^n$	$\dfrac{n}{p}$	$\dfrac{n(1-p)}{p^2}$

The first and second central moments of x are given by

$$m_1 = \frac{1}{i} \frac{d}{d\mu} \phi_x(\mu)\big|_{\mu=0} = \frac{1}{i} \frac{d}{d\mu} \left[\frac{p}{1-(1-p)e^{i\mu}} \right]\bigg|_{\mu=0}$$

$$= \frac{ip(1-p)e^{i\mu}}{i[1-(1-p)e^{i\mu}]^2}\bigg|_{\mu=0} = \frac{(1-p)}{p}$$

and

$$m_2 = \frac{1}{i^2} \frac{d^2}{d\mu^2} \phi_x(\mu)\big|_{\mu=0}$$

$$= \frac{1}{i^2} \frac{d}{d\mu} \left\{ \frac{ip(1-p)e^{i\mu}}{[1-(1-p)e^{i\mu}]^2} \right\}\bigg|_{\mu=0}$$

$$+ \frac{i^2 p(1-p)e^{i\mu}[1+(1-p)e^{i\mu}]}{i^2[1-(1-p)e^{i\mu}]^3}\bigg|_{\mu=0} = \frac{(1-p)(2-p)}{p^2}$$

Thus

$$\sigma^2 = m_2 - m_1^2 = \frac{(1-p)(2-p)}{p^2} - \frac{(1-p)^2}{p^2} = \frac{(1-p)}{p^2} \quad \blacksquare$$

Moment Generating Function

Like the characteristic function, the moment generation function may be defined for discrete as well as continuous random variables:

$$M_x(s) = \sum_{x=-\infty}^{\infty} e^{sx} f(x) \tag{6.96}$$

where $f(x)$ is the probability mass function of x. The moment generating function of a discrete random variable exists only if the series in Eq. (6.96) converges for all s on $(-h, h)$ where h is any nonzero positive number. The moment generating functions for several important discrete random variables are given in Table 6.3.

The central moments of a discrete random variable may be obtained from the moment generating function, if it exists, in a manner identical to that defined for continuous random variables and as given in Eq. (6.49). In a similar manner the moment generating function of the sum of discrete random variables may be obtained from Eq. (6.50).

Example 6.41   Derive the moment generating function of the rectangular random variable x, and from the moment generating function determine the mean of x.

The probability mass function of the rectangular random variable is

$$f(x) = \frac{1}{b - a + 1}, \qquad x = a, a + 1, \ldots, b$$

where a and b are integers and $a < b$. From Eq. (6.97), $M_x(s)$ is defined by

$$M_x(s) = \sum_{x=a}^{b} \frac{e^{sx}}{b - a + 1} = \frac{1}{b - a + 1} \sum_{x=a}^{b} e^{sx}$$

From Table A of the Appendix,

$$\Delta^{-1}[e^{sx}] = \frac{e^{sx} - 1}{e^s - 1}$$

and

$$M_x(s) = \frac{1}{b - a + 1} \left[\frac{e^{s(b+1)} - e^{sa}}{e^s - 1} \right]$$

From Eq. (6.49),

$$m_1 = \frac{d}{ds} M_x(s) \Big|_{s=0}$$

$$= \frac{1}{b - a + 1} \left[\frac{be^{s(b+2)} - (b + 1)e^{s(b+1)} - (a - 1)e^{s(a+1)} + ae^{sa}}{(e^s - 1)^2} \right]\Bigg|_{s=0}$$

As the expression for m_1 is indeterminant, we take the derivatives of the numerator and denominator with respect to s and

$$m_1 = \frac{1}{b - a + 1} \left[\frac{b(b + 2)e^{s(b+2)} - (b + 1)^2 e^{s(b+1)} - (a - 1)(a + 1)e^{s(a+1)}}{2e^s(e^s - 1)} \right.$$

$$\left. + \frac{a^2 e^{sa}}{2e^s(e^s - 1)} \right]\Bigg|_{s=0}$$

The expression for m_1 is still indeterminant and we take first derivatives with respect to s, again yielding

$$m_1 = \frac{1}{b - a + 1} \left[\frac{b(b + 2)^2 e^{s(b+2)} - (b + 1)^3 e^{s(b+1)} - (a - 1)(a + 1)^3 e^{s(a+1)}}{2e^s(2e^s - 1)} \right.$$

$$\left. + \frac{a^3 e^{sa}}{2e^s(2e^s - 1)} \right]\Bigg|_{s=0} = \frac{(b - a + 1)(a + b)}{2(b - a + 1)} = \frac{a + b}{2} \quad \blacksquare$$

SUMMARY

This chapter has dealt with a variety of transform methods useful in operations research, particularly in probabilistic modeling. In defining moments and the convolution of functions all of the transform methods serve the same purpose, except the Mellin transform. To this extent the transforms may be used interchangeably and with equal ease depending upon whether the function considered is continuous or discrete.

The most widely used of the continuous transforms presented is the Laplace transform. Its application to problems in all fields of engineering, the physical sciences, as well as operations research is well documented. Undoubtedly the extent of its use is the result of the extensive tabulation of Laplace transform pairs in many references, which facilitates definition of the inverse of the transform.

Among the discrete transforms, the geometric transform is probably used more extensively than the others presented. Analytic inversion of the geometric transform can be accomplished through successive differentiation of the transform. Thus the inversion process is less complicated than in the case of the other continuous and discrete transforms, although it may still prove a tedious task.

The Mellin transform is uniquely useful in dealing with the prdoduct or ratio of continuous independent random variables. However, as extensive tables of Mellin transform pairs are not available, the process of defining the inverse of the transform may prove difficult.

PROBLEMS

1. Find the Fourier transforms of the following:

   (a) $f(t) = t, t > 0$;
   (b) $f(t) = \int_0^t (t - y)^{n-1}/(n - 1)! e^{-y} dy, t > 0$.

2. Derive the Laplace transforms of the following functions:

   (a) $\cos(ct)$;
   (b) $\sin(ct)$;
   (c) $t \cos(ct)$;
   (d) $t \sin(ct)$.

3. If $L(s)$ is the one-sided Laplace transform of $f(t)$, show that the nth moment of $f(t)$ about zero is as given in Eq. (6.19).

4. If $L(s)$ is the Laplace transform of $f(t)$ and $y = t + \alpha$, show that $\mathcal{L}[f(y)] = e^{\alpha s}L(s)$

5. Show that

$$\mathcal{L}\int_0^t [f(x) \, dx] = \frac{1}{s} L(s)$$

where $L(s) = \mathcal{L}[f(x)]$.

6. Show that

$$\mathcal{L}[f^2(t)] = s^2 L(s) - sf(0) - f'(0)$$

7. Solve the following differential equations using the Laplace transform:

  (a) $f^2(t) + 8f'(t) = e^{4t}$, $f'(0) = 1$, $f(0) = 4$;
  (b) $2f^3(t) + f^2(t) + 2f'(t) = 0$, $f^k(0) = 1$, $k = 0, 1, 2$;
  (c) $f^4(t) - 16f(t) = e^t$, $f^k(0) = 0$, $k = 0, 1, 2, 3$.

8. Solve the following differential equations:

  (a) $f^2(t) + f(t) = 2t$, $f(0) = 1$, $f'(0) = -2$;
  (b) $f^3(t) + f'(t) = 2[\cos(t) - \sin(t)]$, $f(0) = 1$, $f'(0) = 0$, $f^2(0) = 2$;
  (c) $f'(t) - \int_0^t f(t - x)\cos(x)\,dx = \cos(t)$, $f(0) = 0$.

9. The probability density function $f(x)$ satisfies the differential equation given by

$$f^2(x) + f'(x) - \lambda^2(\lambda - 1)f(x) = 0$$

  where $f(0) = \lambda$, $f'(0) = -\lambda^2$, $f^2(0) = \lambda^3$. Define $f(x)$.

10. Find the probability density function $f(t)$ satisfying the differential equation

$$f^2(t) + 2\lambda f'(t) + \lambda f(t) = \lambda^3 e^{-\lambda t}, \qquad 0 < t < \infty$$

  where $f(0) = f'(0) = 0$.

11. Let x be a continuous random variable with probability density function $f(x)$ of x, and let y be a function $\psi(x)$ of x. Show that the characteristic function of $\psi(x)$ is given by

$$\phi_{\psi(x)}(\mu) = \int_{-\infty}^{\infty} e^{i\mu\psi(x)} f(x)\,dx$$

  by showing that

$$\phi_{\psi(x)}(\mu) = \int_{-\infty}^{\infty} e^{i\mu y} g(y)\,dy$$

  where $g(y)$ is the probability density function of y.

12. Derive the characteristic functions for the following random variables and find the mean and variance of each from the characteritic function: (a) normal; (b) gamma; (c) uniform; (d) Laplace.

13. Passengers arriving at an airline ticket counter may require ticketing and baggage checking. The time to service those requiring ticketing only is exponentially distributed with parameter λ_1 while passengers requiring ticketing and baggage checking are serviced in an exponential fashion with parameter λ_2, $\lambda_2 < \lambda_1$. If the proportion of customers requiring ticketing only is p, $0 < p < 1$, then service time is hyperexponentially distributed with probability density function

$$f(x) = p\lambda_1 e^{-\lambda_1 x} + (1 - p)\lambda_2 e^{-\lambda_2 x}, \qquad 0 < x < \infty$$

  Derive

  (a) the characteristic function of x,
  (b) the moment generating function of x,

  and compute the mean and variance of x from each of the transforms.

14. The random variable x is uniformly distributed on the interval (a, b). Let

$$F(x) = \int_a^x \frac{dx}{b - a}$$

  where $F(x)$ is the cumulative distribution function of x. Using characteristic functions, show that $F(x)$ is uniformly distributed on the interval $(0, 1)$.

15. The random variables x is uniformly distributed on the interval $(0, 1)$. Let

$$y = \frac{1}{\lambda} \ln(1 - x)$$

Show that y is exponentially distributed with parameter λ using the moment generating function.

16. The probability density function of the truncated exponential random variables is

$$f(x) = \frac{\lambda e^{-\lambda x}}{1 - e^{-\lambda t}}, \qquad 0 < x < t$$

Derive

   (a) the characteristic function of x,
   (b) the moment generating function of x.

Define the mean and variance of x using the transforms in parts (a) and (b).

17. Solve Problem 12 using the moment generating function.

18. The random variable x is uniformly distributed on the interval $(0, 1)$. Let

$$y = -\frac{1}{\lambda} \ln(1 - x)$$

Using the characteristic function, find the probability density function of y.

19. The distribution of waiting time for a single server queue with Poisson arrivals is both discrete and continuous. That is the probability mass density function is given by

$$f(x) = \begin{cases} (1 - \rho), & x = 0 \\ \lambda(1 - \rho)e^{-\mu(1-\rho)x}, & 0 < x < \infty \end{cases}$$

where λ is the arrival rate of customers, μ is the service rate, and $\rho = \lambda/\mu$. Develop the moment generating function of x and determine the mean waiting time for customers.

20. The probability density function of the noncentral chi-square random variable is

$$f(x) = e^{-\lambda} \sum_{i=0}^{\infty} \frac{\lambda^i x^{(1/2)(n+2i) - 1} e^{-x/2}}{i! 2^{(1/2)(n+2i)} \Gamma[(n + 2i)/2]}, \qquad 0 < x < \infty$$

Show that the moment generating function of x is given by

$$M_x(s) = e^{-\lambda} \sum_{i=0}^{\infty} \frac{\lambda^i}{i!} (1 - 2s)^{-((n/2)+i)}$$

21. Let $x_1, x_2, \ldots, x_k$ be independent normal random variables with means $\mu_1, \mu_2, \ldots, \mu_k$, respectively, and each with unit variance, and let

$$x = \sum_{i=1}^{k} x_i^2$$

Show that x has a noncentral chi-square distribution using the moment generating function (see Problem 20).

22. Let $x_1, x_2, \ldots, x_n$ be independent, identically distributed uniform variables on the interval $(0, 1)$, and let

$$y = -\frac{1}{\lambda} \sum_{i=1}^{n} \ln(1 - x_i)$$

Using the moment generating function, find the probability density function of y.

23. The probability mass function of the random variable x is given by

$$f(x) = \frac{6}{\pi^2 x^2}, \qquad x = 1, 2, 3, \ldots$$

Show that the moment generating function of x does not exist.

24. Develop the Mellin transforms for the following random variables: (a) exponential; (b) uniform; (c) F; (d) gamma.

25. Develop the Mellin transform of the noncentral chi-square random variable with probability density function given in Problem 20.

26. The probability density function of the noncentral F random variable is

$$f(x) = e^{-\lambda} \sum_{i=0}^{\infty} \frac{\Gamma(2i + n + m/2)(n/m)^{(1/2)(2i+n)}\lambda^i}{\Gamma(m/2)\Gamma[(2i+n)/2]i!} \frac{x^{(1/2)(2i+n-2)}}{[1 + (nx/m)]^{(1/2)(2i+m+n)}}$$

where $0 < x < \infty$. Show that the Mellin transform of x is

$$F_{M_x}(s) = e^{-\lambda} \sum_{i=0}^{\infty} \frac{\Gamma[(n/2) + 2 + i - 1]\Gamma[(m/2) - s + 1](m/n)^{s-1}}{\Gamma(m/2)\Gamma(2i + n/2)} \frac{\lambda^i}{i!}$$

27. Let x_1 be a noncentral chi-square random variable with parameters λ and n and let x_2 be a chi-square random variable with parameter m. Show that

$$x = \frac{x_1/n}{x_2/m}$$

has a noncentral F distribution using the Mellin transform (see Problems 20 and 26 for the Mellin transforms of x_1 and x_2).

28. Let

$$f(x) = -\ln(x), \qquad 0 < x < 1$$

Show that the Mellin transform of $f(x)$ is $1/s^2$.

29. Let x_1 and x_2 be independent random variables each uniformly distributed on the interval $(0, 1)$. Using the Mellin transform show that the probability density function of $x = x_1 x_2$ is

$$f(x) = -\ln(x), \qquad 0 < x < 1$$

30. A piece of equipment contains two critical elements which are connected in series. Both elements must operate or the equipment fails. The reliability x_1 and x_2 of the elements is beta distributed with parameters a and $b = 1$. The reliability of the equipment x is given by $x_1 x_2$. Using the Mellin transform, find the probability density function of the reliability of the equipment.

31. The volume of input per hour x_1 to a processing facility is exponentially distributed with parameter λ. Output per hour x_2 is also exponentially distributed with parameter λ. Using the Mellin transform, find the probability density function of the ratio of input per hour to output per hour.

32. Derive the Mellin transform of the Weibull random variable (Table 6.2) and from the transform obtain the mean and variance.

33. The random variable y has a chi-square distribution with parameter n. Let

$$x = \sqrt{y/n}$$

Using the Mellin transform, show that y has a chi-square distribution with probability density function

$$f(x) = \frac{2(n/2)^{n/2}}{\Gamma(n/2)} x^{n-1} e^{-nx^2/2}, \qquad 0 < x < \infty$$

34. Location of a machine tool in the $x - y$ axis is performed automatically. The errors in the coordinate directions x_1 and x_2 are normally distributed with mean 0 and variance 1. Hence the square of the resultant error z is

$$z = (1/2)(x_1^2 + x_2^2)$$

Recognizing that $x_1^2 + x_2^2$ is chi-square distributed with $n = 2$, and using the Mellin transform, show that the resultant error $v = \sqrt{z}$ has the probability density function

$$f(v) = 2ve^{-v^2}, \qquad 0 < v < \infty$$

35. Derive the geometric and z transforms for the (a) binomial random variable, (b) geometric random variable, (c) rectangular random variable.

36. Show that the geometric transform of $\Delta^2 f(x)$ is given by

$$G[\Delta^2 f(x)] = \frac{1}{z^2}\left[(1 - z)^2 G_x(z) - f(0)(1 - 2z) - zf(1)\right]$$

where $G_x(z) = G[f(x)]$.

37. Let $x_1, x_2, \ldots, x_n$ be independent Poisson random variables with parameters λ_1, $\lambda_2, \ldots, \lambda_n$, respectively. Using geometric transforms, show that $x_1 + x_2 + \cdots + x_n$ is also Poisson distributed.

38. Let $x_1, x_2, \ldots, x_n$ be independent geometric random variables each with parameter $0 \leqslant p \leqslant 1$ and $x_i = 1, 2, 3, \ldots$, $i = 1, 2, \ldots, n$. Show that $x_1 + x_2 + \cdots + x_n$ has a negative binomial distribution using geometric transforms.

39. Given the geometric transforms for the random variables in Problem 35, derive their probability mass functions.

40. The random variable x is Poisson distributed with probability mass function

$$f(x) = \frac{\lambda^x}{x!} e^{-\lambda}$$

Derive the geometric transform of $y = x + a$, where a is a positive integer, and define the probability mass function of y from the geometric transform.

41. The geometric transform of the production line failures per day x is given by

$$G_x(z) = \frac{2z[(z - 1)(n + 1)z^n - (z^{n+1} - 1)]}{n(n + 1)(z - 1)^2}$$

Find the probability mass function of x using Eq. (6.64).

42. Show that the sum of m independent, identically distributed binomial random variables, each with parameters p and n is also binomially distributed using (a) geometric transforms, (b) z transforms, (c) characteristic functions, (d) moment generating functions.

43. Show that the sum of independent negative binomial random variables is also negative binomially distributed using (a) geometric transforms, (b) z transforms, (c) characteristic functions, (d) moment generating functions.

44. The probability mass function of the truncated geometric random variable is given by

$$f(x) = \frac{p(1 - p)^{x-1}}{1 - (1 - p)^n}, \qquad x = 1, 2, \ldots, n$$

Derive the (a) geometric transform of x, (b) z transform of x, (c) characteristic function of x, (d) moment generating function of x. Define the mean and variance of x from the transforms given in parts (a)–(d).

45. In Problem 19 assume that k channels provide service instead of a single channel. If each channel provides service in an exponential fashion with parameter μ, then the

probability mass function $f(x)$ of the number of units waiting for service is

$$f(x) = \frac{p_0}{k^m k!} \left(\frac{\lambda}{\mu} \right)^{k+m}, \qquad m = 0, 1, 2, \ldots$$

where p_0 is the probability that there are zero units in the system. Find the geometric transform of $f(x)$ and the mean length of the waiting line.

46. The probability mass function $f(x)$ of x satisfies the difference equation

$$\Delta f(x) + pf(x) = 0, \qquad x = 1, 2, \ldots, n - 1$$

where $\sum_{x=1}^{n} f(x) = 1$. Find $f(x)$.

47. Product demand is Poisson distributed with mean rate λ per week and units are demanded one at a time. If inventory position, on hand inventory plus units on order, falls to -1 units, an order for Q units is placed to replenish inventory. Thus inventory position x may vary from 0 to Q units. If $f(x)$ is the probability mass function of x, then $f(x)$ must satisfy the difference equations given by

$$\lambda \Delta f(x) = 0, \qquad x = 0, 1, 2, \ldots, Q - 1$$
$$f(Q) = f(0)$$

Find $f(x)$ using geometric transforms.

48. Solve Problem 37 using (a) Z transforms, (b) characteristic functions, (c) moment generating functions.

49. Solve Problem 38 using (a) Z transforms, (b) characteristic functions, (c) moment generating functions.

50. Solve Problem 45 using the Z transform.

51. Solve Problem 47 using the Z transform.

52. Let x_k be a Poisson random variable with probability mass function

$$f(x_k) = \frac{\lambda_k x_k}{x_k!} e^{-\lambda_k}, \qquad k = 1, 2, 3, \ldots$$

where $\lambda_k = e^{-k}$. Find the characteristic function of y, where

$$y = \sum_{k=1}^{\infty} kx_k$$

Suggested Further Reading

1. Drake, A. W. (1967). "Fundamentals of Applied Probability Theory." McGraw-Hill, New York.
2. Epstein, B. (1948). Some applications of the Mellin transform in statistics, *Ann. Math. Stat.* **19**, 370–379.
3. Giffin, W. C. (1971). "Introduction to Operations Engineering." Irwin, Homewood, Illinois.
4. Giffin, W. C. (1975). "Transform Techniques for Probability Modeling." Academic Press, New York.
5. Goldberg, S. (1961). "Introduction to Difference Equations." Wiley, New York.
6. Hall, D. L., Maple, C. G., and Vinograde, B. (1959). "Introduction to the Laplace Transform." Appleton, New York.
7. LePage, W. R. (1961). "Complex Variables and the Laplace Transform for Engineers." McGraw-Hill, New York.
8. Lukacs, E. (1960). "Characteristic Functions." Griffin, London.

9. Papoulis, A. (1962). "The Fourier Integral." McGraw-Hill, New York.
10. Parzen, E. (1960). "Modern Probability Theory and Its Applications." Wiley (Interscience), New York.
11. Savant, C. J. (1962). "Fundamentals of the Laplace Transformation." McGraw-Hill, New York.
12. Schmidt, J. W. (1974). "Mathematical Foundations For Management Science and Systems Analysis." Academic Press, New York.
13. Weintraub, S. (1949). "Price Theory." Pitman, New York.
14. Widder, D. V. (1971). "An Introduction to Transform Theory." Academic Press, New York.
15. Wylie, C. R. (1960). "Advanced Engineering Mathematics." McGraw-Hill, New York.

Chapter 7 | Applications in Operations Research

INTRODUCTION

To an author the only thing more difficult than writing the last chapter of a text is writing the first chapter. This is particularly true of books dealing with history, mathematics, science, or engineering, in which there is truly never an ending for any topic but rather an infinite series of new beginnings. In this text we have attempted to provide one element in the series of regimented study which leads, ultimately, to the application of operations research techniques in the design and analysis of operational systems. Our stated objective in preparing this text was to provide a vehicle which facilitated the student's transition between the study of mathematics for its own sake and the application of mathematical methods to the solution of problems arising in operations research. Each individual reader must assess for himself or herself to what degree we have been successful.

There are a number of introductory operations research texts currently available. Even the most narrowly forcused of these is considerably longer than this chapter. And, quite frankly, it is not consistent with our objectives to provide more than the barest introduction to, and illustration of, several elementary models and associated analyses. Our objective in this chapter is to present a selected sampling from the menu of things to come when the reader continues the study of operations research. Hopefully, if your appetite is not already whetted, it will be so now.

The format to be followed in these subsequent sections is quite skeletal. A brief introduction to each class of models will be presented along with the elementary analytical techniques applied to each. Following this, one or more example problems will be given and solved. At the end of the chapter several introductory texts will be listed for further study, and a series of practice problems are provided. We shall begin with an application of linear algebra and end with an application of operational methods.

FIRST-ORDER MARKOV CHAINS

When confronted with a fundamental stochastic system (or process) which exhibits the following properties:

(1) The set of all possible states of the system is finite.

(2) The probability of the occurrence of each state is dependent only on the present state of the system.

(3) The above probabilities remain constant throughout the system's operation—it is convenient to consider modeling such a system, for purposes of analysis, as a first-order Markov chain. The descriptive modifer "first-order" arises from property (2) and manifests itself directly in the model which follows—a linear (first-order) algebraic system.

As the system operates, one or more of its states is sequentially manifested. That is, a transition occurs from one state to another. When a new state is realized (i.e., a new outcome occurs), the system is said to have *stepped*. If we define

$S_i \leftrightarrow$ state i of the system, $i = 1, \ldots, m$,

then we can represent the conditional probabilities of state changes occurring in the system as

$P_{ij} \leftrightarrow$ probability of going from S_i to S_j in one step ($\text{pr}\{S_j \mid S_i\}$).

The collection of all conditional, one-step, state change probabilities can then be conveniently displayed in a square *matrix of transition probabilities*:

$$P = \begin{bmatrix} P_{11} & P_{12} & \cdots & P_{1m} \\ P_{21} & P_{22} & \cdots & P_{2m} \\ \vdots & \vdots & & \vdots \\ P_{m1} & P_{m2} & \cdots & P_{mm} \end{bmatrix}$$

There are two basic classifications of first-order Markov chains: *irreducible* and *absorbing*. A determination can be made from the operational characterisitics of the system being modeled as to which class the model represents. However, this determination is often made more conveniently by an examination of the transition matrix P. Each of these basic classifications is described and illustrated below.

Irreducible Chains

An irreducible chain is representative of a system in which it is possible to go eventually from every state to every other state. That is, regardless of the state in which the system starts, there is a nonzero probability associated with realizing every state of the system. To illustrate this point, if we let $P_{ij}^{(n)}$ represent the probability of going from S_i to S_j in n steps, then

$$0 < P_{ij}^{(n)} < 1 \quad \text{for} \quad 0 < n < \infty$$

If this is true for every S_i and S_j, then the Markov chain is irreducible. As a special case, if for some specific value of $n > 0$, every $P_{ij}^{(n)}$ is nonzero, then the chain is said to be *regular*. The elements $P_{ij}^{(n)}$ can be obtained conveniently by multiplying the transition matrix P by itself n times.

An irreducible chain may possess steady-state behavior. In essence, this means that after a large number of steps $(n \to \infty)$, the probabilities

$$P_{ij}^{(n)} = P_{kj}^{(n)} \quad \text{for every} \quad i \text{ and } k \tag{7.1}$$

Interpreting this characteristic leads to the conclusion that, after a sufficiently large number of steps, the probabilities associated with outcomes (states) are independent of the state in which the system's operation begins. Defining the vector $\mathbf{v}_i^{(n)}$ to represent the ith row vector of the transition matrix after n steps,

$$P^{(n)} = \begin{bmatrix} \mathbf{v}_1^{(n)} \\ \mathbf{v}_2^{(n)} \\ \vdots \\ \mathbf{v}_m^{(n)} \end{bmatrix}$$

then at steady state $(n \to \infty)$,

$$\mathbf{v}_1^{(n)} = \mathbf{v}_2^{(n)} = \cdots = \mathbf{v}_m^{(n)} \tag{7.2}$$

Further, it is also true that, at steady state,

$$\mathbf{v}_i^{(n)} = \mathbf{v}_i^{(n+1)} \quad \text{for all} \quad i \tag{7.3}$$

The last statement leads directly to a means for determining what the steady-state probabilities are for each of the system's states. If we let $\mathbf{v}^*$

represent this steady-state vector, then

$$\mathbf{v}^* P = \mathbf{v}^* \tag{7.4}$$

and since these are probabilities of potential outcomes,

$$\sum_{i=1}^{m} v_i^* = 1 \tag{7.5}$$

Note that (7.4) and (7.5) constitute a system of $m + 1$ simultaneous linear equations in the variables v_i^*, $i = 1, \ldots, m$. Further, the homogeneous subsystem of equations represented by (7.4) is not independent. However, if any of the equations in (7.4) is deleted and replaced by Eq. (7.5), the resulting system contains m independent equations which can be solved to obtain the steady-state vector $\mathbf{v}^*$. The following example illustrates a determination of $\mathbf{v}^*$.

Example 7.1   Jim, Dave, and Geoff each opened "stills in the hills" just west of Del Rio. At the end of their first year's operation, the following things had happened:

(1)   Jim kept 85% of his customers; he lost 5% to Dave and 10% to Geoff.

(2)   Dave kept 90% of his customers; he lost 10% to Jim and none to Geoff.

(3)   Geoff kept 70% of his customers; he lost 15% to Jim and 15% to Dave.

Assuming that the market does not expand (i.e., those who die of lead poisoning are replaced by immigrant alcoholics from Needmore) and that buying habits will not change, predict what the equilibrium market shares will be. That is, in the long run, what percentage of the market will each man have?

The above description indicates that it is possible for a customer of any one of these men to become a customer of any one of the others. Further, if the above percentages (as decimal fractions) are interpreted as the probabilities of a customer either changing vendors or remaining with the original seller, then this liquor market system can be represented as an irreducible (and regular) Markov chain. Defining the states of the system as being the vendor from whom a purchase is made, they can be summarized and identified as follows:

State	Description
1	Jim
2	Dave
3	Geoff

A purchase then becomes a step, and the equilibrium condition arises after a large number of steps (i.e., a steady-state condition). By finding the vector of steady-state probabilities for this system and then interpreting these as percentages of the market, the question of equilibrium market shares is resolved.

The transition matrix is

$$P = \begin{bmatrix} 0.85 & 0.05 & 0.10 \\ 0.10 & 0.90 & 0.00 \\ 0.15 & 0.15 & 0.70 \end{bmatrix} \begin{matrix} \leftarrow & \text{state 1} \\ \leftarrow & \text{state 2} \\ \leftarrow & \text{state 3} \end{matrix}$$
$$\begin{matrix} \uparrow & \uparrow & \uparrow \\ \text{state 1} & \text{state 2} & \text{state 3} \end{matrix}$$

The system of equations to be solved to find v^* is obtained from

$$(v_1^*, v_2^*, v_3^*)P = (v_1^*, v_2^*, v_3^*) \quad \text{and} \quad v_1^* + v_2^* + v_3^* = 1$$

Performing, the indicated matrix multiplication gives

$$0.85v_1^* + 0.10v_2^* + 0.15v_3^* = v_1^*$$
$$0.05v_1^* + 0.90v_2^* + 0.15v_3^* = v_2^*$$
$$0.10v_1^* + 0.00v_2^* + 0.70v_3^* = v_3^*$$
$$v_1 + v_2^* + v_3^* = 1$$

Omitting the first equation above and rearranging the variables to leave constants on the right-hand side of each remaining equation results in the following system:

$$\begin{bmatrix} 0.05 & -0.10 & 0.15 \\ 0.10 & 0.00 & -0.30 \\ 1.00 & 1.00 & 1.00 \end{bmatrix} \begin{bmatrix} v_1^* \\ v_2^* \\ v_3^* \end{bmatrix} = \begin{bmatrix} 0.00 \\ 0.00 \\ 1.00 \end{bmatrix}$$

with solution $v_1^* = 3/7$, $v_2^* = 3/7$, $v_3^* = 1/7$. The equilibrium market shares are approximately

for Jim   → 42.86%
for Dave   → 42.86%
for Geoff   → 14.28% ■

Absorbing Chains

An absorbing Markov chain characterizes a system (or process) which, during its operation, reaches a specified state which causes the system's operations to stop completely or to stop and be restarted in some other state. The state (or states) in which these operational "halts" occur are called *absorbing states*. If a Markov chain represents a process with absorbing states, then there is at least one state, S_k, such that

$$P_{kj} = 0, \quad j = 1, \ldots, m, \quad j \neq k \quad \text{and} \quad P_{kk} = 1$$

In effect, the matrix of one-step transition probabilities P contains at least one probability vector $\mathbf{v}_k$, which indicates that its associated state S_k permits no transitions to states other than itself. However, the presence of an absorbing state does not guarantee that the chain is itself an absorbing chain. One other condition must also be satisfied. That is, it must be possible to go from every nonabsorbing state to at least one of the absorbing states. This need not occur in one step, but it must be possible eventually. In effect, for every nonabsorbing state S_j there must be at least one absorbing state S_k such that

$$P_{jk}^{(n)} > 0, \quad 0 < n \leqslant \infty$$

Generally, the most important questions which arise in the analysis of absorbing chains are, given that the system begins in a nonabsorbing state;

(1) What are the expected number of steps that will occur (how many state changes will take place) before the system stops (before absorption) and, if more than one absorbing state exists?

(2) What is the probability of absorption by each of the absorbing states (what is the likelihood of stopping in each absorbing state)?

To answer these questions, we begin by first rearranging and partitioning the transition matrix P into the following components. First, assume that there are K absorbing states and J nonabsorbing states (i.e., $J + K = m$). Then partition P into the submatrices

$$P = \left[\begin{array}{c|c} I & O \\ \hline B & N \end{array} \right] \tag{7.6}$$

where

$\quad I \leftrightarrow$ a $K \times K$ identity matrix associated with state transitions between the ordered absorbing states,

$\quad O \leftrightarrow$ a $K \times J$ zero matrix associated with the probabilities of going from the ordered absorbing states to the ordered nonabsorbing states,

$\quad B \leftrightarrow$ a $J \times K$ matrix containing the probabilities of going from the nonabsorbing states (in order) to the absorbing states (in order),

$\quad N \leftrightarrow$ a $J \times J$ matrix containing the probabilities of going from each of the nonabsorbing states (in order) to other nonabsorbing states (in order).

We can address the first question raised above by recognizing that it directs attention to the submatrix N. In essence, we would like to know how many transitions (steps) through the states associated with this submatrix will occur before leaving these states for an absorbing state. Recognizing that not all of the probabilities in every row of the submatrix N sum to one (i.e., it must be possible to reach an absorbing state) and further that we must begin in a nonabsorbing state for the system to function at all, it can be seen ultimately (after some large number of steps $n \to \infty$) that

$$N^{(n)} \to |0|$$

Further, this first question is really asking, What is the result of

$$(1)N^0 + (1)N^1 + (1)N^2 + \cdots + (1)N^{(n)} \tag{7.7}$$

The answer is drawn by analogy from the resulting sum in an algebraic power series:

$$\sum_{i=0}^{\infty} (x)^i = \frac{1}{1-x}, \qquad \text{where} \quad |x| < 1 \tag{7.8}$$

Consequently, accepting the analogy,

$$\sum_{i=0}^{\infty} N^i = (I - N)^{-1} \tag{7.9}$$

Let $\hat{N} = (I - N)^{-1}$; then the expected number of steps to absorption, given that the system starts in state S_i, is obtained by summing the elements of $\hat{N}$ along the row associated with state S_i. For example, if the second row of N obtained in partitioning P happened to be associated with state S_3, then the second row of $\hat{N}$ is also associated with state S_3. Summing the elements along the second row of $\hat{N}$ would give the expected number of steps to absorption given that the process starts in state S_3.

A continuation of this interpretation leads directly to a resolution of the second question raised above. Each element in a given row of $\hat{N}$ represents the expected number of times its associated outcome state (column designation) will occur. For example, if the second row (column) of $\hat{N}$ is associated with S_3 and the third row (column) is associated with, say, S_5, then the third column element of row two in $\hat{N}$ ($\hat{n}_{23}$) represents the expected number of occurrences of state five (S_5), given that the system begins operation in state three (S_3). Knowing the number of times a nonabsorbing state will occur once the system begins operating, and knowing the probability of absorption from each of these states by each absorbing state, then to find the probability of absorption by each absorbing state all that is required is that we sum the number of times each nonabsorbing state occurs multiplied by the probability of absorption at each occurrence by the absorbing state in question. It must be remembered that the number of times a nonabsorbing state occurs is dependent on which nonabsorbing state the system begins operating in. However, we can determine this information conveniently for all nonabsorbing states by computing the matrix T, where

$$T = \hat{N}B$$

If we label the rows and columns of T, its interpretation becomes clear.

$$T = \begin{bmatrix} & & & \\ & & & \\ & & & \\ & & & \\ & & & \end{bmatrix} \begin{matrix} \leftarrow \\ \leftarrow \\ \vdots \\ \leftarrow \\ \leftarrow \end{matrix} \begin{matrix} \text{nonabsorbing} \\ \text{states in order} \\ \text{as in } \hat{N} \\ \\ \end{matrix}$$

$$\uparrow \quad \uparrow \cdots \uparrow \quad \uparrow$$
absorbing states
in order as in B

Each element of T then represents the probability of absorption by its associated column state, given that the system begins its operation in its associated row state, i.e.,

$t_{ij} \leftrightarrow$ the probability of absorption by the state associated with column j, given that the system begins operating in the state associated with row i.

The example which follows is intended to illustrate and clarify the above analysis description and its interpretation.

Example 7.2 Below is graphically depicted (Fig. 7.1) a serial production system comprised of four work centers. There is one feedback loop connecting work centers 3 and 4. Parts flow through these work centers as

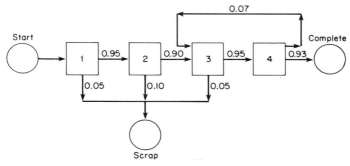

Fig. 7.1 Serial production system.

indicated by the arrows and are either completed or scrapped. The numbers on the arrows indicate the probability that a part will flow between the work centers (including Complete and Scrap) indicated. If 100 parts are processed through this system, beginning in work center 1, each day, how many of these parts on the average will be completed as good parts?

An examination of the structure of this system's operation, as described in the above diagram, leads directly to an awareness that it can be represented as an absorbing Markov chain. If we define the states of the system to correspond to the work centers, scrap bin, and completed parts inventory, then it is apparent that once a part reaches either the scrap bin or the completed parts inventory its flow through the system stops. However, as long as a part is at a work center it can continue to flow through the system. Summarizing and categorizing the states gives

State	Description	Character
1	Work center 1	Nonabsorbing
2	Work center 2	Nonabsorbing
3	Work center 3	Nonabsorbing
4	Work center 4	Nonabsorbing
5	Completed parts	Absorbing
6	Scrap bin	Absorbing

A step in this system corresponds to the flow of a part to a new state. The matrix of one-step transition probabilities obtained from the above diagram, and ordered according to the state designation given above, is

$$
P = \begin{bmatrix}
0.00 & 0.95 & 0.00 & 0.00 & 0.00 & 0.05 \\
0.00 & 0.00 & 0.90 & 0.00 & 0.00 & 0.10 \\
0.00 & 0.00 & 0.00 & 0.95 & 0.00 & 0.05 \\
0.00 & 0.00 & 0.07 & 0.00 & 0.93 & 0.00 \\
0.00 & 0.00 & 0.00 & 0.00 & 1.00 & 0.00 \\
0.00 & 0.00 & 0.00 & 0.00 & 0.00 & 1.00
\end{bmatrix}
\begin{array}{l}
\leftarrow \text{center 1} \\
\leftarrow \text{center 2} \\
\leftarrow \text{center 3} \\
\leftarrow \text{center 4} \\
\leftarrow \text{complete} \\
\leftarrow \text{scrap}
\end{array}
$$

Partitioning the transition matrix gives

$$
\begin{array}{c c}
\begin{array}{c} I \\ \\ \\ A \\ \\ \\ \end{array} &
\begin{array}{c} 5 \\ 6 \\ 1 \\ 2 \\ 3 \\ 4 \end{array}
\end{array}
\left[
\begin{array}{cccccc}
1.00 & 0.00 & 0.00 & 0.00 & 0.00 & 0.00 \\
0.00 & 1.00 & 0.00 & 0.00 & 0.00 & 0.00 \\
\hline
0.00 & 0.05 & 0.00 & 0.95 & 0.00 & 0.00 \\
0.00 & 0.10 & 0.00 & 0.00 & 0.90 & 0.00 \\
0.00 & 0.05 & 0.00 & 0.00 & 0.00 & 0.95 \\
0.93 & 0.00 & 0.00 & 0.00 & 0.07 & 0.00
\end{array}
\right]
\begin{array}{l}
0 \\ \\ \\ N \\ \\ \\ \end{array}
$$

To find the *expected number of steps to absorption*, we need

$$(I - N)^{-1} = \hat{N} \tag{7.10}$$

$$(I - N) = \begin{bmatrix} 1.00 & -0.95 & 0.00 & 0.00 \\ 0.00 & 1.00 & -0.90 & 0.00 \\ 0.00 & 0.00 & 1.00 & -0.95 \\ 0.00 & 0.00 & 0.07 & 1.00 \end{bmatrix}$$

$$\hat{N} = \begin{bmatrix} 1.000 & 0.950 & 0.916 & 0.870 \\ 0.000 & 1.000 & 0.964 & 0.916 \\ 0.000 & 0.000 & 1.071 & 1.018 \\ 0.000 & 0.000 & 0.075 & 1.071 \end{bmatrix}$$

To find the probability of absorption by each absorbing state,

$$T = \hat{N}B = \begin{bmatrix} 1.000 & 0.950 & 0.916 & 0.870 \\ 0.000 & 1.000 & 0.964 & 0.916 \\ 0.000 & 0.000 & 1.071 & 1.018 \\ 0.000 & 0.000 & 0.075 & 1.071 \end{bmatrix} \begin{bmatrix} 0.00 & 0.05 \\ 0.00 & 0.10 \\ 0.00 & 0.05 \\ 0.93 & 0.00 \end{bmatrix}$$

$$= \begin{bmatrix} 0.809 & 0.191 \\ 0.852 & 0.148 \\ 0.974 & 0.953 \\ 0.996 & 0.004 \end{bmatrix} \begin{matrix} \leftarrow \text{state 1} \\ \leftarrow \text{state 2} \\ \leftarrow \text{state 3} \\ \leftarrow \text{state 4} \end{matrix}$$

state 5   state 6

Since each part begins in work center 1 (state 1), the probability of arriving at completed inventory (absorption by state 5) is given by t_{11}. If 100 parts are started each day then $100(0.809) = 80.9$ parts will be completed as good parts, and $100(0.191) = 19.1$ parts will ultimately be scrapped. ∎

LINEAR PROGRAMMING

Linear programming is a name given to the development and analysis of normative, linear mathematical models which can be employed to allocate resources among various activities (programs or products) so as to achieve the most desirable results from these activities. The resources to be allocated are frequently in the form of time, capital, raw materials, equipment, or manpower. The results obtained from employing these resources to a defined set of activities may take the form of units of output product, cost of operation, profit from operation, or some other measure of effectiveness. It is this result, however defined, that is the objective for optimization. Employing a linear programming model for a system's operation assumes that the effect of each activity on the system is described by

(a) a proportionately constant return is achieved per unit of activity accomplished, and
(b) a proportionately constant amount of resource is required to accomplish one unit of each activity.

The mathematical structure of a linear program (in a maximization context) is given by

$$z = \sum_{j=1}^{N} c_j x_j = \max \tag{7.11}$$

$$\text{s.t.} \sum_{j=1}^{N} a_{ij} x_j \leqslant b_i, \qquad i = 1, \ldots, M \tag{7.12}$$

$$x_j \geqslant 0, \qquad j = 1, \ldots, N \tag{7.13}$$

The parameters of this model are defined as

$N \leftrightarrow$ the total number of activities (decision variables) under consideration,
$M \leftrightarrow$ the number of individual resources which are employed in accomplishing the activities,
$z \leftrightarrow$ the value of the objective function at some specified level (quantity) for each activity,
$x_j \leftrightarrow$ a variable representing the level (quantity) of activity j being accomplished,
$c_j \leftrightarrow$ the per unit contribution of activity j to the objective performance,
$a_{ij} \leftrightarrow$ the amount of resource i required per unit of activity j,
$b_i \leftrightarrow$ the total quantity of resource i which is available for allocation.

Recalling the discussion in Chapter 4, we are aware that optimal solutions can be obtained for such problems using classical methods. Unfortunately, for linear programs the number of cases to be examined can be quite large (i.e., $(M + N)!/M!N!$).There is a special technique for solving linear programs known as the *simplex method*, which can dramatically reduce the number of solutions that are tested before an optimum is obtained. This technique will be illustrated, along with the graphical solution of 2-dimensional problems in the discussion which follows. Before beginning a description of solution techniques, the inequality constraints will be converted to equations by introducing M nonnegative slack variables. The resulting linear programming model is then said to be in *canonical form.* First, let $K = M + N$; then the model is

$$z = \sum_{j=1}^{N} c_j x_j + \sum_{k=N+1}^{K} 0 x_k = \max \tag{7.14}$$

$$\text{s.t. } \sum_{j=1}^{N} a_{ij} x_j + x_{N+i} = b_i, \qquad i = 1, \ldots, M \tag{7.15}$$

$$x_j \geqslant 0, \qquad j = 1, \ldots, K \tag{7.16}$$

or in matrix notation,

$$z = \mathbf{c}^T \mathbf{x} = \max \tag{7.17}$$

$$\text{s.t. } A\mathbf{x} = \mathbf{b} \tag{7.18}$$

$$\mathbf{x} \geqslant \emptyset \tag{7.19}$$

It now remains to describe a way of selecting the optimal solution values for the decision variables $\mathbf{x}$. To assist in this determination, there are several fundamental definitions and two basic theorems that will be useful. They are summarized below.

Definitions

(1) A *feasible solution* to a linear programming problem is a solution vector $(x_1, \ldots, x_K)$ which satisfies the linear resource constraints and the nonnegativity constraints.

(2) A *basic feasible solution* is a feasible solution vector in which exactly M variables have positive values.

(3) A *degenerate basic feasible solution* is a feasible solution vector in which less than M variables have positive values.

(4) An *optimal solution* is a solution vector, either basic feasible or degenerate basic feasible, which either maximizes or minimizes the objective function.

(5) A *basis matrix* is an M by M nonsingular matrix formed from some M columns of the constraint matrix.

(6) The collection of feasible solutions constitute a convex set.

Theorems

(1) If a feasible solution exists, a basic feasible solution exists, where the basic feasible solution corresponds to an extreme point of the set of feasible solutions. Also, there exist only a finite number of basic feasible solutions.

(2) If the objective function possesses a finite optimum, then the optimal solution is a basic (or degenerate basic) feasible solution. If it assumes its optimum at more than one extreme point, then it takes on the same value at every point on the line segment joining any two optimal extreme points.

Graphical Solution

Consider the problem

$$z = x_1 + x_2 = \max$$

s.t.

$$x_1 + 2x_2 \leqslant 3$$
$$2x_1 + x_2 \leqslant 4$$
$$x_1, \quad x_2 \geqslant 0$$

As a first step to graphical solution, Fig. 7.2 shows a graph of the *convex polygon* formed by the constraint inequalities. The edges and interior of this polygon define the solution space (shaded area) of the problem. The solution space contains an infinite number of points. However, it can be shown that only one point exists which will maximize the objective function (except in the special case where the objective function is parallel to a constraint line). Figure 7.3 shows the solution space with the objective function graphed for several values of z. These lines, representing different values of the objective function, are referred to as contour lines (analogous to the physical geographer's contour lines on a map). Notice that as the objective function value increases (in an attempt to maximize), the contour lines move away from the origin. The constraint boundaries can be considered as barriers which prevent further movement of the objective function. It is obvious from the graph that to maximize the value of the objective function, it is necessary to move the contour lines as far away from the origin as possible. Since we cannot leave the solution space

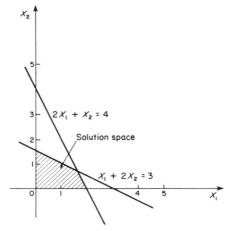

Fig. 7.2 Feasible solution space.

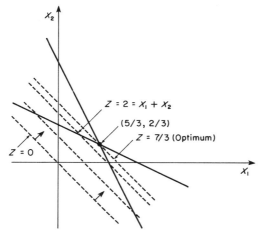

Fig. 7.3 Graphical solution.

(violation of the constraints), it should be apparent that the maximum value for the objective function can only occur at an extreme point of the polygon described. The optimal point for the above example is $x_1^* = 5/3$ and $x_2^* = 2/3$ as shown in Fig. 7.3. Substituting these values into the objective equation yields the optimum

$$z = 5/3 + 2/3 = 7/3$$

For purposes of illustration, the 2-variable problem is quite important because it can be easily solved using graphical methods. Larger problems are more common and an analytical solution technique is necessary.

The Simplex Method

Again consider the problem

$$z = x_1 + x_2 = \text{max}$$

s.t.

$$x_1 + 2x_2 \leqslant 3$$
$$2x_1 + x_2 \leqslant 4$$
$$x_1, \quad x_2 \geqslant 0$$

The analytical method used to solve this type of problem is known as the simplex method. Although this methodology has many attendant ramifications and extensions, only the simplest will be discussed here.

First, it is necessary to convert the inequalities to equalities. Thus, for the above example

$$x_1 + 2x_2 + x_3 \qquad = 3$$
$$2x_1 + \ x_2 \qquad + x_4 = 4$$

Although the nonnegativity constraints are inequalities, rewriting them is not necessary, since the technique implicitly guarantees nonnegativity. The problem now is

$$z = x_1 + x_2 + 0x_3 + 0x_4 = \max$$

s.t.
$$x_1 + 2x_1 + x_3 \qquad = 3$$
$$2x_1 + \ x_2 + \qquad x_4 = 4$$

$$x_1, x_2, x_3, x_4 \geqslant 0$$

Recalling the preceding definitions and theorems, we note that an optimal solution will occur when N of the K variables, called *nonbasic variables*, are set equal to zero. Further, if this is done for any N of the variables, then the constraint equations will be an exactly determined system of equations in the remaining M variables, called *basic variables*. The solution for these M variables is a basic solution, although perhaps not a feasible solution. If this solution also satisfies the nonnegativity restrictions, then it is a basic feasible solution, and consequently, a corner point (or extreme point) of the solution space. The column vectors from A associated with these M variables form a basis for the M-dimensional subspace associated with these variables.

The simplex method begins with the assumption that a basic feasible solution has been found. Although there are several techniques for identifying such a *starting solution*, they will not be discussed here. Note that for problems similar to the one above, it is simple to identify a starting solution. If we select the slack variables x_3 and x_4 as the *basic variables* (i.e., x_1 and x_2 are set equal to zero—and are consequently *nonbasic variables*), then a basic feasible solution is apparent. That is,

$$x_3 = 3, \qquad x_4 = 4$$

while $x_1, x_2 = 0$. Models which exhibit this characteristic, that is, the slack variables constitute a basic feasible solution, are called *primal feasible*.

Having found an initial basic feasible solution, the simplex method provides a mechanism for generating, sequentially, a series of *adjacent extreme points* of the feasible solution space. Each new point represents an improved solution value for z. Moving to an adjacent extreme point is accomplished by exchanging a basic variable with one of the nonbasic variables in a way that ensures that the nonnegativity restrictions are satisfied. To determine whether the objective function can be improved by allowing a nonbasic variable to become a basic variable, the objective function must first be written in terms of the nonbasic variables only. This is done by using the constraint equations to substitute for the basic variables in terms of the nonbasic variables. In summary, there are two fundamental decisions which are made at each iteration of the simplex method:

(1)   Is there a nonbasic variable which would cause the objective function to improve if it were a basic variable?

(2)   If a given nonbasic variable is chosen to enter the basis, which current basic variable should become nonbasic, thereby maintaining a basic feasible solution?

Each of these decision steps will now be illustrated in the context of the above illustrative problem.

Determining Optimality

In order to facilitate both of the above decisions, and as a matter of standard practice, the system of constraint equations will always be written in terms of the basic variables in such a way that their solution values are readily determined and direct substitution for them in the objective function is facilitated. This is accomplished by premultiplying the system of equations by the inverse of the M by M matrix of column vectors associated with the basic variables. If we define this matrix as B, then for the above problem

$$B = \begin{matrix} x_3 & x_4 \end{matrix} \begin{bmatrix} 1 & 0 \\ 0 & 1 \end{bmatrix}, \qquad B^{-1} = \begin{bmatrix} 1 & 0 \\ 0 & 1 \end{bmatrix}$$

and

$$B^{-1}(A \mid b) = \begin{matrix} x_1 & x_2 & x_3 & x_4 \\ \begin{bmatrix} 1 & 2 & 1 & 0 & 3 \\ 2 & 1 & 0 & 1 & 4 \end{bmatrix} \end{matrix} = (\tilde{A} \mid \tilde{b})$$

$$\underbrace{}_{\text{nonbasic}} \quad \underbrace{}_{\text{basic}}$$

Keep in mind that this result represents a uniform transformation of the column vectors of A and b with respect to the current basis. The above result ensures that an identity matrix will always be associated with the basic variables, and further, that since the nonbasic variables are equal to zero, the solution values for the basic variables can be read directly from $\tilde{b}$.

By rearranging the system of equations,

$$\tilde{A}\mathbf{x} = \tilde{\mathbf{b}} \tag{7.20}$$

so that the nonbasic variables appear on the right-hand side, substitution in the objective function for the basic variables is now straightforward.

Let $\tilde{z}$ represent the objective function written in terms of the nonbasic variables. For the problem at hand,

$$\tilde{z} = x_1 + x_2 + 0(3 - x_1 - 2x_2) + 0(4 - 2x_1 - x_2) = x_1 + x_2 + 0$$

In a maximization context, if at any time a basic feasible solution is obtained for which

$$\partial \tilde{z}/\partial x_j < 0 \tag{7.21}$$

for all nonbasic variables x_j, then that solution is the optimum. If this is not the case, then any nonbasic variable x_j for which

$$\partial \tilde{z}/\partial x_j > 0$$

will improve the solution if it becomes a basic variable. For the current problem, the solution will be improved if either x_1 or x_2 becomes a basic variable, since

$$\partial \tilde{z}/\partial x_1 = 1 \quad \text{and} \quad \partial \tilde{z}/\partial x_2 = 1.$$

Arbitrarily, x_1 will be selected as the variable to enter the basis. The procedure employed to define a variable to leave the basis will now be described.

Maintaining a Feasible Solution Basis (The Theta Rule)

Define the variable chosen to enter the basis as x_k. In order to identify the variable x_r, which is to leave the basis, compute for each of the constraint equations the value

$$\theta_i = \tilde{b}_i / \tilde{a}_{ik} \quad i = 1, \ldots, M \tag{7.22}$$

Identify the minimum, nonnegative θ value θ_r as

$$\theta_r = \min\{\theta_i \exists \theta_i \geqslant 0, i = 1, \ldots, M\}$$

This θ_r value is associated with a particular row of the transformed constraint equations. Also, there is a basic variable whose identity element appears on this row; this is the leaving variable x_r. Further, the entering basic variable will have the value θ_r when we compute the new solution values for the new basis (i.e., after this exchange of variables is made). The interpretation of the *theta rule* is really rather straightforward. Recall that the transformed system $(\tilde{A} \mid \tilde{\mathbf{b}})$ can be obtained either by premultiplying the original system by the basis inverse to obtain the desired identity submatrix or by using Gauss–Jordan complete elimination. If this latter method were used to transform the system of equations (7.20) into a system having x_k as a basic variable, then we would first want to obtain a 1 as a row element of the column vector associated with x_k. We would then use elementary row operations to obtain zeros as every other row element in that column. Selecting the minimum nonnegative θ value ensures that the new solution for basic variables (i.e., after the elimination process is completed) will be nonnegative. Also, since this process identifies where the identity element for x_k will appear in this new transformation of equations, it also defines which identity column (and consequently, old basic variable) will disappear when the transformation is completed.

Returning to the example problem, where x_1 is the entering variable, the associated θ values are

$$\theta_1 = \tilde{b}_1/\tilde{a}_{11} = 3/1 = 3, \qquad \theta_2 = \tilde{b}_2/\tilde{a}_{21} = 4/2 = 2$$

Since the minimum nonnegative θ value is associated with row 2, the leaving variable is that variable currently in the basis whose solution value corresponds to $\tilde{b}_2$, that is, x_4. Performing Gauss–Jordan complete elimination on the system of equations given in (7.20) as indicated, or by premultiplying the original system of equations by the new basis inverse,

$$\begin{matrix} & x_3 \quad x_1 \\ B = \begin{bmatrix} 1 & 1 \\ 0 & 2 \end{bmatrix}, & B^{-1} = \begin{bmatrix} 1 & -1/2 \\ 0 & 1/2 \end{bmatrix} \end{matrix}$$

yields the new transformed system

$$\begin{matrix} \tilde{A} & \qquad\qquad \tilde{b} \\ \begin{bmatrix} 0 & 3/2 & 1 & -1/2 & 1 \\ 1 & 1/2 & 0 & 1/2 & 2 \end{bmatrix} \end{matrix}$$

The new solution is then

$$x_1 = 2, \qquad x_3 = 1, \qquad x_2, x_4 = 0, \qquad z = 2$$

The objective function, written in terms of the nonbasic variables only, becomes

$$\tilde{z} = \left[2 - (1/2)x_2 - (1/2)x_4\right] + x_2 + 0\left[1 - (3/2)x_2 + (1/2)x_4\right] + 0x_4$$

Again, since

$$\partial\tilde{z}/\partial x_2 = 1/2$$

this solution is not optimal. If the solution process is completed once more, bringing x_2 into the basis, x_3 is found to be the leaving variable and the consequent solution is optimal and

$$x_1^* = 5/3, \qquad x_2^* = 2/3, \qquad x_3^*, x_4^* = 0, \qquad z^* = 7/3$$

which is borne out by the preceding graphical analysis.

To reinforce and further illustrate the iterative optimization technique described above, consider the following example problem.

Example 7.3   A small fertilizer company produces two kinds of fertilizer: PV-1 and PV-2. These two fertilizers sell for \$2 per pound and \$3 per pound, respectively. Each pound of PV-1 requires 4 ounces of a special mixture and 12 ounces of base waste. Each pound of PV-2 requires 8 ounces of special mixture and 8 ounces of base waste. In order to maximize total revenue from sales, how many pounds of PV-1 and PV-2 should be produced if 1200 ounces of special mixture and 1600 ounces of base waste are available?

The mathematical model is defined by letting

$x_1 \leftrightarrow$ number of pounds of PV-1,
$x_2 \leftrightarrow$ number of pounds of PV-2;

then the objective function and limiting constraints are

$$z = 2x_1 + 3x_2 = \max \quad \text{(revenue from sales)}$$
$$\text{s.t}$$
$$4x_1 + 8x_2 \leqslant 1200 \quad \text{(special mixture)}$$
$$12x_1 + 8x_2 \leqslant 1600 \quad \text{(base waste)}$$
$$x_1, x_2 \geqslant 0$$

Introducing x_3 and x_4 as nonnegative slack variables, and also as the initial basis variables, gives

$$z = 2x_1 + 3x_2 + 0x_3 + 0x_4$$
$$\text{s.t.}$$
$$4x_1 + 8x_2 + x_3 = 1200$$
$$12x_1 + 8x_2 + x_4 = 1600$$
$$x_1, x_2, x_3, x_4 > 0$$

with the initial solution

$$x_3 = 1200, \qquad x_4 = 1600, \qquad x_1, x_2 = 0 \qquad \text{and} \qquad z = 0$$

Since $\bar{z}$ has the same form as z for this initial solution, it is straightforward that

$$\partial \bar{z}/\partial x_1 = 2 \qquad \text{and} \qquad \partial \bar{z}/\partial x_2 = 3$$

Let x_2 be the entering variable (although either x_1 or x_2 could have been chosen), and compute the θ values:

$$\theta_1 = 150, \qquad \theta_2 = 200$$

The minimum nonnegative θ value is associated with the first constraint that has an identity element associated with the current basic variable x_3.

So x_2 will replace x_3 as a basic variable. The basis matrix and its inverse are

$$x_2 \ \ x_4$$
$$B = \begin{bmatrix} 8 & 0 \\ 8 & 1 \end{bmatrix} \quad \text{and} \quad B^{-1} = \begin{bmatrix} 1/8 & 0 \\ -1 & 1 \end{bmatrix}$$

The system of equation $\tilde{A}\mathbf{x} = \tilde{\mathbf{b}}$ transformed by this basis inverse has

$$\tilde{A} = \begin{bmatrix} 1/2 & 1 & 1/8 & 0 \\ 8 & 0 & -1 & 1 \end{bmatrix} \quad \text{and} \quad \tilde{\mathbf{b}} = \begin{bmatrix} 150 \\ 400 \end{bmatrix}$$

Using the transformed equations

$$\tilde{z} = 2x_1 + 3\left[150 - (1/2)x_1 - (1/8)x_3\right] + 0x_3 + 0(400 - 8x_1 + x_3)$$
$$= (3/2)x_1 - (3/8)x_3 + 450$$

and the current solution can be summarized as

$$x_2 = 150, \qquad x_4 = 400, \qquad x_1, x_3 = 0, \qquad z = 450$$

Taking partial derivatives of $\tilde{z}$ with respect to the current nonbasic variables indicates that this solution is not an optimum since

$$\partial z / \partial x_1 = 3/2 > 0$$

Let x_1 be the new entering variable; computing the θ values gives

$$\theta_1 = \frac{150}{1/2} = 300, \qquad \theta_2 = \frac{400}{8} = 50$$

Since θ_2 is the minimum nonnegative value, and x_4 is the current basic variable associated with the second constraint, x_1 will enter the basis and will replace x_4. The new basis matrix and its inverse are

$$B = \begin{bmatrix} 8 & 4 \\ 8 & 12 \end{bmatrix}, \quad B^{-1} = \begin{bmatrix} 3/16 & -1/16 \\ -1/8 & 1/8 \end{bmatrix}$$

The transformed system is then computed as

$$\tilde{A} = B^{-1}A = \begin{bmatrix} 0 & 1 & 3/16 & -1/16 \\ 1 & 0 & -1/8 & 1/8 \end{bmatrix}$$

and $\tilde{\mathbf{b}}^{\mathrm{T}} = [B^{-1}\mathbf{b}]^{\mathrm{T}} = [125, 50]$. Summarizing this new solution, we have

$$x_1 = 50, \qquad x_2 = 125, \qquad x_3, x_4 = 0, \qquad z = 475$$

To check this solution for optimality requires that $\tilde{z}$ be formed:

$$\tilde{Z} = 2\left[50 + (1/8)x_3 - (1/8)x_4\right] + 3\left[125 - (3/16)x_3 + (1/16)x_4\right]$$
$$+ 0x_3 + 0x_4 = 475 - (5/16)x_3 - (1/16)x_4$$

Since $\partial \tilde{z}/\partial x_3 < 0$ and $\partial \tilde{z}/\partial x_4 < 0$, the above solution is the optimum. Summarizing, we have the following. Make 50 pounds of PV-1 and 125 pounds of PV-2 for a total revenue of $475. ∎

DYNAMIC PROGRAMMING

Dynamic programming is an approach that can be used fruitfully in the modeling and analysis of many diverse operational problems. As a modeling tool it provides a framework for building mathematical relationships that describe the operational behavior and performance of multistage decision processes. For example, it can be used to model the sequence of decisions required to define the number of machines, and their individual operating rates, required in each work center of a serial machining system so that total production costs are a minimum. As an analysis tool, it provides a structure whereby a large problem (in terms of the number of decision variables) can be decomposed into a series of interrelated small problems. These small problems are solved sequentially utilizing their interrelationships until, ultimately, the solution to the large problem is obtained. Each of the small problems is associated with a *stage* in the solution process. This staging implies that the problem is separable, that is, can be validly decomposed into such stages.

There are several basic features associated with using a dynamic programming rationale to define an optimal solution to a mathematical programming problem. They are

(1)   The problem can be divided into stages with a policy decision required at each stage.

(2)   Each stage has a number of states associated with it.

(3)   The effect of the policy decision at each stage is to transform the current state into a state associated with the next stage.

(4)   Given the current state of the system in a particular stage, an optimal policy for subsequent stages is independent of the policy adopted in previous stages.

(5)   The solution procedure begins by finding the optimal policy for each state of the last stage.

(6)   A recursive relationship is available which identifies the optimal policy for each state with $N - k$ stages remaining ($k = 0, 1, \ldots, N - 1$).

(7)   Using this recursive relationship, the solution procedure moves backward stage-by-stage, each time finding the optimal policy for each state of that stage, until it finds the optimal policy when starting at the initial stage.

These basic features provide the framework through which a dynamic programming solution is implemented. Having indicated that the problem is to be decomposed into stages, it is important to identify specifically how a typical stage is represented. A typical stage (here denoted the ith stage) can be represented by Fig. 7.4 and is characterized by five fundamental factors:

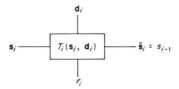

Fig. 7.4 Typical stage diagram.

(1)   an input stage s_i, which gives all relevant information about inputs to the stage; s_i is called the *initial state* of stage i as it gives a description of the system at the beginning of the stage;

(2)   stage transition functions $T_i(\cdot)$, sometimes called the *stage-coupling functions*, which express each component of the output state as a function of the input state and stage decision;

(3)   an output state $\tilde{s}_i$, which gives all relevant information about outputs from the stage; $\tilde{s}_i$ is called the *final state* of stage i as it gives a description of the system at the end of the stage: $\tilde{s}_i = T_i(s_i, d_i) = s_{i-1}$;

(4)   a decision d_i, which controls the operation of the stage;

(5)   a stage return r_i, which is a variable that measures the utility or performance of the stage as a function of the input state and decision: $r_i = R_i(s_i, d_i)$.

If the objective function $F(d)$ is separable into individual stage returns r_i which are additive in their effect on the total objective, that is,

$$F(d) = \sum_{i=1}^{N} r_i$$

then the basic optimization principle of dynamic programming can be stated in a maximization context as follows:

(a)   For every possible input state value s_1 in the first stage of analysis, the optimum decision d_1 will maximize

$$f_1(s_1) = R_1(s_1, d_1) \tag{7.23}$$

and for each of the other stages,

(b)   For every possible input state value s_k in stage k of analysis, the optimal decision d_k will maximize

$$f_k(s_k) = R_k(s_k, d_k) + f_{k-1}^*(s_k, d_k) \tag{7.24}$$

where $f_k(\cdot)$ is the cumulative return for stage k and $f_{k-1}^*(\cdot)$ is the optimal cumulative return from stage $k - 1$ given in terms of each input state to stage k. The key to formation of the cumulative return function is recognizing that each input state of stage $k - 1$ for which f_{k-1}^* is defined can be associated with a specific input state-and-decision pair at stage k. This relationship is explicitly defined by the stage coupling function at stage k. That is,

$$s_{i-1} = \tilde{s}_i = T_i(s_i, d_i) \tag{7.25}$$

It is seldom that the reader readily grasps the mechanics of solving a mathematical programming problem using dynamic programming without the aid of a specific example problem to reinforce the above described concepts. Two examples will follow. The first is an integer linear program, that is, a linear program in which the decision variables take values which are not only discrete but, further, integral. The second example is a separable quadratic program, which is typical of the problems previously described in chapter 4.

Example 7.4 Consider the problem of loading a space capsule having a total weight capacity of $W = 9$ tons with scientific instruments in such a way as to maximize the total value of the payload. Three kinds of items are available for loading into the capsule, where the ith item has weight w_i per unit (in tons) and a value v_i as given in the table below.

We will associate the stages of the problem with each type of equipment so that at each stage we will determine the optimal number of units of a particular type of instrument to load given the weight capacity remaining at that stage.

$w_i \leftrightarrow$ weight of the ith item
$v_i \leftrightarrow$ value of the ith item
$n_i \leftrightarrow$ number of units of item i loaded

i	w_i	v_i
1	5	9
2	4	8
3	3	4

There is a single state variable s_i at each stage which corresponds to the weight capacity which remains available for loading. There is a single decision d_i at each stage, which corresponds to the number of units of item i that will be loaded. The returns associated with each stage are then the number of units of item i loaded multiplied by the value of each item:

$$r_i = v_i d_i$$

The mathematical program corresponding to this problem can be written in expanded form as

$$F(\mathbf{d}) = v_1 d_1 + v_2 d_2 + v_3 d_3 = \max$$

s.t.

$$w_1 d_1 + w_2 d_2 + w_3 d_3 \leqslant 9 \quad \text{(single weight limitation)}$$

$$d_1, d_2, d_3 \geqslant 0, \quad \mathbf{d} \in Z^3 \quad \text{(nonnegative integer restriction)}$$

To illustrate how the problem stages are defined, we will arbitrarily isolate stage 2 in the analysis and give its stage description in detail. Then all three stages will be summarized.

For stage 2, as indicated previously, the return is

$$r_2 = v_2 d_2 = 8 d_2$$

and the stage coupling relationship is

$$s_1 = \tilde{s}_2 = s_2 - w_2 d_2 = s_2 - 4 d_2$$

where if s_2 represents the weight available for loading, then for every unit of item 2 we decide to load (d_2) we use 4 tons from the available weight. The result $\tilde{s}_2$ (or s_1) is then the weight left unused, which is available for use in stage 1. We can go a bit further. Since it is not possible to use more weight than is available,

$$s_2 - 4 d_2 > 0$$

and consequently,

$$d_2 < s_2 / 4$$

In addition, since s_2 cannot exceed the maximum of 9 tons and d_2 must be an integer,

$$d_2 < 9/4 \rightarrow d_2 \in \{0, 1, 2\}$$

We summarize directly on a diagram for stage 2 (Fig. 7.5). Applying a similar reasoning to stages 1 and 3, the complete stage diagram for this problem is described by Fig. 7.6. Now that the problem has been "staged," it is convenient to solve each of the individual stage problems for the optimal cumulative returns $f_k^*(s_k)$ by employing a tabular format. The basic procedure will be to define an optimal cumulative return for each possible input state at each stage, working backward from stage 1 to stage 3. Each of the individual tables of cumulative returns is given below with an illustration of how a specific return in each table is obtained.

In Table 7.1 for a given input state of 6 tons remaining,

$$f_1(s_1 = 6, d_1 = 0) = 0$$
$$f_1(s_1 = 6, d_1 = 1) = 9$$

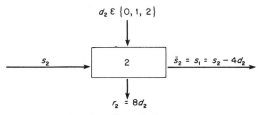

Fig. 7.5 Stage 2 diagram.

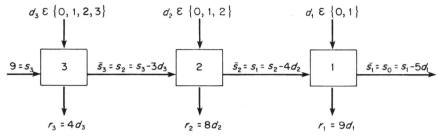

$d_3 \, \varepsilon \, \{0, 1, 2, 3\}$ $d_2 \, \varepsilon \, \{0, 1, 2\}$ $d_1 \, \varepsilon \, \{0, 1\}$

$9 = s_3$ | 3 | $\tilde{s}_3 = s_2 = s_3 - 3d_3$ | 2 | $\tilde{s}_2 = s_1 = s_2 - 4d_2$ | 1 | $\tilde{s}_1 = s_0 = s_1 - 5d_1$

$r_3 = 4d_3$ $r_2 = 8d_2$ $r_1 = 9d_1$

Fig. 7.6 Complete stage diagram.

Table 7.1

Stage 1 Solution[a]

		s_1									
		0	1	2	3	4	5	6	7	8	9
d_1	0	0*	0*	0*	0*	0*	0	0	0	0	0	$\leftarrow f_1(s_1, d_1)$
	1	X	X	X	X	X	9*	9*	9*	9*	9*	

[a] X indicates an infeasible decision given the indicated input state. * indicates the optimum solution for each input state.

In other words, if 6 tons are available and only item 1 remains to be loaded, then if we decide to load none of item 1, the value (return) from this decision is zero and there are 6 tons of unused capacity. However, if 6 tons are available and we decide to load 1 unit of item 1, then we obtain a value of 9 and have only 1 ton of unused capacity. The optimal solution for the case where 6 tons are available and only item 1 remains to be loaded is then

$$s_1 = 6, \qquad d_1^* = 1, \qquad f_1^*(s_1 = 6) = 9$$

In stage 2 (see Table 7.2) it must be remembered that we are not only concerned with the direct return associated with a particular state–decision pair but also the optimal return associated with the output state that results

Table 7.2

Stage 2 Solution

		s_2									
		0	1	2	3	4	5	6	7	8	9
	0	0*	0*	0*	0*	0	9*	9*	9*	9	9	
d_2	1	X	X	X	X	8	8	8	8	8	17*	$\leftarrow f_2(s_2, d_2)$
	2	X	X	X	X	X	X	X	X	16*	16	

from that pair. It is the sum of these two returns that we seek to maximize. To illustrate, consider the case for an input state of $s_2 = 8$.

$$f_2(s_2 = 8, d_2 = 0) = R_2(s_2 = 8, d_2 = 0) + f_1^*(s_1 = 8 - 4(0))$$
$$= 0 \qquad\qquad + 9 \qquad\qquad = 9$$
$$f_2(s_2 = 8, d_2 = 1) = R_2(s_2 = 8, d_2 = 1) + f_1^*(s_1 = 8 - 4(1))$$
$$= 8 \qquad\qquad + 0 \qquad\qquad = 8$$
$$f_2(s_2 = 8, d_2 = 2) = R_2(s_2 = 8, d_2 = 2) + f_1^*(s_1 = 8 - 4(2))$$
$$= 16 \qquad\qquad + 0 \qquad\qquad = 16$$

The optimal solution, considering only items 1 and 2, for an input state of 8 tons available would then be to load 2 units of item 2 and 0 units of item 1 for a total value of 16.

Table 7.3

Stage 3 Solution

		s_3	
		9	
	0	17*	
d_3	1	13	$\leftarrow f_3(s_3, d_3)$
	2	8	
	3	12	

Since we have been told that at the beginning of this allocation process there will be 9 tons available, this is the only state value that need be considered in the last stage of analysis. As with stage 2, here we are interested in identifying the stage 3 decision which leads to a maximum cumulative return from the total allocation process. The entries in Table 7.3 are obtained by

$$f_3(s_3 = 9, d_3 = 0) = R_3(s_3 = 9, d_3 = 0) + f_2^*(s_2 = 9 - 3(0))$$
$$= 0 \qquad\qquad + 17 \qquad\qquad = 17$$
$$f_3(s_3 = 9, d_3 = 1) = R_3(s_3 = 9, d_3 = 1) + f_2^*(s_2 = 9 - 3(1))$$
$$= 4 \qquad\qquad + 9 \qquad\qquad = 13$$
$$f_3(s_3 = 9, d_3 = 2) = R_3(s_3 = 9, d_3 = 2) + f_2^*(s_2 = 9 - 3(2))$$
$$= 8 \qquad\qquad + 0 \qquad\qquad = 8$$
$$f_3(s_3 = 9, d_3 = 3) = R_3(s_3 = 9, d_3 = 3) + f_2^*(s_2 = 9 - 3(3))$$
$$= 12 \qquad\qquad + 0 \qquad\qquad = 12$$

The optimal decision policy for allocating items to the space capsule can be traced back through the stages, beginning with the last stage of analysis, as follows

item 3: $s_3 = 9$; $d_3^* = 0$; $r_3 = 0$; $\tilde{s}_3 = s_2 = 9 - 3(0) = 9$;
item 2: $s_2 = 9$; $d_2^* = 1$; $r_2 = 8$; $\tilde{s}_2 = s_1 = 9 - 4(1) = 5$;
item 1: $s_1 = 5$; $d_1^* = 1$; $r_1 = 9$; $\tilde{s}_1 = s_0 = 5 - 5(1) = 0$.   ∎

Example 7.5   Consider the resource allocation problem with quadratic returns

$$F(\mathbf{d}) = -(d_1 - 3)^2 - (d_2 - 2)^2 = \max$$

s.t.

$$d_1 + 2d_2 \leqslant 3 \qquad \text{(resource limitation constraint)}$$

$$d_1, d_2 \geqslant 0 \qquad \text{(negativity restrictions)}$$

Let each of the decision variables be associated with a stage of analysis. In a similar manner to the preceding example, there is a single state variable which can be associated with the quantity of resource remaining after each decision has been defined. The state transition relationships are then described by

$$s_2 = 3, \qquad \tilde{s}_2 = s_2 - 2d_2 = s_1, \qquad \tilde{s}_1 = s_1 - d_1 = s_0$$

These coupling relationships lead directly to additional restrictions which can be imposed on the decision variables at each stage. Since we cannot allocate more resource to the decisions than is available, we have

$$s_1 \geqslant 0 \qquad \text{and} \qquad s_0 \geqslant 0$$

$$s_2 - 2d_2 \geqslant 0 \rightarrow d_2 \leqslant s_2/2$$

$$s_1 - d_1 \geqslant 0 \rightarrow d_1 \leqslant s_1$$

The stage diagram for this problem is defined as in Fig. 7.7.

The solution proceeds in a backward recursive fashion, as indicated previously, beginning with stage 1.

Stage 1:

$$f_1(\cdot) = -(d_1 - 3)^2 = \max$$
$$0 \leqslant d_1 \leqslant s_1$$

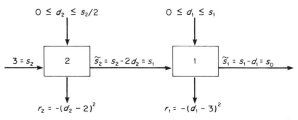

Fig. 7.7 Stage diagram for Example 7.5.

To find the unconstrained optimum for d_1 we take

$$\frac{df_1}{dd_1} = -2d_1 + 6 = 0 \rightarrow d_1^* = 3$$

Although this unconstrained solution satisfied the nonnegativity restriction $d_1 \geqslant 0$, it will only satisfy the upper bound restriction $d_1 \leqslant s_1$ if $s_1 \geqslant 3$. If s_1 is not greater than or equal to 3, then we are prohibited from reaching the unconstrained optimum by the limiting value of s_1. Consequently, the optimal solution for stage 1 is dependent on the value of s_1 and can be summarized as

(1) $d_1^* = 3$; $f_1^* = 0$; $s_1 \geqslant 3$;
(2) $d_1^* = s_1$; $f_1^* = -(s_1 - 3)^2$; $0 \leqslant s_1 \leqslant 3$.

These two state-dependent decisions describe the optimal policy for every possible input state value to stage 1. We can now proceed to the stage 2 analysis.

Stage 2: There are two problems that must be solved in stage 2, one for each of the possible return functions associated with stage 1 [i.e., $f_1(s_1 \geqslant 3)$ and $f_1(0 \leqslant s_1 \leqslant 3)$] which must be added to the direct return in stage 2 to form the cumulative returns function $f_2(s_2, d_2)$. These problems will be addressed in the order indicated above.

The first of these problems is

$$f_2(\cdot) = -(d_2 - 2)^2 + f_1^*(s_1 \geqslant 3) = \max_{0 \leqslant d_2 \leqslant s_2/2}$$

$$= -(d_2 - 2)^2 + 0$$

By recognizing the impact of the stage 2 state transition function on the range of values permitted for s_1, the solution to this problem becomes trivial. Since $s_2 = 3$ and

$$s_2 - 2d_2 = s_1 \geqslant 3$$

then by substitution of the known value for s_3,

$$3 - 2d_2 \geqslant 3 \rightarrow d_2 \leqslant 0$$

which permits only the lower bound value of d_2 as a solution. Consequently,

$$d_2^* = 0, \qquad f_2^* = -4, \qquad s_2 = 3$$

The second stage 2 problem is

$$f_2(\cdot) = -(d_2 - 2)^2 + f_1^*(0 \leqslant s_1 \leqslant 3) = \max_{0 \leqslant d_2 \leqslant s_2/2}$$

$$= -(d_2 - 2)^2 - (s_1 - 3)^2$$

However, we must be able to define $f_2(\cdot)$ in terms of the input state and decision in stage 2. Using the transition function

$$s_2 - 2d_2 = s_1$$

and substituting for s_1, we have

$$f_2(\cdot) = -(d_2 - 2)^2 - [(s_2 - 2d_2) - 3]^2$$

Expanding and then substituting for the known value of s_2 yields

$$f_2(\cdot) = -s_2^2 + 4s_2d_2 - 5d_2^2 + 6s_2 - 8d_2 - 13$$

$$= -5d_2^2 + 4d_2 - 4$$

To find the unconstrained optimum for d_2, we take

$$\frac{df_2}{dd_2} = -10d_2 + 4 = 0 \rightarrow d_2^* = 2/5.$$

Although this solution satisfies the nonnegativity restriction on d_2, we must remember that the cumulative return function being employed requires that a specific range in s_1 be obtained after the decision d_2 has been made. That is,

$$0 \leqslant s_2 - 2d_2 \leqslant 3.$$

In this case, we are ensured of fulfilling this stage coupling restriction, since for $d_2^* = 2/5$,

$$0 \leqslant s_2 - 2(2/5) \leqslant 3$$

whenever $0.8 \leqslant s_2 \leqslant 3.8$. The optimal solution to this second problem is summarized as

$$d_2^* = 2/5, \qquad f_2^* = -16/5, \qquad s_2 = 3$$

We now have two possible solutions, and the optimal policy is defined by the decision policy which is associated with the maximum value for f_2^*. These two policies are

(1) $d_2^* = 0, f_2^* = -4, s_2 = 3,$
(2) $d_2^* = 2/5, f_2^* = -16/5, s_2 = 3.$

Since the second of these policies has the maximum value for f_2^*, it is the one to be followed. Tracing back through the stages, beginning with stage 2, the optimal policy is for

$$s_2 = 3, \qquad d_2^* = 2/5, \qquad r_2^* = -64/25$$

This means that

$$s_1 = s_2 - 2d_2 = 3 - 2(2/5) = 11/5, \qquad d_1^* = 11/5, \qquad r_1^* = -16/25$$

and summing, $r_1^* + r_2^*$,

$$f(\mathbf{d}^*) = -16/25 - 64/25 = -16/5 \quad \blacksquare$$

DIRECT OPTIMIZATION TECHNIQUES

There are numerous specific techniques that have been developed for obtaining optimal solutions, in an algorithmic manner, to mathematical programs. The essence of one of these techniques, the simplex method, has already been described. As with the simplex method for linear programs, each specific technique is usually developed with a particular class of mathematical programs in mind. For example, there is a technique which uses a modification of the simplex method (i.e., a restricted basis entry which is founded on the Kuhn–Tucker conditions) to solve problems with quadratic objective functions and linear inequality constraints. In general, however, these techniques can be classified under two headings: (a) those which make use of the analytical derivatives of the objective function; and (b) those which do not. In the discussion which follows, one of each category will be illustrated. The first will be a derivative-free method for functions of a single variable, the *Fibonacci Search*. The second will be a differential algorithm, the *Method of Steepest Decent*. Each of these techniques relies on the underlying assumption that the function being optimized is unimodal. If not, then the solution obtained is, at best, a local optimum. These techniques will be presented in a minimization context.

The Fibonacci Search

This technique is based on generating a sequence of points x_i, $i = 1, \ldots, N$, along a closed interval in the decision variable: $I_L \leqslant X \leqslant I_U$. The placement of each experimental point and convergence to the optimal solution are both based on evaluating the function at each experimental point, and a specific relationship that exists between these points. The placement of experimental points x_i at which the objective function $F(x)$ is evaluated is determined by the Fibonacci number sequence. This sequence has the form

$$n_i = n_{i-1} + n_{i-2}, \qquad i = 2, 3, \ldots \qquad (7.26)$$

where n_i is the ith Fibonacci number and, by definition, $n_1 = n_0 = 1$.

Define the interval over which the decision variable is defined as $W = I_U - I_L$. It is possible to use this technique to obtain the optimal solution x^* to within a described accuracy δ after a prescribed number of experiments N. Once N is defined, δ can be determined; or once δ is defined, N can be established. The relationships governing N and δ are as follows.

Given a desired accuracy δ, known as the *final interval of separation* or the *interval of uncertainty*, the number of experimental points N required is defined by the Fibonacci number n_N for which

$$\frac{W}{\delta} \leqslant n_N \tag{7.27}$$

Similarly, given a desired number of experimental points N to be generated, the resulting accuracy δ in defining the optimum is again determined by the Fibonacci number n_N:

$$\frac{W}{n_N} = \delta \tag{7.28}$$

The placement of experimental points at which the objective function is evaluated is controlled by the sequence of Fibonacci numbers leading to n_N. Each of the points are placed symmetrically in the interval W until the optimal point x^* is obtained. At each iteration in the solution procedure, either a new value for I_U or a new value for I_L is defined until $I_U - I_L \leqslant \delta$. The placement of experimental points and the convergence characteristic of this technique are best explained in the context of an example problem. It should be noted that the search for an optimum begins by obtaining values for N and n_N either directly or by first specifying δ.

For illustrative purposes consider the simplified problem of minimizing the function

$$F(x) = 2x^2 - 20x + 14$$

where x must be a nonnegative integer between 0 and 21. Since this is an integer-valued function, the global optimum will be found if δ is set equal to 1. For $\delta = 1$, the number of experiments is defined by N such that

$$n_N \geqslant \frac{(21 - 0)}{1} = 21$$

To obtain the Fibonacci number n_N, Eq. (7.26) is used recursively beginning with a definition of

$$n_2 = n_1 + n_0 = 1 + 1 = 2$$

and continuing

$$n_3 = n_2 + n_1 = 2 + 1 = 3$$

until

$$n_7 = 13 + 8 = 21$$

consequently, with seven experimental points the original interval can be reduced to the optimal solution. This is accomplished as follows.

To begin the search process, the function is evaluated at each end point of the original interval ($I_L = 0$, $I_U = 21$). Then the first two experiments are placed symmetrically in the interval at points

$$x_1 = \frac{n_{N-1}}{n_N} (W) + I_L \tag{7.29}$$

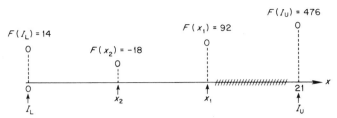

Fig. 7.8 Symmetric test points.

and

$$x_2 = \frac{n_{N-2}}{n_N} (W) + I_L \tag{7.30}$$

Next the function is evaluated at each of these points. In terms of this example, we have

$$x_1 = \frac{13}{21} (21) + 0 = 13, \qquad x_2 = \frac{8}{21} (21) + 0 = 8$$

as shown graphically in Fig. 7.8.

The next step in the solution procedure is to discard a portion of the interval W, and in so doing to redefine either I_L or I_U. The basis for discarding a portion of the interval is as follows: (1) if $F(x_1) < F(x_2)$, then discard the interval $x_2 - I_L$ and set $I_L = x_2$; (2) if $F(x_2) < F(x_1)$, then discard the interval $I_U - x_1$ and set $I_U = x_1$. Observe in Fig. 7.8 for a unimodal function, that if condition (1) holds, then the optimum must lie in the interval x_2 to I_U; and conversely, if condition (2) holds, then the optimum must lie in the interval I_L to x_1.

The next and remaining experimental points are placed symmetrically, with respect to the remaining interior experimental point, in the newly defined interval based on a generalization of either of the above two conditions. If condition (1) occurred, then

$$x_i = \frac{n_{(N-i+1)}}{n_N} (W) + I_L \tag{7.31}$$

If condition (2) occurred, then

$$x_i = \frac{n_{(N-i)}}{n_N} (W) + I_L \tag{7.32}$$

Note that W retains its original value.

After each new experimental point is defined as above ($i = 3, \ldots, N$), the function is evaluated and a portion of the remaining interval is again discarded based on a generalization of the above two conditions. If we let $\hat{x}$ represent the remaining interior experimental point, then (1) if $F(\hat{x}) < F(x_i)$, the interval from x_i to its nearest end point (I_U or I_L) is

Table 7.4

Summary of Test Points[a]

i	x_i	$F(x_i)$	I_L	I_U
1	13	92	0	21
2	8	-18	0	13
3	5	-36	0	8
4	3	-28	3	8
5	6	-34	3	6
6	4	-34	4	6
7	5*	-36	5 or	6
			5	5

[a] In order to terminate the search with a $\delta = I_U - I_L = 1$, an experiment was repeated at $x = 5$.

discarded; (2) if $F(x_i) < F(\hat{x})$, the interval from $\hat{x}$ to its nearest end point (I_U or I_L) is discarded. The result of applying this procedure to the above problem is summarized in Table 7.4.

Method of Steepest Descent

Situations frequently arise in which the techniques described in Chapter 3 are difficult to apply, particularly when the first partial derivatives do not lead to a simple solution for the stationary point. As an alternative, search techniques are often used to find the minimum or maximum of an unconstrained function of several variables. One such technique is called the *gradient method* or *method of steepest ascent (descent)*. In applying the gradient method, one chooses a starting point x_0 and attempts to determine the direction α which will lead to the greatest increase [for maximization of $f(x)$] or the greatest decrease [for minimization of $f(x)$] in $f(x)$. The rate of change in $f(x)$ at the point x_0 in the direction α is given by

$$\Delta_\alpha f(x_0) = \sum_{i=1}^n \alpha_i \frac{\partial}{\partial x_i} f(x_0) \tag{7.33}$$

Each point x in the gradient direction α is given by

$$x^T = [x_{01} + \alpha_1 \quad x_{02} + \alpha_2 \quad \cdots \quad x_{0n} + \alpha_n] \tag{7.34}$$

In applying the gradient technique, the analyst chooses a step of size r such that the next point, x_1, investigated in the search is along the gradient and at a distance r from $\mathbf{x}_0$. Thus

$$r = \left(\sum_{i=1}^{n} (x_{1i} - x_{0i})^2 \right)^{1/2} \tag{7.35}$$

The entire process is then repeated iteratively, letting $\mathbf{x}_0 = \mathbf{x}_1$.

Since $\boldsymbol{\alpha}$ is to the direction of steepest ascent (or descent), we must find $\boldsymbol{\alpha}$ such that the directional derivative at $\mathbf{x}_0$ is maximized (minimized) subject to the constraint given in Eq. (7.35). Hence, the Lagrange function may be expressed as

$$L(\mathbf{x}, \boldsymbol{\lambda}) = \sum_{i=1}^{n} \alpha_i \frac{\partial}{\partial x_i} f(\mathbf{x}_0) + \lambda_1 \left[\sum_{i=1}^{n} (x_{1i} - x_{0i})^2 - r^2 \right] \tag{7.36}$$

Since $x_{1i} = x_{0i} + \alpha_i$, Eq. (7.36) can be expressed as

$$L(\mathbf{x}, \boldsymbol{\lambda}) = \sum_{i=1}^{n} \alpha_i \frac{\partial}{\partial x_i} f(\mathbf{x}_0) + \lambda_1 \left[\sum_{i=1}^{n} \alpha_i^2 - r^2 \right] \tag{7.37}$$

Taking first partial derivatives with respect to α_i, $i = 1, 2, \ldots, n$, and λ_1, we have

$$\frac{\partial}{\partial \alpha_i} L(\boldsymbol{\alpha}, \boldsymbol{\lambda}) = \frac{\partial}{\partial x_i} f(\mathbf{x}_0) + 2\lambda_1 \alpha_i = 0 \tag{7.38}$$

$$\frac{\partial}{\partial \lambda_1} L(\boldsymbol{\alpha}, \boldsymbol{\lambda}) = - \sum_{i=1}^{n} \alpha_i^2 - r^2 = 0 \tag{7.39}$$

and

$$\alpha_i = - \frac{1}{2\lambda_1} f_i(\mathbf{x}_0), \qquad i = 1, 2, \ldots, n \tag{7.40}$$

$$\sum_{i=1}^{n} \alpha_i^2 = r^2 \tag{7.41}$$

Therefore

$$r^2 = \frac{1}{4\lambda_1^2} \sum_{i=1}^{n} \left[f_i(\mathbf{x}_0) \right]^2 \tag{7.42}$$

or

$$\lambda_1 = \pm \frac{1}{2r} \left(\sum_{i=1}^{n} \left[f_i(\mathbf{x}_0) \right]^2 \right)^{1/2} \tag{7.43}$$

Finally,

$$\alpha_i = \pm r f_i(\mathbf{x}_0) / \left(\sum_{i=1}^{n} \left[f_i(\mathbf{x}_0) \right]^2 \right)^{1/2} \tag{7.44}$$

To determine the maximizing and minimizing values of α, we use the sufficient conditions for the Lagrange multiplier technique:

$$\frac{\partial^2}{\partial \alpha_i^2} L(\alpha, \lambda) = 2\lambda_1, \qquad i = 1, 2, \ldots, n \tag{7.45}$$

$$\frac{\partial^2}{\partial \alpha_i \partial \alpha_j} L(\alpha, \lambda) = 0, \qquad i \neq j \tag{7.46}$$

$$\frac{\partial}{\partial \alpha_i} g_{1_j}(\alpha) = 2\alpha_i, \qquad i = 1, 2, \ldots, n \tag{7.47}$$

Thus

$$H_B(x^*, \lambda^*) = \begin{bmatrix} 0 & 2\alpha_1 & 2\alpha_2 & \cdots & 2\alpha_n \\ 2\alpha_1 & 2\lambda_1 & 0 & \cdots & 0 \\ 2\alpha_2 & 0 & 2\lambda_1 & \cdots & 0 \\ \vdots & \vdots & \vdots & & \vdots \\ 2\alpha_n & 0 & 0 & \cdots & 2\lambda_1 \end{bmatrix}$$

Since $m = 1$, we examine the last $n - 1$ leading principal minors of A. Now

$$|H_{B_3}| = \begin{vmatrix} 0 & 2\alpha_1 & 2\alpha_2 \\ 2\alpha_1 & 2\lambda_1 & 0 \\ 2\alpha_2 & 0 & 2\lambda_1 \end{vmatrix}$$

$$= -8\lambda_1 \alpha_2^2 - 8\lambda_1 \alpha_1^2 = -8\lambda_1 \sum_{i=1}^{2} \alpha_i^2$$

Using the cofactor method, we have

$$|H_{B_4}| = \begin{vmatrix} 0 & 2\alpha_1 & 2\alpha_2 & 2\alpha_3 \\ 2\alpha_1 & 2\lambda_1 & 0 & 0 \\ 2\alpha_2 & 0 & 2\lambda_1 & 0 \\ 2\alpha_3 & 0 & 0 & 2\lambda_1 \end{vmatrix}$$

$$= 2\alpha_1[8\lambda_1^2\alpha_1] - 2\alpha_2[-8\lambda_1^2\alpha_2] + 2\alpha_3[8\lambda_1^2\alpha_3] = 16\lambda_1^2 \sum_{i=1}^{3} \alpha_i$$

For general j we have

$$|H_{B_j}| = -2^j(\lambda_1)^{j-2} \sum_{i=1}^{j} \alpha_i^2 \tag{7.48}$$

Thus for $\lambda_1 < 0$, $|H_{B_j}|$ alternates in sign starting with a positive and for $\lambda_1 > 0$, $|H_{B_j}| < 0$ for all j. Since m is odd, the maximizing direction for the search is given by

$$\alpha_i = + r f_i(\mathbf{x}_0) \Big/ \Big(\sum_{i=1}^{n} [f_i(\mathbf{x}_0)]^2 \Big)^{1/2}, \qquad i = 1, 2, \ldots, n \qquad (7.49)$$

and the minimizing direction for the search is

$$\alpha_i = - r f_i(\mathbf{x}_0) \Big/ \Big(\sum_{i=1}^{n} [f_i(\mathbf{x}_0)]^2 \Big)^{1/2} \qquad (7.50)$$

It should be noted that α_i is a positive or negative multiple of the gradient vector depending upon whether the objective is to maximize or minimize the function $f(\mathbf{x})$ and hence the name gradient method.

Example 7.6 Carry out the first five iterations of the gradient search to find the vector $\mathbf{x}$ which minimizes $f(\mathbf{x})$, where

$$f(\mathbf{x}) = b_1 x_1^2 (e^{-x_1} + 1) + b_2 x_2^2 (e^{-x_2} + 1)$$

and $r = 1, \mathbf{x}_0^T = [4 \quad 2], b_1 = 2, b_2 = 10$.
From Eq. (7.33),

$$\Delta_\alpha f(\mathbf{x}) = \sum_{i=1}^{2} \alpha_i b_i x_i \big[(2 - x_i) e^{-x_i} + 2 \big]$$

At $\mathbf{x}_0$, we have

$$f(\mathbf{x}_0) = 78.00, \qquad f_1(\mathbf{x}_0) = 15.71, \qquad f_2(\mathbf{x}_0) = 40.00$$

and

$$\alpha_1 = - \frac{(1)(15.71)}{\sqrt{(15.71)^2 + (40.00)^2}} = -0.37$$

$$\alpha_2 = - \frac{(1)(40.00)}{\sqrt{(15.71)^2 + (40.00)^2}} = -0.93$$

Therefore

$$\mathbf{x}_1^T = [4 - 0.37 \quad 2 - 0.93] = [3.63 \quad 1.07] \qquad \text{and} \qquad f(\mathbf{x}_1) = 42.43$$

Since $f(\mathbf{x}_0) > f(\mathbf{x}_1)$, the first step in the search has led to a reduction in the value of $f(\mathbf{x})$. For the second step let $\mathbf{x}_0 = \mathbf{x}_1$. Then

$$f_1(\mathbf{x}_0) = 14.21, \qquad f_2(\mathbf{x}_0) = 24.81$$

and

$$\alpha_1 = - \frac{(1)(14.21)}{\sqrt{(14.21)^2 + (24.81)^2}} = -0.50$$

$$\alpha_2 = - \frac{(1)(24.81)}{\sqrt{(14.21)^2 + (24.81)^2}} = -0.87$$

$$\mathbf{x}_1^T = [3.63 - 0.50 \quad 1.07 - 0.87] = [3.13 \quad 0.20]$$

Since $f(\mathbf{x}_1) = 21.18$, $f(\mathbf{x}_1) < f(\mathbf{x}_0)$, and the second step in the search has led to further reduction in the value of $f(\mathbf{x})$. For the third step, $\mathbf{x}_0 = \mathbf{x}_1$,

$$f_1(\mathbf{x}_0) = 12.21, \qquad f_2(\mathbf{x}_0) = 6.95$$

and

$$\alpha_1 = -0.87, \qquad \alpha_2 = -0.49$$

$$\mathbf{x}_1^T = [3.13 - 0.87, \quad 0.20 - 0.49] = [2.26 \quad -0.29], \qquad f(\mathbf{x}_1) = 13.24$$

Since $f(\mathbf{x}_1) < f(\mathbf{x}_0)$, the third step has continued to identify a value of $\mathbf{x}$ which reduces the value of $f(\mathbf{x})$. For the fourth step, $\mathbf{x}_0 = \mathbf{x}_1$ and

$$f_1(\mathbf{x}_0) = 8.92, \qquad f_2(\mathbf{x}_0) = -14.68$$

$$\alpha_1 = -0.52, \qquad \alpha_2 = 0.85$$

$$\mathbf{x}_1^T = [2.26 - 0.52, \quad -0.29 + 0.85] = [1.74 \quad 0.56], \qquad f(\mathbf{x}_1) = 12.05$$

Since $f(\mathbf{x}_1) < f(\mathbf{x}_0)$ reduction of the value of $f(\mathbf{x})$ has continued. For the final step, $\mathbf{x}_0 = \mathbf{x}_1$ and

$$f_1(\mathbf{x}_0) = 7.12, \qquad f_2(\mathbf{x}_0) = 15.81$$

$$\alpha_1 = -0.41, \qquad \alpha_2 = -0.91$$

$$\mathbf{x}_1^T = [1.33 \quad -0.35], \qquad f(\mathbf{x}_1) = 7.43$$

Once again the search has identified a point which further reduces the value of $f(\mathbf{x})$. The first five steps in the search are shown graphically in Fig. 7.9. Inspection of $f(\mathbf{x})$ indicates that the minimum point for $f(\mathbf{x})$ is [0 0]. While the gradient search can be expected to find a point near the true minimum, it normally would be terminated before the true minimum is identified. That is, the gradient search, and any other search technique, is reasonably effective in defining a point near a local minimum or maximum. In the case of the gradient method, the proximity of the *indicated* local extreme point to the *actual* local extreme point is a function of the step size r. The smaller the value of r, the closer the indicated local extreme point is likely to be to the actual local extreme point. This point is illustrated in Table 7.5 for the gradient search using values for r of 1.0, 2.0,

Table 7.5

Gradient Search for the Problem in Example 7.6 Using Values of r of 1.0, 2.0, and 0.50

Iteration no.	$r = 1$ x_0	x_1	$f(x_0)$	$r = 2$ x_0	x_1	$f(x_0)$	$r = 0.50$ x_0	x_1	$f(x_0)$
1	[4.00, 2.00]	[3.63, 1.07]	78.00	[4.00, 2.00]	[3.27, 0.14]	78.00	[4.00, 2.00]	[3.81, 1.53]	78.00
2	[3.63, 1.07]	[3.13, 0.20]	42.43	[3.27, 0.14]	[1.11, -0.60]	22.57	[3.81, 1.53]	[3.60, 1.08]	58.15
3	[3.13, 0.20]	[2.26, -0.29]	21.18	[1.11, -0.60]	[0.77, 1.38]	15.11	[3.60, 1.08]	[3.35, 0.65]	42.25
4	[2.26, -0.29]	[1.74, 0.56]	13.24	[0.77, 1.38]	[0.57, -0.39]	27.11	[3.35, 0.65]	[3.04, 0.25]	29.66
5	[1.74, 0.56]	[1.33, -0.35]	12.05	[0.57, -0.39]	[0.36, 1.40]	11.50	[3.04, 0.25]	[2.63, -0.04]	20.48
6	[1.33, -0.35]	[1.03, 0.61]	7.43	[0.36, 1.40]	[0.35, -0.59]	25.45	[2.63, -0.04]	[2.14, 0.04]	14.86
7	[1.03, 0.61]	[0.75, -0.35]	8.62	[0.35, -0.59]	[0.13, 1.41]	10.20	[2.14, 0.04]	[1.64, -0.01]	10.27
8	[0.75, -0.35]	[0.55, 0.63]	4.62	[0.13, 1.41]	[0.08, -0.59]	24.94	[1.64, -0.01]	[1.14, 0.02]	6.42
9	[0.55, 0.63]	[0.37, -0.35]	7.03	[0.08, -0.59]	[0.04, 1.41]	9.82	[1.14, 0.02]	[0.65, -0.05]	3.44
10	[0.37, -0.35]	[0.25, 0.64]	3.42	[0.04, 1.41]	[0.02, -0.59]	24.76	[0.65, -0.05]	[0.22, 0.20]	1.34
11	[0.25, 0.64]	[0.15, -0.35]	6.48	[0.02, -0.59]	[0.01, 1.41]	9.77	[0.22, 0.20]	[0.11, -0.29]	0.90
12	[0.15, -0.35]	[0.09, 0.65]	3.04	[0.01, 1.41]	[0.01, -0.59]	24.74	[0.11, -0.29]	[0.09, 0.21]	2.01
13	[0.09, 0.65]	[0.05, -0.35]	6.46	[0.01, -0.59]	[0.00, 1.41]	9.76	[0.09, 0.21]	[0.04, -0.29]	0.83
14	[0.05, -0.35]	[0.03, 0.65]	2.97	[0.00, 1.41]	[0.00, -0.59]	24.73	[0.04, -0.29]	[0.03, 0.21]	1.97
15	[0.03, 0.65]	[0.02, -0.35]	6.43	[0.00, -0.59]	[0.00, 1.41]	9.76	[0.03, 0.21]	[0.01, -0.29]	0.80
16	[0.02, -0.35]		2.97	[0.00, 1.41]		24.73	[0.01, -0.29]		1.97

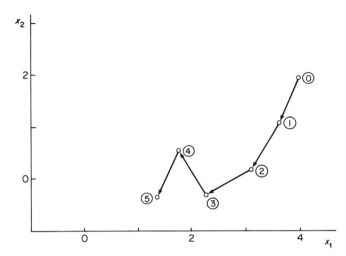

Fig. 7.9 Graph of the gradient search for the value of **x** which minimizes $f(\mathbf{x})$ in Example 7.6.

and 0.50 for the problem in this example. In each case 15 iterations of the search were completed. For $r = 1$ the least value of $f(\mathbf{x})$ identified was at $\mathbf{x} = [0.02 \quad -0.35]$, for which $f(\mathbf{x}) = 2.97$. For $r = 2$ the indicated optimum value of **x** was $[0.00 \quad -0.59]$, yielding $f(\mathbf{x}) = 9.76$. For $r = 0.50$ the indicated minimum value of **x** was $[0.03 \quad 0.21]$, where $f(\mathbf{x}) = 0.80$. It should be noted, however, that as r is decreased the number of iterations required for the search to reach the "vicinity" of the *optimum* will increase. Hence, one usually starts with a relatively large value of r to allow the search to "leap frog" across the space of feasible solutions followed by a reduction in r to refine the search in the vicinity of the optimum. ∎

QUEUEING MODELS

A queueing, or waiting line, system is one in which units or customers arrive demanding a service, may or may not await that service, are served, and leave the system. Typical examples include checkout counters at supermarkets, ticket counters at air terminals, tellers' windows at banks, hospital emergency rooms, and parking lots. The simplest waiting line system consists of a single service channel such as that depicted in Fig. 7.10. More complex systems include service channels in parallel (Fig. 7.11), for which the arriving unit may receive service from any one of several channels, and channels in series (Fig. 7.12), for which each arrival requires

Fig. 7.10 Queueing system with a single service channel.

a sequence of services before leaving the system. Finally, a queueing system may be comprised of a network of waiting line subsystems for which each subsystem consists of one of the systems described in Figs. 7.10, 7.11, and 7.12, the output of one subsystem being the input to another.

In most practical situations neither the occurrence of arrivals nor the time required for service can be predicted with certainty. As a result the time between successive arrivals and the time to complete service are usually considered to be positive-valued continuous random variables. In the most fundamental cases these random variables are assumed to be independent and exponentially distributed with parameter λ in the case of arrivals and parameter μ for service time. That is, if x and y are the times between successive independent arrivals and the time to service an arrival, respectively, then the probability density functions of x and y are given by

$$f(x) = \lambda e^{-\lambda x}, \qquad 0 \leqslant x < \infty \qquad (7.51)$$

$$g(y) = \mu e^{-\mu y}, \qquad 0 \leqslant y < \infty \qquad (7.52)$$

The parameters λ and μ are the mean arrival and service rates. In most

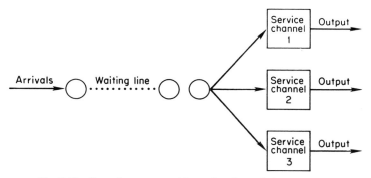

Fig. 7.11 Queueing system with service channels in parallel.

Fig. 7.12 Queueing system with service channels in tandem or series.

cases $\lambda/\mu < 1$. If $\lambda > \mu$ arrivals occur at a higher rate than the system can service and the waiting line will tend to increase without limit.

The purpose in modeling a queueing systems may be to determine the behavior of the system under a variety of conditions, to identify means through which system performance may be improved or simply to better understand the behavior of the system. Examples of measures of system performance include the cost of operating the system, the mean time arrivals spend in the system or the waiting line, the mean length of the waiting line, and the mean idle time for the service channel or channels.

In the first part of this section we shall consider the development of models of simple single-channel waiting line systems (Figure 7.10) where exponential interarrival and service times are assumed. In the last part of this section we shall deal with waiting line systems where there are several service channels in parallel (Figure 7.11). The analysis of more complicated systems is beyond the scope of this text.

Single-Channel Queueing Systems

Consider a single-channel queueing system where service time is exponentially distributed with parameter μ and interarrival time is exponentially distributed with parameter λ, $\lambda/\mu < 1$. It can be shown that the probability of an arrival in Δt is

$$P(\text{arrival in } \Delta t) = \lambda \Delta t \tag{7.53}$$

for sufficiently small Δt. In a similar manner,

$$P(\text{service in } \Delta t) = \mu \Delta t \tag{7.54}$$

given that the system is not empty. Further, the probability of two or more events in Δt is approximately zero.

Now let us consider the system at times t and $t + \Delta t$ and let $P_n(t)$ be the probability that there are n units in the system at time t. Now

$$P_0(t + \Delta t) = P_0(t)P(0 \text{ arrivals in } \Delta t) + P_1(t)P(1 \text{ service in } \Delta t) \tag{7.55}$$

since the probability of two or more events in Δt is zero. Hence

$$P_0(t + \Delta t) = P_0(t)(1 - \lambda \Delta t) + P_1(t) \mu \Delta t \tag{7.56}$$

By a similar argument $P_n(t + \Delta t)$, $n > 0$, is given by

$$P_n(t + \Delta t) = P_{n-1}(t)P(1 \text{ arrival in } \Delta t)$$
$$+ P_n(t)P(0 \text{ arrivals and 0 services in } \Delta t)$$
$$+ P_{n+1}(t)P(1 \text{ service in } \Delta t) \tag{7.57}$$

or

$$P_n(t + \Delta t) = P_{n-1}(t)\lambda\,\Delta t + P_n(t)(1 - \lambda\,\Delta t)(1 - \mu\,\Delta t)$$
$$+ P_{n+1}(t)\mu\,\Delta t, \qquad n > 0 \tag{7.58}$$

Subtracting $P_0(t)$ from both sides of Eq. (7.56) and dividing by Δt yields

$$\frac{P_0(t + \Delta t) - P_0(t)}{\Delta t} = -\lambda P_0(t) + \mu P_1(t) \tag{7.59}$$

Subtracting $P_n(t)$ from both sides of Eq. (7.58) and dividing by Δt, we have

$$\frac{P_n(t + \Delta t) - P_n(t)}{\Delta t} = \lambda P_{n-1}(t) - (\lambda + \mu)P_n(t) + \mu P_{n+1}(t) + \lambda\mu\,\Delta t\, P_n(t) \tag{7.60}$$

Taking the limit of Eqs. (7.59) and (7.60) as $\Delta t \to 0$, we have

$$\lim_{\Delta t \to 0} \frac{P_0(t + \Delta t) - P_0(t)}{\Delta t} = \frac{d}{dt} P_0(t) \tag{7.61}$$

$$\lim_{\Delta t \to 0} \frac{P_n(t + \Delta t) - P_n(t)}{\Delta t} = \frac{d}{dt} P_n(t) \tag{7.62}$$

and

$$\frac{d}{dt} P_0(t) = -\lambda P_0(t) + \mu P_1(t) \tag{7.63}$$

$$\frac{d}{dt} P_n(t) = \lambda P_{n-1}(t) - (\lambda + \mu)P_n(t) + \mu P_{n+1}(t) \tag{7.64}$$

The solutions for Eqs. (7.63) and (7.64) yield transient state relationships for $P_n(t)$, $n = 0, 2, 3, \ldots$. In most cases, however, we are concerned with steady state solutions where $t \to \infty$ and

$$\lim_{t \to \infty} \frac{d}{dt} P_n(t) = 0 \tag{7.65}$$

Hence in the steady state we have

$$-\lambda P_0 + \mu P_1 = 0 \tag{7.66}$$

$$\lambda P_{n-1} - (\lambda + \mu)P_n + \mu P_{n+1} = 0, \qquad n = 1, 2, \ldots \tag{7.67}$$

where

$$P_n = \lim_{t \to \infty} P_n(t) \tag{7.68}$$

Rewriting Eq. (7.67) as

$$\lambda P_n - (\lambda + \mu)P_{n+1} + \mu P_{n+2} = 0, \qquad n = 0, 1, 2, \ldots$$

we will use the geometric transform to solve for P_n. Taking the geometric transform of Eq. (7.68) yields

$$\lambda G_n(z) - \left(\frac{\lambda + \mu}{z} \right)[G_n(z) - P_0] + \frac{\mu}{z^2}[G_n(z) - P_0 - zP_1] = 0 \quad (7.69)$$

and

$$G_n(z)\left[\frac{\lambda z^2 - (\lambda + \mu)z + \mu}{z^2} \right] = \frac{\mu P_0 + \mu z P_1 - (\lambda + \mu)z P_0}{z^2} \quad (7.70)$$

for $n = 0, 1, 2, \ldots$. From Eq. (7.66),

$$P_1 = \frac{\lambda}{\mu} P_0 = \rho P_0 \quad (7.71)$$

where $\rho = \lambda/\mu$ and ρ is referred to as the *utilization factor*. Hence

$$\mu\left[\rho z^2 - (1 + \rho)z + 1 \right]G_n(z) = \mu(1 - z)P_0$$

or

$$\mu(1 - z)(1 - \rho z)G_n(z) = \mu(1 - z)P_0$$

Thus

$$G_n(z) = \frac{P_0}{1 - \rho z} \quad (7.72)$$

From Table C of the Appendix, the inverse transform of $1/(1 - \rho z)$ is ρ^n and

$$P_n = \rho^n P_0 \quad (7.73)$$

Since

$$\sum_{n=0}^{\infty} P_n = 1 \quad \text{and} \quad \sum_{n=0}^{\infty} \rho^n = \frac{1}{1 - \rho}$$

from Table A of the Appendix, we have

$$P_0 = 1 - \rho \quad \text{and} \quad P_n = (1 - \rho)\rho^n \quad (7.74)$$

Example 7.7 The mean or expected number of units in the system L is given by

$$L = \sum_{n=0}^{\infty} nP_n$$

Define L using Eq. (7.74).
From Eq. (7.74),

$$L = \sum_{n=0}^{\infty} n(1 - \rho)(\rho)^n = (1 - \rho)\sum_{n=0}^{\infty} n(\rho)^n$$

From Table A of the Appendix,

$$\Delta^{-1}\left[n(\rho)^n\right] = \frac{\rho}{(1-\rho)^2}\left[(\rho-1)n(\rho)^{n-1} - (\rho)^n + 1\right] \qquad (7.75)$$

Thus

$$\sum_{n=0}^{\infty} n(\rho)^n = \frac{\rho}{(1-\rho)^2}$$

or

$$L = \frac{\rho}{1-\rho} \quad \blacksquare \qquad (7.76)$$

Example 7.8   Find the mean length L_q of the waiting line if P_n is given by Eq. (7.74).

If m is the number of units in the waiting line, then

$$m = \begin{cases} 0, & n = 0, 1 \\ n-1, & n = 2, 3, \ldots \end{cases} \qquad (7.77)$$

Then the mean length of the waiting line is given by

$$L_q = \sum_{m=0}^{\infty} mQ_m \qquad (7.78)$$

where Q_m is the probability that there are m units in the waiting line and

$$Q_0 = P_0 + P_1 \qquad (7.79)$$
$$Q_m = P_{m+1}, \qquad m = 1, 2, 3, \ldots \qquad (7.80)$$

Thus

$$L_q = (0)\left[(1-\rho) + (1-\rho)(\rho)\right] + \sum_{m=1}^{\infty} m(1-\rho)(\rho)^{m+1} = (1-\rho)\sum_{m=1}^{\infty} m(\rho)^m \qquad (7.81)$$

Using Table A of the Appendix, we have

$$\sum_{m=1}^{\infty} m(\rho)^m = \frac{\rho}{(1-\rho)^2}$$

and

$$L_q = \frac{(\rho)^2}{(1-\rho)} \quad \blacksquare \qquad (7.82)$$

In general if λ, μ, and L are known, general relationships defining the mean waiting line length L_q, mean total time in the system (mean time in the waiting line + mean time in the service channel) W, and mean time in the waiting line W_q, may be defined as follows:

$$W = L/\lambda \tag{7.83}$$

$$L_q = L - \rho \tag{7.84}$$

$$W_q = L/\lambda - 1/\mu \tag{7.85}$$

Thus far we have assumed that the waiting line has capacity sufficient to accommodate a limitless number of arrivals. This may of course be an unreasonable assumption. If the system is such that it can handle no more than M customers at one time (one in the service channel and $M - 1$ in the waiting line), then

$$P_0 = (1 - \rho)/(1 - \rho^{M+1}) \tag{7.86}$$

$$L = \rho\left[(1 - \rho^M) - M(1 - \rho)\rho^M\right]/\left[(1 - \rho)(1 - \rho^{M+1})\right] \tag{7.87}$$

$$L_q = \left[\rho^2(1 - \rho^M) - M(1 - \rho)\rho^{M+1}\right]/\left[(1 - \rho)(1 - \rho^{M+1})\right] \tag{7.88}$$

$$W = \rho\left[(1 - \rho^M) - M(1 - \rho)\rho^M\right]/\left[\lambda(1 - \rho)(1 - \rho^{M+1})\right] \tag{7.89}$$

$$W_q = \left[\rho^2(1 - \rho^M) - M(1 - \rho)\rho^{M+1}\right]/\left[\lambda(1 - \rho)(1 - \rho^{M+1})\right] \tag{7.90}$$

It should be noted that in this case the system is stable even if $\rho > 1.0$.

Multiple Channels in Parallel

We will now consider the system depicted in Fig. 7.11, where s service channels are available, service time in each channel being exponentially distributed with mean rate μ. Again interarrival time will be assumed to be exponentially distributed with parameter λ. We will assume unlimited capacity for the waiting line. As in the case of the single-channel queueing system, we will first develop differential equations involving $P_n(t)$ and then define the steady state equations for P_n by letting $t \to \infty$.

Since interarrival time is assumed to be exponentially distributed with parameter λ,

$$P(\text{arrival in } \Delta t) = \lambda \Delta t \tag{7.91}$$

If there are m units in service, $m \leqslant s$, then

$$P(\text{service in } \Delta t) = m\mu \Delta t \tag{7.92}$$

since a service may occur in any one of the m busy channels. If all s channels are busy, then

$$P(\text{service in } \Delta t) = s\mu \Delta t \tag{7.93}$$

As in the preceding section, the assumption of exponential arrivals and services precludes the possibility of two or more events in Δt for sufficiently small Δt.

From Eqs. (7.91), (7.92), and (7.93), we have

$$P_0(t + \Delta t) = (1 - \lambda \Delta t)P_0(t) + \mu \Delta t \, P_1(t) \tag{7.94}$$

$$P_n(t + \Delta t) = \lambda \Delta t \, P_{n-1}(t) + (1 - \lambda \Delta t)(1 - n\mu \, \Delta t)P_n(t)$$

$$+ (n + 1)\mu \Delta t \, P_{n+1}(t), \qquad n = 1, 2, \ldots, s - 1 \tag{7.95}$$

$$P_n(t + \Delta t) = \lambda \Delta t \, P_{n-1}(t) + (1 - \lambda \Delta t)(1 - s\mu \, \Delta t)P_n(t)$$

$$+ s\mu \, \Delta t \, P_{n+1}(t), \qquad n = s, s + 1, \ldots \tag{7.96}$$

Subtracting $P_0(t)$ from both sides of Eq. (7.94) and $P_n(t)$ from both sides of Eqs. (7.95) and (7.96) and dividing the three resulting equations by Δt leads to

$$\frac{P_0(t + \Delta t) - P_0(t)}{\Delta t} = -\lambda P_0(t) + \mu P_1(t) \tag{7.97}$$

$$\frac{P_n(t + \Delta t) - P_n(t)}{\Delta t} = \lambda P_{n-1}(t) - (\lambda + n\mu)P_n(t)$$

$$+ (n + 1)\mu P_{n+1}(t), \qquad n = 1, 2, \ldots, s - 1 \tag{7.98}$$

$$\frac{P_n(t + \Delta t) - P_n(t)}{\Delta t} = \lambda P_{n-1}(t) - (\lambda + s\mu)P_n(t)$$

$$+ s\mu P_{n+1}(t), \qquad n = s, s + 1, \ldots \tag{7.99}$$

Taking the limit in Eqs. (7.97), (7.98), and (7.99) as $\Delta t \to 0$, we have the following:

$$\frac{d}{dt} P_0(t) = -\lambda P_0(t) + \mu P_1(t) \tag{7.100}$$

$$\frac{d}{dt} P_n(t) = \lambda P_{n-1}(t) - (\lambda + n\mu)P_n(t)$$

$$+ (n + 1)\mu P_{n+1}(t), \qquad n = 1, 2, \ldots, s - 1 \tag{7.101}$$

$$\frac{d}{dt} P_n(t) = \lambda P_{n-1}(t) - (\lambda + s\mu)P_n(t)$$

$$+ s\mu P_{n+1}(t), \qquad n = s, s + 1, \ldots \tag{7.102}$$

and the steady state solutions are obtained for $t \to \infty$ and are given by

$$-\lambda P_0 + \mu P_1 = 0 \tag{7.103}$$

$$\lambda P_{n-1} - (\lambda + n\mu) P_n + (n+1)\mu P_{n+1} = 0, \qquad n = 1, 2, \dots, (s-1) \tag{7.104}$$

$$\lambda P_{n-1} - (\lambda + s\mu) P_n + s\mu P_{n+1} = 0, \qquad n = s, s+1, \dots \tag{7.105}$$

In this case we will solve iteratively for P_n, defining P_n as a function of P_0 and then solving for P_0, noting that $\sum_{n=0}^{\infty} P_n = 1$. From Eq. (7.103),

$$P_1 = \rho P_0 \tag{7.106}$$

where $\rho = \lambda/\mu$. For $n = 1 < s$ in Eq. (7.104),

$$P_2 = \frac{\lambda + \mu}{2\mu} P_1 - \frac{\lambda}{2\mu} P_0 = \frac{\rho^2}{2} P_0 \tag{7.107}$$

For $n = 2 < s$,

$$P_3 = \frac{\lambda + 2\mu}{3\mu} P_2 - \frac{\lambda}{3\mu} P_1 = \frac{\rho^3}{3!} P_0 \tag{7.108}$$

Continuing in this manner, we have

$$P_n = \frac{\rho^n}{n!} P_0, \qquad n = 1, 2, \dots, s \tag{7.109}$$

For $n = s$ in Eq. (7.105),

$$P_{s+1} = \frac{\lambda + s\mu}{s\mu} P_s - \frac{\lambda}{s\mu} P_{s-1} = \frac{\rho^{s+1}}{s\,s!} P_0 \tag{7.110}$$

and for $n = s + 1$,

$$P_{s+2} = \frac{\lambda + s\mu}{s\mu} P_{s+1} - \frac{\lambda}{s\mu} P_s = \frac{\rho^{s+2}}{s^2 s!} P_0 \tag{7.111}$$

Thus for $n = s + m$,

$$P_{s+m} = \frac{\rho^{s+m}}{s^m s!} P_0, \qquad m = 1, 2, \dots \tag{7.112}$$

Now

$$\sum_{n=0}^{\infty} P_n = P_0 + \sum_{n=1}^{s} \frac{\rho^n}{n!} P_0 + \sum_{n=s+1}^{\infty} \frac{\rho^n}{s^{n-s} s!} P_0$$

$$= P_0 \left[\sum_{n=0}^{s} \frac{\rho^n}{n!} + \frac{s^s}{s!} \sum_{n=s+1}^{\infty} \frac{\rho^n}{s^n} \right] = 1 \tag{7.113}$$

or

$$P_0 = 1 / \left[\sum_{n=0}^{s} \frac{\rho^n}{n!} + \frac{s^s}{s!} \sum_{n=s+1}^{\infty} \left(\frac{\rho}{s} \right)^n \right]$$

$$= 1 / \left[\sum_{n=0}^{s} \frac{\rho^n}{n!} + \frac{\rho^{s+1}}{s\,s!\,(1 - \rho/s)} \right] \tag{7.114}$$

where $\sum_{n=s+1}^{\infty} (\rho/s)^n$ converges if and only if $\rho/s < 1.0$. In summary, then,

$$P_n = \begin{cases} P_0, & n = 0 \\[2mm] \dfrac{\rho^n}{n!} P_0, & n = 1, 2, \ldots, s \\[3mm] \dfrac{\rho^n}{s^{n-s} s!} P_0, & n = s + 1, s + 2, \ldots \end{cases} \tag{7.115}$$

From Eqs. (7.114) and (7.115) L, L_q, W, and W_q may be defined as follows:

$$L = \lambda \mu s \rho^s P_0 / \left[s! \, (s\mu - \lambda)^2 \right] + \rho \tag{7.116}$$

$$L_q = \lambda \mu s \rho^s P_0 / \left[s! \, (s\mu - \lambda)^2 \right] \tag{7.117}$$

$$W = \mu s \rho^s P_0 / \left[s! \, (s\mu - \lambda)^2 \right] + 1/\mu \tag{7.118}$$

$$W_q = \mu s \rho^s P_0 / \left[s! \, (s\mu - \lambda)^2 \right] \tag{7.119}$$

Example 7.9 A maintenance department has the responsibility for repair of production equipment. The time between equipment failures is exponentially distributed with $\lambda = 4$ per day. The time required for a repair crew to service equipment upon failure is exponentially distributed with $\mu = 2$ per day. If the maintenance department provides s repair crews, the mean daily cost of maintenance is given by

$$C(s) = 8000 \left\{ \lambda \mu s \rho^s P_0 / \left[s! \, (s\mu - \lambda)^2 \right] \right\} + 400s$$

Find the number of repair crews s which will minimize mean daily cost of maintenance.

If s^* is the number of repair crews which minimizes $C(s)$, then

$$C(s^* - 1) \leqslant 0 \leqslant C(s^*)$$

or s^* is the smallest integer such that $C(s^*) \geqslant 0$. The solution for s^* is summarized in Table 7.6, where $s^* = 5$. ∎

Table 7.6

Solution for s^* in Example 7.9

s	$C(s)$
3	-1255.47
4	-670.93
5	152.05

SUMMARY

The models which have been presented in this chapter represent only a limited sampling of the most elementary forms encountered by the operations researcher. Further, the analyses which were presented represent the most basic approach to resolving the problems to which these models apply. Currently, both theoretical and applied research in optimization theory (as represented here by linear and dynamic programming and search techniques) as well as stochastic processes (as represented by Markov chains and queueing models) are producing significant advances in the design and analysis of operational systems. The references presented at the end of this chapter should be viewed as sources of information to which the reader can now turn to further his or her understanding of topics in operations research.

PROBLEMS

1. You are a member of the notorious High Tor bank-robbery gang. The gang is planning to rob the Last Exchange Bank of Luxembourg. From your past experience, and that of other less successful gangs, you have obtained the following information about your chances on this job. There is a 10% chance that you will trip one of the alarms on entering the bank and will be apprehended. If you get past the alarms, there is a 15% chance that you will be spotted by a guard and be captured. If you should reach the vault, you have a 95% chance of opening it and escaping with $1 million it contains. If you do not get the vault open, you can escape empty-handed. Describe your situation as a Markov chain and answer the following questions.

   (a) What is the probability that the robbery will be a success, and what is your a priori expected return from this robbery?
   (b) What is the probability that you will leave the bank empty-handed but undetected?
   (c) If you tried to rob this bank 10 times under the same circumstances, how many times would you get past the guards?

2. Find the vector of steady-state probabilities for

(a)

	state 1	state 2	state 3
state 1	0.7	0.0	0.3
P = state 2	0.6	0.3	0.1
state 3	0.2	0.5	0.3

(b)

$$P = \begin{bmatrix} 0 & 0 & 1 \\ 1/3 & 1/3 & 1/3 \\ 1/2 & 1/4 & 1/4 \end{bmatrix}$$

(c)

$$P = \begin{bmatrix} 0.8 & 0.2 & 0.0 \\ 0.2 & 0.4 & 0.4 \\ 0.0 & 0.5 & 0.5 \end{bmatrix}$$

3. A market survey was done on 3 brands of breakfast foods: X, Y, Z. Every time a customer purchased a new package, he might buy the same brand or switch to one of the other brands. The following estimates have been obtained.

	Next brand purchased		
Present brand	X	Y	Z
X	0.7	0.1	'0.2
Y	0.3	0.5	0.2
Z	0.2	0.4	0.4

What will be the market equilibrium of customers?

4. A machine operates with a probability of failure during any given time period of 0.2. Sixty percent of the time the failure can be fixed in exactly one time period, and in all other cases it will require exactly two time periods for repair. Assume failures occur at the *end* of a time period. Down time costs $40 per period.

   (a) Formulate this problem as a Markov chain, describe the states, and develop a transition matrix.

   (b) For $15 per time period, an extra mechanic can be added so that a failure is always repaired in one time period. Should this be done?

5. Consider the network routing problem of Fig. 7.13. What is the optimal path from state 1 to state 10? (Costs are given on the arcs.)

6. Given the following tabular stage coupling relationships and return functions maximize $\sum_{i=1}^{3} r_i$ and indicate the optimal policy and returns for $s_3 = 3$.

   (a) $s_{n-1} = T_n(s_n, d_n)$:

Stage 3						Stage 2						Stage 1				
		d_3						d_2						d_1			
		1	2	3	4			1	2	3	4			1	2	3	4
	1	3	2	1	4		1	–	2	5	1		1	1	2	1	–
	2	4	3	3	4		2	3	4	3	–		2	4	3	2	–
s_3	3	3	1	2	4	s_2	3	4	5	4	–	s_1	3	5	3	4	2
	4	2	4	2	1		4	3	4	2	3		4	–	4	3	4
													5	–	–	5	5

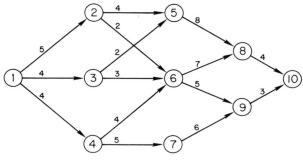

Fig. 7.13

(b) $r_n = R_n(s_n, d_n)$:

	Stage 3					Stage 2					Stage 1			
	d_3					d_2					d_1			
	1	2	3	4		1	2	3	4		1	2	3	4
1	3	4	1	4	1	–	1	5	4	1	2	1	3	–
2	2	4	3	3	2	5	4	2	–	2	4	3	2	–
s_3 3	3	4	5	4	s_2 3	2	3	3	–	s_1 3	3	5	4	3
4	4	2	3	2	4	3	5	4	2	4	–	4	5	3
										5	–	–	4	3

7. Given the following three-stages-of-solution problem, find the optimal decision policy. Identify the solution values for the decision variables and the value of the cumulative return function:

$$\sum_{i=1}^{3} r_i = \max$$

s.t.

$$
\left.
\begin{array}{l}
s_{i-1} = T_i(s_i, d_i) = 0.6s_i + 0.4d_i \\[4pt]
0 \leqslant d_i \leqslant s_i \\[4pt]
r_i = R_i(s_i, d_i) = 0.7s_i - 0.3d_i \\[4pt]
s_3 = 50
\end{array}
\right\} \quad i = 1, 2, 3
$$

8. A consulting firm has four different projects under consideration. Each of these projects requires a fixed number of the firm's employees, devoted full time, to accomplish project activities, and a definable amount of the firm's operating capital. Further, each of these projects has the same estimated time duration. The cost of each project and manpower requirements are given below.

Project #	Cost ($1000)	Employees
1	2	1
2	4	2
3	3	2
4	5	3

The firm has \$9000 of operating capital available and five employees that are available for assignment. If the revenue generated from each of these projects is as follows, what is the optimal policy?

Project #	Revenue (\$1000)
1	4
2	7
3	6
4	10

9. Use dynamic programming to solve the following problem:

$$F(\mathbf{d}) = d_1^2 + 5d_1 + d_2^2 - 3d_2 + 8 = \min$$

s.t.

$$2d_1 + d_2 \geqslant L$$
$$3 \leqslant L \leqslant 6$$
$$d_1, d_2 \geqslant 0$$

Identify the optimal decision values and objective function values over the range of L indicated.

10. Use dynamic programming to solve the following constrained optimization problem:

$$F = d_1^2 + d_2^2 + 2d_1 - 5d_2 + 7 = \min$$

s.t.

$$d_1 + d_2 \geqslant K$$
$$d_1, d_2 \geqslant 0$$
$$2 \leqslant K \leqslant 6$$

11. Four different items are available for loading into a freight car which has a weight limitation of 17 tons. The table below indicates the per unit value v_i and weight w_i of each item.

i	v_i	w_i
1	1	1
2	8	4
3	4	3
4	1	2

At least one and not more than four units of item 4 must be loaded, and not more than three each of items 2 and 3 should be loaded. Using dynamic programming, determine how the freight car should be loaded in order to maximize the total value represented by its cargo. Also, what is the effect of removing the restriction that at least one of item 4 must be loaded?

12. Find the optimal decision policy and returns for the initial value problem

$$\sum_{i=1}^{4} r_i = \max$$

s.t.

$$
\left.
\begin{aligned}
r_i &= S_i + 3d_i \\
S_{i-1} &\equiv \tilde{S}_i = 2S_i - 0.2d_i \\
0 &\le d_i \le S_i
\end{aligned}
\right\} \quad i = 1, \ldots, 4
$$

$$S_4 = 100$$

13. Consider a simplified economy of the following sort. Each dollar of capital invested in heavy goods industry at the beginning of a year yields, at the end of that year, $2 of capital and $1 of consumer's goods. Each dollar of capital invested in consumer goods industry at the beginning of a year yields, at the end of that year, $1.8 of capital and $4 of consumer's goods. The present government of the country is operating with the above economy. This government has an election coming up in 5 years and wants to maximize the total production of consumer's goods over the next 5 years. How much of the available capital should be invested in consumer goods industry each year if C dollars of capital are available at the beginning of the 5-year period?

14. A production process must be scheduled over five periods. The production during each period is restricted to integral numbers of units and the maximum production per period is 4 units. The following table gives the total cost of production (in hundreds of dollars) for the different numbers of units that may be produced per period. In addition to these production costs, there is an inventory cost of $100 per unit per period. The inventory cost may be taken into account for complete periods only (including the period of production). The units are inventoried until the end of the last period. What is the optimal production schedule if demand is (a) 18 units, (b) 15 units, (c) 13 units, (d) 10 units?

Period		I	II	III	IV	V
	0	2	2	3	5	3
	1	3	4	4	6	8
Production	2	7	6	8	8	10
Quantity	3	10	11	13	17	15
	4	11	12	14	21	18

15. Solve the following linear programming problems:

   (a)

$$z = x_1 + 2x_2 + x_3 = \max$$

   s.t.

$$x_1 - x_2 + x_3 \le 4$$
$$2x_1 + 4x_2 - x_3 \le 3$$
$$x_1, x_2, x_3 \ge 0$$

(b)

$$z = x_1 + x_2 = \max$$

s.t.

$$x_1 + 3x_2 \leqslant 5$$

$$2x_1 + x_2 \leqslant 4$$

$$x_1 \leqslant 3$$

$$x_1, x_2 \geqslant 0$$

16. A winery manufactures two types of liquor, red and white. Red sells for $25 per quart, and white sells for $35 per quart. There are 16 hours per day available for mixing these liquors. Red takes 3 hours per quart to mix and white takes 5 hours per quart. In addition the winery is permitted to reinforce its liquors with alcohol up to a maximum of 20 ounces per day. Red is fortified with 4 ounces per quart, and white is fortified with 3 ounces per quart. How many quarts of each liquor should the winery make per day to maximize dollar sales?

17. Minimize $F(x) = x_1^2 - 28x_1 + 24$ using the Fibonacci search over the interval $5 \leqslant x \leqslant 60$.

18. The cost of inventorying units of a product is given by the following function

$$F(x) = cx + \frac{Kx}{2} + \frac{SR}{x}$$

where $x \leftrightarrow$ the number of units ordered. Define the optimum order quantity using a Fibonacci search if (a) $S = 5$, $R = 50$, $C = 5$, $K = 5$; (b) $S = 8$, $R = 12$, $C = 10$, $K = 3$; (c) $S = 10$, $R = 50$, $C = 2$, $K = 10$.

19. Given the following function of a single variable, $F(x) = x^4 - 3x^3 + 17$

   (a) optimize using the Fibonacci search, where the original interval of search is $1 \leqslant x \leqslant 5$ and the desired final interval of separation is $\delta \leqslant 0.1$.

   (b) What is the actual, final interval of uncertainty?

20. Use the method of steepest descent to minimize

$$F(\mathbf{x}) = 3x_1^2 + x_2^2 - 12x_1 - 6x_2.$$

Start your search at $\mathbf{x}^0 = \begin{bmatrix} 1 \\ 1 \end{bmatrix}$.

21. Use the method of steepest descent to minimize the function

$$F(\mathbf{x}) = 2x_1^2 - x_1x_2 + 3x_2^2 - 6x_1 - 12x_2$$

Start your search at $\mathbf{x} = \begin{bmatrix} 0 \\ 0 \end{bmatrix}$.

22. A conveyor feeds units of product to a work station for packaging. Units are packaged one at a time and on a first-come, first-serve basis. Spacing of units is in an exponential fashion at a mean rate λ of 400 per hour. Packaging time is exponentially distributed with parameter $\mu = 500$ per hour. Determine P_0, L, L_q, W and W_q.

23. For the single-channel queueing system, P_n is given by Eq. (7.74). Show that no solution exists for P_n if $\rho \geqslant 1$.

24. Derive an expression for P_n for a single-channel queueing system for which interarrival time and service time are exponentially distributed with parameter λ and μ, respectively, and the capacity of the waiting line is $M - 1$.

25. Derive Eq. (7.87) based upon the expression for P_n in Problem 24.

26. Derive Eq. (7.88) based upon the expression for P_n in Problem 24.

27. Noting that $L = \sum_{n=0}^{\infty} nP_n$, derive Eq. (7.116).

28. Noting that $L_q = \sum_{n=1}^{\infty}(n-1)P_n$, derive Eq. (7.117).

29. In Problem 22 suppose that the cost of the packaging operation is a function of λ and is given by

$$C(\lambda) = C_1 W_q + C_2/\lambda$$

Find the conveyor feed rate λ which minimizes $C(\lambda)$ if $C_1 = \$10.00$ and $C_2 = \$4.00$.

30. Customers arrive at a carwash in an exponential fashion with mean rate 20 per hour. The time to wash a car is also exponentially distributed, but with mean rate 22 per hour. Space for waiting cars is to be provided so that the probability of a customer being rejected from the carwash (no space available) is to be 0.07 or less. How many spaces are required to meet this criterion?

31. In Problem 30 suppose the mean hourly cost of operation of the carwash is given by

$$C(M) = C_1 \lambda P_M + C_2 M$$

where λ is the mean customer arrival rate, P_M the probability that no space is available in the waiting line, M the capacity of the system (number in the waiting line plus the service channel), $C_1 = \$1.00$, and $C_2 = \$13.00$. Find the value of M which minimizes $C(M)$.

Suggested Further Reading

1. Beightler, C. S., Phillips, D. T., and Wilde, D. J. (1979). "Foundations of Optimization," 2nd ed. Prentice-Hall, Englewood Cliffs, New Jersey.
2. Cooper, R. B. (1972). "Introduction to Queueing Theory." Macmillan, New York.
3. Dreyfus, S. W., and Law, A. M. (1977). "The Art and Theory of Dynamic Programming." Academic Press, New York.
4. Hillier, F. S., and Lieberman, G. J. (1974). "Operations Research." 2nd ed. Holden-Day, San Francisco, California.
5. Himmelblau, D. M. (1972). "Applied Nonlinear Programming." McGraw-Hill, New York.
6. Kleinisch, L. (1975). "Queueing Systems. Vol. 1: Theory." Wiley, New York.
7. Kleinisch, L. (1976). "Queueing Systems. Vol. 2: Computer Applications." Wiley, New York.
8. Phillips, D. T., Ravindran, A., and Solberg, J. J. (1976). "Operations Research—Principles and Practice." Wiley, New York.
9. Shamblin, J. E., and Stevens, G. T., Jr. (1974). "Operations Research—A Fundamental Approach." McGraw-Hill, New York.
10. Taha, H. A. (1976). "Operations Research—An Introduction," 2nd ed. Macmillan, New York.
11. Wagner, H. M. (1969). "Principles of Operations Research." Prentice-Hall, Englewood Cliffs, New Jersey.
12. White, J. A., Schmidt, J. W., and Bennett, G. K. (1975). "Analysis of Queueing Systems." Academic Press, New York.

Appendix

Antidifference Table $\Delta[\Delta^{-1}f(x)] = f(x)$

$f(x)$	$\Delta^{-1}f(x)$
a	ax
x	$x(x-1)/2$
x^2	$x(x-1)(2x-1)/6$
x^3	$[x(x-1)]^2/4$
x^4	$x(x-1)(2x-1)[3x(x-1)-1]/36$
a^x	$\dfrac{a^x-1}{a-1}$
xa^x	$\dfrac{a[(a-1)xa^{x-1}-(a^x-1)]}{(a-1)^2}$
$\dfrac{1}{x(x+1)}$	$\dfrac{x-1}{x}$
$\dfrac{1}{x(x+2)}$	$\dfrac{(x-1)(3x+2)}{4x(x+1)}$
$xx!$	$x!$
$x(x!)^2(x+2)$	$(x!)^2$
$\dfrac{x}{(x+1)!}$	$-\dfrac{1}{x!}$
$\dfrac{(x+1)(2x)!}{x!}$	$\dfrac{(2x)!}{x!}$
$(2x-1)^2$	$\dfrac{(x-1)[4(x-1)^2-1]}{3}$
$(2x-1)^3$	$(x-1)^2[2(x-1)^2-1]$
$\binom{x}{n}$	$\binom{x}{n+1}, x>n$
$\binom{n+x-1}{n}$	$\binom{n+x-1}{n-1}$
$\dfrac{1}{(1+ax)[1+a(x+1)]}$	$\dfrac{x-1}{(1+a)(1+ax)}$
$\dfrac{a^{x-1}}{(1+ba^{x-1})(1+ba^x)}$	$\dfrac{1}{1-a}\left(\dfrac{1}{1+b}-\dfrac{a^{x-1}}{1+ba^{x-1}}\right)$
$\dfrac{x^2+x-1}{(x+2)!}$	$-\dfrac{x}{(x+1)!}$
$\dfrac{(4x+5)(x+1)!}{(2x+3)!}$	$-\dfrac{x!}{(2x+1)!}$

Table B

Laplace Transform Pairs $\mathcal{L}[f(t)] = L(s) = \int_0^\infty f(t)e^{-st}\,dt$

$f(t)$	$L(s)$	$f(t)$	$L(s)$
$cf(t)$	$cL(s)$	c	$\dfrac{c}{s}$
$f^1(t)$	$sL(s) - f(0)$	$\dfrac{c}{\Gamma(n)}\,t^{n-1}$	$\dfrac{c}{s^n}$, $n>0$
$f^n(t)$	$s^n L(s) - \sum\limits_{j=1}^{n} s^{n-j}f^{j-1}(0)$	e^{ct}	$\dfrac{1}{s-c}$
$e^{at}f(t)$	$L(s-a)$	$\dfrac{e^{ct}t^{n-1}}{\Gamma(n)}$	$\dfrac{1}{(s-c)^n}$, $n>0$
$\int_0^t f(x)\,dx$	$\dfrac{1}{s}L(s)$	$\dfrac{e^{c_1 t} - e^{c_2 t}}{c_1 - c_2}$	$\dfrac{1}{(s-c_1 s-c_2)}$
$\int_0^t f(x)g(t-x)\,dx$	$\mathcal{L}[f(t)]\mathcal{L}[g(t)]$	$\dfrac{(a+c_1)e^{c_1 t} - (a+c_2)e^{c_2 t}}{c_1 - c_2}$	$\dfrac{s+a}{(s-c_1)(s-c_2)}$
$-tf(t)$	$L^1(s)$	$\sin(ct)$	$\dfrac{c}{s^2 + c^2}$
$(-t)^n f(t)$	$L^n(s)$	$\cos(ct)$	$\dfrac{s}{s^2 + c^2}$
$\dfrac{1}{t}f(t)$	$\int_s^\infty L(x)\,dx$	$e^{c_1 t}\sin(c_2 t)$	$\dfrac{c_2}{(s-c_1)^2 + c_2^2}$
$f(t-c),\ t>c$	$e^{-cs}L(s)$	$e^{c_1 t}\cos(c_2 t)$	$\dfrac{s - c_1}{(x-c_1)^2 + c_2^2}$
$t\cos(ct)$	$\dfrac{s^2 - c^2}{(s^2 + c^2)^2}$	$\sinh(ct)$	$\dfrac{c}{s^2 - c^2}$
$t\sin(ct)$	$\dfrac{2cs}{(s^2 + c^2)^2}$	$\cosh(ct)$	$\dfrac{s}{s^2 - c^2}$
$t\sinh(ct)$	$\dfrac{2cs}{(s^2 - c^2)^2}$	$e^{c_1 t}\sinh(c_2 t)$	$\dfrac{c^2}{(s-c_1)^2 - c_2^2}$
$t\cosh(ct)$	$\dfrac{s^2 + c^2}{(s^2 - c^2)^2}$	$e^{c_1 t}\cosh(c_2 t)$	$\dfrac{s - c_1}{(s-c_1)^2 - c_2 2}$

Table C

Geometric Transform Pairs $G[f(x)] = G_x(z) = \sum_{x=0}^{\infty} z^x f(x)$

$f(x)$	$G_x(z)$	Remarks
$g(x) + h(x)$	$G[g(x)] + G[h(x)]$	
$\Delta f(x)$	$(z^{-1} - 1)G_x(z) - z^{-1}f(0)$	
$\Delta^2 f(x)$	$\dfrac{(1-z)^2 G_x(z) - f(0)(1-2z) - zf(1)}{z^2}$	
$\Delta^n f(x)$	$\sum_{i=1}^{n} (-1)^{n-i}\binom{n}{i} z^{-i}\left[G_x(x) - \sum_{k=0}^{i-1} z^k f(k)\right]$ $+ (-1)^n G_x(z),\ n > 0$	
$f(x + i)$	$z^{-i}\left[G_x(z) - \sum_{k=0}^{i-1} z^k f(k)\right],\ i > 0$	
$\sum_{k=0}^{x} g(k)h(x - k)$	$G[g(x)]G[h(x)]$	
a	$\dfrac{a}{1-z}$	
a^x	$\dfrac{1}{1-az}$	
x	$\dfrac{z}{(1-z)^2}$	
x^k	$z\dfrac{d}{dz} G(x^{k-1})$	
$\dfrac{a^x}{x!}$	e^{az}	
$\dfrac{a^x}{x}$	$-\ln(1 - az)$	
$\binom{x+k}{k}a^x$	$(1 - az)^{-(k+1)}$	
$p^x(1-p)^{1-x},\ x = 0, 1$	$[pz + (1 - p)]$	Bernoulli p.m.f.
$\binom{n}{x}p^x(1-p)^{n-x},\ x = 0, 1, \dots, n$	$[pz + (1 - p)]^n$	Binomial p.m.f.
$\dfrac{\lambda^x}{x!}e^{-\lambda x},\ x = 0, 1, 2, \dots$	$e^{-\lambda(1-z)}$	Poisson p.m.f.
$p(1-p)^x,\ x = 0, 1, 2, \dots$	$\dfrac{p}{1 - (1-p)z}$	Geometric p.m.f.
$p(1-p)^{x-1},\ x = 1, 2, 3, \dots$	$\dfrac{pz}{1 - (1-p)z}$	Geometric p.m.f.
$\binom{n+x-1}{x}p^n(1-p)^x,\ x = n, n+1, \dots$	$\left[\dfrac{pz}{1 - (1-p)z}\right]^n$	Negative binomial p.m.f.
$\dfrac{1}{b-a+1},\ x = a, a+1, \dots, b$	$\dfrac{z^a - z^{b+1}}{(b - a + 1)(1 - z)}$	Rectangular p.m.f.

Table D

Z Transform Pairs $Z[f(x)] = Z_x(z) = \sum_{x=0}^{\infty} z^{-x} f(x)$

$f(x)$	$Z_x(z)$	Remarks
$g(x) + h(x)$	$Z[g(x)] + Z[h(x)]$	
$\Delta f(x)$	$(z-1)Z_x(z) - zf(0)$	
$\Delta^2 f(x)$	$(z-1)^2 Z_x(z) - z(z-2)f(0) - zf(1)$	
$\Delta^n f(x)$	$\sum_{i=1}^{n} (-1)^{n-i} \binom{n}{i} z^i \left[Z_x(z) - \sum_{k=0}^{i-1} z^{-k} f(k) \right]$ $+ (-1)^n Z_x(z),\ n > 0$	
$f(x+i)$	$z^i \left[Z_x(x) - \sum_{k=0}^{i-1} z^{-k} f(k) \right],\ i > o$	
$\sum_{k=0}^{x} g(k) h(x-k)$	$Z[g(x)] Z[h(x)]$	
a	$\dfrac{az}{z-1}$	
a^x	$\dfrac{z}{z-a}$	
x	$\dfrac{z}{(x-1)^2}$	
x^k	$-z \dfrac{d}{dz} Z(x^{k-1})$	
$\dfrac{a^x}{x}$	$\ln(z) - \ln(z-a)$	
$\binom{x+k}{k} a^x$	$\dfrac{z^{k+1}}{(z-a)^{k+1}}$	
$\dfrac{a^x}{x!}$	$e^{a/z}$	
$p^x (1-p)^{1-x},\ x = 0, 1$	$\dfrac{(1-p)z + p}{z}$	Bernoulli p.m.f.
$\binom{n}{x} p^x (1-p)^{n-x},\ x = 0, 1, \ldots, n$	$\dfrac{[(1-p)z + p]^n}{z^n}$	Binomial p.m.f.
$\dfrac{\lambda^x}{x!} e^{-\lambda},\ x = 0, 1, 2, \ldots$	$e^{-\lambda}\left(\dfrac{z-1}{z} \right)$	Poisson p.m.f.
$p(1-p)^x,\ x = 0, 1, 2 \ldots$	$\dfrac{pz}{z-1+p}$	Geometric p.m.f.
$p(1-p)^{x-1},\ x = 1, 2, 3, \ldots$	$\dfrac{p}{z-1+p}$	Geometric p.m.f.
$\binom{n+x-1}{x} p^n (1-p)^x,\ x = n, n+1, \ldots$	$\left[\dfrac{p}{z-1+p} \right]^n$	Negative binomial p.m.f.
$\dfrac{1}{b-a+1},\ x = a, a+1, \ldots, b$	$\dfrac{z^{-a+1} - z^{-b}}{(b-a+1)(z-1)}$	Rectangular p.m.f.

Index